The Microprocessor and its Application

The Microprocessor and its Application

An advanced course

Editor and Course Director
D.ASPINALL

Main Contributors
W.A.CLARK, A.J.T.COLIN, D.DACK, E.L.DAGLESS, R.D.DOWSING,
J.K.ILIFFE, C.A.OGDIN, M.VANNESCHI

Invited Specialists
I.M.BARRON, C.A.R.HOARE

CAMBRIDGE UNIVERSITY PRESS
Cambridge
London · New York · Melbourne

Published by the Syndics of the Cambridge University Press
The Pitt Building, Trumpington Street, Cambridge CB2 1RP
Bentley House, 200 Euston Road, London NW1 2DB
32 East 57th Street, New York, NY 10022, USA
296 Beaconsfield Parade, Middle Park, Melbourne 3206, Australia

© Cambridge University Press 1978

First published 1978

Printed in Malta by
Interprint (Malta) Ltd.

ISBN 0 521 22241 9

621·3819'5835

MIC

C O N T E N T S

CONTENTS

CONTENTS

CONTENTS

CONTENTS

PREFACE

1. INTRODUCTION

In 1972 the electronics engineer received data on a new component - the Microprocessor. This was seized upon as a means to implement low cost complex information processing products for large markets. It was realised that the skill of programming these components must be acquired. By 1975, the sales seminars of the semiconductor component manufacturers were being complemented by independent teaching courses which endeavoured to introduce the electronics engineer to the characteristics of the processing element as a component and the discipline of a structured programming strategy in its use. The computer scientists were much slower to react to the new development, being preoccupied with the large main frame computer system and the problems inherent in its proper use and management.

The continued development of microelectronics, which provides a wide spectrum of components from basic gates and flip-flops through medium-scale integrated circuits to memory, uncommitted logic arrays, programmable logic arrays, arithmetic/logic units, "bit-slice" sets, microprocessors, and microcomputers, has forced a re-appraisal of the skills and knowledge of the electronics engineer. These now include the interworking of a circuit of complex components and a program which, together, translate the general purpose processor component into a piece of equipment to meet a special requirement. This interworking activity, which represents the convergence of electronic engineering and computer science, was previously the concern of a few manufacturers of computer systems and was of no concern to the vast army of computer users. The low cost of the components and the widening possibilities for their application mean that this interworking will be the concern of a much wider community, including both electronics engineers and computer scientists.

The need to bring representatives of these two groups together, to study the body of knowledge necessary to support a professional approach to the design and implementation of equipment based upon the new microelectronics components, was recognised by the Computing Science Committee of the Science Research Council and the C R E S T – ITG Committee of the European Economic Commission. Together they sponsored the Advanced Course entitled "The Microprocessor and its Application" at the University College of Swansea in the University of Wales, from the 5th to 16th September 1977.

This volume has been compiled from the handbook of this Advanced Course.

2. COURSE STRUCTURE

All the main contributors participated with the Course Director in planning the structure and content both of the course, and of this volume. Early in the planning, it was realised that the course should have two main strands of formal lectures, with discussion periods, plus a workshop activity in which the participants would design, develop, and demonstrate a piece of information processing equipment based upon a microprocessor component.

The course of lectures was divided into six sections :

1. Hardware Components
2. Software Techniques
3. Microprocessor Project Management
4. Design Exercise
5. Microprogrammable Microprocessors
6. Future Developments

2.1 Hardware Components

This section attempted to introduce the computer scientist to the technology of microelectronics and to characterise the various microprocessor and ancillary components of large-scale integration. Wesley Clark brought a lifetime of experience, in the design of computers and modular digital equipment, to bear on the preparation of a pithy presentation of the underlying principles of microelectronic technology and an introduction to the manufacture of basic components and their use. Erik Dagless presented the characteristics of microprocessor components based upon an active study of their application and the development of teaching material for postgraduate, undergraduate, and post-experience courses for electronics engineers at the University College of Swansea.

2.2 Software Techniques

The electronics engineer needs reminding that the familiar disciplines for the design and development of hardware must have a parallel when the product is software. Roy Dowsing, a computer scientist, has been involved in the teaching of electronics engineers for some time, both in the Computer Technology undergraduate course and in the post-experience courses at the University College of Swansea. This experience is reflected in his contributions on the underlying principles of the design of complex information processing systems. Andrew Colin, formerly an engineer, and now a computer scientist, has developed high level languages which are being used in the design of practical microprocessor-based systems. His contribution summarised the role of high level languages and the disciplines for their use.

2.3 Microprocessor Project Management

Projects which involve the interworking of software and hardware to meet the specification of a complex information processing product require careful management. Carol Anne Ogdin has been involved with many such projects during her career. She introduced the total management problem and discussed strategies to solve it. She gave an account of the various techniques and tools which are available to execute a successful project.

2.4 Design Exercise

When a complex subject is in its infancy and general theory to support good design practice has not been developed, then one must teach by case study and design exercise. David Dack has developed several microprocessor-based electronic instruments which are on the market. As an electronics engineer, he has learnt the need to combine new computer skills and disciplines in his work. He presented the design exercise in a way which illustrated the general principles involved, so that the reader may see the relevance to his own particular situation. During the course, the presentation also included the specification of the product to be developed by the participants in their workshop activity.

2.5 Microprogrammable Microprocessors

The preceding sections have been concerned, in the main, with the ramifications of the single fixed instruction set microprocessor. They have been ordained by the realisation that the designer has little or no chance of influencing the instruction set or architecture characteristics of the microprocessor components offered by the semiconductor manufacturers, and he, or she, must learn to use those which are available.

There is an alternative approach. Microelectronics technology also makes available the components which make up a processor based upon microprogrammed control of separate data path circuits. These are the true microprocessors of micro-code, as described by Wilkes in 1950.

Marco Vanneschi has studied the subject of microprogramming for some time, and presented an account of the basic principles and how they relate to the available microelectronic components. John Iliffe needs little introduction as a distinguished contributor to computer science. In recent years, he has been concerned with the architecture and design of computer systems which match the users' need. His contribution on interpretive machines teaches much about the structure of computer systems and suggests ways to use the emerging technology in a wide range of applications.

2.6 Future Developments

The sub-title for this section could be "Microprocessors in Concert". In it are three contributions on the future developments made possible by the new technology. David Aspinall pointed out that electronics engineers will naturally build circuits in which many separate processing elements are interconnected to work concurrently. Before this can be done in a professional manner, they will need methods to identify concurrency and techniques to provide reliable interconnections. Identification of concurrency will require a new way of thinking which breaks away from the traditional sequential state machine approach. Tony Hoare presented a seminal paper which identified the need for a language to enable concurrent description of solutions as opposed to the present sequential descriptions. A language is described which is a first step on the road to this objective. Iann Barron gave a summary of microprocessor development and heralded the emergence of a new component, the Transputer, the processing element of the future, to enable the implementation of concurrent information processing systems.

2.7 Syndicate Discussion Sessions

The course participants were divided into small syndicate groups, to enable general discussion with the lecturers and the preparation of material for a discussion session, involving all participants, each day. These activities afforded opportunities for a ready interchange between engineers and programmers. They confirmed the need for a course of this nature, and resulted in certain changes to the edited material in this book. Provision was not made for considered reporting of these sessions which, on reflection, would have provided a valuable addition to this volume. However, the discussion on the final day, led by Iann Barron, on the implications of the new technology, was memorable, and some brief record needs to be made.

2.8 Implications of the New Technology

The revolution in microelectronic technology, which we have been considering, presents a crisis to our industrialised society.

It presents a threat to large sections of established manufacturing industry. Products which were previously based upon electro-mechanical components may now be replaced by new products based upon microelectronics. Jobs in these manufacturing industries are at risk. There will be a proliferation of automation products which will place other jobs at risk in the wider manufacturing industries. The lower cost of storing, processing, and communicating information by electronic means will affect both the manufacturing and service industries. There will be a fall in the demand for stationery, books, and newsprint. What will happen to the forests which were planted to provide us with paper? What will happen to the lumberjack and the postman?

Any crisis presents not only a threat but also an opportunity for advancement. The opportunity here is to restructure manufacturing industry to exploit the potential of the new technology by retraining the existing workforce and adopting new attitudes to working conditions. There will be improved access to communications media, which should lead to greater opportunities for the dissemination of information to all. There are opportunities to decentralise the computer systems of the administrative bureaucracies, enabling a more personal interface between the administered and the administrator. There is a challenge facing all who work in the application of this technology to use their skills and knowledge to benefit society.

2.9 Workshop Activity

Teaching experience in the University College of Swansea had demonstrated the value of practical work with a microprocessor development system in support of lectures and discussions. During the pre-course planning meetings, David Dack suggested a design exercise which the participants could undertake in the teaching laboratory of the Department of Electrical & Electronic Engineering. Erik Dagless took the design exercise, supervised modifications to the equipment in the laboratory, and organised the necessary support facilities to enable the workshop activity. During the course, he supervised the workshop periods and the team of demonstrators. This team comprised : P.Allman, M.Barton, B.Davies, R.Davies, M.Edwards, N.Graves, D.Harvey, J.Proudfoot and D.Tudhope.

The participants made full use of the practical facilities available in the workshop. Some completed the exercise and were able to demonstrate a working system by the end of the course. All benefited from the experience, and went away from the course with a clear idea of the problems of a microprocessor-based project and an appreciation of the ways to solve them.

PREFACE

2.10 Site Visit

The participants visited the chemical plant of B.P.Chemicals
Ltd., Baglan Bay, Swansea, where they viewed the practical application of computer technology. The visit was preceded by a presentation by Dr.T.Robbins during which he described the role of the
computers in the plant.

3. ACKNOWLEDGEMENTS

As Course Director, as well as Editor of this book, I wish to
take this opportunity to thank all the contributors and demonstrators for their efforts in planning and executing this task. Also,
I wish to thank John Mason who assisted with the administration
before and during the course. The workshop facilities were enhanced
by the technical services staff of the Department of Electrical &
Electronic Engineering, notably Mrs.L.Jones and Mr.G.Gunn. There
was much documentation provided to the participants; not only the
course notes but also a laboratory handbook for the workshop
facilities. These were prepared in the reprographic centre of
the School of Engineering, ably staffed by Mrs.J.Pugh, Mrs.A.McGairl,
and Mr.D.Gabriel.

None of this would have been possible but for the patient,
diligent, and creative secretarial support of Mrs.Ethel Phillips.

In conclusion I wish, on behalf of all participants, to
acknowledge the sponsorship of the Science Research Council and
C R E S T - ITG of the European Economic Commission.

D.ASPINALL

Swansea
January, 1978

CONTRIBUTORS TO C R E S T - I T G ADVANCED COURSE

The Microprocessor and Its Application

University College of Swansea

SEPTEMBER 5 - 16, 1977

COURSE DIRECTOR :

D.ASPINALL,
Department of Electrical and
  Electronic Engineering,
University College of Swansea,.
SWANSEA, SA2 8PP.

MAIN CONTRIBUTORS

W.A.CLARK,
1572 Massachusetts Avenue,
Cambridge,
Massachusetts 02138,
U.S.A.

R.D.DOWSING,
Department of Computer Science,
University College of Swansea,
SWANSEA, SA2 8PP.

A.J.T.COLIN,
Department of Computer Science,
University of Strathclyde,
George Street,
GLASGOW, C.1.
Scotland.

J.K.ILIFFE,
Visiting Fellow,
Department of Computer Science
  and Statistics,
Queen Mary College,
Mile End Road, LONDON E1 4NS

D.DACK,
Research & Development Dept.,
Hewlett Packard Limited,
South Queensferry,
West Lothian, EH30 9TG
Scotland.

C.A.OGDIN,
Software Technique Inc.,
100 Pommander Walk,
Alexandria,
Va 22314,
U.S.A.

E.L.DAGLESS,
Department of Electrical and
  Electronic Engineering,
University College of Swansea,
SWANSEA, SA2 8PP.

M.VANNESCHI,
Istituto di Scienze dell'
  Informazione,
Universita di Pisa,
Corso Italia, 40,
56100 PISA,
Italy.

INVITED SPECIALISTS

I.M.BARRON,
"Greyfriars",
The Common,
REDBOURNE,
Herts.

C.A.R.HOARE,
Programming Research Group,
Oxford University Computing Laboratory,
45, Banbury Road,
OXFORD, OH2 6PE

I.A.   ASPECTS OF INTEGRATED CIRCUIT HARDWARE:
         FROM ELECTRON MOBILITY TO LOGICAL STRUCTURE

                  Wesley A. Clark

             Cambridge, Massachusetts, USA

1 INTRODUCTION

Anyone who has used a plastic pocket-comb on a cold dry day
has at least a basic knowledge of electricity: electric charge can
be moved from place to place, and there is a force between two
charged objects that decreases as the distance separating the objects is increased. On a dry day, evidently, the comb removes and
retains some of the electric charge found on the surface of hair.
This leaves the hair electrified by virtue of a charge deficit
while electrifying the comb with a charge surplus. The balance of
nature is disturbed momentarily and some observable forces result:
hairs having a similar charge-imbalance repel one another but are
attracted to the comb, which now has an imbalance of the opposite
kind. In the further experience of grasping a metal doorknob after walking across a carpet on that same dry day, one is memorably
persuaded that metallic objects if not good retainers of charge
are certainly excellent charge *conductors*, and that the human body
itself is a fair conductor of electricity.

Electronic computers operate, of course, by coordinating the
conduction of charge from place to place along numerous pathways:
now opening a gate here or closing a gate there to regulate the
flow; now charging or discharging component parts; now merging,
amplifying, and so on - always heating up the surroundings and
occasionally producing observable forces useful to man.

In today's astonishing microprocessor the workhorse or perhaps
demon of this busy enterprise is the *transistor*, a carefully made
microscopic device that is inseparably integrated with many of its
kind into inexpensive electrical circuit modules. These integrated
circuit modules are available in many different forms and at various levels of complexity, utility and cost, and thus present a
sizeable array of possibilities for contemplation.

The intent of this chapter is to offer the reader - presumed
conversant in the idiom of computer science but possessed of limited enthusiasm for the contemplation of its engines - a brief

                          1

and limited glimpse of the 'high' technology of large-scale integrated circuits. The road from Electron to Logic is well paved
and well marked, and those who make the present journey are prom-
ised a minimum of Dielectrical Materialism along the way.

2 THE DESIGN OF INTEGRATED TRANSISTOR CIRCUITS

The principles underlying the design and operation of integrated circuits with their myriad transistor devices are easily
grasped if one is prepared to begin with a short excursion into
the domain of atoms and molecules, from which all of the known
properties of matter arise. Since our objective is an understanding of computer *hardware*, we can limit our interest to the properties of appropriate solid objects.

2.1 Physical properties of solids

In the atomic domain the attraction of unlike charges holding
an atom together is identified as an attraction between a massive
positively-charged nucleus and a number of much less massive neg-
atively-charged electrons, which surround the nucleus and balance
the whole thing electrically. When atoms combine to form molecules, crystals or other matter, the nature of the inter-atomic
attraction is somewhat more complicated. Each atom has preferred
groupings of electrons, loosely thought of as concentric shells
each capable of holding so many electrons and no more. In balancing the nuclear charge, electrons fill inner shells first and become inaccessible but may or may not complete the outermost shell.
Molecules, crystals or other solids form when two or more atoms
having incomplete outer shells come just close enough to share
their accessible outermost or *valence* electrons with one another
in an attempt to complete all shells, locking together by establishing *covalent bonds*. Full removal of electrons from an atom
leaves the atom with a net positive charge, of course, while addition of electrons leaves it with a net negative charge. Such
electrically unbalanced atoms are called *ions*, and they too have
a role to play in repulsion and attraction.

So much we know from basic physics and chemistry. Now to the
substance of the matter:

2.1.1 Insulators, conductors and semiconductors. With regard to
electrical substance, solid matter can be classified as *insulators*
(dielectrics), *conductors,* or something in-between called *semiconductors*. We will ignore superconductors. In insulators such
as combs, carpets and hair, electrons are so tenaciously bound to
atoms that they can be torn free only by relatively large forces
and at that, generally, only from the surface of the solid. Electrons within the solid cannot move about in an attempt to compensate such a loss and the surface of a 'stripped' insulator thus

2

remains charged at the fixed ionized sites created by the loss until new electrons are reintroduced from without.

In conductors, on the other hand, valence electrons are quite
easily separated from their atoms under the least provocation and
travel freely throughout the conductor in all directions at high
speed, frequently colliding or otherwise interacting with the
atoms fixed within the solid but generally keeping their distance
from one another. If extra electrons are somehow crammed into a
conductor having no escape pathway they quickly distribute themselves throughout in the manner of a diffusing gas. But with an
escape pathway provided by a closed electrical circuit, electrons
injected into one end of a conductor almost immediately push electrons out of the other, and are themselves crowded along and finally out unless the injection stops or the circuit is opened. The
mobility of the electrons depends on properties of the conductor;
the *number* of electrons pushed along per second depends on how
hard they are being pushed and how crowded they become - factors
measured by the gradient of population pressure from the injection
end to the escape end, the cross-sectional area of the conductive
corridor, and finally, by the electron mobility.

Semiconductors are yet another matter. Certain elements -
among them *silicon*, the one to be discussed here - have valence
shells that are half full. Silicon has four valence electrons and
readily bonds with four neighbors to form a solid lattice in which
interior atoms have completed shells (Fig.1). With the addition
of a bit of energy (for example, the thermal agitation energy of
free electrons in a comfortably heated room) it will be found that
an extremely tiny fraction of these bonds are always breaking
apart here and there. The electrons thus released are free to jit-
ter about in search of other bond-deficient ionized sites to fill.
But it is vastly easier for a bond-deficient pair simply to *borrow*
an electron from a neighbor, which then borrows from *its* neighbor
and so on, de-ionizing one site at the expense of another.

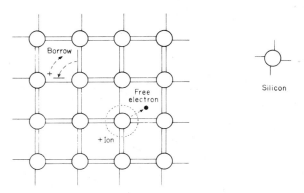

Fig. 1. Covalent bonds in silicon crystal; breaking and borrowing.

3

Semiconductor specialists like to refer to bond-deficiencies as *holes*. They observe that these 'holes' can be said to wander about and to repel one another just as electrons do, each hole momentarily defining a positive ion which inhibits the intrusion of other holes into its vicinity. In practical silicon crystals the mobility of such holes is about one-third that of free electrons, but charge can be 'carried' by either or both. Inasmuch as these charge carriers are so very few in number, silicon crystal will conduct only weakly and is therefore said to be a *semi*conductor. Since the breaking of any bond gives rise to exactly one hole and one free electron while the balancing opposite process involves the capture of one free electron by one hole (taking both temporarily out of the action), the number of holes is always equal to the number of free electrons in pure silicon crystals. There appears to be no such thing as completely pure crystalline silicon, but no matter; as pure crystals, semiconductors seem to have no electrical properties of great utility.

Ah, but semiconductor crystals can be enriched in either *holes* or *free electrons* by somehow embedding within the lattice just a pinch of atoms of certain other elements, and it is this fact that makes it possible to build useful devices.

2.1.2 <u>Charge-carrier enrichment of semiconductors</u>. An atom of phosphorus has five valence electrons; an atom of boron, three. Atoms of either kind can be locked into the silicon lattice, and when they take up residence at even a minute fraction of sites their contribution becomes dominant. The awkward fifth valence electron of each phosphorus atom is promptly freed (Fig.2a) while each boron atom's embarrassing deficit is no less promptly covered by a neighborly silicon atom (Fig.2b), which takes a hole in exchange and passes it on. With enough tenants per crystal, the number of free electrons or holes in general circulation is enhanced *a million-fold*.

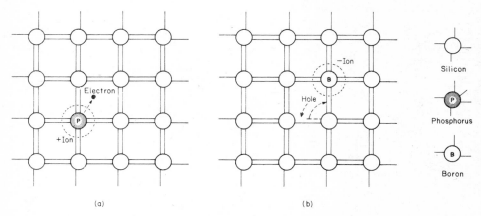

(a)   (b)

<u>Fig. 2</u>. Enrichment of silicon in: (a) electrons; (b) holes.

This process of substituting other atoms for some of the semiconductor atoms is called *doping*. Semiconductors doped with electron donors such as phosphorus are said to be of *n*-type; boron
doping, which results in extra holes, produces semiconductors of
p-type. (The letters *n* and *p* stand for *negative* and *positive*; our
physicists had already appropriated *e* and *h* for worthy purposes.)
Doping elements, though they give semiconductors extraordinary
characteristics, are referred to as impurities - rather like calling orchids *weeds* if they are found growing in a cabbage patch.
Doping of silicon is easily accomplished by adding just the right
amount of the doping element to molten silicon and allowing the
result to cool and crystallize; or by diffusing the dopant as a
vapor through the surface of the crystalline solid at high temperature, when everything is vibrating so much in all directions that
the intruders can find accommodations in minor lattice defects without greatly upsetting the overall structure. In the shorthand of
the specialists, heavily-doped material is referred to as n^+ or p^+
- an unfortunate choice, perhaps, but there it is. The heavier
the doping, the better - i.e. more metallic - the conductivity.

The underpinnings of exposition are now all in place and we
are ready to move on to a consideration of their practical consequences. The reader who is disquieted by the informality and im-
precision of the foregoing discussion or who is motivated to learn
more of the underlying theory is encouraged to examine Grove (1967)
or perhaps Carr and Mize (1972).

2.2 Semiconductor devices

2.2.1 The semiconductor junction: CHARGE WARS. Consider, for
example, what happens when blocks of n-type and p-type semiconductors are joined (Fig.3). Assuming a perfect union, electrons

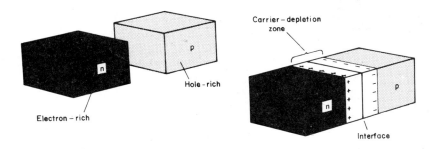

Fig. 3. Charge-carrier depletion in the semiconductor junction.

and holes immediately begin to swarm across the interface to anni-
hilate one another. This war would spread throughout the entire
composite crystal were it not for the fact that as they enter the
fray at the interface, electrons from the n-region leave behind

them a thickening barrier of immobile phosphorus ions whose positive charges are no longer compensated by the departed free electrons. Similarly, holes entering from the p-region leave behind
a thickening barrier of uncompensated negative boron ions. These
defensive walls quickly become so strong that they cannot be
breached in great numbers without extraordinary force; the nega-
tively-charged wall on the p-side repels the invading negative
electrons, while the positively-charged wall on the n-side repels
the counter-invading positive holes.

There the matter sits; the battle neatly confines itself to a
narrow zone in which the charge carriers are quite depleted and
the rate of recruitment just balances the rate of desertion on
either side. If one side is more heavily doped than the other, it
prevails only to the extent of shifting the battle zone towards,
and in the limit just inside, enemy territory.

Fresh troops can be sent in from abroad (by a battery, for example), electrons into the n-region and holes into the p-region
(Fig.4b). After some attrition through skirmishes along the way
with oppositely-charged *guerillas*, which constitute a very small
minority in each region, most of these suicidal charge carriers
reach the front where they too are annihilated. Now since a backward flow of holes is equivalent to a forward flow of electrons,
there is a net flow of negative charge in the n-to-p direction.
The increase in population pressure narrows the depletion zone.

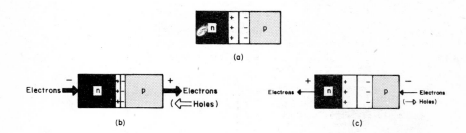

(a)

(b)   (c)

Fig. 4. Conduction through a semiconductor junction: (a) at
rest; (b) with majority-carrier injection; (c) with majority-carrier removal (charge flow negligible in practice).

On the other hand, an attempt to *withdraw* troops leads only to
a strengthening of the walls because of the further decompensation
of fixed ions (Fig.4c). Therefore, only a tiny negative charge
will flow in the p-to-n direction. It is usually ignored.

This remarkable one-way-flow property of semiconductor junctions appears in the operation of practical devices in essentially
two different ways: first, under suitable external conditions, to
isolate one semiconductor region *from* another region of opposite

majority-carrier polarity, thus permitting charge to flow within
the one without escaping into the other; second, on the basis of
external conditions, to <u>modulate</u> the flow of charge *between* two
regions of opposite polarity. Devices of the first kind are said
to be <u>unipolar</u>; devices of the second kind, <u>bipolar</u>. Conduction
through a semiconductor junction is a *bipolar* process.

Devices of either kind can be made in great batches by using
the high temperature vapor diffusion method of doping. Indeed it
is the efficiency of batch fabrication that gives us the inexpensive products characteristic of semiconductor technology. Diffused regions are created near the surface of a thin substrate of
pre-doped silicon; windows cut into a covering layer of s•licon
dioxide permit entry of the vapor (Fig.5a). Phosphorus vapor, for
example, will then form a bounded n-region in a boron-doped substrate (Fig.5b) when introduced in a quantity sufficient to overwhelm the contribution of the boron ions already in residence. A
few crafty holes will survive to become guerillas. Silicon dioxide, by the way, is an excellent insulator.

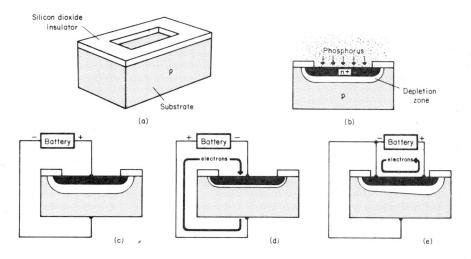

Fig. 5. The diffused junction: (a) substrate and diffusion window;
(b) formation; (c) & (d) bipolar behavior; (e) unipolar behavior.

Additional regions of differing polarities can be formed by
changing the diffusion times and diffusing vapor compositions,
thus creating more complex layered structures. In practice, sub-
strates are roughly one-hundred times thicker than the diffused
regions and therefore the resulting structures can fairly be characterized as *planar*. Two of these more complex planar structures
are shown in Fig.6, the diffusion layer structures of TTL (Tran-
sistor-Transistor Logic – Fig.6a) and CMOS (Complementary Metal-
Oxide-Semiconductor – Fig.6b) transistors.

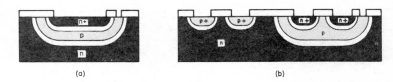

Fig. 6. Diffusion layers in (a) TTL and (b) CMOS transistors.

Before we proceed to discuss transistor devices, the reader is invited to contemplate one last form of semiconductor junction, a form at once charming in simplicity and extraordinary in utility:

The field-induced junction provides the basic unipolar control mechanism of all MOS integrated circuits. It arises in the following way: A semiconductor substrate (p-type in the illustration) is covered with an insulating layer of silicon dioxide - actually glass and therefore a very old friend of man, though in the degree of purity required we know it as quartz. On this is laid a conductive plate (Fig.7a). An electrical force field is now created between substrate and plate by connecting each of them to opposite poles of a battery, plate-to-plus. Some of the plate's free electrons are conducted away to the battery, leaving the plate with a net positive charge (Fig.7b):

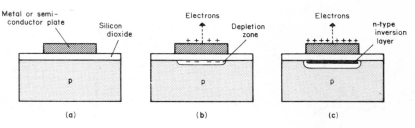

Fig. 7. Field-induced junction: (a) rest; (b) onset; (c) junction.

In the substrate beneath the glass, a number of subtending holes are induced to retreat just far enough for their abandoned ions to form a counter-balancing negative image of the plate, thus creating a carrier-depleted zone at the glass boundary. Nearby negative guerillas begin to cluster as well, though their very small minority position at the outset precludes much of a contribution to the formation of the counter-image. But as the battery pressure increases to a threshold value or beyond, almost all of the holes are pushed away from the boundary and the guerillas suddenly find themselves in the majority within a very thin boundary-layer of semiconductor material. The layer is thus, for the moment, inverted from p-type to n-type (Fig.7c). (Although this example is based on the use of a p-substrate, the expected complementary junction would have been formed had we made the appropriate reversal of all charge-mechanism polarities - a fact generally

true throughout our discussions.) If the battery is now disconnected, the plate will become electrically isolated and its trapped positive charge will maintain the junction. But if the pressure of a connected battery falls to a sub-threshold level, or if
electrons are allowed to return to the plate by some other route,
the field-induced junction will collapse and disappear.

Very, very nice. The *existence* of junctions can be controlled
dynamically, and there is even a hint of possible memory applications. We have only to discover the means.

2.2.2 TTL and MOS transistors. In digital circuits, 'transistor'
primarily means 'switch' - a device that either conducts charge to
the best of its ability or not at all, depending on whether it is
'on' or 'off'. At present there are many circuit families; each
manufacturer develops his own techniques and nurtures his own family and its market. A partial list would include the TTL, MOS and
CMOS families mentioned above, as well as the CCD (Charge-Coupled
Device), ECL (Emitter-Coupled Logic) and I^2L (Integrated Injection
Logic) families, to name but a few more. Some of these come in either p- or n-flavors (CMOS, in both at once) and some in both high-
and low-power or speed versions, further lengthening the list.
The discussion will be limited to TTL and MOS transistors, and at
that, TTL will be given short shrift in order to get on with an
introduction to the simpler, unipolar MOS technology.

The MOS transistor was the first to appear. It was invented
by J.E. Lilienfeld about fifty years ago in the course of experi-
mentation with the use of the field effect in semiconductors to
achieve charge-current amplification (Lilienfeld, 1928). Although
the device appeared to work to some extent, an adequate theoretical basis was not possible until the late 1940's; but it was at
about that time that J. Bardeen, W.H. Brattain and W. Shockley invented the Bipolar Junction Transistor (Bardeen and Brattain, 1948,
and Shockley, 1949), and for more than a decade attention was diverted instead to the development of this remarkable device.

Early bipolar transistors were clumsy, unreliable, and expensive - yet very promising. Following the lead of the Bell Laboratories work, commercial interest expanded with increasing rapidity
and useful numbers of devices became available to the circuit designer. Germanium rather than silicon was the basic ingredient of
these first transistors, and products were far from perfect. The
designer's task involved the combination of many transistors and
other circuit components and a great deal of wire in an attempt to
correct device deficiencies, often with brilliant success but always with added complexity. With the development of the diffusion
methods of doping silicon, planar structures became possible and
the extremely small sizes necessary for sub-microsecond switching
were finally achieved. Today's transistors are marvels of reliability and low cost, representing an enormous investment in both

engineering effort and manufacturing skill.

Interestingly enough, when attention was finally focussed once again on MOS it was found, contrary to theory, that the practical devices failed to work as well as expected. It then took a great deal of study and many years of frustrating and exacting effort to discover that the culprit was *common table-salt*. The salt, which is nearly ubiquitous on our planet, had been contaminating the silicon dioxide in almost non-existent amounts, thereby impairing the ability of the oxide to act as a proper insulator. Toughening up the standards of cleanliness and purity - already at exceptionally high levels - finally solved the problem.

TTL transistors are all of the *npn* form shown below but appear as functionally distinct units embedded in the surface of a broad underlying substrate of p-type semiconductor material not shown.

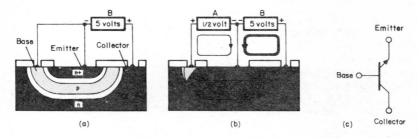

Fig. 8. The TTL transistor: (a) *off*; (b) *on*; (c) symbol.

The unit's three participating regions are named the *emitter*, the *base* and the *collector*. If a battery, B, is connected to these regions as in Fig.8a, a few charge troops will be withdrawn from both base and collector but the depletion zones at the emitter-base and base-collector frontiers of the eternal Charge Wars prevent the flow of currents of significant size along any pathway. But if as shown in Fig.8b we now connect another battery, A, having a pressure or *voltage* of, say, one-tenth that of B, then two different currents begin to flow: holes are introduced into the base by A, while electrons are sent into the emitter by both A and B. The emitter-base battle immediately intensifies; energetic electrons pushed by both batteries crowd across the northern frontier into the base region.

The principal electron casualties are those taken out of the action by some of the holes. But the base region is very thin and most of the electrons, pressed forward by endless incoming ranks, quickly pass through enemy territory unscathed and cross over the southern frontier into the collector, where they join their comrades in a withdrawal to battery B for another try. If A ceases to operate or is removed from the circuit, the two frontier battles become deadlocked once again and all flow immediately stops.

Thus the flow of a very small current in the A-loop modulates the flow of a current many times its size in the B-loop. In TTL circuits, the A-loop of one transistor generally appears as but one of several branches of the B-loop of another which in turn is 'driven' as part of the job of a third transistor, and so on.

The symbol used to represent an npn-transistor is shown in Fig.8c. Note that its arrowhead points upstream, like a boat with a bow-anchor, rather than in the direction of electron flow.

MOS transistors are unipolar and simple. The figure below shows an n-carrier version and is almost self-explanatory. Two separate n-regions, the *source* and *drain*, are diffused into the surface of a p-substrate through windows in a thin covering of silicon dioxide and are bridged by an insulated plate, the *gate*. With substrate and gate both anchored electrically as in Fig.9a,

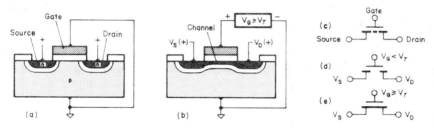

Fig. 9. The n-channel MOS transistor: (a) *off*; (b) *on*; (c-e) symbols. Voltages: *source*, V_S; *gate*, V_G; *drain*, V_D; *threshold*, V_T.

the source and drain will be isolated from the substrate, and thus from one another, by depletion zones - provided that neither is ever forced to become more negative than the anchor when included in external circuits not shown. If we now (Fig.9b) connect a battery having a voltage at least as great as that required to establish a field-induced junction under the gate - about 1 volt - the source and drain will be interconnected by the resulting inversion layer. Electrons will thus have a conductive n-*channel* through which to flow from source to drain when pushed by external means; which is source and which is drain depends only on flow direction.

The channel is not the best of conductors. It is inherently several orders of magnitude more resistive to flow than either the source or drain because it presents a much smaller cross-sectional area to the current and because it supports many fewer charge carriers. Furthermore, as the electrons jostle their way through the channel considerable energy is lost to the crystalline substrate through collisions with its fixed atoms; it will appear as unwanted heat. Weakened ranks of electrons emerge from the channel to continue on their way down remaining pathways to an energy-infusing battery or its equivalent, generally through other 'resistors' along the way. Long narrow channels are *more* resistive to flow; short broad ones, *less*. There are lower limits to both length and breadth, but no upper limits within the confines of the surface. The general shape of the channel is arbitrary.

2.3 MOS Integration

In 1952 the British engineer, G.W.A. Dummer, made the following remarkable prediction in an invited paper presented at a Washington, D.C. symposium on electronic components:

> "With the advent of the transistor and the work in semi-conductors generally, it seems now possible to envisage electronic equipment in a solid block with no connecting wires. The block may consist of layers of insulating, conducting, rectifying and amplifying materials, the electrical functions being connected directly by cutting out areas of the various layers." (quoted in Wolff, 1976)

Within a few years, work was begun both in England and in the United States in search of Dummer's device. Dummer himself exhibited a model in 1957 that demonstrated how silicon might be used in integration, but the first working monolithic circuit was made by the American, J.S.C. Kilby, in the following year. The device as we now know it derives from fabrication methods developed by R.S. Noyce. An example is shown in Fig.10, a few-hundred MOS-transistor integrated circuit 'chip' designed by E.K. Cheng and C.A. Mead (1975) for pipeline multiplication:

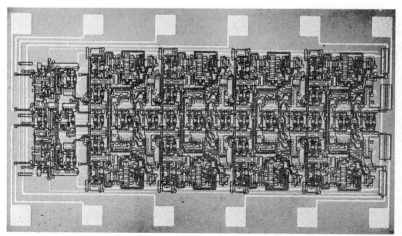

▤ Actual size

Fig. 10. Dual-product pipeline multiplier MOS chip. Large squares, aluminum; on the right, broad low-resistance output transistors.

12

2.3.1 The physical structure of MOS. The n-channel silicon-gate transistor is currently the preferred form in unipolar integration technology; the name MOS survives an earlier period in which gates were made of metal. Polycrystalline silicon ('poly') is sputtered or otherwise deposited over the surface of oxide covering the sub-.strate. It is then etched selectively to form gates and useful pathways. As we shall see, these polysilicon features are doped during manufacture and this improves their conductivity. Aluminum remains the metal-of-choice for all high-conductivity pathways, though unlike the older aluminum/oxide/semiconductor sandwich that provided only two topological levels on which to make interconnections, the newer silicon-gate structures provide three and are therefore more compact and correspondingly faster.

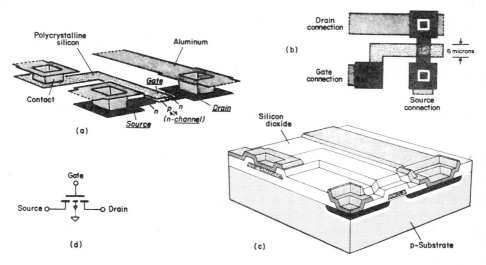

Fig. 11. An n-channel silicon-gate transistor: (a) topological levels; (b) planar layout; (c) structure; (d) symbol (arrow optional).

The three topologically distinct levels defined by the manufacturing process are shown in Fig.11a. The middle level of polysilicon is insulated by interposed oxide from both the upper aluminum level and the lower diffusion level and therefore may be used to provide pathways that cross under the aluminum without touching it if required, though the figure shows the poly and aluminum in contact. Such cross-under pathways can also be defined on the diffusion level, but wherever the designer's layout requires a diffusion level path to cross under a polysilicon path as in Fig.11b, the process establishes a transistor! Note that the polysilicon strip, in its glass tunnel, dips down to a physical level almost in contact with that of the substrate (Fig.11c). The thinner the tunnel floor at this point, the lower the field-effect threshold of the transistor; but if the floor is too thin, the transistor will be turned on too easily. The designer, however, follows only a set of simple rules dealing with relative sizes and spacings of planar features, and depends on the manufacturing process to take care of the third dimension. The planar layout in Fig.11b is typical. It is scaled to a gate-width of 6 microns - about ten wavelengths of visible light! - and follows design rules established by Mead for experimental work at the California Institute of Technology. In Fig.11c the surface-layer thicknesses are exaggerated for clarity; the thickness of the aluminum layer, for example, is approximately one-half of one micron. MOS structures are small and thin.

Yet *not all that planar*, our glassy Lilliput; poly-filled tunnels and deeply pitted highways of aluminum run over hill and vale in this fragile, wrinkled domain resting upon a vast plateau of warring crystal, where manifold subterranean battles are fought futilely on and on by agitated electrons against mythical holes. Quite an interesting gadget, actually, even without the battery; but how in the world does one go about making such a thing?

2.3.2 <u>Fabrication of MOS integrated circuits</u>. One starts by growing a large silicon crystal ingot, the larger the better. This is done by attaching a small crystal, the *seed*, to the end of a rod, dipping the rod into a vat of molten silicon containing the requisite pinch of boron, and then withdrawing the rod very, very slowly. Oriented, polished wafers are made from this ingot, each one about a third of a millimeter thick and ten centimeters in diameter. A few-hundred replicas of the circuit to be made will be built up simultaneously on each of several wafers - each replica, many thousands of transistors and their interconnections. Under various kinds of atmosphere and degrees of temperature, phosphorus is diffused, oxide is grown, and polysilicon and aluminum are deposited - each at a different step in the process.

Planar features are created by a combination of photographic and etching processes. A set of photomasks defining the arrayed replica patterns to be etched into the various layers is carefully prepared from the designer's layout, one mask for each level of structure or kind of feature. Levels to be etched are first coated with a light-sensitive emulsion called *photoresist*, then exposed to light through the appropriate mask, and finally immersed in acid or other strong solution to etch away either the exposed or the unexposed part of the pattern depending on whether positive or negative photoresist had been used. A bath follows.

Microstructure fabrication is a tricky business in which many things can go wrong. Finished wafers are never perfect. Obvious flaws are identified and marked, the wafers are carefully scored with a sharp tool, and with something like a kitchen rolling-pin the individual replicas - now chips - are broken apart from one another. Marked chips are discarded; unmarked ones are mounted in a small plastic or ceramic case. Tiny gold wires are maneuvered into position under a microscope and then bonded to aluminum pads on

the chip, connecting the circuit to convenient metal pins along
the edge of the case. A lid bearing the manufacturer's emblem is
sealed on and the finished package is tested. Bad packages are
discarded or sold at a discount; good ones are shipped to the customer, sometimes filling hollow plastic or metal 'sticks' which
then cost about a million dollars a cord. Large packages such as
microprocessors are sent along in more dignified containers.

Planar features, already near the resolution limit of the light
used in their definition, cannot easily be made much smaller by
optical means. Even so, the manufacturing tolerances maintained
throughout the process are phenomenal. Mask alignment is routine-
ly held to one micron in ten centimeters, an accuracy of one part
in 10^5 quite without precedent in industrial practice. If a ten-
centimeter wafer is scaled up conceptually to 264 kilometers or
164 miles – the distance from Swansea to London – one micron becomes the *length of the hour hand on the clock face of Big Ben*.

We will follow our simple planar layout through the process.
Definition of physical structure begins with a masking step on an
oxide-covered substrate:

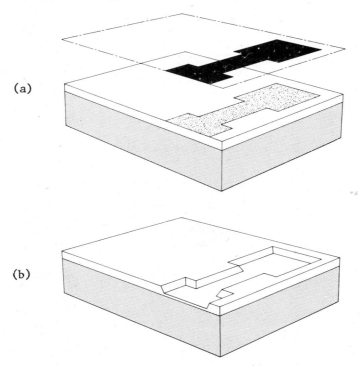

(a)

(b)

Fig. 12. MOS fabrication steps: (a) Diffusion Mask defines planar
features on a photoresist-coated oxide layer; (b) etching removes
unexposed oxide. A thin floor is formed to insulate the gate.

The first two steps (Fig.12a,b) establish the tunnel floor and the source and drain areas. The next three steps (Fig.12c,d,e) form the transistor itself, but leave it bare and unconnected:

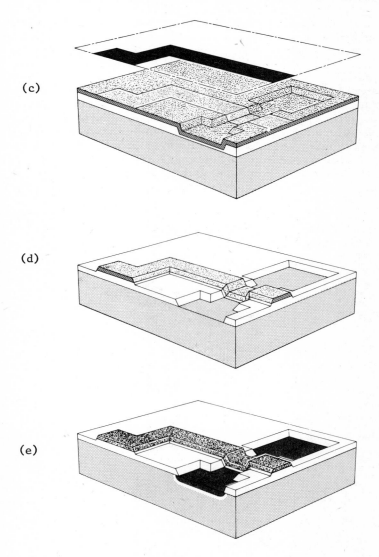

(c)

(d)

(e)

Fig. 12 (continued). MOS fabrication steps: (c) Poly Mask defines features on a photoresist-coated layer of polycrystalline silicon; (d) etching of *exposed* poly forms the gate structure. Additional oxide is removed to uncover the substrate areas defined earlier; (e) phosphorus is diffused into all uncovered silicon thus forming source and drain regions and improving the conductivity of the gate structure. Gate-oxide blocks diffusion into the substrate.

The reader has not failed to notice that the transistor itself is a very small part of the whole, namely just that part of the gate structure which has the thin tunnel floor, together with a thin slice of substrate just below it. It occupies less than 3% of the area of our layout, and much less than .03% of the volume of underlying substrate. All else serves either to support it, to isolate it, or to connect it into the circuit. Transistors can be packed more closely than this implies if pathways are efficiently routed on all three levels, but most of the area of any integrated circuit remains committed to interconnections or 'wires'; and our chip has yet to be wired into its case, and the case, into the computer. Electronic computer circuits are *made* of wire.

In any case, our fabrication surface must now be covered once again with oxide in order to insulate the bare semiconductor areas from the final uppermost pathways. Windows must then be cut to provide access to the gate, source and drain regions wherever required for circuit connections (Fig.12f,g):

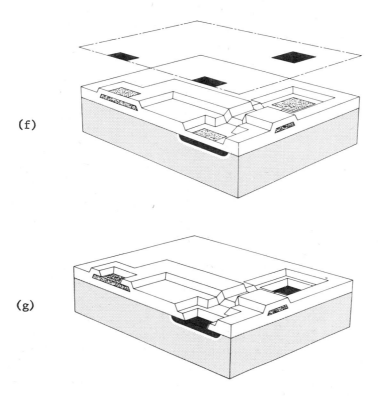

(f)

(g)

Fig.12 (continued). MOS fabrication steps: (f) Contact Mask defines cutout areas on a photoresist-coated oxide covering; (g) etching removes *unexposed* oxide to uncover contact areas on the poly and diffusion levels for circuit connections.

We are ready to build the uppermost pathways. At the places where connections are to be made, areas are enlarged somewhat to assure good inter-level contact even when masks are not in perfect registration; all pathways are otherwise made as small as possible in order to conserve area. Note, by the way, that the task of aligning the Poly and Diffusion Masks is made a bit easier by the fact that it is only their *intersections* – wherever they occur – that define transistor boundaries. This self-alignment feature is partly responsible for the success of silicon-gate technology.

A thin covering of aluminum is now deposited over the entire surface of oxide, now quite complex in structure. Etching then removes all but the requisite 'wires' and contacts (Fig.12h,i):

(h)

(i)

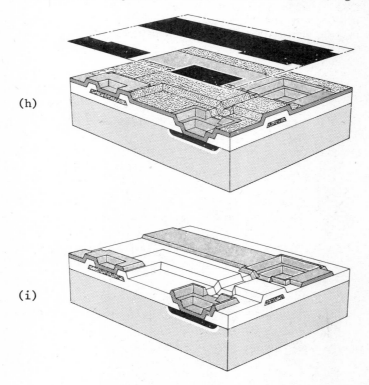

Fig. 12 (concluded). MOS fabrication steps: (h) the Aluminum Mask defines pathways on a photoresist-coated layer of aluminum; (i) etching of *exposed* metal forms 'wires' and their contacts.

The final steps, not illustrated, involve covering the surface with oxide once again and then etching giant windows to gain access to the giant aluminum bonding pads, to which giant gold wires will be attached. On our present scale of things, the final package is *Gargantuan*.

Before we leave the subject of fabrication, it is a good idea to point out that MOS transistors do not have to be so tiny even though much effort is devoted to making them as small as possible for greater packing density and higher speed. Indeed, MOS output-transistors *must* be large (broad) if they are to supply enough current to operate other packages holding power-hungry circuits such as TTL. Fig.13 shows the four-mask set and a composite computer-plot of a pair of giant serpentine-gated output-transistors surrounding a bonding pad, all attached to a second pad nearby:

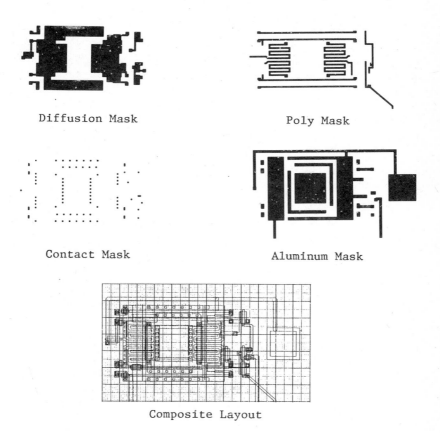

Diffusion Mask   Poly Mask

Contact Mask   Aluminum Mask

Composite Layout

<u>Fig. 13</u>. An MOS output amplifier circuit: photomask set and composite layout (a computer plot). Smaller staging transistors appear near the left and right edges of a pair of large serpentine-gated output-transistors surrounding a bonding pad. A second pad nearby is attached. Multiple contacts share the current-load.

Computer aids to design and layout are essential. Most of the circuit above was obtained by calling forth one plotting-program subroutine for TRANSISTOR, another for PAD, and so on. The amplifier itself was designed by I.E. Sutherland.

19

The word *large* in *large-scale integration* refers not to the size of the transistors, of course, but rather to the number of transistors on one chip. Chip size is limited by a consideration of yield: the larger the chip, the greater the probability of surface flaws and therefore the slimmer the chances of finding enough good chips per wafer to make batch-production profitable. A good deal of effort thus goes into the development of efficient structures that lead to high packing densities. Chips holding ten thousand transistors have already been produced; large-scale indeed, these digital systems one can hold, to use Professor Aspinall's apt phrase, "between finger and thumb".

The microcircuit industry is inclined to protect its huge investment by minimizing risk. Mistakes are very costly and progress towards higher levels of integration is made cautiously. But the industry is now at a turning point: X-ray lithography or electron-beam technology must take the place of photolithography if devices are to be made significantly smaller, though the almost incredible problem of mask alignment stands in the way of their full use. One-mask structures already are being made by means of these new techniques and demonstrate the feasibility of feature densities two or three orders of magnitude *greater* than those achieved under ultraviolet light.

We began the discussion of integration with Dummer's prediction. We will close it with another, and then move on to consider aspects of the organization of microstructural units. Sutherland, Mead and Everhart (1976), after a very thorough review of the work of many U.S. laboratories aimed at producing devices of sub-micron dimensions, arrive at the following startling conclusion:

> "There is every reason to believe that the integrated circuit revolution has run only half its course: the change in complexity of four to five orders of magnitude that has taken place during the past 15 years appears to be only the first half of a potentially eight-order-of-magnitude development. There seem to be no fundamental obstacles to 10^7 to 10^8 device integrated circuits."

One hundred *million*. Ultrasystem chips in which microprocessors as we now know them, rather than transistors, become the operative units? Powerful storage arrays with integral processing? The designers of complex algorithmic systems face a very important challenge. Let us hope that they do their job well and that we all learn how to make good use of their work. One hundred million is a large number, and devices will be very small indeed. On the Swansea-to-London scale, today's transistor is perhaps the size of a room; tomorrow's transistor may be the size of a book.

3 THE LOGIC OF MOS CIRCUITS

We must now discover transistor combinations that can be made to do the work of logic. Only a few basic forms are required for the synthesis of useful complex structures. We proceed:

3.1 Basic combinations

3.1.1 The Inverter. The MOS transistor is essentially an on-off switch with a bad connection; it can be turned completely 'off' but not completely 'on'. The transistor's channel resists the flow of electrons so that they become less numerous (though a bit speedier) towards the drain end. In bumping through a chain of conducting channels, negative electron-ranks become thinner link-by-link; the relative positivity of the inter-channel pathway correspondingly increases. Broad, 'easy' channels increase the positivity less; narrow, 'hard' ones, more. The Inverter is based on these facts.

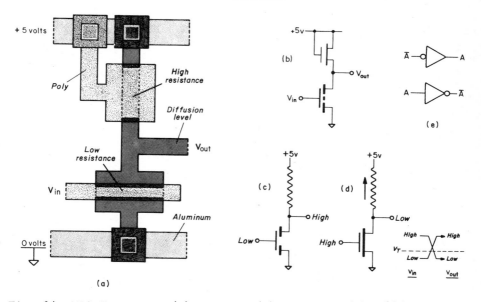

Fig. 14. MOS Inverter: (a) layout; (b) circuit; (c) *off*; (d) *on*; (e) logic symbols. The upper-link symbol is simplified in (c) and (d).

In the two-link Inverter, the upper channel, long and narrow, has a high resistance; the lower one, short and broad, a low resistance. Uppermost gate and drain are connected via an aluminum pathway to the positive side of a 5-volt battery (Fig.14a); the lowermost source is connected to the negative side and anchored to establish a zero-voltage reference level. The upper transistor serves only to provide a fixed high-resistance link since it is always 'on' by virtue of its highly-charged gate, a fact emphasized

21

by the use of a simplifying zig-zag symbol. The lower transistor, on the other hand, will be 'on' only when its gate voltage, V_{in}, is given a value above the general 1-volt threshold. When this happens, the output voltage, V_{out}, takes on a <u>low</u> relatively-positive value as electrons are pushed by the battery through the low-resistance link of the completed chain and flow past the mid-chain output point as shown in Fig.14d. V_{out} otherwise takes on a relatively <u>high</u> value (but of course not more than 5 volts) as some of the un-anchored output-pathway's electrons are pulled away to the battery through the fixed 'pull-up resistor' (Fig.14c). Thus, a *high* V_{in} implies a *low* V_{out} and vice versa. Proper choice of both battery-voltage and channel-resistance-ratio ensures that *high* and *low* are values in turn well above- and below-threshold so that one Inverter will drive another reliably. In logic symbols (Fig.14e), we identify *high* with 'one' or 'true'; *low*, with 'zero' or 'false'. If A is true then its inverse, NOT-A (written $\bar{A}$), is false.

3.1.2 <u>Not-AND (NAND) and Not-OR (NOR) circuits</u>. Simple elaborations of the Inverter chain give us the two basic 'logical' gating elements of coordinated charge flow, the NAND and NOR Gates. In the NAND circuit of Fig.15a, the output will be *low* only when both of the inputs, A and B, are *high*, for only then will a conductive pathway to the zero-anchor be established. In the NOR circuit of Fig.15c, the chain is a bifurcated one and a *high* on either of the inputs, A or B (or on both, of course), will do the trick. The expression 'A and B' is written AB; the expression 'A or B', A + B.

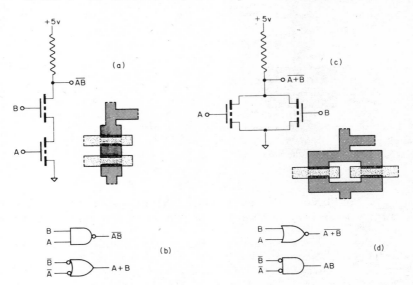

Fig. 15. NAND and NOR Gates: (a) NAND circuit; (b) NAND Gate and its equivalent Low-input-OR Gate logic symbols; (c) NOR circuit; (d) NOR Gate and its equivalent Low-input-AND Gate logic symbols.

The principles observed in designing such combinational circuits are simple ones: a single pull-up resistor must be fixed
'above' the point of output and a network of variable-gated transistors attached 'below'; the ratio of fixed-resistance to maximum
'on' variable-resistance must be made about equal to that of the
Inverter, about ten- or twenty-to-one; the size of the overall
structure generally must be kept small for greater speed. Fig.16
shows a somewhat richer example:

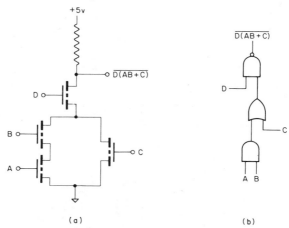

(a)   (b)

Fig. 16. A combination of logic gates: (a) circuit; (b) logic net.

Combinational circuits based on switching devices have been
studied thoroughly since the publication of the classic paper on
the subject by Shannon (1938). In the pre-transistor years much
activity was devoted to the development of techniques for circuit
synthesis, first in the design of telephone relay networks and
later in the design of digital computers. In modern integrated
circuit layouts the logical is nicely related to the physical, and
we see wires and switches at a glance - or perhaps a *stare*, when
matters become just a bit complicated as in Fig.17:

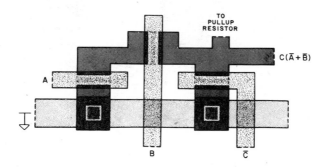

Fig. 17. A planar layout of a combinational circuit
with cross-under pathways and inverted logic terms.

3.1.3 <u>Flip-Flops</u>. Seldom as lively as its name implies, the Flip-Flop is in fact a bi-stable circuit that will hold itself in one of two preset states so long as the battery remains in operation. Bi-stability is provided by a trick of cross-connection between negating logic combinations. Fig.18 shows a version based on a pair of NOR Gates, often known as a Latch:

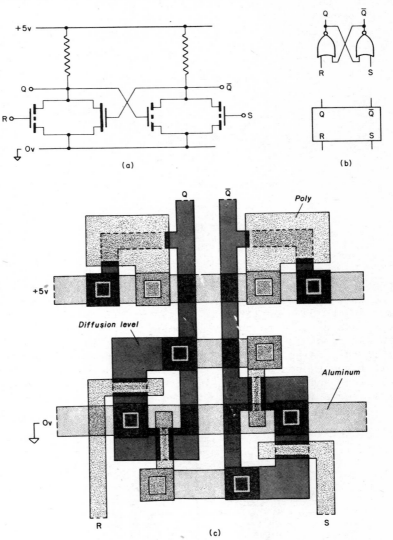

Fig. 18. An RS Flip-Flop (Latch): (a) circuit; (b) logic form; (c) planar layout. ˙ Poly level and Diffusion level features are connected to one another via the Aluminum level. Q and Q̄ outputs appear on all three levels thus simplifying later integration.

Fig.18a shows the circuit initially locked in its Q-Low state by the cross-connected $\bar{Q}$ output, which is 'un-anchored' and there-fore *high*. Circuits external to the figure provide R (Reset) and S (Set) inputs in such a way that either R or S, but not both at once, can be raised momentarily to a high level. If S is now made *high*, output $\bar{Q}$ is 'anchored' and becomes *low*; the cross-activated link in the R-side NOR Gate is broken, and output Q promptly be-comes *high*. This Q-High signal crosses back to establish a second anchoring pathway in the S-side NOR Gate and will continue to hold $\bar{Q}$ *low* after the momentary S input signal disappears. Circuitous! The circuit now appears locked in its Q-High state. A momentary *high* on the R input will reset the circuit to its initial Q-Low state. It is clear that R and S must never be made *high* at the same time if the circuit is to be well-behaved. There will be more to say about this shortly.

The so-called D Flip-Flop (Fig.19) is often a more convenient design element. It is a bi-stable circuit in which the changes of state can occur only during specific intervals of time established by an externally generated 'clock' signal:

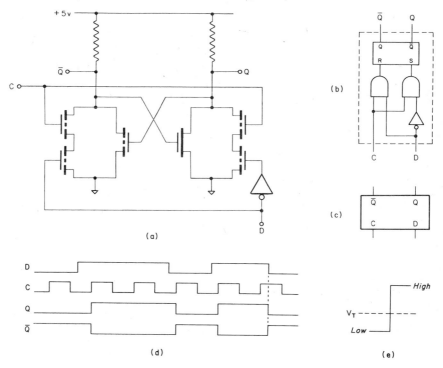

(b)

(c)

(a)

(d)

(e)

Fig. 19. The D Flip-Flop: (a) circuit; (b) logic form; (c) symbol; (d) timing diagram; (e) voltage 'swing'. When the C (Clock) input is *high*, Q and $\bar{Q}$ outputs match the D (Data) input and its inverse.

The timing diagram (Fig.19d) shows the final transition of the D input signal as occurring while the C input is *high*, an event resulting in out-of-step outputs. Clearly, the briefer the 'high C' intervals, the better the time definition of the outputs. There is a limit, of course: if these high intervals or clock pulses are too brief, the circuit will fail to 'flip' or 'flop'. An alternative way to improve time resolution involves the addition of other elements to the D Flip-Flop circuit so that it will ignore the D input signal once the *low*-to-*high* C-transition has been made, and will attend further D input changes only after the subsequent 'safe' *high*-to-*low* C-transition. These more complex Flip-Flops, said to be leading-edge triggered, make possible the reduction of timing uncertainty to a minimum — though not to zero, of course, since electron mobilities are finite.

Many other Flip-Flop forms of even greater complexity are possible. In one robust version, for example, Q outputs are led back to input steering gates in such a way that presentation of a 'true' value at transition time results in a complementing of the state of the Flip-Flop. All such complex Flip-Flops, however, are relatively large and are used only when they simplify or are essential to the overall design.

Now pay attention! There is a short DETOUR at this point:

Regardless of complexity, no Flip-Flop is predictably well-behaved when triggered by marginally adequate signals. This is no less true of integrated circuit Flip-Flops than it is of any other form of bi-stable device that one is able to contrive; in the view of Holt (1977), the problem is intrinsic to the decision process itself and thus one that challenges our most profound concepts of choice and cause. From some of the earliest perceptions of difficulty (Gray, 1963; Catt, 1966; Ornstein, 1966; and Littlefield and Chaney, 1966) to the more recent experimental work and rigorous theoretical analysis (Mars, 1968; Chaney and Molnar, 1973; Couranz and Wann, 1975; and Hurtado, 1975), the subject has grown to maturity and — surprisingly — considerable controversy.

Thus, the following story has been told in many other contexts. It is recounted here in the spirit of that alarmed politician who, two thousand years ago, took advantage of every oratorical opportunity to call for the precautionary destruction of Carthage; for it seems that the potential for instability in what we would like to regard as bi-stable mechanisms cannot be brought to our attention often enough.

In a clocked Flip-Flop, marginal triggering can occur whenever a data input, for some reason, happens to change just at the moment of clock transition. In an RS Flip-Flop, marginal triggering can occur whenever Reset and Set signals are presented concurrently and then withdrawn nearly simultaneously. Instead of recording 'YES' or 'NO' with convincing authority, the marginally-triggered Flip-Flop can become vacillatory or perhaps meta-stable, its confused outputs interpretable as 'neither Yes nor No', or worse, 'Yes *and* No'. Furthermore, <u>it is impossible to predict the durations of any such periods of indecisiveness</u>; one can know only that such periods are more likely to be very short than very long, the odds at best falling exponentially with length in a way that varies from circuit to circuit. The logician groans.

These occasional dicey outcomes, known in some cultures as 'glitches', are unavoidable in systems having more than one clock or timing basis. Synchronizing circuits can be interposed between independently timed subsystems to trap most of the misbehavior and thereby reduce the scope of unwanted effects. Fig.20 illustrates one method of synchronization in the context of the interaction between a randomly-thrown switch and a clocked subsystem:

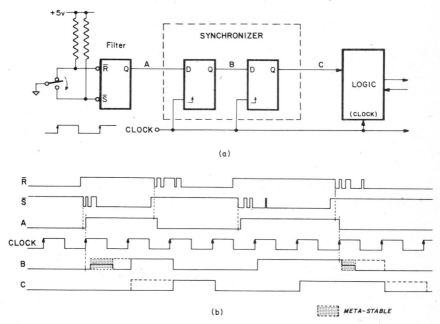

(a)

(b)   ▒▒▒▒ *META-STABLE*

<u>Fig. 20.</u> Clock synchronization of a randomly timed signal.

Actually, two independent processes are depicted in Fig.20. In the first, an $\overline{\text{RS}}$ Latch is used to tidy up the signals produced by operation of the switch when its mechanical arm bounces against the 'target' contact before coming to rest; the resulting filtered output, A, is indeed quite tidy but is not at all in step with the clock pulses. In the second, a pair of edge-triggered D Flip-Flops attempts to reconstruct an authoritative clock-cycle-quantized approximation of signal A; successful or not, it sends its result, C, to the clocked logic subsystem.

27

The timing diagram in Fig.20 shows small delays between causes
and effects in order to clarify sequential dependency. For example, the Latch (cross-connected NANDs) responds to the first ap-
pearance of a *low* on either the $\overline{R}$ or $\overline{S}$ input lines after a characteristic small delay. In other respects the A, $\overline{R}$ and $\overline{S}$ tracks are
grossly foreshortened in the diagram; mechanical switching and
bouncing epochs typically span many tens-of-thousands of clock cycles. The first rising and last falling A-transitions are shown
as happening to coincide with clock triggering edges thereby creating two B-glitches, both of which happen to resolve to a final
low after a fairly short period of instability.

The principle of glitch-trapping synchronization is this:
Owing to its exponential time-dependency, the probability that a
B-glitch created on one clock transition will survive long enough
to cause a C-glitch on the following clock transition can readily
be reduced to any arbitrary acceptable value by setting the clock
rate sufficiently low. By the same consideration, synchronizers
run at increasingly <u>high</u> rates will fail dramatically. In any
event, it is clear that synchronization introduces both delay and
pulse-width uncertainty.

An Asynchronous Arbiter is a circuit combining synchronizers
and decision elements in such a way that it can withhold a change
in, or validation of, its output signals until stability appears to
be assured. For this service it demands the sacrifice of decision
time predictability. Not all Asynchronous Arbiters work well.

Right, then. Back to the main discussion:

3.1.4 <u>Drivers</u>. Where speed of operation is important, fairly powerful (i.e., low-resistance) combinations are required to supply
charge current simultaneously to the many gates often found connected to a clock line or other pathway. Three of the forms such
Drivers take in current practice are shown in Fig.21. In the simplest form (Fig.21a) both upper and lower transistors of a tandem
pair are given low-resistance channels; an Inverter ensures that
only one of the two will be 'on' at a time to force the output
voltage to a high or low level. All CMOS elements, by the way,
are based on this tandem-pair principle but avoid the heat-produc-
ing Inverter altogether by including one *low-on* and one *high-on*
transistor in each pair as foreshadowed earlier in Fig.6b.

If the gating network of Fig.21b is now added it becomes possible to disconnect the output line from the output transistors
altogether, thereby giving us a useful 'third state'. Another
such '3-state-output' driver can be attached to this same output
line, and another, and another, so that signals from many different originating nodes can now be sent along the same signal bus
pathway, provided that only one node is licensed or enabled to
drive at any one time. The final form (Fig.21c) provides for both

sending <u>and</u> receiving by combining a 3-state-output Driver with an
Inverter and a Low-input AND Gate:

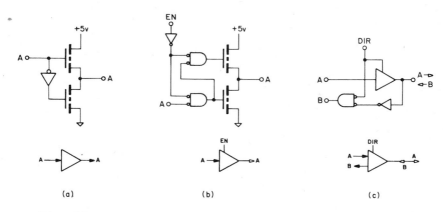

(a)   (b)   (c)

Fig. 21. Drivers: (a) simple Driver (non-inverting);
(b) a 3-state-output Driver; (c) a 3-state-output
Driver/input Receiver. EN, *enable*; DIR, *direction*.

While we're on the subject of Driving, the reader surely will
excuse the need for a few steps backward at this point in order to
see how a trick of fabrication - Ion Implantation - results in a
significant increase in driving capability and a general decrease
in physical size. The trick involves the deliberate alteration of
the characteristics of the transistor so as to produce an inherent-
ly-inverted rather than a field-inverted channel. This is accomplished early in the fabrication sequence for n-channel MOS by
using an elaborate ion-accelerating gun to shoot phosphorus ions
into some of the channel areas of the substrate. Additional masking and processing steps are necessary. Ion-Implant Mask areas
overlap those of the partially completed transistor candidates;
the additional steps create temporary access windows through which
ion bullets can be shot into the substrate. The ions are then ac-
celerated to a velocity just high enough so that they lodge themselves in the selected future channels to a carefully controlled
depth. Subsequent standard processing steps will then build transistors that are normally-'on' rather than normally-'off' around
each of these implanted channels. The standard MOS transistor,
normally-'off', is turned 'on' by application of a gate voltage
that is greater than some positive threshold value. The implanted-
ion transistor, normally-'on', is turned 'off' by application of a
gate voltage that is less than some negative threshold value. But
inasmuch as negative gate voltages never appear in our circuits,
one can read 'always on' for 'normally on'.

Why is it advantageous to use these normally-on transistors in
design? The simple answer is that they form better pull-up resistors when used in a certain way, but a full explanation of the

improvement would take us farther back than we care to go. We
would have to examine the notion of channel resistance in more detail, for example, and would immediately find that our pull-up resistor is not in fact a purely resistive component (for which, in
a careful exposition, the zig-zag symbol would strictly have been
reserved). A purely resistive component would exhibit the linear
relationship between current, I, and voltage, V, known as Ohm's
Law (Fig.22a) whereas our pull-up 'resistor', formed by connecting
together the gate and drain of a standard MOS transistor, would be

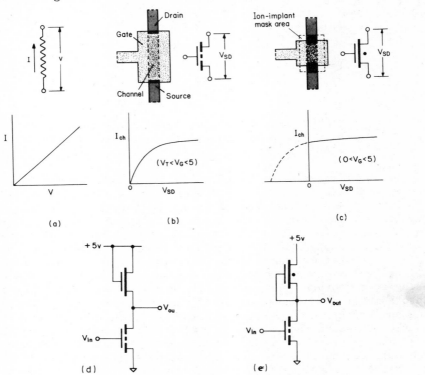

Fig. 22. Comparison of 'resistors': (a) pure resistor and
linear current/voltage characteristic; (b) a standard MOS
transistor and characteristic for gate connected to drain;
(c) an Implanted Ion MOS transistor and characteristic for
gate connected to source (the dotted symbol denotes 'normally on'); (d) Inverter circuit with standard MOS pull-up 'resistor'; (e) Inverter with Implanted Ion pull-up 'resistor'.

found to exhibit a markedly non-linear relationship (Fig.22b), as
would the 'resistor' based on an implanted-channel transistor in
which the gate is connected to the source (Fig.22c). We would then
have to call upon the mathematical tools of circuit analysis for a
clear understanding of the input/output behavior of basic Inverter

configurations with non-linear components. Our reward would be the discovery that the 'implanted' Inverter (Fig.22e) requires an upper-to-lower size ratio of only five-to-one for an adequate output voltage swing, while the 'standard' Inverter (Fig.22d) requires a ratio of ten-to-one or greater. We would also learn that the implanted Inverter 'swings' more crisply, and therefore drives more capably, than does its counterpart.

3.2 Logic Arrays

The basic circuits can be combined in many different ways to form more or less regular arrays of logical structure. Combinational logic circuits may or may not assume regular form; storage elements almost always do. But in any case, simple 'linear' Shift Registers as well as complex Memories and Logic are all teased into geometrical forms having felicitous planar projections. The catalog of structures is a very large one, and we can look at only a few of its illustrations.

3.2.1 Decoders. In its simplest form, a Decoder is essentially a set of logic gates with several outputs, each output asserting the presentation of a specific pattern of input values. A delightfully compact Decoder structure has been illuminated by Sutherland. It is based on the observation that the Implanted Ion transistor defined by Poly and Diffusion pathways that cross in an implanted zone as in Fig.23a will nicely preserve the continuity of signal flow on both levels, since it will always be 'on' for all proper signals on the crossing Poly level. This structural feature — what we may call an *Ion Cross* — can then be used to great advantage in Decoder matrix forms when combined with standard transistor 'crosses' as in Fig.23b.

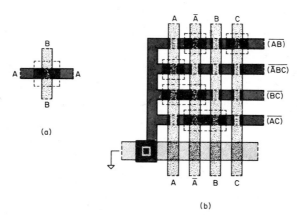

Fig. 23. Decoder matrix using Implanted Ion transistors: (a) an Ion Cross, showing continuity of signal pathways on Diffusion (AA) and Poly (BB) levels; (b) a combined matrix. Dashed lines enclose the Ion Implant Mask areas.

3.2.2 Shift Registers.

Due to their simplicity and regularity of structure, Shift Registers were among the earliest candidates for large-scale integration. Two main families, termed *Static* and *Dynamic*, have been developed. In the Static Shift Register family, information can be held for indefinitely long periods in the absence of clock pulse activity. In the Dynamic Shift Register family, periodic or occasional clock pulses are required to prevent loss of information, an inconvenience justified by a concomitant reduction in the overall size of the structure.

One Static Shift Register makes use of D Flip-Flops in pairs, with one pair per bit (Fig.24). Trains of non-overlapping clock pulses, C_1 and C_2, alternately transfer data from the Input and the upper rank of Flip-Flops into the lower rank, and from the lower rank into the upper and to the Output:

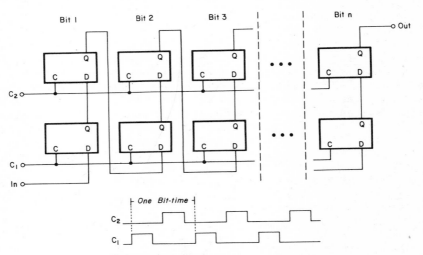

Fig. 24. D Flip-Flop Static Shift Register

Each pair of clock pulses shifts the information along one bit-position. Time must be allowed between C_1 and C_2 pulses to permit the Flip-Flops to stabilize before passing information onwards. Big but effective; each bit inhabits a 20-transistor 'cell'.

The Dynamic Shift Register shown in Fig.25 has a 6-transistor cell. Its operation is based on the storage of charge on electrically isolated pathways. Recall that when a gate pathway is somehow disconnected from all other pathways after some of its electrons have been removed by application of a *high* signal, the positive charge thus trapped above the gate-oxide will sustain the field-induced channel in the substrate below until electrons are reintroduced by application of a *low* signal. Unfortunately, such isolation is never perfect; electrons wander back onto the 'isolated' structure along a number of unplanned and unwanted yet

unavoidable minor routes, thus leading to a gradual loss of the
gate's positivity and the collapse of its field. Any information
held in place by the field must be passed on or otherwise regen-
erated in a timely fashion. Charge is retained long enough, however, to make possible the following simple arrangement:

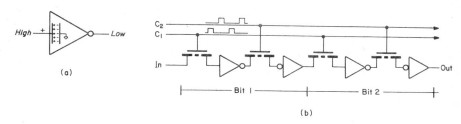

Fig. 25. Simple Dynamic Shift Register: (a) charge
storage at the Inverter input gate; (b) circuit.

Two ranks of Inverters are operated by two trains of non-overlapping clock pulses. In Fig.25 the two ranks are shown interleaved in order to emphasize structural linearity. C_1 pulses control 'pass' transistors which establish pathways across the cell
boundaries; C_2 pulses establish pathways within the cells. Alternation of pulses therefore shifts information along; failure to
apply pulses often enough results in information loss.

Simplification of the Static Shift Register follows directly
(Fig.26) by extension of this technique. C_1 and C_2 pulse pairs
shift information along as in the previous example. Bi-stability
is provided by adding a *feedback* pass transistor to each cell; it
is turned 'on' by a third clock pulse, C_3. Small delays between
pulses allow Inverters to stabilize. So long as C_2 and C_3 are
both held *high*, the Inverters within each cell are cross-connected
and information will remain in place without further attention.

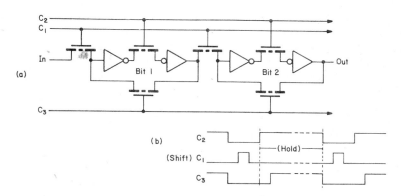

Fig. 26. Simple Static Shift Register. Information remains in place so long as C_2 and C_3 signals are held *high*.

3.2.3 Read-Only-Memory (ROM).

Structurally very regular, ROM is made in many forms. Fig.27 shows one simple form in which stored information is represented by the presence or absence of transistors in a storage matrix.

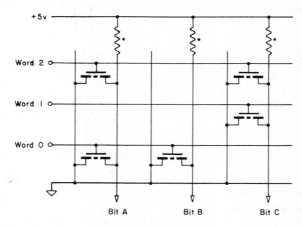

Fig. 27. Read-Only-Memory (ROM) matrix. Word lines select partially filled rows of transistors arranged in NOR columns. Absence of a transistor corresponds to *high* output.

When a *high* signal is applied to a selected Word line, *high* signals will appear on only those Bit-output lines for which the corresponding matrix-element transistor sites are unfilled. In *mask-programable* ROM manufacture, variants of one basic chip are produced by specifying different patterns of filled and unfilled sites, a matter of relatively easy alteration of just the Diffusion mask.

Other ROM forms of greater complexity provide for alteration of stored patterns by means of externally applied 'programming' signals. In one popular form, selected matrix elements are permanently disabled by energetic signals. In another ROM form, the information storage mechanisms are such that stored patterns can be erased by ultraviolet light, which shines down upon the transistor plane through a transparent window thoughtfully built into the lid of the integrated circuit package.

3.2.4 Programmed Logic Array (PLA).

By connecting two ROMs in tandem, we obtain a structure that generates outputs in canonical 'sum of products' form in response to the presentation of sets of input signals. Although both ROMs have the same NOR Gate composition as that of the previous example, we view the input ROM as the AND (logical product) generator for *low* input signals and the output ROM as the OR (logical sum) generator with *low* outputs as in Fig.28a. PLA combinations typically provide Inverters so that both 'true' and 'false' values can be included in the static logic

expressions developed by such a pair of ROMs. They can be extended to sequential operation - in a direct implementation of the
well-known Finite State Automaton - by incorporating Flip-Flops
having outputs fed back to some of the PLA inputs, as in Fig.28b.
An appealingly simple AND-OR structure based on the transistor-
cross matrix is shown in Fig.28c. It omits the 'OR' ROM altogether but may require some duplication of AND terms, as illustrated
on the middle two rows of the matrix.

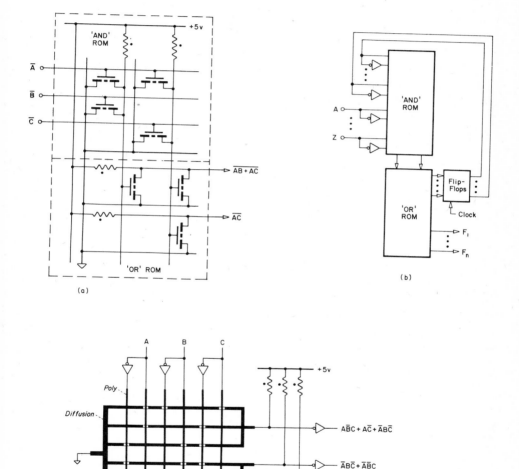

Fig. 28. Programmed Logic Arrays (PLA): (a) ROM pair; (b) typical
PLA form; (c) transistor-cross matrix with 'wired-OR' outputs.
'White' crosses, standard transistors; all others, Ion Crosses.

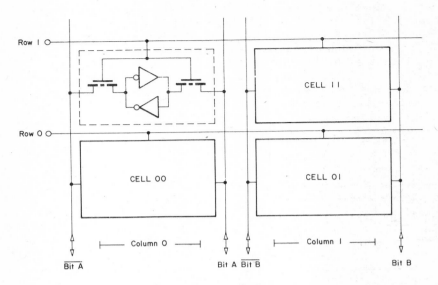

Fig. 29. Static Read Write Memory (RWM) array. In addition to Row-select and Bit in/out lines, zero- and +5-volt lines (not shown) connect all cells to operate the Inverter pairs.

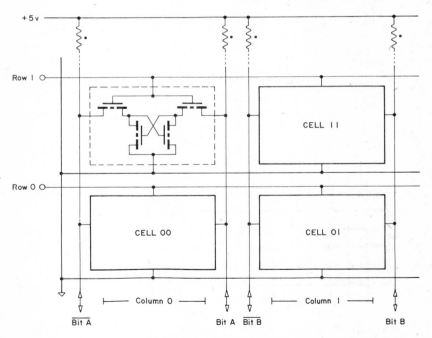

Fig. 30. Dynamic Read Write Memory (RWM) array. Occasional *high* signals on the Row-select lines refresh information.

3.2.5 Read Write Memory (RWM). Both static and dynamic forms of Read Write Memory arrays are made. The Static RWM cell shown in Fig.29 illustrates the use of a bi-stable pair of Inverters as the storage element. Pass transistors connect opposite sides of the pair to Bit lines for reading and writing. Quite indifferent to the direction of flow, those pass transistors turned 'on' by a *high* Row Select signal will conduct information into the cell if either the Bit or Bit line is driven *low* externally, but will otherwise conduct information out of the cell. The bi-stable pair either assumes the state forced by the Bit line signals or else puts its own signals onto the Bit lines without changing state.

In order to expose some of the ideas involved in simplification, we will take only the first step down the path that leads ultimately to a 1- or 2-transistor storage cell: the 6-transistor Static RWM cell can be simplified directly by removing all Inverter pull-up components to a zone outside the array, from which a single pair can be time-shared by all cells within the same Bit column. The resulting Dynamic RWM cell array is shown in Fig.30. The occasional *high* signals on the Row Select lines which are presented during normal readout operations temporarily reconnect the selected row of cells to the set of shared pull-ups, and thus refresh the information stored along the row. Logic circuits not shown provide extra background reference-signals to ensure that each row is selected often enough to prevent information loss.

Addressing the above arrays is a simple enough matter of Decoders and further pass-transistor gating of Bit lines (Fig.31):

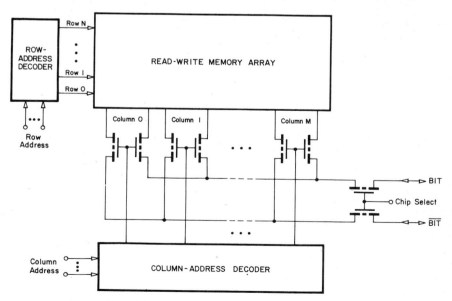

Fig. 31. Addressing an MxNx1-bit memory array.

3.3 Microprocessors

Well ... microprocessors, after all, are the subject of our larger inquiry and are to be studied in considerable depth and in many variations in the remaining chapters, are they not? A single picture will suffice to make the following introductory point: Microprocessors are little more than further combinations of the basic elements and arrays that we have already seen.

Fig. 32. Composite n-MOS photomask set for the OM1, a 16-bit microprogramable microprocessor.

Fig.32 shows the composite mask set for one such microprocessor, the 16-bit OM1, a forerunner of a coordinated group of modules (Johannsen and Mead, 1977). Several arrays can be seen in the interior; to the left, two 16 x 16-bit Dynamic RWM sub-arrays, with address Decoders above and below and read-write circuits on either side; to the right of center, a 16 x 16 array of data pathway offset gates for high-speed shifting; to the far right, the Arithmetic Logic Unit (ALU), with other PLA structures above and below. Drivers and Driver/Receivers are seen near the edges. The names of the designers, Mead, Carroll, Johannsen and Matsumoto, are registered as minute engravings on the polycrystalline silicon level of a thousand chips.

––––––––

4 CONCLUSION AND PERSPECTIVE

There you have it: out of the ceaseless irregular bustling of jittery electrons, the statistical orderliness of controlled circuit flow; out of the happy coincidence of just the right properties of matter and the innate inventiveness of man, a miniscule but powerful apparatus to serve the methodology of logic. It all hangs by a circumstantial chain: silicon just happens to have an accommodating lattice structure that can be altered in useful ways; insulating glass just happens to bond well to silicon; some chemical etchants just happen to eat glass while others eat non-glass; the right sort of aluminum just happens to bond well to both silicon *and* glass, the right sort of gold, to aluminum.

In learning how to create and use the tiny no-man's land between opposed regions of enriched semiconductive material we have contrived to build practical devices of extraordinarily small size. In learning how to partition and distribute electron population pressures we have developed a set of techniques for controlling the movement of charge in minute physical structures. A grasp of control principles has given us the ability to analogize increasingly complex expressions of logic, from the 'and' and 'or' of propositional calculus to the machinery of algorithmic systems. The family of microprocessors lives on top of this growing peak of technical achievement.

The tools of fabrication are costly and elaborate marvels of technology: crystal growers, orienters, slicers and polishers; diffusion furnaces, vacuum deposition chambers and ion accelerators; high-precision cameras with ultra-stable indexing mechanisms; micro-manipulators and micro-welders; injection molders; inspection and test equipment; accounting departments.

The integrated circuits themselves are amazingly cheap and almost too plentiful. Through the sorcery of a very advanced technology we will soon be able to produce powerful circuit modules in quantities far greater than we can assimilate. And remember, *the integrated circuit revolution has run only half its course!* We have much to learn and much to keep in careful perspective; yet with the relentless quickening of the pace of development and the almost inevitable decline in our ability to master our most complex artifacts, will not we sorcerer's apprentices make too many brooms anyway? What are we going to do with them all?

It is always a pleasure to acknowledge the help of friends. Mr. Amar Archbold - a man of unlimited enthusiasms - gave me the title and therewith my theme; Prof. David Aspinall, boundless editorial patience; Profs. Ivan Sutherland and Carver Mead, a princely welcome into their delightful world of microscopic logic. To these good gentlemen and scholars goes my deepest gratitude.

E. L. Dagless

University College, Swansea

1. INTRODUCTION

A computer based information processing system contains two main components, the computer mainframe and its peripherals (fig. 1). In large and expensive installations many man years

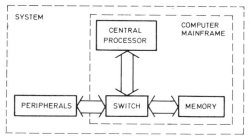

Fig.1. Computer system

of skilled effort by the computer engineer is devoted to producing an efficient mainframe computer, which is then provided with the peripherals necessary to interface to the user. The systems designer using a microcomputer mainframe is usually faced with the reverse situation. The external environment which is to be monitored or controlled usually exists first and a mainframe must be selected to meet the requirements of the processing function, which is the algorithm or algorithms necessary to transform the information, the information flow rate from the external transducers and the response time of the computer system in servicing critical time dependent events.

A microcomputer is basically an assembly of a few components formed around one or more integrated circuits called a micro-processor. The user has considerable scope for arranging these components to suit a specific application, a degree of freedom denied to the conventional mainframe user. Thus the system designer may select a suitable standard microcomputer mainframe, alternatively he can choose the best components and organise them optimally, to produce his own dedicated computer. Within the mainframe of the microcomputer the four main components that require more detailed consideration are (a) the processor, which executes the programmed instructions (b) the memory which stores the program and the information the program manipulates (c) the input-output system, which provides the link between the mainframe and the peripherals, and finally (d) the switch, which performs the routing of information between the three main components above. Because of the interrelated nature of these components they will be discussed under three main headings.

a) Processor - Memory - Switch (PMS) level concentrates on the processor-switch interface, the switch-memory interface, and the memory system.

b) Instruction Set Processor (ISP) level concentrates on the processor architecture and the instruction set, Chapter I.C.

c) Input Output presents the features of the peripheral-processor interface and the special requirements of this interface for efficient information flow and control of critical events, Chapter I.D.

2.   BACKGROUND

The microcomputer evolved as the natural progression upwards from the production of medium scale integrated (MSI) circuits (IC) for digital computers. When the semiconductor manufacturer had the capability to fabricate an IC with 500 gates or more he had to find a component that would sell in large volume. The product was called a microprocessor, possibly erroneously, and the term is now used for almost any processing 'component' of one or at most a few integrated circuits. The constraints of having to place a complex component on a single integrated circuit can have a significant influence on the characteristics and behaviour of the final product. The restrictions imposed by limited pin out (between 18 and 64 signal connections on the chip), chip size (limits the number of gates on the device), power consumption (a typical package can only dissipate about 1 watt without elaborate cooling techniques), circuit technology (affects number of gates, voltage levels, clock signals) and the need to produce a general purpose product will always be, in some way, responsible for machine architecture and detailed operational features. Since there is no one 'correct' solution to such a complex set of constraints, many individual, unusual diverse answers exist in the 30 or so microprocessors currently available. Any attempt to rationalise these into a coherent statement will have flaws and faults but some general

'truths' can be identified through the progression of products
seen to date, and many important fundamental principles can be
presented which differ only in detail from product to product.

Fixed Instruction Set Processors

By far the greatest majority of 'microprocessors' produced
are of the fixed instruction set type, many of them on a single
integrated circuit. This is also the simplest and easiest
classification to make. The fixed instruction set processor
can be explained by reference to the hypothetical processor and
memory shown in fig. 2. The processor fetches from the memory

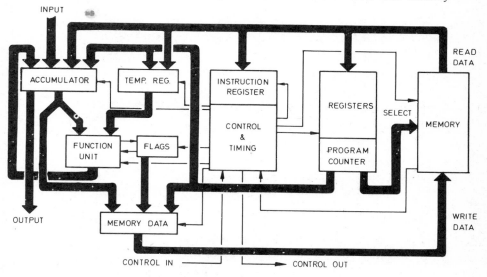

Fig.2. Small central processor and its memory

instructions which are loaded into the instruction register.
This information then controls the activity of the processor as
it executes the instruction. Operations on data in registers or
memory are effected through the function unit and the accumulator,
the results being returned to the registers or to locations in
memory. All of the actions in the processor are controlled by
the control and timing unit which can be implemented with random
logic gates, read only memory or programmable logic arrays. A
processor has a fixed instruction set if the control circuitry
cannot be changed by the user. Almost all microprocessors
made in MOS technology are of this type. The manufacturer
defines the instruction set and usually fixes it during the
fabrication of the integrated circuit. Alternative approaches
are described elsewhere in this course. The characteristics
of the instruction set are elaborated in Chapter I.C.

Processor Types. If the material presented here only related
to a single processor then the general principles could not
easily be abstracted, and a biased view of the market would be
presented. However there are well over 30 products and a
complete description of all would only be a duplication of the
manufacturers' (in most cases) bulky literature and probably
very boring reading. Where possible, different devices are
mentioned when they have important characteristics that may or
may not conform to what seems to be the norm. Over the years
certain devices have achieved industry standard status and
these will be used for examples where reference to many would
become confusing. Particular emphasis will be given to the
Intel range from the 8008, 8080, 8085, to 8048 because it
covers 3 generations of a recognisably generic product range,
and shows some important trends in current thinking.

3. PROCESSOR-MEMORY-SWITCH

     A processor provides an address which the switch uses to
select a location in the memory to perform a read or write
cycle using the basic data routes shown in fig. 3.

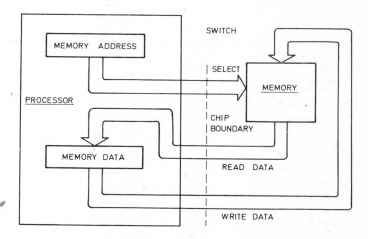

Fig.3. Processor - memory: Basic routes

     There also exists a number of control signals which manage
the transfer of data across the switch boundaries, which are
implied here but considered in more detail later. To
emphasise the importance of the chip boundary, which need not
coincide with the processor switch interface, a hashed line is
drawn on the diagrams. A column in the tables contains the
pin count at this boundary. In the system of fig. 3 the only
switch action consists of selecting a single location in the

memory, an action common to all memory systems, so this will be implied on all the subsequent diagrams.

Since the memory can only be either reading or writing the two data routes can be merged to one to produce the bidirectional data route shown in fig. 4. Two drivers (one each side of the

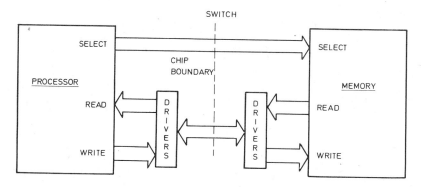

Fig.4. Processor – memory: Bidirectional data

chip boundary) provide a bidirectional drive capability, one receiving while the other transmits and vice versa when the direction of flow changes. Since both have the ability to transmit, the drivers must be of the open collector or three state type so the receiving device can have its transmitters disabled. The processor must generate a signal (usually read (RD) because it enables a memory read) which crosses the chip boundary, and enables or disables the external driver without enabling both drivers together. Table 1 shows the processors with this basic arrangement and the column for pin count (Npn) is given by $Npn = Na + Nw + 1$, where Na is the length of the address in bits, and Nw the word length and the extra pin is required for the read signal.

The pin count can be reduced further by multiplexing the information by transferring it across the chip boundary in consecutive time intervals. All the data routes are combined inside the chip by a multiplexer-driver combination and externally these are demultiplexed by the appropriate latch circuits and control signals. Two situations are shown in fig. 5. If $Na = Nw = Np$ where Np is the width of the data port (normally equal to Nw) two beats will complete the transfer of the address and the data. The arrangement of fig. 5a illustrates this and the pin count is given by $Npn = Np + 2$; one of the control signals is for read and a further one is required to load the latch. A variation on this (fig. 5b) is required if $Na > Np$, because the memory address must

45

Table 1. Processor-memory : Bidirectional data

Processor	Word length (Nw)	Address length (Na)	Memory size (Kwords)	Pin count (Npn)
8080	8	16	64	25
6800	8	16	64	25
6501/2	8	16	64	25
6504	8	13	8	22
6503/5	8	12	4	21
EA9002	8	12	4	21
PP S-8	8	14	16	23
Z80	8	16	64	25
2650	8	15	32	24
TMS9900	16	16	32*	33

* byte addressing allowed.

be transmitted in two beats. The pin count is now $Npn = Np + 3$, the extra control signal being required to load the second address latch. Processors with a single multiplexed bus are shown in Table 2.

Table 2. Processor-memory : Single multiplexed bidirectional route

Processor	Word length (Nw = Np)	Address length (Na)	Latch length (Nl)	Memory size (K words)	Pin count (Npn)
GI-1600	16	16	16(a)	64	18
PACE	16	16	16(a)	64	18
MPS-1600	16	16	16(a)	64	18
CRD-8	8	16	8 + 8(b)	64	11
8008	8	14	8 + 6(b)	16	11
IM 1600	12	12	12(a)	4	14
8048 (DATA)	8	8	8(a)	1/4	(14)
F 100	16	15	15(a)	32	18

When $Na > Nw$, an intermediate solution is possible which improves on the speed of fig. 5, but needs extra pins. One of the two data routes of fig. 4 is used to multiplex

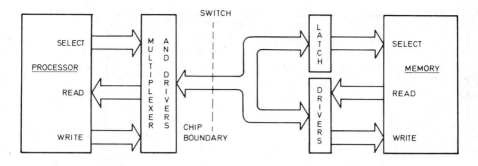

(a) Address and data words of equal length

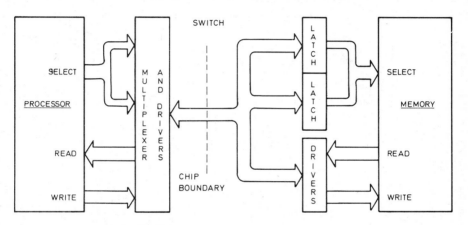

(b) Address word length greater than data word length

Fig.5. Processor - memory: Single multiplexed
bidirectional route

part of the memory address; the multiplexed data route is shown
in fig. 6a, while the multiplexed address route is shown in
fig. 6b. Both require a single latch of length N1 and one
extra control signal to load the latch. The pin count for both
solutions is Na - N1 + Nw + 2 provided N1 ⩽ Nw for (a) and
2N1 ⩽ Nw for (b). The processors using this switching method
are shown in Table 3.

Bank Switching

Bank switching is a method of extending the basic
addressing capability of a processor to provide a larger
memory, which some processors have as an inbuilt switch

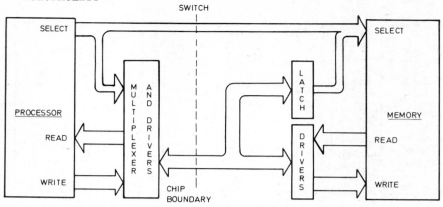

(a) Multiplexing on the data route

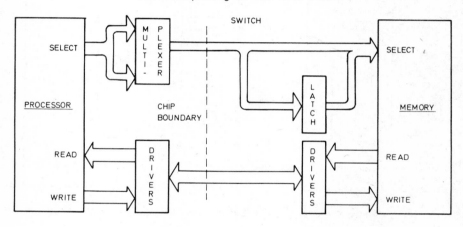

(b) Multiplexing on the address route

Fig.6. Processor – memory: Multiplexed address with
bidirectional data

Table 3. Processor – memory: Multiplexed address with
bidirectional data

Processor	Word length (Nw)	Address length (Na)	Multiplexing latch length (Nl)	route A or D	Memory size (Kwords)	Pin count (Npn)
8085	8	16	8	D	64	18
8048 (PROG)*	8	12	8	D	4	14
COSMAC	8	16	8	A	64	18
MK5065	8	15	8	D	32	17
*Bank switch internally.						

48

function. The address issued by the processor is concatenated with Nb bits of the bank register (fig. 7) to produce the full memory address. A special bank switch instruction is used to

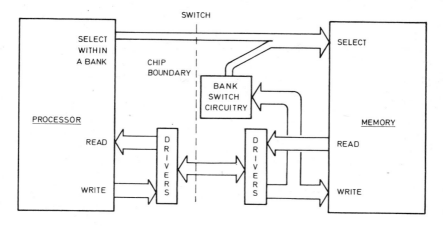

<u>Fig.7.</u> Processor - memory: Bank switched addressing
with bidirectional data

load the bank register. Difficulties arise in maintaining program continuity when switching banks, and so the method is not used frequently, those that do are shown in Table 4, and the pin count is Npn = Na - Nb + Nw + 2 where the extra control signal loads the bank register.

<u>Table 4.</u> Processor - memory: Bankswitched addressing with
bidirectional data

| Processor | Word length (Nw) | Address length | | Memory size | | | Pin count (Npn) |
		Total (Na)	Bank (Nb)	Banks	Bank size (Kwords)	Total	
SC/MP	8	16	4	16	4	64K	22
CDP1801	8	16	8	256	1/4	64K	18

Bankswitching can be used with any switch configuration to enlarge the memory of a processor, but the user must provide the bank switch mechanism.

The 8048 uses bankswitching internally (the user is unaware of it at the PMS level) to extend the program address range from 2 to 4K words. However the technique has been cleverly applied so that the bank switch change can be programmed at any time but it only occurs on the next jump instruction. The processor also stores the full address, including bank switch bit, when storing a subroutine return address.

Summary

The tables and diagrams show the main features of the P-S-M organisations found on most microprocessors. The 8048 appears in two because the program memory and data memory are separate and use different arrangements for each. The popularity of the arrangement of fig. 4 is obvious, the fast memory access it offers is appealing (all the accepted industry standards are in this class), and the memory interface is simple. The high speed of this organisation is essential for the efficient execution of instructions in the TMS9900 with its memory to memory operations but the huge 64 pin package may be embarrassing to many users.

Intel's successor to the 8080, the 8085, and the new single chip computer, the 8048, both use the arrangement of fig. 6a, with no apparent loss of speed and the gain of 7 extra pins, although the status information provided in the 8080 is no longer available. With a simple latch, the 8085 can be matched to the memory interface of the 8080.

Except for TMS9900 all the 16 and 12 bit word machines use the single bidirectional route (the intermediate of fig. 6 is of no benefit here), requiring a large address latch outside the chip and operating at the lower speed expected of this organisation.

The pin count proposed for each organisation may be hypothetical because many pins have multiple functions and although the signal functions described must be present they may in fact be provided indirectly. For example in Table 2 the 8008 has a 6 bit latch on an 8 bit route; the other two bits provide the read/write information.

Additional Switch Information

Many processors provide additional switching information to indicate instruction fetch (usually means the first word of a multiword instruction), the most common, data read, data write and stack access either read or write (pop or push). A further distinction can occur between program and data memories in some processors (8048 for example), which differs from the instruction fetch mentioned earlier. The status information is usually provided early in the memory cycle to provide a 'look ahead' for the switch, which can be useful in multiple processor configurations or where memory access checking is performed by the switch prior to requesting a memory cycle. Because of the exclusive nature of these signals they can be optimally coded; i.e. two pins could provide 4 signals, so the overhead is not large.

4. SWITCH SIGNALLING

The switch signalling or control information that has been implied so far is remarkably similar in its pin requirements (3 or 4) from processor to processor but virtually every combination possible has been used through the range of micro-processors studied. The signalling information is used to validate the data and address information from the processor and to synchronise the transfer of information between processor and its memory. The situation is complicated because, to simplify the memory interface, the microprocessor designer has incorporated memory control signals into the switch signalling, so more pins are required than would normally be needed for the latter function alone.

Processor Read Cycle. Fig. 8 shows the signalling cycle for a memory read on the Z80 processor. The machine cycle is the

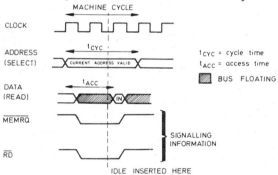

Fig.8. Read cycle: Bidirectional data

interval between one memory access and the next. The time tcyc depends on the clock frequency and the instruction type, the one shown being typical. The address (select) information is generated and a memory request (MEMRQ) issued indicating that the address is valid. The read signal (RD) becomes active when the internal drivers on the processor have reached the high impedance state (three state outputs) and is used to enable the drivers of the selected memory block. The memory has a time of t_{ACC} seconds to get the data ready for the critical period shown. The data must be held by the memory until RD and MEMRQ terminate the cycle. If the memory is unable to perform an access in the time t_{ACC} then the processor

must be prevented from reaching the critical point by making
it idle. Most processors provide an input, often called ready
(RDY), which if inactive makes the processor idle. When the
memory is ready it makes 'ready' active and the machine cycle
continues. Some processors also generate a wait status upon
entering the idle state, and by connecting this to the ready
signal a single idle period can be generated for every memory
access. Except for exceptionally slow memories this would
normally be adequate.

Processor Write Cycle. The write cycle is illustrated in
fig. 9, the only difference being that the processor now
generates the data for the memory, the memory drivers being
disabled by RD being inactive. After a time the
write active signal is generated which is normally used to

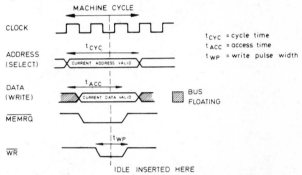

Fig.9. Write cycle: Bidirectional data

load the memory on the rising edge. The delay from the data
valid time to the active write signal is to allow for the
setting up of the data in the memory. Many processors provide
this type of signal to simplify memory circuits. For slower
memories an idle state can be generated.

Loading of Processor Signals. The outputs of microprocessors
can normally drive between 1 and 2 standard TTL loads and for
small systems this may be adequate. But when the capacitance,
signal line lengths or loading become larger, all the signals
from the processor will need buffering to increase the drive.
This decreases the available access time for memories because
the outward and inward signals are delayed by one gate each
at the processor. These factors must be considered when
designing the system and calculating the performance.

5. MEMORY SYSTEMS

If microcomputer systems differ from their larger brothers
anywhere it is most marked in their memory systems. With

modern LSI memory devices the user has considerable scope for tailoring the memory to any application, both for the program memory and the data memory, which are usually quite separate entities in the final production system. A wide range of products exist, competition is fierce and prices are attractive to the customer. For every processor purchased at least 2K bytes of memory are also required, so the profits are to be made in selling memory components not microprocessors. This is not the situation in the minicomputer market where the user is tied to one or at most two suppliers, but these suppliers have to support large maintenance teams - a problem not faced by the semiconductor manufacturers.

Core Stores

Core stores are used with microprocessors particularly where the ability to retain data after power failure is important. They cannot compete with semiconductor memories in small tailored systems, and they are larger than semi-conductor systems. For this reason they will not be considered further.

Standard Read Only Memories

Many microcomputer applications require two types of memory component. A read only memory (ROM) or permanent memory is used for the program and fixed data, while a read write memory stores the data that is modified during program execution. By using a permanent store for the program, the computer will always be in an operationally ready state after switch on, thus avoiding papertape readers or the other more conventional permanent storage media found in larger computer systems.

A memory component is classed as read only if the writing time is significantly longer than the reading time. Although ROM's can be written during the fabrication of the IC (mask programmed), this is only economical for large quantities of the same program. The ultra violet erasable and electrically programmable read only memory is far more popular for small production runs and development work. Special facilities are required for programming which takes 100 secs for 1000 words. If incorrect they may be erased by exposing to ultra violet light of an appropriate frequency for 10 to 20 minutes.

In the read mode these devices have an access time of between 400 and 1500 nano seconds, ideal for microprocessor systems. A typical arrangement for a single 256 x 8 memory device is shown in fig. 10. 8 bits of address enter directly and are decoded inside the chip to select one word of 8 bits (justifying the earlier decision to ignore this function in

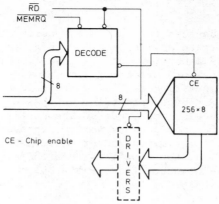

<u>Fig.10</u>.   Organisation of read only memory

fig. 3 onwards). The residual address bits (8 for a 64K word
memory address) must be decoded externally (see a later section)
to select a single block of memory. If MEMRQ and RD are active
and the address is correct the decoder enables the memory
(chip enable CE) which activates the three state drivers at
the output, thus many memories can be commoned together to
form a larger memory, each having a separate enable signal.
In small memory systems the drive capability of the ROM outputs
will be adequate but for larger systems additional drivers will
be required as shown. The timing of the memory is shown in
fig. 11. The access time t_{ACC} is the critical parameter and

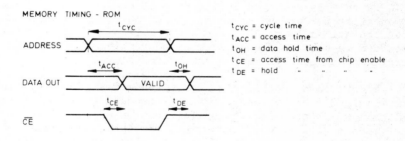

<u>Fig.11</u>.   Timing waveforms for a memory read cycle

must be small enough to ensure that the data is available when
the processor requires it. There may be additional signals on
the memory chip for programming but these have been omitted for
clarity.

Standard Read Write Memory

Read write memory circuits can be dynamic or static. The
former must be cycled regularly to refresh the stored energy

which gradually leaks away, but the memory cell is compact so dynamic memories contain more bits than static memories of the same generation. This refreshing can be inconvenient and requires additional logic circuits making it unpopular in small systems. The Z80 processor provides a refreshing facility thereby simplifying the use of dynamic memories.

The static memory, whose storage cell is a bistable, does not require refreshing and is more common in medium to small memory systems. The organisation of a read write memory using static 1K x 1 bit memories is shown in fig. 12. An eight bit word is achieved by placing 8 devices in parallel and routing the data paths accordingly. A device with

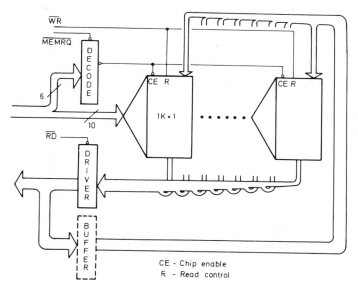

Fig.12. Organisation of read-write memory

separate input and output paths is shown and drivers disable the output to the data route on a write cycle (the chip outputs are active whenever the memory is enabled). Ten address bits are decoded within the device, the rest are decoded externally to produce a unique enable line for every memory bank. MEMRQ controls this decoder and RD controls the three state drivers. The timing for a read cycle is identical to the read only memory cycle shown in fig. 11. In a write cycle the information on the data route, which may be buffered in large system organisations, is written into the memory register on the rising edge of the write signal (WR) shown in fig. 13. This signal is normally generated directly by the processor so simplifying memory circuit designs.

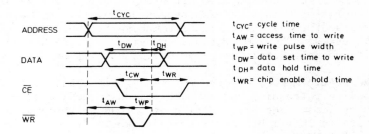

Fig.13. Timing waveforms for a memory write cycle

For yet smaller memory systems 256 x 4 or 128 x 8 bit organisations are available and an example of the former is shown in fig. 14. To reduce the pin count on these memories

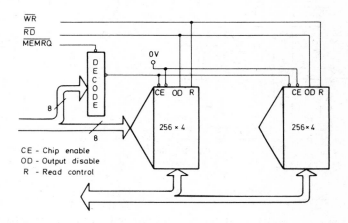

CE - Chip enable
OD - Output disable
R - Read control

Fig.14. Organisation of read-write memory with bidirectional data

the data route is bidirectional and can be connected directly to the switch. The RD signal now controls the output disable signal on the memory device, everything else remaining the same. A small system containing read only memory (fig.10), and read-write memory (fig.14) is simple to design and has a low component count.

External Decoder

The switch implementation is completed by the external decoder shown in figs. 10, 12, 14. Complete or full decoding involves producing a unique enable signal for each combination of the residual address bits, and although this is the safest solution extra circuits may be needed (fig.15a). A simpler though less foolproof solution is to partially decode some or

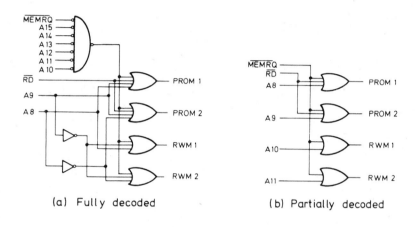

(a) Fully decoded   (b) Partially decoded

Fig.15. Comparison of a full and partial address decoder

all of the address bits. Only one or two address bits are used to enable a memory block. (See Table 5, and the circuits of fig. 15b.) The partial decoder is particularly convenient in small systems when the decoder circuit is inside the memory device. For example in fig. 14 two address bits can be directly connected to the enable pins on the memory devices to give direct decoding. Great care is required in programming to ensure that only one bank of memory is selected and expansion of memory is difficult, particularly if contiguous blocks of memory are required. In Table 5a the four blocks form a continuous memory address field, but this is not the case in Table 5b.

Special Memory Devices

Some manufacturers produce special memory circuits for their microprocessors. The examples described above refer to standard products available from many different manufacturers and the systems can be placed within the memory shown in figs. 3-7. Special memory chips are provided where it is advantageous to

Table 5. Examples of memory arrangements

15	8	7	0			
0 0 0 0 0 0 0 0		8 bit address		256	PROM	1
0 0 0 0 0 0 0 1		"				2
0 0 0 0 0 0 1 0		"		256	RWM	1
0 0 0 0 0 0 1 1		"				2

a) Fully decoded

15	8	7	0			
X X X X X X X O		8 bit address		256	PROM	1
X X X X X X O X		"				2
X X X X X O X X		"		256	RWM	1
X X X X O X X X		"				2

b) Partially decoded

include part or all of the switch logic to reduce the package
count. The most common arrangement is to include the switch
drivers of fig. 4 within the memory chip. (E.g. see fig. 14.)
In the F8 system the program counter, the memory registers
and the complete memory switch are included in every memory
chip. This approach has severe drawbacks since without the
memory the processor is incomplete and the memories are not
very useful in their own right. This explains the exclusion
of the F8 from the earlier tables.

The memories being offered for the 8085 and 8048 series
have the memory address latches of fig. 6a inside, giving two
distinct advantages. The pin count is drastically reduced
releasing pins for other functions, and the system is greatly
simplified because the processor chip boundary and the memory
chip boundary are coincident in small memory configurations.
The spare pins are used to provide input-output facilities.

Both the F8 and the Intel systems provide very compact
small processing systems.

The ultimate step is to place the processor, memory and
input output on the same chip - this is the approach in the 8048.

I. C. PROCESSING ELEMENTS – THE INSTRUCTION SET PROCESSOR

E.L.Dagless

University College, Swansea

1. INTRODUCTION

The fixed instruction set processor is the most complex of the components that make up the computer mainframe. Its many facets include the architecture, word length, processing power, power consumption, physical size, and finally, the instruction set – probably the most important, easily the most complex – all are relevant to the system designer. When the processor is fabricated using a single large-scale integrated circuit, other aspects become relevant, like the pin count, power dissipation, chip size, reliability (the internal components cannot be repaired), among many others. The aspects to be considered here are, principally, the machine architecture, which introduces the instruction set ideas presented elsewhere.

With many devices available, and so many factors to consider, comparison is difficult; detailed description of all, impossible. Further difficulties arise when the end user is considered. The designers of a jet turbine controller and the hospital instrument will have contrasting views concerning the important features essential for his use, while the semiconductor manufacturer has to produce a product with an extremely wide appeal, to justify the huge investment in development. Some of the most salient features will be discussed, but only a cursory sketch of any individual device can be provided here

2. POWER & CLOCK REQUIREMENTS

The most apparent influence of the integrated circuit technology on the processor is in the clock and power supply requirements. The voltage levels vary between -15 v to $+15$ v, and many devices require two or three voltages to achieve TTL compatibility; a very desirable feature. Power consumptions are typically between $\frac{1}{2}$ watt and 1 watt; a very acceptable level for many applications. The clock signals which vary from nothing (except an external crystal), to a four-phase non-overlapping clock, are directly a function of the logic technology used in the chip. The latest trends are towards a single supply with an internal clock generator;

the former reduces power supply costs, the latter simplifies the circuit requirements and reduces the package count. This may also reduce the pins required for these functions, although if the clock is generated internally, a clock signal must emerge for external control and timing. The timing element can be a crystal (XTAL), a resistor-capacitor combination (RC), a capacitor (CAP), or an external clock. The latter is desirable in a multiple processor configuration where all the processors are driven from the same clock to simplify the system logic. These details are summarised in Table 1.

Table 1   Power and Clock Requirements

Processor	CLOCK				POWER SUPPLIES	
	No. of Phases	Voltage (V)	Frequency Max(MHz)	Special Chip	Voltages (V)	Power (W)
8008	2	5	0.8	Yes	+5, -9	1.0
8080	2	12	3.12	Yes	+5, +12, -5	1.5
Z 80	1	5	2.5	No	+5	1.1
6800	2	5	1.0	Yes	+5	1.2
2650	1	2.2	1.25	No	+5	0.75
9900	4	12	3.0	No	+5, +12, -5	1.2
CDP 1802 CD	1	5	3.2	No	+5	0.008
CDP 1802 C	1	10	6.4	No	+10	0.04
CP 1600	2	12	5.0	No	+5, +12, -3	1.1
5065	1	+5 to -12	1.4	No	+5, -5, -12	0.9
F 100	1	1.6	$\simeq 14$ M	No	+5*	1.35

(a) External Clock Circuit

Processor	CLOCK			POWER SUPPLIES	
	Type	Clocks Out	Frequency Max (MHz)	Voltages (V)	Power (W)
8085	XTAL,RC,EXT	1	1 (avge)	+5	1.5
8048	XTAL,RC,EXT	1	0.4	+5	1.5
F 8	XTAL,RC	2	2	+5, +12	0.7
IM 1600	XTAL	Many	2 (typ)	+5	0.005
IM 1600A	XTAL	Many	2 (typ)	+10	0.012
SC/MP	XTAL,CAP	-	1	+12	-

(b) Internal Clock Circuit

The IM 1600 is notable for its very low power consumption and the fact that the A version is C-MOS logic compatible.

* Connections for regulator included

3. WORD LENGTH

The processor word length affects all aspects of the computer mainframe. The size of the chip which affects yield - thereby cost - is probably the most sensitive factor since an increase in word length increases the size of almost every element of the processor. It also influences the pin count, the size of the system interconnections, and the width of memory and input-output registers. Increasing width may adversely affect the total system cost and reliability (it is more reliable to use one pin twice than have two pins), but the user benefits in increased throughput and computational power. A long word gives greater freedom and scope for designing a powerful instruction set, and numbers can be represented more accurately. Short word length machines must have extra instructions to enable the programmer to achieve numerical precision; unfortunately, in a situation where the scope for a rich instruction set is already rather limited. These machines popularised the use of multiple word instructions to overcome these limitations. The principal features of the word length are shown in Table 2.

Table 2   The Features of Word Length

Word Length	n	8	16
Number range: Unsigned	0 to $+(2^n-1)$	0 to +255	0 to +65535
Signed	-2^{n-1} to $+(2^{n-1}-1)$	-128 to +127	-32768 to +32767
No. of words for 10^6	-	3	2
No. of: Binary variables	n	8	16
States	2^n	256	65536
No.of words for 64K Memory	-	2	1

Since it is usual for the data and program to be stored in the same memory, the word length selected for the data operations will directly influence the instruction length; hence, the instruction set.

4. PROCESSOR ARCHITECTURE

The instruction set of a processor can be more readily interpreted if the processor architecture is examined; in particular, the components present on the processor chip. Here there is little commonality, except in the family based on the 8008, which includes the 8080, 8085, and the Z80. Some processors use memory as an extension of the processor to reduce the hardware on the chip, as in the case of the 9900 , or as in the 8048 and F8, to rationalise the read-write registers in the system.

The structure of a simple hypothetical processor is shown in Fig.2 of Chapter I.B, and this illustrates how the basic units, the register array, arithmetic and logic unit (function unit), and control unit, might be connected. In this section, the arithmetic and register units will be discussed in detail, but the data paths that interconnect them are best illustrated by a description of the instruction set.

<u>Function Unit</u>

The function unit is an n-bit wide arithmetic and logical unit (ALU) which executes the operations of the processor. It can perform unary operations using only one source register, while a binary operation has two. Increment register X is an example of the former, while Add A to B is an example of the latter. Table 3 is a complete list of the operators seen in microprocessors to date.

<u>Table 3</u>   Arithmetic and Logical Operations

binary type (b)	unary type (u)
Add	Increment
Add with carry	Decrement
Add decimal	Negate
Add floating point	Complement
Subtract	Decimal Adjust
Subtract with borrow	Rotate
Subtract decimal	Variable Rotate
Subtract floating point	Test
Multiply	
Multiply floating point	
Divide	
Divide floating point	
AND	
AND NOT	
OR	
EXCLUSIVE OR	
Compare	

Add with Carry, and Subtract with Borrow, are only present in 8-bit word processors, to allow multiple word operations to increase numerical precision. Floating point operations have not appeared in the basic instruction set, although external floating point function units are beginning to appear, whereas the multiply and divide operators are present in some 16-bit machines, e.g. 9900 and F 100. The logical operators are common to many machines.

Decimal arithmetic is effected with the Decimal Add and Subtract operations and Decimal Adjust, the latter being the most common. Rotate describes all single-bit Shift Left and Shift Right operations, while the variable rotate covers multiple bit shifts.

Condition Flags

The results of operations in the function unit are computed and stored in a register called the condition flag register. The state of the ALU result, i.e. the flag identity, is shown with a selection of processors, in Table 4. Carry, Sign, and Zero are the most common – the first being essential in 8-bit machines. Half-carry and Subtract are stored for use in the decimal adjust operation and, unlike the rest, are not usually available for condition testing. The 5065 and IM1600 appear to be devoid of condition flags; the latter tests the accumulator directly. The logical greater than (GT), arithmetic greater than and equal conditions, are far less common as flags, although they are frequently provided as conditional tests since all three are simply derived from sign, carry and zero.

Table 4   Condition Flags

ALU State	8008	8080	8085	8048	Z80	9900	650X	CP1600	6800	F8	2650	COSMAC
Carry	*	*	*	*	*	*	*	*	*	*	*	*
Zero	*	*	*		*		*	*	*	*	*	
Sign	*	*	*		*		*	*	*	*	*	
Parity	*	*	*		*	*			*			
Overflow				*	*	*	*	*	*	*	*	
Logical GT						*						
Arith. GT						*						
Equal						*						
Half-carry	*	*	*	*							*	
Subtract				*								

Auxiliary Arithmetic Unit

Some of the generically older 8-bit processors include an auxiliary arithmetic unit which operates on 16-bit quantities, usually on pairs of 8-bit registers or 16-bit memory address registers. Considerable improvements in performance are achieved both in computation speed and code reduction. It is not required in 12 and 16-bit machines, since the main function unit has the requisite processing width. The functions are typically, Add, Subtract, Increment and Decrement.

Register Unit

The second major unit of the processor architecture is the register array, which is separate from the main memory, and usually on the processor chip itself. The speed advantage this provides is significant, since only internal chip transit times are involved when accessing the register, and the much slower accesses to external memory are avoided. The register array contains two types of information: data representing numerical or logical variables, and addresses for accessing the data and program stored in the memory. The complexity of a processor is primarily due to the variety of addressing mechanisms. Table 5 describes the registers for some processors, giving the number and length of each.

Data Registers

The accumulator register (ACC), which is the result register for
the arithmetic and logic unit, is often a single dedicated register.
Sometimes, many accumulators are available, but in some cases –
like the Z 80, 5065 and 8048 – they are selected by a switch
from one bank of registers to another, so only a single accumulator is accessible at any time. The table entries show this; for
example, the 5065 has three 8-bit accumulators

General purpose (GP) registers are data registers which can store
numerical or logical variables of any type, and have no special
function in the machine architecture. Where registers have a dual
or multiple function, the most powerful is shown, while the subsi-
diary functions are given in parenthesis.

Table 5   Register Architecture

Processor	ACC	GP	PC	MR	IR	AIR	SP	F
8008	1,8	4(2),8	1,14	1,14	–	–	3(INT)	1,4
8080	1,8	(6),8	1,16	3,16	–	–	16	1,5
8085	1,8	(6),8	1,16	3,16	–	–	16	1,5
Z 80	2 x 1,8	(2 x 6),8	1,16	2 x 3,16	2,16	–	16	2 x 1,6
8048	1,8	2 x 6(2),8	1,12	2 x 2,8	–	–	3(INT)	1,4
6800	2,8	–	1,16	–	1,16	–	16	1,6
9900	–	–	1,16	–	1,16[+]	–	–	1,7
5065	3 x 1,8	–	3 x1,16	–	–	–	8	–
CP 1600	8,16	(5),16	1,16	3,16	–	2,16[*]	16	1,4
IM 1600	1,12	–	1,12	–	–	–	–	–
650 X	1,8	–	1,16	–	2,8		8	1,7
		* increment only			[+]workspace pointer			

Address Registers

The most important address register is the program counter (PC) or
instruction address register. The length of the program counter
determines the size of memory that can be directly accessed as program space.

The memory address registers (MR) are registers whose contents are
used to address memory. The length is given, but the number
available is particularly important since the programmer has
greater freedom if many are provided. The instruction set will
clarify whether there is great freedom in the use of these.

Index address registers (IR) are used to address memory, but an
offset address is added to the contents of IR before the access
is made. This mechanism simplifies table accessing, especially if

a variety of offsets are available. Again, the instruction set clarifies this, but not many processors have this facility on the chip.

Auto-increment/decrement address registers (AIR) are even more powerful, since they enable a software stack to be generated. Here, it is assumed that on Read (or Write), an increment is performed before accessing the memory, while for a Write (or Read), a decrement is performed after accessing the memory. No processor to date has this complete operation on the chip.

The final address register is the stack pointer, which is used mainly for storing subroutine return addresses, but sometimes - usually when the stack is external - data can be stored, particularly for a context switch due to interrupt (see Chapter I,D). Some have the stack inside the processor, in which case size restrictions are acute, and only a small stack (hence, limited nesting of subroutines) is available. The 5065 and 650X processors have an 8-bit stack which references the first 256 locations in memory.

Summary of Register Array :

The discussion above concerns the registers present on the processor chip, and any special functions associated with them. These functions may also be operated on data and addresses stored in memory, in which case the number is near infinity. This is the approach in the 9900 (almost no registers are present on the chip); the work-space pointer, IR, acts as a base address for a 16-word register array in memory. This pointer also functions as stack pointer indirectly, since the old pointer, program counter, and status register, are stored automatically when the pointer changes.

The register array can provide a valuable insight into the processor operation, but this only forms part of the picture that is the instruction set processor.

5. INSTRUCTION SET

The instruction set of a fixed instruction set processor defines how the component parts, i.e. operator and operand, are combined as an operational entity. A classification of instruction sets, aimed at making comparison easier, is described.

The author acknowledges the fact that the sales literature describing the Microprocessors mentioned in these chapters provided much of the information used in the tables and diagrams, but the list is too extensive to cite in detail.

I.D.   PROCESSING ELEMENTS - INPUT, OUTPUT AND CONCURRENCY

E.L. DAGLESS

University College, Swansea

1. INTRODUCTION

A computer communicates to external peripherals through its input-output system. Unlike the processor-memory interface the facilities provided at the processor-peripheral interface are varied and may be complex; the choice depends on the peripheral type, its response time and the data transfer rate. The switch associated with this interface will include functions present in the memory interface and in addition provide a range of other dedicated functions implemented with special hardware units which link processor and peripherals. The system designer has considerable freedom in arranging the input output to suit his own particular problem. However, some degree of standardisation is being achieved with the appearance of integrated circuits which provide the data paths and perform the switch function of the input-output system.

Such circuits reduce the package count, increase flexibility, since most have programmable functions, and simplify the hardware design. The more complex components reduce program overheads by performing, in hardware, tasks otherwise executed by software which allows concurrent operation of the system functions. A trend towards concurrent operation on a function division basis is apparent in the manufacturers' product plans, a topic discussed later.

2. INPUT-OUTPUT DATA ROUTES

The input-output system provides (a) a route for information flow between a peripheral device and the processor (b) the switch mechanism to select the appropriate input-output channel (decoder) and (c) the control functions which ensure valid information transfers occur. The data routes, the first two items above, are shown in fig.1 while the control lines, which are implied, are omitted for clarity. The input-output address register contains the address of the selected channel and the data register is the source or destination for output and input respectively. On an

67

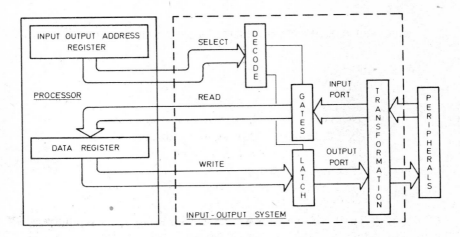

Fig.1. General input-output
system

input cycle one word of binary information at the input of the
gate is loaded into the data register while an output operation
transfers the contents of the data register to the latch which
stores one word of information and presents it, in binary, to the
transformation unit. The decoder, which may be a full or partial
decoder, selects the appropriate channel. For many applications
digital ports are adequate, in which case the transformation unit
is omitted.

Drive and Loading

The drive capability, i.e. the voltage and current levels, is
determined by the type of latch which in turn specifies the type
of load that can be placed at the output. For example TTL latches
can drive light emitting diodes directly but extra power gain
would be needed to drive relays.

Similar considerations apply on the input side, again TTL
voltage levels are common, but the current requirements can vary.
Care must be exercised in ensuring that the peripheral device can
generate the drive and with TTL extra care is needed to avoid high
voltages which can irreversibly damage the gates. Consideration
must also be given to the unused inputs which may have to be
connected to one of the power lines for reliable system operation.
(A floating TTL input can be very sensitive to noise and during an
input operation oscillations may occur which could affect the
other input lines.) The data sheets of the input-output devices
must be studied carefully to determine the drive and loading
conditions.

PROCESSING ELEMENTS - INPUT, OUTPUT AND CONCURRENCY

Transformation Unit

Some peripherals communicate in serial form, e.g. teletypes, cassettes or floppy discs, while others require analogue or continuously varying signals. Special circuits transform the parallel binary information into a form suitable to output to the peripheral, others transform peripheral signals into digital form for input. The most common transform unit is one which generates the serial information for a teletype (TTY) or visual display unit (VDU). The outputs of the transformation unit may not provide the voltage and current levels needed by the peripherals in which case buffering circuits must be inserted.

Analogue to digital converters and digital to analogue converters are special transformation units that provide analogue or continuous information channels. These are becoming available in a microprocessor compatible form for small minimum package count systems.

The data routes and transformation unit when present are combined to form the input-output system.

This unit is commonly called a peripheral interface unit, since it matches the processor to a specific peripheral device.

Accessing the Input-Output Registers

The two registers shown in fig.1 can be duplicated to produce an array of discrete input-output registers that present to the processor a digital image of the total peripheral information, and is referred to often as the peripheral image memory. The difference between the memory and the more conventional memory is that (a) read and write (input and output) operations at the same address can access different information (b) the information in the memory is input from external devices while output is fed to external devices, and so the registers must be accessible to the peripheral system and to the processor. The array of image memory registers can be located in either the conventional memory space of the processor (memory mapped) or in an extra image memory.

Memory Mapped Input-Output   If the image memory is located in the normal addressing space of the processor then these registers can be regarded as ordinary memory locations. The decoder must distinguish between accesses to the input output registers and the read only and read-write memory, and the system must match the switch configuration of the processor concerned. An input-output system for the bidirectional data route processor is shown in fig.2. The memory address is decoded to select the appropriate input or output port. Many latch and buffer circuits can be added provided the loading rules are obeyed, and the buffers are open collector or three state devices so they can release the data route when not selected.

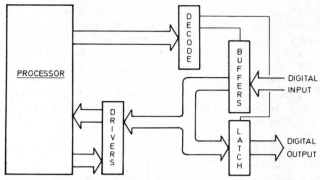

Fig.2. Peripheral Image Memory: Memory Mapped

Memory mapped input-output offers the programmer the complete repertoire of memory reference instructions as input-output instructions, giving a great deal of freedom in the selection of source and destination registers and the operations performed on the input-output registers. Because the image memory is fragmented direct addressing is popular, which for most processors needs a 16 bit operand address in the instruction. So this method may be costly in space and slow in execution time; the more sophisticated addressing modes may be even slower due to the increased number of memory accesses. Memory mapping reduces the space available for program and data and can be the cause of spurious program execution if a fault causes the processor to obey the peripheral image registers as if program space. Any processor whose address route is accessible can have memory mapped input output.

Extra Image Memory: Parallel Many processors provide a smaller directly addressed memory dedicated to the input-output registers. To reduce the pin count the memory switch arrangement is normally used to provide the data routes while control signals distinguish between an input-output cycle and a memory cycle. The circuit is similar to fig.2, but the decoder is only enabled on an output or input cycle, and only a few of the address bits are used (typically 8 bits). The COSMAC is an exception; it uses the same data route but has a separate peripheral address route of 3 bits. In both cases the decoder will be smaller since the total address space is less (typically 256 registers, see table 1).

A limited number of instructions will access the extra image memory, but their size and execution time will be less than general memory reference orders used for a memory mapped solution. Table 1 shows the processors with an extra image memory capability. Devices with input-output facilities on the processor chip are

Table 1   Peripheral Image Memory: extra-image
memory

Processor	Width (bits)	Number of Ports		Number of Instruc- tions
		I	O	
8008	8	8	32	1
8080	8	256	256	2
8085 EXT	8	256	256	2
8085 INT	1	1	1	2
Z80	8	256	256	12
8048 INT	8	2		4
8048 EXT	4	16		3
9900 INT	1	1	1	5
CDP 1802	8	7	7	2
MK 5065	8	16	16	4
2650	8	256	256	2
IM 6100	12	64	64	6
F8	8	256	256	4
INT - INTERNAL: REGISTERS ON THE CHIP				
EXT - EXTERNAL:				

shown.   The Z80 has a rich set of input-output instructions,
some of which perform block data transfers between memory and
input-output register. The 8048 has two 8 bit ports on the chip
and an external 4 bit port capability; the latter presumably
for driving digital displays.

Extra Image Memory: Serial   Serial input-output is provided on
some processors; the 8085, and 9900 are notable. In the latter
the complete circuit of fig.1 is enclosed in the chip including
an internal serial to parallel converter. This saves pins but
proves rather cumbersome when, as in this case, it is the only
input-output mechanism. External hardware converts back to the
parallel form. The serial facilities on the 8085 essentially
provide fast conditional testing or simple serial scanning;
there is no mechanism in the hardware for serial to parallel
conversion.

Input-Output Timing

    For memory mapped input-output and the majority of extra
image memory systems, the timing requirements are identical to
the memory timings in figs. 8 and 9 of Chapter I.B. When the gate
and latches are from a fast logic family there should be no
timing problems and if special input-output devices are used these

will be designed to operate with the relevant processor. If the input-output chips of one processor system are connected to another processor then the timing characteristics must be studied very carefully to ensure compatibility.

The only significant point to remember on the timing is that the latch is loaded and output data is present on the rising edge of WR (see fig.9, Chapter I.B) and that input data will be present on the data route for the complete duration of MEMRQ active (fig.8, Chapter I.B) for memory mapped systems or while IORQ is active during an extra image memory cycle (note IORQ is similar to MEMRQ). Because of delay times through the gates, switch and processor the input signals should be stable while the control signals are active. The example in fig.3 illustrates this point.

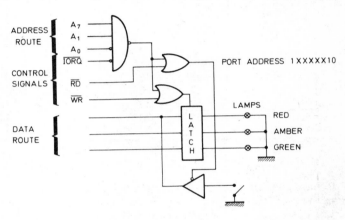

Fig.3. Simple Traffic Light Interface

Example

A simple light and switch system is illustrated in fig.3 which is interfaced to the Z80 processor. IORQ signals that an input-output cycle is in progress and enables the latch if write or the three state buffer if read, provided address bits A_7, A_1 and A_0 are 1,1 and 0 respectively.

3. CONTROL OF INPUT-OUTPUT TRANSFERS

In the example just described, the timing of the information transfer across the processor-peripheral interface is not controlled by the peripheral. Consider a paper tape reader loading the processor with a string of 8 bit characters at a continuous rate. The processor must only read the tape when the character is positioned over the read head. This timing information or control signal is provided by the sprocket hole. Special hardware circuits could be designed so that when an input is performed the processor is made to wait until a sprocket hole is detected, it is then allowed to proceed to read the character; this is the input-output equivalent of the ready-wait handshake described in Chapter I.B. This approach requires dedicated hardware and special precautions to avoid locking up the processor if the paper tape reader fails to operate.

If the sprocket signal is fed to another input port the processor can examine the status of the paper tape reader by reading the image memory. The processor can idle under program control by testing for the presence of the sprocket signal. This process can be taken a stage further with an incremental reader because now the processor must instruct the reader to advance one character and this signal can be generated at an output port.

The introduction of a control word and status word into the image memory means that, by suitable program design, external devices can dictate the actions of the program and ensure that only correct information is transferred (see fig.4). This offers the programmer considerable freedom in controlling the peripheral devices and is now a standard method of input-output design.

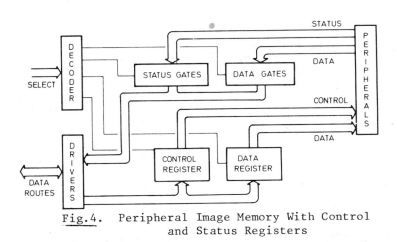

Fig.4. Peripheral Image Memory With Control
and Status Registers

Special Input-Output Circuits

The arrival of LSI input-output devices extended this concept to the point where the processor can, by program, control the organisation of the input-output interface. There are three main types of device available for general purpose use, the parallel interface, the serial interface and the timer.

73

<u>Parallel Input-Output Devices</u>   Two or three input-output ports
are provided on a single device together with part of the switch
logic.   An example of the Motorola MC6820 is shown in fig.5, which
shows it   memory mapped with a partial decoder, and two bits A_1
and A_0 fully decoded.   The MC6820 was one of the first devices
available and is typical of the rest.   There are four registers
addressed by A_0 and A_1, two are the ports A and B and the others
the control and status words (one pair for each port).   The ports
are quasi-bidirectional, the input or output direction must be
programmed prior to using the port.   Writing a particular code in
the control register causes special hardware in the device to fix
the direction of the port.   After initialising the port it may be

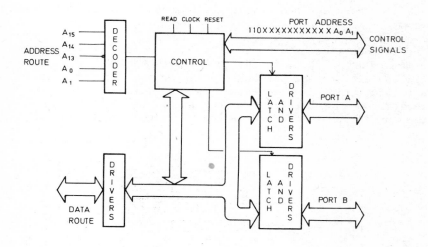

<u>Fig.5</u>.   Block Diagram of Parallel Input-Output
Device (Motorola type 6820)

accessed in the conventional manner.

   Control and status signals are provided at the peripheral
interface which are accessed through the control and status
registers.   This arrangement is very economical in port addresses
and simplifies the system design.   Peripheral devices like a
paper tape reader can be easily interfaced to such products.   Other
chips with a parallel interface capability are listed in table 2.

<u>Serial Input-Output Devices</u>   The earliest LSI circuit made from
random logic gates was the serial-parallel, parallel-serial
converter for asynchronous or synchronous transmission of
characters;   the UART or USART.   These devices predated micro-

Table 2   Special Input Output Devices

Device No.	Parallel Ports				Processor family	General purpose
	Width	In	Out	I/O		
Z80-PIO	8			2	Z80	Y
6820/6821	8			2	6800	Y
8155 (RWM)	8,8,6			3	8085	N
8755 (ROM)	8			2	8085	N
8255	8			3	8080	Y
8243	4			4	8048	N
TMS 5501	8	1	1		8080	N
F8(3850)	8			2	F8	-
3851(ROM)	8			2	F8	N
8048	8			2	8048	-
	Serial Ports					
	No.	SYN	ASYN			
Z80-SIO	2	*	*		Z80	Y
8251	1	*	*		8080	Y
TMS 5501	1		*		8080	N
6850	1		*		6800	Y
6852	1	*			6800	Y
6854	1	*			6800	Y
	Timers					
	No.	Length (bits)				
8155	1	14			8085	N
8253	3	16			8080	Y
TMS 5501	5	8			8080	N
8048	1	8			8048	-
6840	3	16			6800	Y

processors so they were obvious candidates for peripheral interface products. Many are available and all have very similar
features and characteristics.   Control words are used to set up
the transmitted and received format, to select synchronous or
asynchronous mode and many other functions. The status word
indicates character sent, character received and any error
conditions. Some have full V.24 standard compatibility and these
signals are available through the control and status words. A
limited selection of these products are listed in Table 2. Few
devices generate the voltage and current levels needed for transmission along lines so buffering circuits are usually needed on
the serial input and output lines.

E.L.DAGLESS

Timing Input–Output Devices   In real time applications time
information is required for a variety of reasons. Timing with a
program is extremely tedious and never very accurate. The timer
is a counter, driven by an external clock, usually the processor's,
which is read or written by the processor for setting programmable
time intervals. A selection of circuits is shown in Table 2.

Summary of Special Input–Output Devices   Table 2 lists some of the
wide range of products presently offered. Most are designed for
specific processors but where they may have more general use this
is indicated. The TMS5501 has an appealing specification but is
inflexible because it is closely tied to the 8080 processor, so
much so that it is not compatible to the 8085 or the Z80, both
very close relatives of the 8080. Processors and memories with
integral input–output are included.

4.   CONCURRENCY

    Consider the problem of controlling with a processor, a drill
head that moves under the direction of a program being read from
paper tape. The processor has to control two concurrent activities,
reading characters from the paper tape and positioning the drill.
How may this be achieved?   A similar problem faced the large
computer manufacturers many years ago when faced with many
peripheral devices serving on expensive mainframe. There are three
ways of sharing the mainframe resource between many tasks, polling,
interrupt and direct memory access (DMA).

Concurrency by Polling

    Returning to the example, assume that the tape is feeding
continuously, and that the time between characters is T_{sr}, the
service time. The critical time, T_{cr}, is the time during which
the character is valid after the sprocket hole signal is true.
The drill can be started and stopped and has a position indicator
all being accessible to the processor. The drilling accuracy is
determined by the feeding speed, which is fixed, and the time, T_{cd},
between the drill reaching the endpoint and the processor stopping
it. The drill service time, T_{sd}, depends on the total drill
movement. The program actions are:

        start: if character ready   then   read character
                                       else   idle for equal time
                 if endpoint reached   then   stop drill and initiate
                                                 new action
                                       else   idle for equal time
                 jump to start

76

If reading the character takes less than T_{ar} and the stopping of
the drill and restarting takes less than T_{ad} then the worst loop
time $T = T_{ar} + T_{ad}$ if the times for testing are ignored. For
correct operation $Tcr > T < Tcd$ i.e. the loop time must be less than
the critical times of both peripherals. The idle periods provide
a regular cycle time, but this pedantic polling can be speeded up
by removing the idle periods, but this has no real benefit under
these circumstances since the idling is now replaced by a very
fast poll which does nothing. If the service times are long,
$T \ll Tsr$ or Tsd, then the processor is idling most of the time.
This mismatch between service time and crisis time can sometimes
be improved by double buffering. If the sprocket signal loads the
data into a register, storing it while the tape progresses, then
the crisis time is now equal to the service time, thereby removing
any mismatch. This technique is common in the serial input-output
devices discussed earlier and is appearing in some digital to
analogue converters. It can only be used, however, when there are
no problems caused by delaying the information. There is no such
remedy with the drill control cycle.

If Tcr is much larger than Tcd, but Tar and Tad are similar,
then the drill could be polled many times while the
reader is polled only once: e.g. if the loop time is $T' = Tar$
$+ 4Tad$ the worst case service time for the drill is T but T' for
the reader.

There may be circumstances where the processor must perform a
large computation while performing input-output tasks, e.g.
determining machining shapes from coordinates on the tape. The
computation, C, must be subdivided into actions C1, C2 to Cn, where
the execution time of each is less than Te, then the critical
service time becomes $T = Te + Tar + Tad$ and the program action
is now

```
Start:    do   next portion of C
          if   character ready then read character
          if   endpoint reached then stop drill and initiate
                                          new action
          jump to start
```

Since the actions of the poll may use the registers and flags
required by C, these must be stored or 'dumped' before executing
the poll, and restored at the end of the poll. By combining this
with a rapid poll of inactive inputs, the computation efficiency
is increased, but the critical service time must still provide
for the worst case time, T, above.

Polling benefits if the total task can be subdivided into a set of subtasks that can be scheduled for execution in a tidy sequential manner. Its advantage is that the program designer is in complete control of the actions of the system.

Concurrency by Interrupt

If the tasks cannot be readily subdivided or the execution sequence is random then polling must be replaced by interrupt. Interrupt is a hardware poll performed by the processor at the end of each instruction e.g.:

> start: execute next instruction
> if interrupt then   execute interrupt routine
> jump to start

where interrupt is a signal from the interrupting peripheral which enters the processor hardware. By polling so frequently, the processor can respond very quickly to a request for service.

A Single Interrupting Device   By using interrupt in the earlier example the computation, C, and polling the drill can proceed until the reader requests service by generating an interrupt request when a character is ready. The processor state (its registers and flags) is stored before entering the interrupt service routine and is restored at the end. With polling, only the registers being used are stored, but for interrupt, all registers must be stored because the interrupting routine has no prior knowledge of the state of the processor, so the latter process is slower than the former.

Storing the processor state is simple and quick if another bank of vacant registers is available as in the 5065 (3 banks), the Z80 (2 banks), 8048 (2 banks), or the 9900 (2K banks). The latter is rather elegant because it has a workspace pointer addressing the 16 working registers in memory which are stored simply by storing the pointer contents and loading it with a new value.

The 6800 stores the processor state automatically on interrupt and restores it on return from interrupt. The majority of the rest execute a call instruction, either automatically or after external hardware forces it into the processor, and the program then stores the registers using move orders. (Note:- in all cases the first interrupt instruction does not increment the program counter.)

If the time to store the processor state is Tst, and the time to execute the interrupted instruction is Ti, then the worst case service time, Ts, is given by Ts = Tst + Ti.

PROCESSING ELEMENTS - INPUT, OUTPUT AND CONCURRENCY

Many Interrupting Devices Two or more interrupts in a system
creates five problems for the system designer. The identification
of the interrupting device is the first and locating its service
routine the second. If two devices request service at the same
time then some ranking or priority must be applied to select the
successful one. Once an interrupt is being serviced, two actions
can be taken should another arrive. The active routine can
disable interrupts preventing further interruption and a pre-emptive
mechanism can be provided which allows only higher priority requests
to interrupt.

Identification of the Interrupting Device Normally a single
interrupt signal enters the processor and the signals from the
peripherals are wire ORed together, so the processor must somehow
locate the requesting device. The simplest method is to poll round
the status words examining the interrupt bits as in the 6800 but this
increases the service time. An alternative solution is for the
processor to issue an acknowledgement which stimulates the interrupting device to signal its identity (used in 8080, 8008, 8085,
Z80) usually on the data bus during the instruction fetch of the
interrupt cycle. A variation, if pins are available on the processor,
is for the interrupting device to identify itself when requesting
service as in the 9900. After identifying the source of the interrupt the processor must translate the identity into the unique start
address of the associated service routine, a slow process if performed
by software.   The identification information may be used directly as
the address, or part of the address, of the service routine enabling
the processor to jump directly or indirectly to the correct program.
This technique is called a vectored interrupt and is present in the
9900, Z80, 8080, 8085 processors.

Ranking of Interrupt Requests The last section deals with the
problem of many interrupts which do not interact, i.e. two never
occur together and another interrupt does not occur while the
processor is already serving one. Unless the interrupt routines
are extremely short and the service time is incredibly long, the likelihood of avoiding these situations is remote. What can the system
designer do?

     If two interrupts arrive together then a priority must be
assigned to both so that the highest claims the service. A
popular solution is to 'daisy chain' the peripherals together,
and when the processor acknowledges an interrupt this passes to
the closest, who passes it to the next if a request is not
pending, and so on until it reaches the device requesting service.
This device then claims the acknowledgement, so preventing it
reaching the lower priority levels. Another solution is to route
all the requests to a priority circuit, like the 74148, where the
active input with the highest priority is indicated by a 3 bit code

which can be examined by the processor. In both cases the successful peripheral must remove its request before the lower priority request can be served.

What happens in the case above after the high priority interrupt request is removed? Either the low priority request is served, in which case the high priority routine is suspended, or the low priority request is inhibited by some mechanism. Both solutions will increase the service time to one peripheral. Obviously the former solution is undesirable since the high priority peripherals will be continuously interrupted by subsequent requests. So the system designer must categorise peripherals as either urgent or non-urgent and ensure that urgent interrupts cannot be interrupted by non-urgent ones while urgent interrupts can interrupt non-urgent ones.

The simplest solution is to let the urgent routines disable interrupt until the service routine is complete, while the non-urgent ones are prevented from disabling interrupts. An example of the resulting activity is shown in fig.6. Many processors

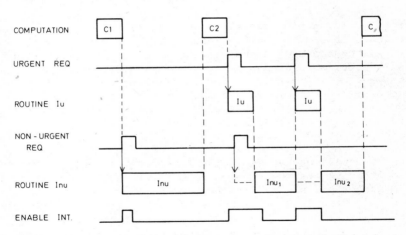

Fig.6. Interrupt Servicing For a Two Level Priority:
Urgent and Non-Urgent

have a maskable interrupt; some also include a non-maskable interrupt for very urgent interrupts (e.g. power failure interrupt). The 8085 has five interrupt levels, a non-maskable interrupt and four maskable interrupts with a descending priority.

Multiple Level Priority The approach above is fine if only two levels are required, for multiple level systems the priority of the interrupt being serviced is stored so that when another interrupt occurs its priority can be compared with the current priority. If higher it interrupts otherwise nothing happens until the priority of the current interrupt being serviced becomes

lower than the priority of the suspended request. The 8214
priority interrupt controller performs this function for the 8080
processor, and a simplified block diagram is shown in fig.7.
The device also includes logic for cascading many devices together

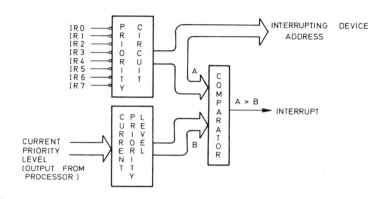

Fig.7.   Interrupt Logic For An Eight Level Priority
System (from 8214)

and is matched to the 8080 switch structure but these signals
are omitted for clarity.

The TMS9900 provides this function internally for single
requests from sixteen sources, but should two or more requests
occur simultaneously these must be resolved as described earlier
using a priority decoder. Intel now produce a more elegant
solution in the 8259 interrupt controller which performs the
multi-level priority function with programmable vectoring for each
of the eight interrupts the chip services. Other facilities
are available but the device is closely related to the 8080 and
8085 since it generates the call instruction as part of the
interrupt cycle.

Concurrency by Direct Memory Access

In the interrupt and polling methods it is assumed that the
processor can service the information rate of the input-output
channel, and interrupt is used only if the processor's response to
requests is too slow in the poll mode. If the processor cannot
service, by program, the rate of data transfer, for example data
from a high speed disc, then direct memory access (DMA) must be
used. In a DMA system dedicated hardware controls the transfer
of complete blocks of data from memory to peripheral or vice versa.
The DMA controller is given, by the processor, the address in the
memory of the beginning of the block, it must then gain control of
the address and data routes, transfer the data into sequential

locations until the complete block is transferred, then inform the processor, probably by an interrupt, that the transfer is complete. To gain control of the address and data routes it must request the processor to release the bus which it does by putting the address and data lines in the high impedance state. This action is strictly a switch function which is included in the processor chip. The processor will acknowedge this action and then idle until the DMA controller releases the routes. Although in large computer systems there are many methods for interleaving the DMA access with the processor accesses thereby achieving real concurrency, with most microprocessors the DMA request causes the processor to idle while the transfer occurs.

If many DMA channels are required then hardware must be provided, as with interrupt, to decide which channel gains control. The 8257 DMA controller which is compatible with the 8085 and 8080 provides this logic for up to 4 channels and contains the registers for address initialisation and the address incrementing logic.

Summary of Polling and Interrupt

If the system specification is bounded and explicit then it should be possible to devise a program structure, based on polling, that will work. The writing and testing of such a program should be relatively straightforward since the sequence of actions is well defined.

There is, however, a strong temptation to use the interrupt techniques provided by the processor systems, particularly when the manufacturers stress this aspect so heavily. The pedantry of the polling system may seem wasteful of processor power particularly where many diverse peripherals are involved. If many of the devices are active most of the time, the multitude of nested levels that could occur together with the unpredictable behaviour due to the asynchronous nature of the system could cause insurmountable problems during the testing phase. Although it may be argued that the interrupt driven system can be handled as a set of independent tasks, without automatic protection and dynamic store allocation there is every likelihood that corruption of one routine by another, indeterminacy, or even deadlock will occur.

One may be tempted, by the overtures of the salesman, to develop interrupt based systems to achieve the system concurrency, but perhaps these same overtures, viewed from a different perspective, may yield a better solution. With the cost of the processor being such an insignificant portion of the overall cost, maybe more processors should be purchased to produce true concurrency rather than the apparent concurrency attained by using interrupt.

Many of the special input-output devices have interrupt signals, whose operational features are very varied. The manufacturers' literature should be consulted for this information.

5. CONCLUSION

An example of a complete system is illustrated in fig.8. The switch is replaced by a bus connecting the system components while the switch logic is distributed amongst them. The control lines are usually bussed as well, but these are shown separately to explain their function more clearly. The structure is modular and very flexible, each unit is added only when required for the system being implemented.

The interrupt identity and current interrupt priority are shown as input-output channels because this is often the logical implementation; however, the input output logic may be included in the controller chip. The DMA controller contains data, control and status, hence the two address connections and the input-output control lines. For memory mapped systems, the input output control lines are replaced by the memory control lines.

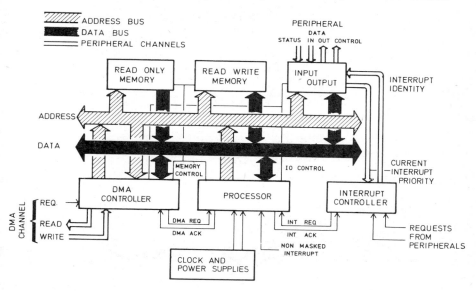

Fig.8. Complete Microprocessor Mainframe

Many manufacturers are fast approaching the situation where each major block of fig.8 can be obtained in a single integrated circuit, so that a high throughput computer mainframe can be assembled from 6 or so packages.

II.A.   THE HARDWARE-SOFTWARE SPECTRUM

A.J.T.Colin

University of Strathclyde

1. INTRODUCTION

Microprocessors are devices for handling and processing information. Any application of a microprocessor is governed by an algorithm or set of rules, which specify exactly how the information is to be dealt with under all possible circumstances.

To give an example, consider an 'instantaneous' fuel consumption meter for a car (Fig.1).

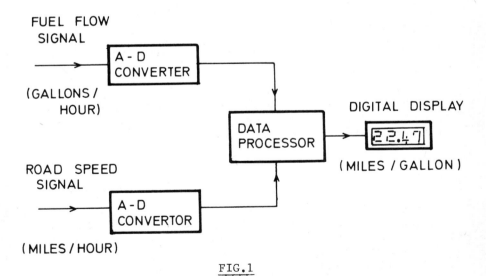

FIG.1

A suitable algorithm would be :
(1) Sample road speed signal. Call this quantity 's'
(2) Sample fuel flow signal.   Call this quantity 'f'
(3) If f=0, displya ---- (four minuses) and go back to step (1)
(4) Otherwise, divide s by f and display the result; then go back to step (1).

85

Step (3) is necessary because, if the car's engine is not running and the fuel flow is zero, the fuel consumption is determinate, and cannot be displayed as an ordinary number.

Once it has been designed, an algorithm can usually be implemented in many different ways. The variants can be placed on a spectrum. At one end, the method relies entirely on hardware; that is to say, the rules are 'wired in' to a set of relays or a network of logic and storage elements. At the other extreme, the algorithm is expressed as a set of instructions, to be executed by a general-purpose computer. Such sets of instructions are usually called programs or pieces of software, and may be compared to pieces of music, which are composed and written down but must be played on an instrument to produce the desired effect.

Computers all have certain important properties in common :

(1) Every computer has an arithmetic/logic unit (A L U) which contains a number of registers, each of which can contain an item of information such as a number of character code. The ALU also includes data handling mechanisms which allow the information to be manipulated and transferred between the registers. Such simple operations as addition, subtraction, comparison, and the various functions of Boolean logic are all available.

(2) Every computer includes a store consisting of cells which are numbered or addressed, usually from 0 upwards. Each cell in the store can hold an item of information, which can be transferred to or from the registers in the CPU.

(3) Every computer has certain registers which act as communication links with the outside world. For example, the apparent 'contents' of such a register at any moment may be the state of the push-buttons in a lift.

(4) Every computer runs by executing a sequence of instructions. The instructions are of two basic kinds:

   (a) Data Transfers. In a data transfer instruction, the computer will take the contents of certain register(s), carry out a specified arithmetic or logic operation, and put the result in another given register. This instruction is inevitably followed by the next in the sequence; that is, it has only one possible successor.

   (b) Jumps. Here, the machine uses the value of the data in a designated register to make a decision, between two successor instructions, one of which is followed if a particular condition is true, and the other if it is not.

(5) The instructions which govern the algorithm are stored, in coded form, in the cells of the store. Since the instructions

themselves determine their successors (either implicitly like data transfers, or explicitly like jumps), the sequence may skip or repeat certain sections of the program with complete flexibility.

This basic structure is very powerful. Even though the number of different instructions is limited, a suitable sequence can be devised to execute any well-defined algorithm (Shakespeare used only 26 letters!). This is why computers are called 'general-purpose'. Thus, a computer with a fruit-machine program in its store forms the control mechanism for a one-armed bandit; the same computer with different software can be at the heart of a monitoring system for a patient in an intensive care unit.

We can now contrast some of the properties of hardware versus software for the implementation of data processing algorithms:

Hardware	Software
Designed by an engineer, who must know the physical limitations (fan-out, propagation delay, heat dissipation, etc.) of the components he is using	Designed by a programmer, who must understand his machine as an abstract mathematical object with formal properties, but needs no detailed knowledge of the hardware.
•Capable of fast operation if necessary.	Speed limited by: (a) algorithm; (b) design of computer.
•Every system is unique.	All systems use standardised hardware, but every program is unique.
•Complexity limited to reasonably simple algorithms, because very complex systems use so many components that problems of reliability arise.	Complexity apparently unlimited by hardware.
•Design method uses finite state machines, and logic diagrams.	Design method uses flow charts, mnemonic codes, etc.

As a general observation, it may be added that, given designers of comparable experience and skill, it is usually quicker to implement any algorithm in software than in hardware.

To illustrate these points, consider the implementation of the division algorithm which would be needed for the fuel consumption meter we mentioned earlier. The hardware solution will involve shift registers, a parallel adder/subtractor unit, a counter, a number of flip-flops to indicate the current 'control state', and gating to make the device follow the right sequence of states. A schematic diagram, which assumes 16-bit binary numbers, would be as in fig.2.

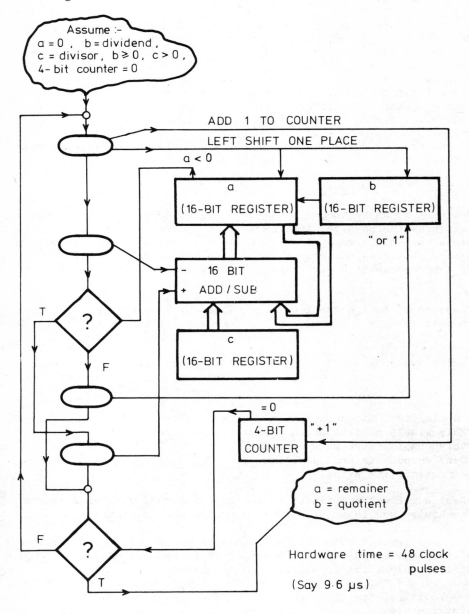

FIG.2. Division Algorithm.

The software equivalent for one computer (the PDP-11) would be something like:

```
LOOP:    ASL  RO  ⎫
         ASL  R1  ⎪ Shift a, b, one place left
         ADC  RO  ⎬
         SUB  RO,R2 ⎭
         BGE  .+6
         ADD  RO,R2
         BR   .+4
         INC  R1
         INC  R3
         BNE  LOOP
```

Total time - 130 instructions (say 300 μs)

Both solutions need a knowledge of the relevant detail for full understanding. The hardware solution is not in its final form; before handing it over to be constructed by a technician, the design engineer would have to elaborate it considerably, making creative use of his knowledge of electronics and of the components currently available.

The software solution is also not directly usable; but here, all that is necessary is to translate the symbolic representations of the instructions into their coded binary form and to load them into the store of the general-purpose computer. This is a trivial exercise, and there exist fully automatic ways of doing it.

In comparing the two methods of implementing algorithms, we conclude that software is considerably slower in running than hardware, but it is very much faster to design and write, and that it can handle more complex algorithms. This seems to make it preferable in most circumstances.

Until the introduction of L S I, computers were expensive; this made it uneconomic to use them, in spite of their advantages, in systems costing less than £50,000 or so, overall. Recently, however, the cost of basic components has fallen to a figure which is almost negligible, so that computers and computer-like devices can be used in a wide variety of cheap products.

The structure of a microprocessor is identical to the A L U and sequence control mechanism of a computer, so that we can make it into a general-purpose computer merely by attaching some random-access store. In most practical applications, this is not the best way to proceed, for two reasons: first, microprocessor systems are usually dedicated; that is, they are built into a piece of equipment and only ever require to implement one algorithm. This makes it feasible to put the controlling program into read-only memory, where it is protected from damage by power failures and other faults.

Secondly, we note that the designer who uses a general-purpose computer is obliged to use the machine exactly as he finds it, without the possibility of hardware modifications. On the other hand, the designer who uses a microprocessor is usually responsible for assembling the entire system from its components. This gives him a great deal of freedom; for example, he may choose to use several microprocessors working in parallel on different parts of the algorithm, or he may decide to implement certain sections of his device in pure hardware, so as to comply with time constraints. We conclude that :

(a) the designer must be familiar with both software and hardware to arrive at a good solution to his problem.

(b) the solution will in general contain both software and hardware components, and will occupy an intermediate place in the software-hardware spectrum.

2. WRITING SOFTWARE

In the first part of this Chapter, the impression you have been given is that writing satisfactory software is easy. In fact, as many people know to their great cost, it is extremely hard. The main difficulties seem to be as follows :

Psychological Optimism

Almost everyone can write really simple programs - say of 30 instructions or less. It is often falsely concluded that to write larger programs, all that is needed is a linear scaling of the time required. In reality, as a program increases in size, its complexity (in terms of possible interactions between its several parts) grows very rapidly, and soon the point is reached where the behaviour of the program as a whole is no longer comprehensible to its writer. Unfortunately, this state is far from obvious to the programmer himself. He embarks on a series of tests and modifications and clings to the belief - often in the face of months of evidence to the contrary - that there is 'one last bug to be found'. He 'knows' that the program will run correctly tomorrow.

In reality, such a program will never be correct. If, somehow, it passes the tests set for it by the programmer, it will fail after being put in to service, with much more serious consequences.

Misunderstanding of Failure Modes

Hardware failures usually arise when, due to dry joints or other physical causes, the equipment ceases to work in the way intended by the designer. The reliability of hardware can therefore be much improved by duplication or other methods involving redundancy.

On the other hand, software is not degraded by physical causes; any failure must have been potentially present from the time the equipment was first programmed. Simple duplication therefore gives absolutely no protection against software error, since both systems are bound to fail in the same way at the same instant. The redundancy needed for comparative safety is of a much more complex type.

Poor Documentation

Programmers detest writing full descriptions of their programs, and often this essential part of the development work is never done. The eventual results can be catastrophic; even though the original program may have been correct, any attempt to modify it, or to adapt it for a slightly different environment, brings it crashing in ruins. Such programs are euphemistically called 'fragile'. The most common reason for this kind of failure is that the original writer made a set of assumptions about the environment, which may have been true at the time, and which were so obvious to him that they did not need to be stated (for example, 'everyone' knows that all keyboard devices communicate at 10 cps, and 50% of the world is convinced that $\emptyset$ means letter 'Oh' (the other 50% knows that $\emptyset$ is digit Zero)). If these assumptions are not documented, violation of them in a different context may be very hard to detect.

This represents only a selection of the problems which arise when software is being written. The most promising remedy is the wholesale adoption of the techniques of software engineering, a newly emerging discipline. Some of the principles involved are :

- High-level languages, which separate the abstract algorithm from the computer which has to execute it.

- Structured programming, which imposes strict conventions on the way programs are written, and makes possible the proper control of complexity.

- Rules for documentation, which ensure that programs and their environments are fully described.

- Guidelines for testing programs, to reduce the chances of failure whilst actually in service.

- The recognition of programming as a genuine profession which requires years of experience in which to achieve a high standard; instead of, as at present, a refuge for the inept, and a brief stepping-stone for the competent.

II.B.   INTRODUCTION TO SYSTEM DESIGN

R. D. Dowsing

University College of Swansea

1. NATURE OF THE TASK

With any large scale task, as, for example, developing the software and hardware of a microprocessor system for a particular application, the problems which arise are due, directly or indirectly, to the complexity of the task. The human brain is unable to deal competently with more than a certain amount of information at any one time (Miller, 1956). The only way in which a large scale task may be comprehended and solved is by breaking it down into a set of smaller tasks in a logical manner so that the subtasks are of a size which may be completely comprehended. The process of decomposing a task into these smaller subtasks is one of analysis.

The process of system design is essentially the problem of translating the problem specification in a high level language notation, quite probably a natural language, meant for comprehension by a human being into the problem solution in a lower level language notation, usually ranging in complexity between a high level programming language and a hardware logic design language, which is meant to be understood by the implementation system, hardware and software. Since the translation is usually too complex to be performed in one stage it is normally split up into a number of smaller translation steps, each step lowering the level of the language used for the specification and the complexity of the system needed to understand it. Each of these stages can therefore be thought of as producing a set of instructions for a processing system or, in computing terms, for an abstract machine. Hence the decomposition of the problem solution may be thought of either in terms of abstract languages or in terms of abstract machines or a mixture of the two.

It has been the recognition of degree of complexity in computing and the methods of resolving the complexity (Dijkstra, 1972) which have been one of the major advances in the field of software engineering over the past fifteen years. With the advent of the microprocessor and other L.S.I. devices, the degree of complexity in each hardware device has increased and, because of the low cost, systems are being contemplated which are very

complex both due to the relatively simple hardware of each device
and due to cheapness which invites the production of systems with
a large number of components. For these type of systems there
is an overwhelming need for some type of design system to help
contain the complexity of the system so that the final product
has a high probability of fulfilling its design aims.

Before considering the process of problem solution design in
more detail it is interesting to consider what quantities the
designer has to deal with in the design of a system. The overall objective is to produce a system which is the most cost-
effective one to solve the given problem and which satisfies the
customer. This involves making tradeoffs such as the classical
space-time tradeoff. The designer also has to make tradeoffs
between the efficiency of his design and its clarity and correctness; for example to divide by 2 should he use a divide instruction for clarity or a shift right instruction for efficiency.
In many cases the only guidelines which can be given are that
"good engineering principles" should be followed. In view of
the fact that many of the problems arise directly due to the
complexity of the problem then it is probably wiser for the
designer to err on the side of clarity and correctness in the
first instance, rather than concentrating on efficiency.

One of the most important aspects of any design is the quality
of its documentation (Fitzgerald and Fitzgerald, 1973). Design is
an art and so involves making personal choices and tradeoffs. In
order to communicate amongst a group of designers on a large
project it is necessary not just to provide the solution to the
problem but the reasons why the particular design decisions were
taken. This necessitates a designer producing full documentation giving, as well as the design decisions, the reasons for
them and their consequences on the rest of the design, for example
that a sparse matrix will be stored in a linked list data structure to save storage space but this may increase the access time
to any element. Few, if any, designers like producing documentation, as may be seen from much present day computer system
software documentation, and so some automated aids are very helpful, if not essential. Frequently the maintainer of the software is not the originator and the absence of documentation or
its poor quality adds greatly to the cost and ease of maintenance
and modification.

The process of design may be split into a number of subtasks:-

Problem Specification

In order for a problem to be solved, the first requirement is
an unambiguous, rigorous, detailed specification of the problem.
The production of this specification is normally both demanding
and time-consuming unless the person with the problem and the

problem solver are the same person, since the specification must
be detailed enough for a correct solution to be produced but not
over detailed with irrelevant information. There has been relatively little research into this branch of problem solving although
recently a number of papers have appeared (Teichroew, 1972; Ross,
1977; Davis and Vick, 1977; Teichroew and Hershey, 1977) addressing
this particular problem, requirements specification.

These techniques, however, still suffer from the basic
problem that the person with the problem has to know or learn the
formalism or else the initial problem has to be communicated to
another person. It would seem at present as though a natural
language is probably the way in which a typical user would wish
to communicate his problem and so any of the automated aids to
problem specification will be used to communicate between the
customer systems analyst and the rest of the problem solving
organisation but not for the initial statement of the problem.

Logical Design of the Problem Solution

Having produced a specification of the problem, the next task
is to decide on the method, the algorithm, for solving the
problem. This involves trying a variety of different methods to
discover which is the "best" for the particular task in hand.
Much of this depends on the skill of the designer as an incorrect
choice of algorithm usually leads to a poor solution to the problem and only experience can help in deciding what are the
relevant weights of the various factors influencing the choice of
algorithm.

Having decided on a method of solving the problem, the next
task is to produce a formal definition of the problem solution
using the chosen algorithm in a clear unambiguous notation from
which the solution may be implemented with the available
implementation tools, either hardware or software or a mixture of
the two. This task is, therefore, a decomposition of the high
level problem description provided from the specification stage
into a lower level description containing more implementation
dependent details. The object of this decomposition is to
resolve the complexity of the problem by providing a formal framework and guidelines of how to decompose the problem description
in a structured manner.

Implementation

The result of the logical design phase should be a specification which can be directly implemented, for example by direct
interpretation by the implementation system corresponding to the
abstract machine implied by the lowest level of the logical
design. If the implementation system is at a lower level, then
further levels of refinement will be necessary.

One of the major problems of the implementation phase is to
map the logical design on to the implementation system. The
logical design produces a specification of the solution for an
abstract machine with a given amount of resources. If the
implementation system does not mirror this system then one of the
tasks of implementation is to map the abstract machine on to the
actual implementation system. This is frequently carried out by
an operating system. The object of this phase of the problem
solution is to map the logical design on to the implementation
system so that the implementation system appears as the lowest
level abstract machine implied by the logical design.

Testing

Since there are so many intermediate stages and designers
involved in the design phase it is very likely that the final
design is incorrect in some sense, that is, it will not satisfy
"the customer". These errors may be classified into several
types. Firstly, the original specification may be incorrect
thus leading to an incorrect solution. This is frequently the
case especially regarding the problem constraints, for example,
the solution must stay within given cost constraints. Secondly,
errors may have crept into the logical decomposition of the
problem which may be manifest because the design no longer makes
sense at the implementation phase (syntax or semantic errors),
for example, misspelt identifiers, or because of incorrect
results. A dangerous form of error may occur where the results
cannot be predicated beforehand and hence incorrect results are
very difficult, or impossible, to detect. A further form of
incorrectness may occur at the implementation level because the
solution does not fit the problem constraints with respect to
time or use of resources. In all of these cases iteration around
the design process has to be performed to solve the problem.

In order to detect these errors, two separate systems are
required, one to test the logic of the design and another to
check the use of resources against the problem constraints. In
both these cases the testing could be left to the implementation
phase but this is undesirable for several reasons. Firstly, the
sooner an error is detected the easier it is to correct and the
less effort expended. Secondly, many of the errors which could
occur do not depend on all the details of the solution but only
on a subset of them. There is less chance of an error being
"hidden" by other problems if the testing is performed before
complete elaboration of the problem. Hence simulators for
various levels of abstract machine are required in order to detect
the different types of error which may occur at the different
levels. The object of this phase of the solution is to detect
errors as soon as possible in order to provide easier correction
and to save design effort.

Optimisation

Optimisation is not strictly part of the design phase of the problem solution but is an important technique for mapping from one abstract machine to another. For example, to implement the result of the logical design on to the implementation system, the obvious technique is to emulate (simulate) the abstract machine defined by the logical design phase on the implementation system.   This may or may not be an efficient method of implementation depending on the architecture of the two systems.   For example, if the logical design implies an abstract stack machine and the implementation system is not stack oriented then the implementation is unlikely to be efficient if the technique outlined above is used.   In those cases where the mapping is not efficient enough then special techniques, optimisations, have to be employed to improve the mapping.   Hence if the problem solving constraints cannot be met at any stage then it may be possible to modify the design using some optimisation procedures rather than a complete redesign using a different algorithm, the worst-case situation.   The object of this phase of the problem solution is to modify the design so that the resource requirements of the problem solution may be met.

The design process is an iterative procedure around the tasks outlined above with the specification, testing and, if necessary, optimisation taking place at each stage of the problem solution elaboration.   If errors are detected at any stage, then the design process has to revert back one or more stages until the error can be corrected.   It is the task of the designer to ensure that too great steps are not taken at any stage since this increases the complexity and likelihood of errors.   This expertise can only be gained by practice and experience.

2.   SYSTEM DESIGN AND THE MICROPROCESSOR

It is pertinent here to consider the specific ways in which a design system relates to the microprocessor.   With the advent of these low cost L.S.I. components, a large complicated system may be built very cheaply, considering only the component costs. The software and hardware development costs for such a system may well be several orders of magnitude higher than the component costs and even then there is a fair likelihood that the system will not perform satisfactorily.   There are a number of questions which should be answered before these type of systems are built, such as which is the most cost effective method of implementing a specific function, hardware or software ?   In order to answer these questions in a satisfactory manner, they have to be considered at the relevant place in the design and implementation of the system.   Because of the extra choice given to the designer with the development of L.S.I. components, it is even more important that some systematic method of design is adopted which allows and constrains the designer to consider the relevance of the microprocessor to the cost effectiveness of his design at the appropriate stage. One important feature of the design system should be its ability to allow, or coerce, the designer to think in terms of parallelism or concurrency in the design since one of the major benefits of L.S.I. components is the possibility of multiprocessor or multicomputer systems. Hopefully trends in this direction will help the designer by simplifying the implementation of the final design.

Finally it is worthwhile considering what the total objectives of a design and implementation system such as described here are. Firstly, to be of use in the design and implementation of microprocessor systems, the cost of using the design aids should not be too high and the benefits to the user should be made obvious so that the user has every incentive to use them. Secondly, the system should constrain the user into structuring his problem solution in a well-defined manner and help him to modularise his design to help contain the complexity at every stage. Thirdly, it should help the designer by keeping detailed documentation of the design, stage by stage, to help to make the design comprehensible to others. Lastly, the system should attempt to provide as much checking as possible, as soon as possible, in order to isolate errors before they propagate through the design.

II.C.   LOGICAL DESIGN

                         R. D. Dowsing

                University College of Swansea

1. INTRODUCTION

   The logical design phase of system design is the elaboration
of the problem solution from a high level definition to a lower
level one.   Neither the "height" of the high level nor the low
level are defined for the general problem, only for specific cases.
For example, the high level could be natural English and the low
level a high level programming language such as ALGOL 68.   The
object is to end up with the problem solution defined in some
language understood by the implementation system and in a form
which is easy to understand, debug and modify.

   It has been realised for a number of years that the key to
"good" program design is structure.   In order for the human being
to understand the complexity of a problem, the explanation has to
be structured in some sense.   Exactly what this structuring
should be is not fully understood although various guiding
principles (Dijkstra, 1972; Wirth, 1971 a) have been proposed and
used for system and program design.   One of the keys to the
structure is modularisation, the process of splitting the problem
into a series of subproblems, modules, and defining the interface between them.   Again, exactly how the original problem
should be subdivided is not clear although several workers
(e.g. Parnas, 1972a; Parnas, 1972b) have given some guidelines
for this decomposition.

2. CONTROL & DATA STRUCTURES

   The logical design phase is concerned with two features of the
problem: control and data.   The control specification defines
the actions to be performed on the data and their ordering.   The
data specifications define the type of data manipulated by the
control specification and the flow of data through the problem
solution.   Most of the work on structured programming and
similar techniques has concentrated on the structure of the

                              99

control specification and has led to the specification of a number of design constructs to facilitate structured decomposition. Many of these constructions (all in some methodologies) are limited to one control entry and one control exit. The object is to elaborate the design in such a way that it is easily modifiable and understandable and this form of control structure leads to hierarchical design with the desired properties. It has also led to the suggestion that statements such as GOTO should be eliminated (Dijkstra, 1968) or their use severely restricted in design languages. This suggestion arises because of the possibility of unstructured design when using such constructions. Although situations have been found where these constructions are required, such as error exits, they are relatively infrequent.

There has been less research into the structure of the design as far as data is concerned (Hoare, 1972 a); **Schneiderman and Scheuerman, 1974).** Much of the research is concerned with regarding the data and the actions on the data as a complete entity with the data only being accessed by reference to one of the actions which may be performed on the data, that is, direct access to data is only allowed to the primitive actions on the data (Hoare, 1974). This is in contrast to the functional division of a problem into the different tasks to be carried out. In this case the problem is organised around the transformations of the data objects rather than the operations to be performed. These methods are essentially the same but with different emphasis on the two parts, control and data. Many of the newer present day programming languages (e.g. Wirth, 1977) attempt to deal with one or both of these techniques of design.

3. DESIGN STRATEGY

As well as the rules and constructions for producing a structured design there also has to be some overall strategy for tackling the problem solution. The two most obvious approaches to design are top-down **(McCowan and Kelly, 1975)** and bottom-up. At one end of the design there exists a high level description of the problem solution in a few statements, whilst at the other extreme there exist a number of statements in a low level description language. Obviously one could be mapped on to the other starting from either end. The advantage of top-down over bottom-up is that at every stage the overall design is known and the interfaces are defined at the beginning whereas in a bottom-up design the interfaces may be designed later, are certainly implemented later and the overall structure of the design is not apparent until the last step is taken. Conversely much of the design may be performed in parallel and so it might seem that the design could be produced faster but the interfacing problems are usually enough to outweigh any concurrent design gains. In view of this, several workers (e.g. Hewitt, 1974) have suggested other methods of decomposing the design such as middle-out and outside-in. All of these methods are acknowledging the fact that it is necessary to have an overall view in all directions for successful design. The crucial point in any design exercise is to take note of important facts and to "ignore" the rest and this "window" of what is important moves with the progress of the design. It has also been shown in the recent past that the idea that all design is hierarchical, that is, tree structured, is in fact not true and that other structures are more appropriate in some cases. This also means that the methods of designing using these structures are different. Parnas (1972 a & b) has pointed out another relevant feature when attempting to decompose a problem solution into modules. This is the idea of "information hiding" which is concerned with hiding as much information as possible from the outside world inside a module, that is, the module interface should be as simple and small as possible and should be designed on the basis of what the outside world "needs to know".

4. REPRESENTATION METHODS

In order to represent the various stages of the logical design process some form of "language" is required. There has been a great deal of discussion and contention, about the form which this "language" should take. Many designers prefer to use some form of graphical notation (e.g. Rose and Bradshaw, 1971; Ross, 1977) rather than a textual form although the textual form is usually more concise and allows some ideas, for example, recursion, to be expressed much more easily than the graphical notation. Basically there is no difference between the two notations and it is simply a matter of which is easiest for the particular designer to use. However, there are an ever-increasing number of formal representations which may be used as some form of mathematical model so that the properties of the resulting design may be analysed. Perhaps the most common model at present in use is that of Petri nets (Petri, 1962) for which there are a wide range of properties known. Many of the other representation schemes have been shown to be equivalent to Petri nets and properties for these models deduced in this manner.

5. ALTERNATIVE METHODS OF LOGICAL DESIGN

Previous sections of this paper have dealt with the more familiar methods of logical design. This section considers some rather different methods.

The object of the control structure is to define the sequencing of actions to be performed on the data and to this end it contains constructions to specify concurrency and sequentiality. This

implies that the actions on the data are synchronised to occur in
the stated order.   What is actually defined by the control structure is a set of possible control paths, one of which will be
executed for a particular set of starting conditions.   One method
of specifying this set of control paths is by means of path
expressions (Campbell and Haberman, 1974).   The objective of
path expressions is to bring the design of the concurrency
restrictions to a higher level.   The language of path expressions
allows the user to specify, in a convenient notation, the allowable paths of execution of operations on a shared object.   As
such, path expressions are included in the type definition of the
shared object.   An example of a path expression is:-

<u>path</u>   a;   (b + c);   d   <u>end</u>

which represents execution sequences containing an arbitrary
number of the sequence given by a followed by either b or c
followed by d.   For example, this might specify that an operation
a (deposit) must occur on a shared buffer followed by either
operation b or c which modifies the information in some manner,
followed by operation d (remove) which clears the buffer.

Another, contrasting, method of specifying synchronisation is
by means of message transfer expressions (Riddle, 1973).   Path
expressions are essentially a generative method of specifying
execution sequences;   that is, they specify rules which allow
particular sequences to be generated.   Message transfer expressions, however, are a template solution to the problem, that is,
they specify the form of allowed sequences without specifying the
rules for generating them.   An example of a message transfer
expression is:-

(DALAD × DAALD × DAADL)*

where × denotes exclusive alternation and * indefinite repetition.
This specifies that the messages in the system should appear in
one of the orders specified, that is, it specifies the possible
states of the system with respect to message transfers.   Whilst
both path expressions and message transfer expressions are concerned with synchronisation, message transfer expressions are
really the user's view of a design, that is, they specify the
possible sequences of messages which may be generated by the
system whereas path expressions are the programmer's/designer's
tools to specify how to generate the correct control paths through
the design.   It is worthwhile noticing that both of these methods
deal with the problem of synchronisation in terms of the data
objects involved and the design technique used is to think of the
design in terms of the data objects primarily.

Riddle (1974) has attempted to classify the types of
behavioural specification schemes.   These schemes, such as

predicate calculus assertions, path expressions and message transfer expressions, are methods of providing extra specifications
of the intended purpose of the system, that is, what the system
should do.   They provide redundancy in the problem solution to
allow for error checking and correctness checks.

6.   RELEVANCE TO MICROPROCESSORS

As has been stated previously from the point of view of software microprocessors are very similar to mini and mainframe
processors and so the ideas of structured programming and other
design methods are equally relevant to them.   However, the
specific difference of microprocessors is that they are cheap and
hence a large multiprocessor system, distributed or otherwise,
may be built very cheaply and one of the main areas of research
at the moment is to discover how to build and use such a network
of microcomputers to see if this is a more cost effective method
of problem solving than the use of the more powerful minicomputers
and mainframe processors.   Since there is this tendency to build
multimicroprocessor systems a method is required for constructing
the complete system in a logical manner, that is, we need a
logical design methodology for the whole system.   This means that
the methodology needs to be applicable to both hardware and
software, since at the implementation phase the design may be
mapped on to either hardware or software or a combination of both.

7.   DESIGN TECHNIQUES FOR CONCURRENCY

Since many microprocessor systems will comprise of several
microprocessors much of the current research into design methodology is directed towards concurrent systems.   There appear to
be two different methods of producing a design with a high degree
of concurrency.   One approach, typified by Ramamoorthy and
Gonzalez (1969), is to design the problem solution in exactly the
same manner as for a single processor and then apply a technique,
usually in the form of a program, to this design to determine
which parts may be executed concurrently.   The other approach is
to design the problem solution specifically for multiprocessor
implementation by including constructions in the design language
to express concurrency (Brinch Hansen, 1975).   This is the
approach taken by Hoare elsewhere in this book (Chapter VI.B).
By comparison with Knuth's (1971) study on the efficiency of
FORTRAN programs and Brinch Hansen's (1977) comments on the
amount of an operating system written in a language involving
concurrency, it is probable that only a small part of many designs
need to be specified in terms of concurrency.   For this reason
it is probably more cost effective to leave the concurrency design
to the designer rather than an automatic system.

As well as the actual technique of specifying the concurrency there is the difficult problem of identifying concurrency in the problem solution at any level. For example, in many cases, a different algorithm would be chosen for problem solution in the case of multiprocessor as opposed to single processor implementation. Also, frequently, a different view of the problem leads to a solution with a different amount of concurrency. This aspect of design is also being investigated at present to see if there are any methods of approach which are especially useful in multiprocessor system design.

II.D.   DESIGN SIMULATION AND OPTIMISATION

R. D. Dowsing

University College of Swansea

1. INTRODUCTION

Simulation is one of the most powerful tools for investigating errors and mapping strategies during the process of system design. One view of design is that it is the elaboration of a problem solution by a series of specifications of instructions for abstract machines whose definition becomes more detailed as the design progresses.   At each stage of the design, therefore, a specification of the solution exists for a machine which may not exist. ' There are two ways to implement the design; by elaborating the design to the level at which the actual machine does exist or by simulating, or emulating, the abstract machine on the real machine.   In this chapter it is the latter of these methods which will be considered.

At each level of design elaboration errors may be introduced. These errors should be detected at the highest level since it is only at this level that a precise, relevant error message may be given.   To discover these errors it is necessary to "execute" (understand) the design at each level of elaboration.   Since each level of design only elaborates a few features, then the testing only needs to be confined to these features.   The easiest method of providing this test facility is by means of simulation.

At the lowest level of design the problem is how to map the design on to the implementation system.   There may be several different mappings and the designer may well need to know the features of each so that he can make the correct tradeoffs for his particular implementation.   This could be provided by actually implementing all the alternatives and measuring the various parameters but this is usually quite difficult and time-consuming.   It is usually much easier to simulate the implementation system in software and experiment on the simulator. Frequently these models have been rather poor but recent work suggests that realistic models can now be built.

R. D. DOWSING

Hence there are really two types of simulator required; one
to simulate an abstract machine to test mainly the logic of a
design and another to aid the mapping of the final design to the
implementation system.

Logical Simulators

At each level of design the previous stage is elaborated in
more detail.   To provide consistency within the design the levels
of elaboration need to be checked against one another to ensure
that they are self-consistent.   Remembering that the logical
design consists of control and data structures, the logical
simulator should be designed to deal with these two different
structures.   One method of providing this checking is by means of
a state graph approach (Lister, 1974).   If a module, a design
unit, is thought of in terms of its interface to the rest of the
design then the two things to be checked are that this interface
is correct i.e. it is identical to the previous design stage
both in respect to the control and to the data paths and that the
actions defined by the module are identical semantically to the
previous elaboration.   It is relatively easy to check that the
interfaces are syntactically identical but this only provides
static checking.   To ensure the consistency of the interface at
run time dynamic checks are necessary unless the design language
is very restrictive.   This type of check may be provided by a
simulator which can check the interface requirements at run time.
As to checking that the module actions are semantically correct,
this can only be done by some form of theorem proving technique
(London, 1975).   These techniques are still in the research
stage and, although they are important and will hopefully be of
practical use in a few years' time, they will not be considered
here.   As well as the logical properties of the module there are
other properties such as deadlock and determinacy which need to
be checked for in the design.   Since these are, in general,
dynamic properties concerned with the control of resources in the
most general sense, some form of simulator or implementation is
needed to detect them.

What are the properties associated with the design which are
required for the logical simulator ?   In essence the logical
simulator simulates the flow in the control graph whilst considering each associated module in the data graph as being a single
composite action, hence representing a state.   At the next level
of elaboration the module itself is decomposed into a control
and data structure.   The logical simulator needs to know details
of the control and data flow in and out of each module so that the
flow of control in the system can be simulated.   The logical
simulator then takes the form of a state graph producer.   In
order to characterise the states a high level description of each
module is required i.e. the transformation of the inputs to the
outputs.   Each module is then regarded as a state transformer and

the actions of the system can be defined in terms of the state transformation of the inputs to the outputs for the complete system. The user may interrogate this system by inputting various state conditions to see if they may ever occur e.g. deadlock is a state which may be entered but not exited and is not a termination state. Also, by definition some states may not exist e.g. an action of reading and updating data at once, and the existence of these states may be checked for.

Since most systems will generate a large number of states, this type of checking will have to be performed in a hierarchical manner. This implies that there has to be a sensible way of breaking down the graph into small sections to be tested. In general this cannot be done, and has to rely on the design philosophy to produce a sensibly structured graph which may be broken down in a hierarchical manner, for example, the tree structured hierarchy produced by top-down design.

Resource Simulator

A second type of simulator required is one to explore the different mappings of the design on to a real implementation system. This is equivalent to the task of mapping the user's abstract machine on to the actual machine architecture and since these two will almost certainly be different then there will be several different methods of implementation. The designer will wish to determine the various tradeoffs to be made between cost and efficiency of these different implementations to determine which is the best mapping for his purpose. Hence the simulator required for this purpose has to be given the two machine architectures as data input together with the design in order to produce cost-performance - efficiency comparisons as output. Since both cost and performance are difficult to define precisely for all purposes, then the simulator may decide on more concrete measures such as resource utilisation, throughput and job time to produce as measures of the "goodness" of the mapping strategies.

In an ideal situation the simulator would also produce as output details of the mapping algorithm decided upon as best by the designer to drive the actual implementation on the final system, for example, the resource scheduling algorithm. In many cases several of the mapping parameters are already fixed, for example, in a multiprocessing, multiprogramming operating system environment, and it is only a few which are variable. For this reason automatic mapping via a simulator is not frequently performed.

2. OPTIMISATION

If the resource simulator indicates that the design does not meet its requirements with respect to resource usage or time, then the designer has to produce another design to satisfy these needs. He may either rework his design from a previous level of elaboration, or from the beginning, or he may decide to modify his design to optimise those features which do not meet the specification. If the designer chooses this latter approach it is likely to be because his design does not meet one of the time requirements. If it does not meet the resource usage requirements, for example, memory space, there is little, apart from minor tidying, that can be done without modifying the basic algorithm and hence reworking the design from the beginning. Assuming that it is a time constraint which has not been met, for example real time requirements, then one of the major optimisations which may be made is to make use of any processing concurrency in the implementation system. There are two schools of thought about this, one believing that an automatic system should detect the concurrency (Ramamoorthy and Gonzalez, 1969) whilst the other believes that concurrency should be specified by the designer (Brinch Hansen, 1975). Since for microprocessor systems a relatively cheap solution to the problem is required and a solution where the performance of the system may be estimated at every stage, a system where the designer is in control at every stage of design is a necessity so a fully automatic system is a distinct disadvantage.

What types of concurrency can the designer look for ?

1. Parallelism.
2. Overlapping processing and input-output.
3. Pipelining and overlapping.

Parallelism

Any inherent parallelism in the design should have been specified at the logical design level using the parbegin-parend type of construction (Dijkstra, 1968). However, this depends on the designer thinking in this manner which is not common at the present moment and a review of the current design is probably worthwhile to see if any extra parallelism exists. At this stage an automatic aid may be of some help since it has no preconceived ideas of the amount of parallelism and may detect some not obvious to the designer.

Overlapping processing and input-output

The extent to which input-output may be overlapped with processing depends to a large extent on the implementation system. Input-output processing requires a certain amount of intelligence

or processing power in order to perform the operation. Some of
this intelligence may be provided in the input/output device
itself or it may be provided by a central processor and the
extent to which input/output may be overlapped depends to some
extent on how much intelligence is provided in the device itself.
Since the control of input/output devices is usually complex, for
example, time dependent, it is usually provided by some form of
operating system which means that the degree of concurrency in
overlapping input/output and processing cannot be determined by
the designer of a user system.

Pipelining and overlapping

Another form of concurrency which the designer may make use
of in optimising his design is pipelining (Aspinall et al, 1977).
If part of the design is a loop, for example repeat ... until,
then instead of executing the loop serially each iteration of the
loop may be able to be activated before the previous iteration
has finished. In the limit this becomes a parallel loop but
there are usually restrictions which imply a partial ordering of
operations. The optimum pipeline is a pipeline where every
stage has the same execution time. To achieve this, the problem
has to be split up into equal execution-time units. This is
frequently not possible and one way of overcoming this problem is
to overlap processing of the longer stages of the pipeline so
that the effective execution time of these stages is lowered.
In this manner it is possible to speed up the execution of loops
which is frequently where bottlenecks occur in design.

Thus the designer has a number of methods of optimising the
design. Since the problem constraints are implementation constraints, the design has to be implemented, or simulated, before
it is discovered that optimisation is necessary. This means
that a number of measurements need to be taken on implementation
to measure the critical parameters, the performance, of the system.
These measurements may then be used as the basis of any optimisation which is required. What features of the implementation
need to be measured and what aids are required for this ? The
two main parameters of the implementation are time and use of
resources. The designer wishes to know how efficient the design
is, that is, is it efficient in use of resources, and whether or
not it meets any timing constraints. Both of these measurements
then give him some measure of the "cost" of execution. In order
to measure these parameters some form of monitoring system is
required. This is described in the chapter on implementation.
One form of monitoring device which is very useful to the designer
is an execution time profile which provides the cost of execution
of the various parts of the design. Since it has been shown
(Ignalls, 1971) that in typical FORTRAN programs 50% of the
execution time is spent in 3% of the code it is reasonable to
suppose that in order to optimise a design, if necessary, the

designer need only concentrate on a small proportion of his design and an execution time profile helps him to focus his attention on the critical section.

It is worthwhile re-emphasising here that optimisation is not required in many, or most, cases and is only a useful technique when the designer's "final" abstract machine design is sufficiently different from the real implementation system for there to be scope for improving the obvious mapping strategy.

3. IMPLICATION TO MICROPROCESSOR SYSTEMS

As far as microprocessor systems are concerned, there are several specific requirements of the simulation systems. Firstly, most microprocessors being used at present are in simple dedicated systems and these simple systems do not provide many aids to testing the initial system thoroughly, since neither the hardware of the microprocessor nor its associated equipment contain appropriate error detection checks. Hence the best method of testing the logic of microprocessor software systems is via a simulator or an emulator.

At the present time, microprocessors are used mainly in dedicated environments to perform a specific task. There is, therefore, not so much emphasis in implementation on resource sharing, since resources are dedicated to a given task, but more on exploiting concurrency to meet design objectives. Also, since microprocessors are relatively cheap, there is less need to make efficient use of them providing that the resulting system is still cost-effective.

Optimisation techniques become quite important with micro-processor systems, since present-day microprocessors are relatively slow and so many designs may fail because of time constraints. By using the fact that microprocessors are cheap and hence multi-processor systems may be produced quite cheaply a design may be optimised to bring it within the time constraints by exploiting concurrency in the implementation system.

II.E.   DESIGN IMPLEMENTATION

                          R. D. Dowsing

                 University College of Swansea

1. INTRODUCTION

At some level the design has to be implemented on a hardware/
software system.   The designer's final product specifies
sequences of operations for an abstract machine.   The task of
the implementation phase is to realise this abstract machine on a
real hardware/software system.   This realisation may be produced
by one of two mechanisms.   The implementation system may either
present the design with its abstract machine, for example, by
microprogramming, so it may be directly executed or it may transform the user design into one which uses the given implementation
system as its "abstract machine".   In practice mixtures of these
two techniques may be used (cf. compilers and interpreters).

As well as these two different methods of performing the
mapping, there are two mapping strategies which differ in the
time of binding;   the operation of associating resources of the
abstract machine with the implementation system.

The mapping may be performed statically in which case the
mapping is performed on the final design before execution.   This
suffers from the problem that the actual concurrency, dynamic
concurrency, in execution has to be predicted from the static
concurrency expressed in the design.   This is difficult to predict accurately since it involves knowing factors such as the
timing for each part of the design which may be data dependent and
hence not predictable before execution.   These problems may be
alleviated by the alternative method of dynamic mapping where the
mapping is left until execution time.   In this case the mapping
is performed when required and the actual concurrency may be
determined by the mapping system at that time.   This dynamic
solution to the problem is the classic operating system solution.

2. IMPLEMENTATION TASKS

Before looking at the various implementation techniques in more detail, it is worth considering the tasks associated with design implementation. Firstly, there has to be some form of mapping performed to transform from the designer's abstract machine solution to the real implementation system. This implies that the mapping system has a knowledge both of the real implementation system and the designer's abstract machine. In many cases the mapping system knows very little about the designer's abstract machine and it has to build up a picture of the machine as execution progresses. It is this feature which gives rise to such problems as deadlock and determinacy which occur because the mapping system cannot predict in advance how to map the designer's abstract machine on to the real implementation system. In order to improve the mapping, either the mapping system or the designer must be given more information about the efficiency of the mapping. To obtain information about this efficiency, some form of monitoring of use of resources is necessary in the mapping system. A further task which is necessary is to detect any errors which occur. Since this may be the first instance of executing the design it is only to be expected that errors will occur. The task of error detection is to detect the various errors as soon as possible and to attempt to provide error messages which indicate the exact nature of the error. This depends very much on the information provided by the designer, since the only methods of detecting an error are either that two specifications of the problem conflict or that the implementation will not map on to the implementation system since its resource requirements are too large.

Static and Dynamic Mapping

The mapping task is crucial if a cost effective system is to be produced (Sayne, 1969). The main mapping task is that of resource management. If the design can be mapped to the implementation system with no sharing then there are very few problems. The majority of problems are associated with the sharing of real resources and these can be classified as synchronisation and mutual exclusion problems. Synchronisation is concerned with the ordering of actions in time whereas mutual exclusion is concerned with the control of a re-usable resource so that it is never in use by more than one task at a time.

The policy of sharing may be determined either statically or dynamically, although the mechanism will be implemented dynamically since it must include some synchronisation and/or mutual exclusion features, such as semaphore manipulation. To map the user's design to the implementation system may require that the user's design be modified because not enough real resources are

available.   The design may have to be modified so that some
resources are shared, for example, processors.   In order to
share a resource, synchronisation for use of the resource must be
stated together with any mutual exclusion, if necessary.   This
implies that some policy, for example, scheduling, has to be
decided upon as to how to use the synchronisation and mutual
exclusion of resources.   A static policy would decide solely on
the design, a static object, how to map this on to the implementation system.   A dynamic policy would decide at execution time
how to direct the mapping.   Since the object is to map the
execution time graph on to the implementation system the dynamic
policy, in general, produces a more efficient mapping at the
expense of some execution time overhead.   This may not mean that
the actual design utilisation of the resource is more efficient
since the mapping process requires the use of resources.   In a
number of cases the mapping overhead may outweigh any gains in
the efficiency of the mapping.   The implementor has the difficult
problem of deciding how to make the tradeoffs between cost and
efficiency and the overheads of the different mapping strategies.
Since the most efficient scheme with the least mapping overhead
is where the implementation system is the designer's final
abstract machine, then ideally no sharing is required.   However,
this may not be the most cost effective way of providing an
implementation system, especially if the hardware system costs are
high.   It has traditionally been the situation that the hardware
costs of, for example, processors have been high and hence high
utilisation must be made of them for cost effective performance.
This gives rise to the concept of sharing and produces the
complications of a large complicated operating system to keep
hardware utilisation high.

In the case where hardware costs decline the balance between
the overheads of sharing and the cost of the resource changes
and at some point it becomes more cost effective to provide more
hardware to reduce the overheads of sharing.   In the case of
microprocessors this point is, or has, rapidly been reached and
there is a good case, in many situations, for abandoning the
traditional, dynamic, operating system approach and adopting a
static mapping technique with enough hardware so that little, if
any, sharing is required.   This implies that the emphasis is
more on producing a simple error free system with minimal software costs than on producing high utilisation of resources such
as processors.   In fact, the most cost effective technique for
producing the complete system, hardware and software may well
produce a system where processor utilisation is low.

Interrupts

One aspect of implementation which causes a good deal of
problems is the use of interrupts.   Interrupts are essentially

a technique to implement the sharing of the use of a resource, a processor, between a set of competing processes. If sharing is not required, then interrupts are also not required. However, in many situations, there are several processes, both input, output and processing taking place concurrently, and there are more active processes than processors.

The object of interrupts is to inform the mapping system (operating system) of some change in the state of the system of which it needs to be aware e.g. termination of message transfer. The main reason this is required is to switch the processor (pre-emption) between one of several tasks it is conceptually running in parallel. If the tasks are actually running in parallel, then no switching is required, only communication between the processor and its resources. For this polling may be used since this is the basis of interrupts in any case. If a processor is dedicated to a task e.g. controlling a disc then, assuming no sharing, it has only one task to perform at any one stage and the signal from a resource does not have to interrupt it since it will be waiting for the signal. So from the hardware viewpoint, the objective is for no sharing which means that the processing becomes distributed, that is, the processing becomes closely associated with a particular piece of hardware and the tasks of synchronisation and mutual exclusion are pushed back to the system designer, that is, to a higher level where it is easier to see and comprehend exactly what is happening. These are the types of computer system which will become more numerous as hardware becomes cheaper. Interrupts may be used for some specific purposes in these systems, such as very fast response, but their use will be restricted due to the software complications.

Portability

One of the most important features of a design if it is to be implemented on a number of different systems is portability; the ease with which the design can be implemented on a different system. There are a number of well known techniques for produc-ing portable systems (Brown, 1977). If the final design is specified for a general purpose abstract machine, then it is likely that it can be implemented on a variety of implementation systems. The ease of portability depends on how easy it is to map the abstract machine on to the implementation system and on this also depends the efficiency of the implementation. The design then becomes a tradeoff between making it general purpose for portability and special purpose for efficiency; that is, at which level of design should implementation be effected. As well as the design itself being portable the implementation aids also have to be portable, for example, compilers, interpreters and operating systems, to enable implementation on a variety of different systems.

DESIGN IMPLEMENTATION

As the proportion of software cost to system cost rises, then portability becomes more important since replication of already existing software is a major expense in any new system.

Protection

If a design is to be implemented on a system where design sharing is allowed, a multiprogramming system, then the implementation system has to provide some form of protection, either in software or, preferably, hardware. The object of this protection is to prevent interaction between the different programs. It means that each real resource may only be used by one program over a given period of time; this period depending on the type of access to the resource and whether mutual exclusion is necessary. In essence, therefore, this problem is exactly the same problem as the single program designer has in mapping the design to the implementation system, the sharing of real resources.

The protection mechanisms employed can range from the very simple such as no sharing of the addressing space with simple base-limit checks to the very complex such as capability systems (England, 1974). The problems with these systems are that they usually degrade the performance by a significant amount and the more complex systems are relatively expensive. For this reason, many of the cheaper computer systems provide little in the way of protection features in the hardware.

Error Detection

Allied to the problem of protection is the problem of detecting the various types of errors which may occur on design implementation. Error detection relies on the fact that the system has at least two definitions of the problem, at least one of which is assumed to be correct. For example, if the design is produced in ALGOL 68, the implementation system must know the rules of ALGOL 68, both syntax and semantics, which it uses to check the design against. Similarly, correctness proofs depend on the fact that the system is given two definitions of the problem solution which are then checked for equivalence.

The types of error which may occur depend upon the level at which the design is implemented. For example, in a high level programming language it is usually impossible for the programmer to generate actual machine addresses. The translation to actual addresses occur during the compilation phase so that the real address space is only referenced by the translator which can insert checks at the relevant places to check for illegal memory accesses, for example, accessing outside the bounds of an array. The most difficult type of error which exists is where an answer is produced which is incorrect due to some logical error in the design but which appears to be correct. There is little help which may be given for this situation at the present time assuming that program proving schemes are not viable at present. Any other types of error which may be detected, either syntactic or semantic, should be reported to the designer in a form which he will understand. The problem with many systems is that the implementation level is lower than the final design level so that a transformation has to take place before implementation. When errors are detected on implementation, they should be transformed back in to a form which may be related to the original design. In many systems this is not done, so giving rise to incomprehensible error messages.

3. TESTING THE IMPLEMENTATION

Since the process of proving the design by theorem proving techniques is still in its infancy, the designer has to rely on testing the design with sets of test data (Hetzel, 1973; Gerhart, 1977). The object of this is to test all the data and control paths in the design. Since this is normally impractical due to the large number, a number of sets of "typical" input data are used to test the design. The selection of these sets of data is very difficult and the choice has a critical effect on the performance of the system. For this reason there has been a good deal of effort expended into attempting to automate this selection process (Howden, 1976; Ramamoorthy et al., 1976). In fact, even in the automated case, these error detection strategies rarely exceed a 70% error detection rate.

Assuming that the design cannot be properly tested by these means and will therefore contain errors, another approach is to attempt to take correcting action when errors are found in executing the tested design. This is done by specifying alternative methods of performing various parts of the design which may be used if the primary method fails. This is the method used in the "recovery block" method described by Randell (1975). To make this technique effective, special hardware is needed to save and restore the program state on entry to a recovery block.

Monitoring

Even with all the normal implementation aids it is often difficult for the implementor to predict the exact performance of the system on implementation. It is therefore necessary for some form of monitoring, hardware or software or both, to be included in the system so that the designer is provided with the information to allow him to improve the implementation. In order to do this it is normal to take a snapshot of the state of the system

from time to time together with a log of any external events and
to process this after the execution of the design to produce
relevant statistics. These tasks may be performed by an operating system if dynamic mapping is being performed but must be built
into the design or the mapping primitives if static mapping is
used.

4. RELEVANCE TO MICROPROCESSOR SYSTEMS

Microprocessor hardware costs are relatively low so the
objective of not sharing a processor but providing one for each
active process becomes a possibility. Similarly the objective
of removing interrupts also becomes a possibility. This means
that many microprocessor systems will be multiprocessor systems
either closely coupled or loosely coupled, distributed systems.
These should provide simpler, cheaper overall systems since the
necessity for large complicated operating systems is removed.

Also, present microprocessor systems incorporate few, if any,
hardware protection mechanisms so any sharing of resources can
result in corruption unless time consuming software protection is
employed. This is another reason why multiprocessor systems
where little, if any, sharing is required are to be preferred.
Most of the present day microprocessor systems similarly provide
few error detection aids making it difficult to debug programs
on the real hardware. For this reason the use of simulators has
been widespread and the use of sophisticated monitoring devices
(Payne, 1977) for debugging real time systems have been employed.

At the present little thought has been given to the problems
of portability and microprocessor systems although this will
become increasingly important especially since the software costs
are much higher in relationship to the hardware costs in these
systems. Portability is helped by the fact that efficiency, in
terms of resource usage, is not so important in these systems,
although the widely differing microprocessor architectures do not
make it easy to produce machine independent designs which can be
easily and efficiently transported. This subject will undoubt-
edly be the subject of extensive research in the near future.

A.J.T.Colin

University of Strathclyde

1. INTRODUCTION

A high-level language is a notation for expressing an algorithm
in software; but, unlike machine or assembly code, it does not
make use of the detailed structure of the target machine but relies
on abstract entities such as variables, expressions, procedures,
and so on. To illustrate the point, consider an algorithm for
division, first in assembly code for the PDP-11, and second, in a
high-level language (ALGOL 68) :

```
          CLR  RO           rem:=0
          MOV   -20,R3       to 16
LOOP  :   ASL  RO             do left shift(rem, dividend);
          ASL  R1                rem:=rem-divisor;
          ADC  RO             if rem   0
          SUB  RO,R2          then rem:=rem+divisor
          BGE  .+6            else dividend:=dividend+1
          ADD  RO,R2          fi
          BR   .+4           od
          INC  R1
          INC  R3
          BNE  LOOP
```

(Assembly code)   (ALGOL 68)

When the algorithm has been written in a high-level language,
it must still be translated into the code of the target machine.
The translation can be done automatically by a special program
called a 'compiler'.

High-level languages offer two important advantages over
machine and assembly codes. In the first place, the programmer is
freed from having to remember the precise arbitrary details of the
target machine he is writing for, and can direct his full attention
to the problem he is trying to solve. This makes programming
easier and much faster - factors of 10 have been reported.

HLL's are therefore often caled 'Problem-Orientated Languages'. Secondly, the algorithm is not related to any particular design of machine and can therefore run on any computer or microcomputer for which a suitable compiler exists. Such programs are called portable. Portable software has an in-built advantage over the kind that is limited to one computer; it can be sold in a much larger market, and can help 'own equipment manufacturers' to change the suppliers of their computing machinery as they think fit, instead of being 'locked in' to a particular design.

To offset these advantages, high-level languages do have certain drawbacks. In general, the translation process is not perfectly efficient, and a program which has been compiled from a high-level language source usually runs slower and needs more storage than one which has been effectively coded by hand. The difference may be as high as 50%. Another disadvantage, which mainly affects certain archaic languages such as FORTRAN and COBOL, is that they lack the facilities for expressing certain operations which are commonly needed in microprocessor applications.

2. ABSTRACT MACHINES

When a program written in a high-level language is compiled, every element in the program must be mapped onto the target computer. For example, a decimal number like '16' must be converted into its binary form, and the symbol + must somehow become an instruction for addition.

In the ideal case, every feature of the high-level language would be exactly mirrored by a corresponding facility of the target machine so that, for instance, the ability to write a division symbol ÷ in the source code would be reflected in the presence of hardware to do division. Such an ideal computer is called the 'abstract machine', which corresponds to the language. A compiler for an abstract machine could be completely efficient, producing code as good as that which could be written by hand.

In practice, engineers must use existing micro-computers which may be quite different from the ideal abstract machine. On such systems, the high-level features can only be translated crudely and inefficiently by circumlocutions, and the resulting programs are bulky and slow.

3. SOME BASIC FEATURES

In the rest of this chapter, some important features of high-level languages will be discussed, and how they can be mapped onto some existing microprocessor architectures will be shown.

HIGH LEVEL LANGUAGES

3.1 Quantitites and Modes

All high-level languages involve quantities, and in most cases the programmer may select the type or mode of any quantity he uses. Common modes are :

Boolean	(True or false)
Integers	(Whole numbers up to certain size limits)
Characters	(Usually 6 or 8 bits, ASCII or EBCDIC codes)
Floating Point	(For numerical work)

Most machines are constrained to handling bits in groups of 4, 8, 12, or 16, called words. Thus, the obvious mapping of a Boolean variable is onto a single binary digit, but in many practical cases, it is awkward to use each digit of a word for a separate Boolean quantity, and the whole word is inefficiently assigned to a single variable.

Integers can be efficiently handled so long as numbers within the range implied by the high-level language can fit into single words. Otherwise, integers can only be represented as groups of words, each one of which must be handled individually when the integer is referred to. The same is broadly true of floating-point numbers.

3.2 Storage Assignment

A variable is a quantity which must be 'remembered' for part of a calculation, and must therefore be stored. Most high-level languages allow two kinds of variable: global and local.

A global variable exists for the whole duration of an algorithm (that is, all the time in a dedicated system), and the storage space for it can easily be allocated when the program is compiled. On the other hand, each local variable is associated with only a particular part of the algorithm, and need not exist when that part is not being executed. This opens up the possibility of using the same storage locations for different local variables at different times.

It turns out that the easiest (although not the only) way of organising the storage of local variables is to use a stack. This is an array of storage, together with a pointer, i.e. a special register containing the address of one of the cells (fig. 1).

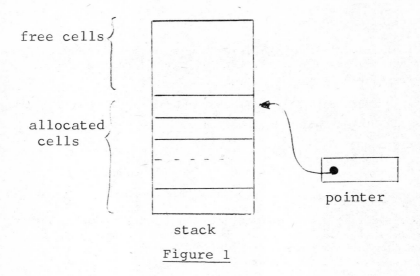

free cells

allocated
cells

pointer

stack

Figure 1

Whenever the program starts, part of the algorithm which needs a local variable, it moves the pointer up by one cell (or by more than one if the variable was of a mode which needed several words).

Eventually, the program ends with this particular variable. The space is returned to the general pool by moving the pointer down by the necessary number of cells. The values remaining in the cells freed can be regarded as 'rubbish'.

If a microprocessor has a 'stack' mechanism, then space allocation by this method is simple and fast; otherwise it is a tedious chore.

3.3 Operators

A prominent feature of every high-level program is its use of operators such as + - * ÷ AND , OR. Semantically, these operators signify what is to be done to the various quantities in order to achieve the result of the calculation.

If the operators can be translated directly into single machine code instructions, the program will be fast and compact. Usually, however, some of the operators must be represented by whole sequences of instructions, which are very much slower. For example, consider a language which needs 16-bit binary integers running on a microprocessor with 8-bit words. Each integer must use two words, which we can call the 'least significant' and 'most significant' halves. To add two such integers, the rules are :

(1) Add the least significant halves. Remember if there is an 'overflow'.

(2) Add the most significant halves. Add in a 1 if there was an overflow when the least significant halves were added.

On one 8-bit microprocessor – the 6800 – this takes several instructions. On another – the 8080 – there is a single instruction called 'double-length add' which achieves the same effect, rather more quickly and compactly.

The lack of more complex operators such as multiplication and division is not necessarily a serious drawback. If speed is not at a premium, then these functions can be provided by subroutines which are permanently placed in the store and called whenever they are needed. If speed is essential, special fast IC's can be brought and added to the system as 'peripherals'.

3.4 Arrays

A vital component of every HLL is its use of arrays. An array in its simplest form is a list or table of values, with a common name. Individual elements in the list can be selected by supplying a 'subscript'; one can refer to the first, second, third,...., n'th element in the array. The subscript may be written as a variable quantity, so that repetitions of the same piece of program will refer to different elements. Here, for example, is part of a program to add values in an array of 100 elements :

$$s:=0;$$
$$\text{for } j \text{ to } 100 \text{ do } s:=s+array[j] \text{ od}$$

As j takes the values 1, 2, 3,...., 100 on successive repetitions, so the elements used are array[1], array[2],..., array[100].

In the target machine, arrays are always allocated to blocks of store. The address of the first element is called the base address, and the address of any other – say the j'th – must be calculated by using the base address, the value of j, and the size of each element, in words. This calculation must be repeated every time that the program needs access to an array element, and almost invariably involves integers of 12 bits or more. It follows that a micro-computer which cannot do such arithmetic easily must be somewhat slow and ineffective for handling arrays.

3.5 Sequencing

In most simple algorithms, the individual steps must be executed one by one, and followed in the correct sequence.

A.J.T.COLIN

Modern high-level languages give four main rules for sequencing;

(1) Simple sequence : When actions x and y are written in that order, they should be executed in that order.

(2) Choice of alternatives : It should be possible to test a Boolean condition and to select one of two courses of action, depending on the outcome.

(3) Repetition : It should be possible to execute a section of program repeatedly until some condition is no longer true.

(4) Subroutines : It must be possible to transfer control to a subroutine (a self-contained section of code elsewhere in the program) and eventually to return to the original location. Once a subroutine has been written, it should be possible to regard it as a new 'primitive function' which can be involved without formality.

In translation, simple sequencing is carried over because it is implicit in the machine code program. The other facilities can be mapped using conditional and unconditional jumps. Some systems have conditional skips, which always transfer control forward by one extra instruction if the condition is true. They are slightly more awkward to use than conditional jumps.

Again, subroutine calls are easily handled by a stack, and rather more clumsily by other mechanisms.

3.6 Input/Output and Concurrency

In no field is there less agreed opinion than in the area of input and output. Every computer architect seems intent on arranging matters in his own personal way. For this reason, the more old-fashioned high-level languages such as ALGOL 60 and CORAL 66 made no provision for input/output other than allowing the programmer to supply his own assembly code routines for the purpose.

More modern languages provide somewhat simpler and more portable facilities. Physically, most input and output takes place in 8-bit groups called 'characters'. Many languages allow simple character I/O on any of a number of 'channels', which can be mapped onto physical input and output devices.

In most computer architectures, every I/O device is 'modelled' by a communication register which mirrors its current state. These registers may be mapped onto part of the main memory, or occupy their own separate address space. In either case, high-level languages sometimes permit these communication registers to be

124

given symbolic names and manipulated just like any other variable quantity.

It is usual for I/O operations to overlap each other, and maybe computation as well. In practice, therefore, input/output is inseparable from ideas of concurrency.

Today, most systems handle concurrency by 'processes'. A process is a 'stream of consciousness' - a strictly sequential set of operations usually governed by a section of program. A system can include any number of processes all of which - at least at the conceptual level - can be active simultaneously. Thus, for instance, there will be one process for each peripheral device.

To achieve proper synchronisation, processes must communicate. This can be done by various high-level mechanisms, including shared variables, 'messages', and semaphores.

The mapping of processes and concurrency onto given pieces of hardware is notoriously difficult, and usually needs complex resident pieces of software called 'operating systems'. An operating system has to use interrupts - a very low-level concept - to control the flow of information and to work out the appropriate interaction between the processes. In a system where there are fewer processors than processes, there is also the problem of deciding how the available processors should be allocated. Furthermore, the operating system has the responsibility of ensuring that processes do not interfere with one another except through the established, official, channels. It is not surprising that operating systems tend to be huge.

To conclude, it has been shown that high-level languages are a good way of programming microprocessors, except in the rare event that run-time efficiency outweighs all other considerations; but not all languages are equally suitable. Similarly, any high-level language program can be mapped onto any microprocessor, but with widely varying efficiency; it depends on how close the microprocessor's order code is to the abstract machine of the high-level language.

A.J.T.Colin

University of Strathclyde

1.   INTRODUCTION

Correctness in programs is a simple aim to state, and a diffi-cult one to achieve. Very simple programs may be 'obviously' correct, but this intuition on the part of the programmer misleads him as programs increase in size. The comprehensive testing of really large-scale programs is virtually impossible, and it is now part of the accepted wisdom that large software systems will always contain residual errors.

Software errors in dedicated systems are particularly serious. First, the system may be 'out in the field' when the error occurs, and it is unlikely that there will be a knowledgeable programmer present to put things right. Second, the software in a dedicated system is usually stored in a R O M. Any corrections will need the manufacture of a new mask, and will be extremely expensive.

Programs can suffer from three kinds of error, of increasing seriousness.

The simplest species of mistake in programming is the syntax error. This is a straightforward violation of the rules of grammar of the language being used, or possibly a spelling mistake. Some examples are mismatched brackets, putting '++' for '+', or 'BEIGN' for 'BEGIN'. Most assemblers and compilers will detect and report such errors immediately. Certain systems (notably FORTRAN) are designed not to detect spelling mistakes, but to assume that the programmer meant something entirely different. A rocket launching a satellite is said to have crashed, at huge expense, because a programmer wrote :

DO5J=1.7

instead of :   DO5J=1,7

In summary, syntax errors need present no worry so long as a well-designed programming language is used. Most modern languages

127

are satisfactory in this respect.

The second kind of programming error is one which leaves a program grammatically correct but which shows up in the production of wrong answers (or no answers) when the program is tested. A very simple example of such a mistake could be the omission of a term from a formula, or the incorrect control of a looping mechanism, so that the number of repetitions is wrong.

Once such a mistake is detected, the cause is usually easy to find if the program has been carefully written and documented.

The third kind of error is one which escapes the test procedures and may never be detected. It is worth illustrating: Consider a system for keeping records on incoming airline flights and answering queries about them. The system is a computer with a data entry terminal and several enquiry terminals. The flight controller puts in data such as:

Flight 047 from Paris due at 1320

Flight 394 from Moscow delayed

Flight 777 from Madrid diverted to Manchester

The enquiry terminals give replies to such queries as :

"When is the next plane due from Oslo?"

"How many planes have been delayed in the last 24 hours?"

The programmer assumed that all the flight numbers are in the range 000 to 999, and planned his store layout accordingly (Fig.1).

The whole system checked out when tested, and worked well for months. One day, however, the harassed controller mistakenly entered a flight number as 2009 instead of 209. The system constructed a record for 'flight 2009' and stored it in 2009 locations from the one for flight 000; that is, right in the middle of the area reserved for the program. The program was now corrupted. However, the section to be spoiled was one which dealt with an obscure type of query and was rarely used. The system appeared to work correctly for several days, only to collapse when someone actually asked the obscure query affected. It was then far too late to connect the failure with its original cause. Since the programmer who investigated the failure could not reproduce it, he dismissed it as a 'sudden severe fluctuation in the mains voltage'.

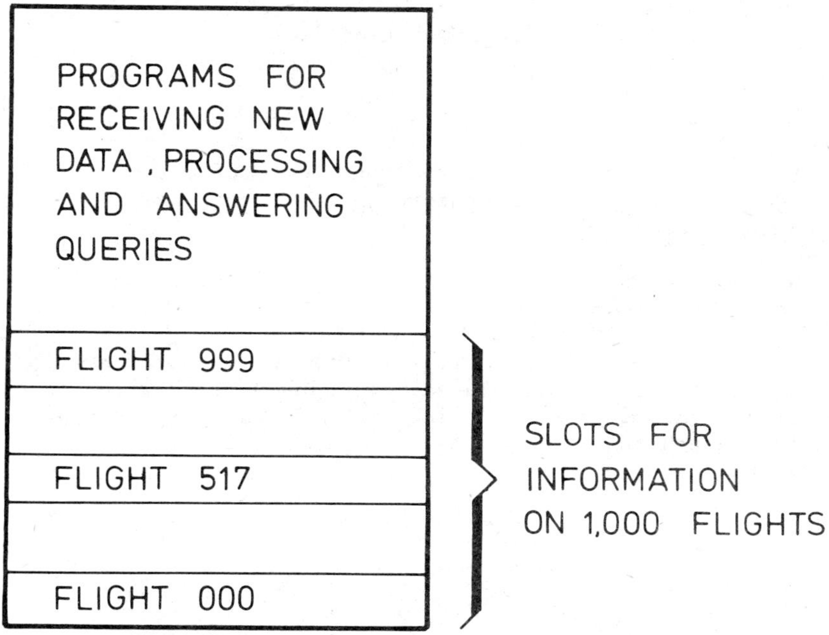

PROGRAMS FOR RECEIVING NEW DATA , PROCESSING AND ANSWERING QUERIES
FLIGHT 999
FLIGHT 517
FLIGHT 000

SLOTS FOR INFORMATION ON 1,000 FLIGHTS

FIG.1

2. STRUCTURED PROGRAMMING

In Engineering, it is a well-accepted principle that any complex machine is best constructed from sub-assemblies which can be designed, built, and tested on their own. This principle can also be applied to software, where it gives rise to the rules of structured programming.

A well-structured program is composed of modules, often called procedures or routines, each of which does some simple and well-defined job. The module should have certain important properties:

(a) It should be small enough for its correctness to be genuinely 'obvious', and not only to the programmer who wrote it.

(b) It should avoid using the tangled control paths implied by labels and 'goto' instructions. Instead, it should use the four sequencing primitives listed in Chapter II.F.

> Simple sequence
>
> Choice of alternatives
>
> Repetition
>
> Calling of subroutines

(c) It should be impossible for a routine to affect anything out-side its own orbit,except through its formal channels of communication.

(d) The routine must always terminate; that is, it must never get 'stuck in a loop'.

The overall design of a program involves the sub-division of the algorithm into a suitable set of modules, each with its own special responsibility. This is done on an hierarchic basis, usually starting at the top, as shown in fig.2.

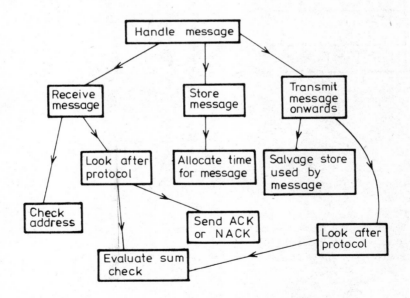

FIG.2

CORRECTNESS IN DEDICATED SYSTEMS

The hierarchic structure of such a system implies that some of the statements in the higher routines can be subroutine calls to lower ones. This does not destroy their simplicity of concept since, once a particular routine has been specified, its function – no matter how complex – can be viewed as a single 'elementary' action.

The best method of passing information between routines is by 'parameters' and 'results'. Consider two routines, A and B, and suppose that A calls B. Then A will give B certain values or 'parameters' to work on, and B will eventually return a 'result' to A. For example, B could be a routine which calculates the square root of a number x. Here, the parameter would be x, and the result would be $\sqrt{x}$.

Routines can have many parameters, and they can be of different modes. Thus, a navigational instrument might have a routine to find the Great Circle Distance between any two points. Such a routine would have 4 parameters: two longitudes, and two latitudes.

Parameters can also be arrays, or the addresses of arrays and other data structures. The result of a routine can also be of any mode, and in some circumstances (such as an output routine), there is no need to supply one at all.

Most procedures need variables as temporary stores for intermediate values. These variables should be declared locally, so that they cannot be accessed or interfered with by any other part of the program.

The correct frame of mind for writing a routine for a structured program is one of distrust and cynicism. You should insist on a detailed written specification for the routine which lays down :

(a) What it should do.

(b) What the parameters represent.

(c) What the ranges of the parameters are supposed to be.

In the routine itself, the first group of statements should check that the parameters supplied do, in fact, conform to the ranges defined in the specification, and generate error messages if they do not; for example :

if x <0 then print("SQUARE ROOT OF -VE NO ASKED FOR") fi

or

if n <1 then print("NUMBER OF LETTERS IN NAME MUST BE ≥ 1") fi

As you write the routine, you should place no more confidence in your own abilities than in the reliability of the programmer who sends you parameters. Whenever you believe that 'so-and-so must be the case', put in a test - perhaps as follows :

```
if (condition a) then x:=1
    else if(condition b) then x:=2
        else            x:=3
    fi
```

later :

```
if x<1 or x>3 then print("IMPOSSIBLE HAPPENED")fi
```

In principle, if all is correct, this error message is never printed. In practice, such redundant and 'unncessary' coding is of great value in tracking down residual errors.

The overall design of structured programs is something of an art which must be learned by practice. The essential guiding principles are :

(1) Use a high-level language which supports routines with parameters, and gives the maximum possible protection against syntax errors.

(2) Let each module be small and have a well-defined task.

(3) Let the interfaces between the modules (that is, the parameters and results) be as narrow as possible.

(4) Let every module and its interface be fully documented.

3. TEST PROCEDURES

As a general rule, most programmers believe that the code they have just written is correct. They will not test it at all unless suitable pressure is applied.

If a large program is written without structure, there are so many different combinations of input data and timing, so many different possible paths, that exhaustive testing is not a feasible proposition. Such a program will always be unreliable.

If a program is structured into modules, testing is much more satisfactory.

To begin with, each module should be tested on its own. For testing, a module can be fitted with a 'driver program' which supplies various combinations of parameters and prints out the results for checking. The driver program may include, if necessary, other modules which have already been tested.

The test parameters should be very carefully chosen so as to exercise each logical path through the module at least once. They should include 'illegal' values so that the routine's checking mechanism can itself be verified.

A useful adjunct at this stage is a 'program profile generator'. This is a special compiler which arranges for the computer to count the number of times that each statement is obeyed. If, after an exhaustive test run, a statement is found not to have been obeyed at all, this casts doubt either on the selection of test cases, or on the logic of the module being tested.

Once tested, each module of a structured program can be relied on to do its job clearly, without interfering with the function of any other module. It follows that a program composed of such modules should run correctly. Once the program has been assembled from its modules, testing need only be concerned with checking out that the assembly is correct. This process is greatly assisted by the error checks built into the modules themselves.

Well-structured programs are vastly more reliable than their unstructured counterparts. Nevertheless, they may still contain residual errors. Among the more esoteric ways of finding obscure mistakes is the technique of 'be-bugging'. You take a program which has been tested, and is supposed to be error-free, and carefully insert a subtle mistake in it. You then give the program to several other programmers, asking them to find the mistake. Frequently, the errors they find are not the ones you planted!

Where reliability is of the utmost importance (as in, say, an unmanned satellite), there is a need for exceptional precautions. There are two current developments, both of which are in the research stage :

(1) Techniques are emerging for constructing mathematical proofs of program correctness. The procedures are long and complex and have so far been applied mainly to simple algorithms, like sorting. Whilst a purported proof is no guarantee of correctness (there may be an error in the proof), it is a great deal more reliable than a programmer's unsupported intuition.

(2) Programs can be written so as to make them tolerant of failure. An approach being developed by B.Randell (1975) at Newcastle University consists of giving each routine a primary algorithm, an assertion (which is true only if the routine has done its job correctly), and one or more alternative algorithms to be used if the primary algorithm fails. When invoked, the routine uses its primary algorithm to work out a result, and then checks

it with the assertion. If all is well, the value is returned. Otherwise, the routine tries one of the alternative algorithms, and again checks the result. This process continues (at least in theory) until all the algorithms have been tried and found wanting; only then does the routine return a failure message.

To give an example, consider a routine which accepts two parameters x and y; it divides x by y to yield a quotient q and a remainder, r. The assertion would be :

$$(r \geq 0 \text{ and } r < y \text{ and } q * y + r = x)$$

The 'main algorithm' would use a long division method which involved subtraction, shifting, and testing. The alternative algorithm (there would only be one) would use repeated subtraction; a poor method, but one acceptable as a fallback.

It is worth noting that this scheme is tolerant not only to software errors, but to certain hardware failures as well. Thus, an intermittent error in the shift circuits would sometimes make the routine use its alternative algorithms, but would not produce an overall failure.

In Randell's scheme, these tolerant routines call each other hierarchically, so that a total failure at one level need only cause an alternative algorithm to be called at a higher level.

Of course, a program with redundancy of this kind is larger, slower, and more expensive to run than one which is not. Reliability has to be paid for.

II.H.   IMPLEMENTATION OF HIGH LEVEL PROGRAMS

A.J.T.Colin
University of Strathclyde

1. INTRODUCTION

In this chapter it will be assumed that a program for some
algorithm has already been written in a high-level language. The
various ways of actually implementing the program on a particular
microprocessor will be discussed.

The difficulty arises because, in most cases, the order code
of the microprocessor is not the same as that implied by the high-
level language; as explained in Chapter II.F, the high-level
algorithm has to be mapped onto the low-level device.

2. MANUAL TRANSLATION

A primitive way of mapping an algorithm is to map it by hand.
This takes several steps :

(1) Study the target microprocessor carefully.

(2) Decide how to map the high-level variables onto the store of
    the target machine. For example, a 16-bit integer can be
    mapped onto two 8-bit words, or a real number might use one
    16-bit word for its exponent and three for its mantissa.
    Draw diagrams showing the exact layout of each kind of variable,
    as in Figures 1 a and 1 b .

(3) Obtain (or design, if necessary) instruction sequences to
    implement the elementary operations on various kinds of
    variable. The list will usually include input, output, the
    arithmetical and logical operations, conditional jumps, and
    array access. Appropriate sequences will nearly always be
    found in published program libraries.

    All the code sequences (except those which consist of only one
    or two instructions) are made into subroutines and assembled
    into a 'run-time package'. This package can, of course, be

135

used for any program written in the original high-level language.

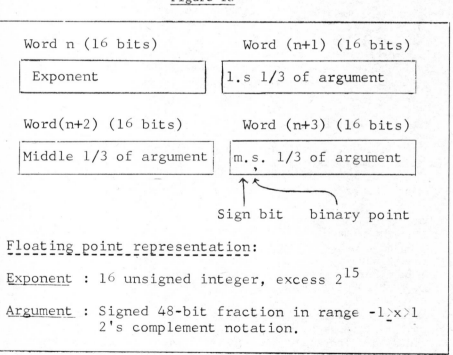

Word n (8 bits) | Word (n+1) (8 bits)
Most significant half | Least significant half

↑
Sign digit

Integer representation : 16 bit 2's complement

Figure 1a

Word n (16 bits) | Word (n+1) (16 bits)
Exponent | l.s 1/3 of argument

Word(n+2) (16 bits) | Word (n+3) (16 bits)
Middle 1/3 of argument | m.s. 1/3 of argument

Sign bit   binary point

Floating point representation:

Exponent : 16 unsigned integer, excess 2^{15}

Argument : Signed 48-bit fraction in range $-1 \geq x > 1$
2's complement notation.

Figure 1b

(4) Now turn to the individual program to be translated. Decide
which section of store is going to be used for the variable
quantities, and allocate the appropriate number of words to
each variable. Maintain a table which shows the exact type
and address of each variable.

To be safe, it is best to use a different set of locations
for each variable. Where certain variables are used only
locally, in principle, the same space for several such quantities may be used provided that they do not co-exist in time.
In practice, such a policy is an open invitation for trouble;
it makes for fragile programs with failure modes which are
difficult to diagnose.

(5) Translate each instruction of the source program into a corresponding sequence of machine code. The result will be a
mixture of calls to sub-routines in the run-time package and
'in-line' code for those operations whose sequences are very
short.

The translation process is not entirely straightforward since
re-ordering and the use of temporary storage will often be
needed. For example, the ALGOL 68 instruction :

$$a := (b*c)+(d*e)$$

must become: (1) form $b*c$ and place in temporary store

(2) form $d*e$

(3) add contents of temporary store

(4) store result in a

Similarly, conditional statements which involve jumps ahead
are awkward since the destination address cannot be filled
in until the translation has actually reached the point concerned. It is necessary to keep a list of 'unfilled references'.

(6) Finally, if time permits, review the written code. 'Polish'
it to remove obvious inefficiencies.

3. COMPILATION

In practice, it is extremely unusual to carry out the translation process manually. This would be exceedingly laborious,
particularly since the first few versions of the source code are
seldom correct, and the translation would have to be done several
times. Fortunately, the entire process is well enough understood
to be susceptible of automation in a program called a 'compiler'.
The various steps needed so as to give some idea of the complexity

of this kind of automatic translation have been outlined. Nevertheless, there is no 'magic' about a compiler. It reads data, transforms it according to fixed rules, and generates results like any other data processing program; the 'data' is the source code, and the 'results' are the corresponding object program. This implies that a compiler can be written in any suitable language (including a high-level language) and run on any computer with a sufficiently large store.

In their general structure, compilers are all similar to one another, but in detail they vary widely. Each high-level language has its own rules of grammar, and a compiler has to take account of these rules when translating source code. Similarly, every target machine has its own peculiar characteristics, which determine the details of the code actually produced. This suggests that if we consider m different high-level languages, and n target machines, we would need m n compilers to allow us to run any program on any machine.

Designers are often faced with the choice of a high-level language for some applications. The two most important considerations are, of course, the suitability of the language for the problem, and the degree to which the programmers are already familiar with it. However, the properties of the compiler are also worth considering. Some of the significant features are listed below :

3.1 Cross- and auto-compilers

Compilers for microprocessor languages usually run on mainframes or minicomputers, in which case they are called 'cross-compilers'. Sometimes, the kit used for developing and testing programs has enough store to support a compiler by itself. This is usually preferable, since not everyone has ready access to a larger machine. Recompilations, which are a frequent feature of program development, can be obtained without delay.

3.2 Listings

A good compiler will provide its users with a great deal of information: lists of variables and references to them, details of space allocation, and a listing of the translation into assembly or machine code. However, such listings should only be used for tracking down hardware faults, since the best place to find software errors is the source program.

3.3 Diagnostics

A good compiler will :

(a) Detect all grammatical errors in a program

(b) Report them in a comprehensible way

(c) Recover after each error to continue translating and report further faults.

For programs which have no grammatical errors, the compiler should provide optional facilities for :

(d) Tracing : a trace is a blow-by-blow account or audit trail of what the computer actually does when executing a program. This often helps to decide where and how the program has gone wrong.

(e) Post-mortems : when a program has failed, a post-mortem will print out the values of all the variables. This again helps to track down the error.

(f) Program profiles : when a program stops for any reason, the profile indicates how many times each statement has been obeyed. This is useful for exhaustive testing, and in deciding which part of an algorithm is using the lion's share of the CPU time.

An alternative way of getting the information in (d), (e) and (f) is to use a <u>simulator</u>. This is a program which forms an exact model of a microprocessor system (except for its speed), but also provides a 'window' through which various aspects of the program's behaviour can be observed. Nevertheless, the compiler's own monitoring system has the major potential advantage that it can generate its results in terms of the source program, using the original variable names, statement numbers, and so on.

3.4 <u>Efficiency</u>

It is accepted that the code generated by a compiler is not usually as good as the best possible hand-coded version. The compiler produced program may use up more space, or run slower, or both. Nevertheless, most compilers probably produce rather better code than the 'average' hand programmer, and it is more profitable to compare compilers with each other than with the mythical 'perfect' coder.

Some compilers are said to produce 'optimised' code. This means that the object code has been 'polished'. The most obvious sources of inefficiency (such as moving the contents of a register to a storage location and then immediately bringing it back again) have been removed. The process of optimisation is laborious, and optimising compilers are large and slow. Optimisation is a relative term, since certain 'optimised' compilers are out-performed in every respect by compilers which make no claims to produce specially good code.

3.5 Portability

A program which can be run on many different machines is called portable. Portability of software confers a deal of flexibility on manufacturers and widens the scope for the software builders' products. One way of achieving portability of a language (and therefore of all programs in that language) is to have a compiler for each of many target machines. By this rule, FORTRAN, CORAL 66, and STAB are portable, whereas PL/M (designed specifically for the INTEL 8080) is not.

Genuine portability is only achieved if the various target machines use the identical language. Even minor differences of dialect (such as I/O provision) rapidly make program transfer impossible.

3.6 Machine Code Interface

A good high-level language is supposed to handle every possible type of command. Nevertheless, occasions arise when the designer wants to put part of his algorithm into machine code. This might be necessary to handle a new type of peripheral, or it might confer a small but vital speed advantage in a critical part of the program.

A good compiler will allow certain parts of programs to be written in assembly code, and will simplify the interface between the two types of coding by allowing the use of symbolic variable names. Nevertheless, such a facility should only be used with great caution, as a last resort, because it destroys the portability of the program and by-passes the disciplined structure imposed by the high-level language.

3.7 Maintenance and Documentation

The responsibility for maintaining a compiler should have been accepted by a reputable body. There must also be a good set of training manuals.

4. INTERPRETERS

A compiler is part of a two-stage process of implementation: first, a program is translated and later, when the translation is complete, the program is executed.

In an interpretive system, these two phases are interleaved. The program is stored in its source form, and each statement is translated (or retranslated) every time it is executed. Consider :

Program	Compiler System No. of times		Interpreter System No. of times	
	Translated	Executed	Translated	Executed
s:=0;	1	1	1	1
for j to 100 do	1	100	100	100
s:=s+a[j]	1	100	100	100
od;				
print(s)	1	1	1	1

At first sight, this appears monstrously wasteful of CPU time. It is true that interpretive execution is very slow, but when speed is not critical (or which the primitive operations take longer than the translation process, as in, say, a matrix manipulation language), the system has certain marked advantages:

(1) The source form of the program is usually more compact than the corresponding object code. Although there is a constant overhead of the interpreter (the software which translates and executes the statements of the source program), there is still a saving of space in large systems. For some microprocessors, the interpreter can be bought cheaply as a stock item, in a standard ROM chip.

(2) The program can be altered and retested without the overhead of recompiling. It is also possible to change a program while it is running; but this is strongly discouraged!

The best known interpretive language is BASIC.

5. ABSTRACT MACHINE IMPLEMENTATIONS

A line of development which has been pursued at Strathclyde University (amongst others) is to combine the ideas of compilation and interpretation. The notion rests on the following premises :

(1) A high-level language (in our case, STAB-1) is defined.

(2) An abstract machine is designed which conforms exactly to the requirements of the high-level language. Our abstract machine is called STAB-12. A compiler is written to give an efficient translation of STAB-1 programs into STAB-12.

(3) The abstract machine is then realised by any of three methods:

    (a) Interpretation of the abstract machine code. This gives compact code with slow execution, but forms a fast way of transporting STAB to a new environment, since the STAB-12 interpreter is a very simple program.

(b) Translation of the abstract machine code to the object
code of the target machine. The translation can be
polished to give highly streamlined efficient code, and
this is worthwhile if the programs are to be heavily used.

(c) Certain computers can be microcoded to implement the
STAB-12 abstract machine directly. This gives the most
effective system of all.

Overall, this method confers :-

Portability (and access to a large library of existing
software).

Conscious control over the space-speed trade-off.

Simplicity in transferring the system to a new machine.

AIDS TO PROGRAM MAINTENANCE

A.J.T.Colin

University of Strathclyde

1. INTRODUCTION

Programs are abstract mathematical objects, and do not deter-
iorate like mechanical devices. There is obviously no need for
preventive maintenance, or regular attention like a '3000 mile
service' on a car. Nevertheless, program maintenance is an
essential and expensive part of the service supplied by anyone
who sells software, or even devices with software components.

Program maintenance implies the alteration of an existing
system. Maintenance as such begins when the product is completed
and sold, but there is much that can be done during the design to
make maintenance easier.

2. REASONS FOR MAINTENANCE

There are three separate reasons for maintaining programs :

(1) The correction of residual errors. No matter how carefully
a program is written and tested, there remains the possibility
that parts of the software are not completely right, and will
fail under unusual conditions. If a small system (such as a
calculator) is used extensively without any errors coming to
light, then it is probably correct. On the other hand, the
construction of large programs totally without errors seems
to be an impossibility – at least at present. Whilst the
total number of residual errors must remain unknown, the
performance of these very large systems is measured by the
'mean time between software faults'. The fault rate is deemed
acceptable whenever it is substantially less than the hardware
error rate on the same equipment, and maintenance is concerned
with reaching this state.

(2) Changing requirements. In all branches of engineering a
great deal of design work consists of adapting existing
designs to new and different requirements. In software, the

changes may be as trivial as changing the number of I/O ports
in a message-switching system, or more radical, such as replacing the control algorithm in a real-time system.

(3) Changing the underlying hardware. All software is designed to
run on a system with particular characteristics. In the
present explosive phase of micro-electronics, new systems
appear constantly, making older ones obsolete. To remain
competitive, a device may have to change its microprocessor
several times in its lifetime.

In their advertisements, manufacturers claim that the successive 'generations' of their microprocessors are software compatible. In practice, this is a half-truth. Consider a program
which is developed to run on Model 1. Eventually, Model 2 is
announced. It is cheaper, and has an enhanced performance,
because it provides new 'extra' instructions and a small area
of 'scratchpad' store. The original program may well run
without alteration on the Model 2, but this confers no advantage, because none of the new features is used. To make conversion to the new model worthwhile, extensive program changes
will be needed. This kind of program maintenance is often
thought of as 'running to stand still'.

Program maintenance is the most unpleasant aspect of the programmer's job. It is boring, but demands great intellectual
effort and attention to detail, so that it cannot be done in a
semi-automatic way like a more routine task. Finding and correcting errors confers almost no stimulus to one's sense of creativity
and, by its very nature, the job exposes the programmer to the
possibility of a great deal of blame and no praise.

Finding staff to do program maintenance is always a severe
problem. The obvious solution - which is to have the maintenance
done by the original programmer - is not feasible in a free
society. Programmers,hired only for maintenance,will usually
leave as soon as their training period is completed. One possibility is to share out maintenance among all programming staff as a
weekly chore.

3. GUIDING PRINCIPLES

These difficulties naturally suggest that every precaution
should be taken to make maintenance as easy and simple as possible.
Fortunately, there are a number of ways in which this can be done
at the original design and implementation stage. There are three
guiding principles :

(1) Careful Documentation

Use detailed, careful documentation throughout the project.

Thus, the first phase of the program development should be a detailed program specification which describes, in English or in mathematical terms, exactly what the program is supposed to do. The specification should be thoroughly discussed between the user, the programmer, and the chief project designer. Then it should be frozen; the only changes or additions permitted being those which correct actual errors. Any such changes to the specification must be made by a formal mechanism such as a written amendment, signed by all the users concerned.

If these rather rigid rules are not followed, there is a great danger of 'unwritten understandings' arising to the effect that this or that part of the specification is not exactly right, and that the program need not conform to it. Such understandings do not survive changes of personnel, and can cause endless difficulty in maintenance.

Next, the program itself should be accompanied by four sorts of documentation :

First, there should be an overall description of the algorithm and a 'tree', showing how it is broken down into its component parts.

Second, there should be an exact description of the variables used, including their type, purpose of scope (i.e. the parts of the program which are permitted to use or change them). If the program is complex enough to use data structures, then this part of the documentation should include diagrams which show exactly how the structures are mapped onto the store.

Third, each subroutine or procedure of the program should be documented, with the following items:

Its exact purpose.

The significance of the input data : the modes and meaning of the input parameters.

The exact form of the result.

Any 'side-effects' or changes which the procedure may cause outside its own orbit. This would include changing the values of global variables or altering the status of peripheral devices.

An estimate of performance such as :

"200-300 μs on Model 1 microprocessor".

Any limitations which the programmer may be aware of, such as "Parameter A must be positive" or "Array X must not exceed 500 items in length".

Fourth, the source text of the program should be spiced with plenty of comments. If the other documentation is respectable, the comments can be brief, but they should be informative; for example :

a:=a+1   ↑ Advance pointer to next device state vector

<u>not</u> a:=a+1   ↑ Add 1 to a

Finally, when the program is debugged, the test runs together with sample sets of input and output should be collected together to form a body of evidence to show that the program fulfils its specification.

(2) Defer Decisions

Defer all decisions as far as possible. This is the second principle of good programming. If a specific decision is avoided, then the solution - at least in that respect - will have to be written in a general way. This makes it much more amenable to alteration.

Consider the following example: Suppose that the software for a concentrator is being designed and that it is under-stood that, initially, there will be 6 terminals. An amateur programmer will use the explicit number 6 in various places in the program, such as the device scanners. He might put :

<u>for</u> j <u>to</u> 6 <u>do</u>
    <u>if</u> a[j]=0 <u>then</u> ------
       <u>od</u>

Suppose now that the system is to be expanded to handle 7 con-soles. Every occurrence of the '6' in the program will have to be changed to '7'. If done by hand, there is a danger of missing some 6's out. If done by an automatic text editor, there is a risk of changing too much. If the program has a machine code segment with a line like :

BYTE=316,317,240,317,306,240,326,301,314,325,305,323

it will suddenly begin to type :

OO OG WALUES   instead of   NO OF VALUES

This difficulty is avoided by <u>parameterising</u> the number of consoles. Initially the program written with a symbolic name for the quantity (say 'nc'):

<u>for</u> j <u>to</u> nc <u>do</u>
    <u>if</u> a[j]=0 <u>then</u> ....
       <u>od</u>

In the first version of the program, the parameter is assigned a value by an equation like <u>int</u> nc=6.

To expand the system to 7 consoles, all that is necessary (apart from checking that the increased load is still acceptable) is to alter the equation to: <u>int</u> nc=7.

What has been done is to defer the decision as to how many consoles are actually to be used.

The basic principle has many applications :

Decisions about the layout of store variables can be deferred by using symbolic addresses.

The choice of the actual microprocessor to be used can be deferred by writing in a high-level language.

Fixing the details of the interface to each procedure may be deferred by specifying that the necessary information will be supplied at runtime as a parameter. Thus, a procedure can be specified to accept numbers from a keyboard in radix r (where r is a parameter), instead of just decimal numbers.

The exact hardware configuration can be deferred by writing a self-adaptive program. When started, such a program will scan its environment, see how much store and other resources it has access to, and adapt itself accordingly. The overheads – perhaps some 100 instructions – are well worth paying for a program which runs efficiently on a wide range of configurations without any alteration.

The one decision which cannot be deferred is the purpose of the program you are writing.

(3) Programming Style

Pay attention to programming style. The general rule is to use structured programming (because structured programs are easier to understand), and to plant safety traps in all critical places. These traps are analogous to fuses or cut-outs in an electric system: as long as all is well, they serve no useful purpose, but when things go wrong, they protect and help one to find the fault.

Every procedure should check the validity of its parameters, and input commands should verify that the data read is acceptable. Loops which depend on the convergence of two mathematical expressions for termination should have an 'emergency' exit which is invoked if the expressions have not converged after a given number of cycles.

Lastly, programmers are prone to invent 'clever tricks' which capitalise on their detailed knowledge of the program and of

the processor, to produce minor improvements in efficiency.
To give a somewhat extreme example, suppose that a quantity in
the accumulator of a microprocessor has to be incremented by
a constant (perhaps the number of lines in a telephone exchange).
Writing in assembly code, a good programmer would set up this
constant by an equation, and then use it as an argument :

NO OF LINES = 97 ↑ SET NUMBER OF LINES

and then: ADI NOOFLINES   ↑ ADD NUMBER OF LINES

An enthusiastic, but less professional, coder might notice
that the function code for the 'Add' instruction was 97, and
he would know that, at least initially, the number of lines
entering the exchange was also, coincidentally, 97. He would
write :

XYZ: ADD   XYZ

Such a program might well pass its initial test, but it would
be fragile. Being incomprehensible (even to its writer after
he has spent a few weeks on a different project), it would not
be capable of being maintained.

Fortunately, high-level languages are less amenable to tricks
of this kind. The programmer feels that the advantages of an
unusual piece of coding are overwhelming; he must include a
comment giving a detailed explanation and an alternative in
conventional code which will do the same job, albeit more
slowly.

In conclusion, it has been shown that maintenance is difficult
and boring, but it is also a vital part of any activity which
involves software. The problems of maintenance can only be managed
by careful planning and the application of engineering (that is,
rational principles).

III.A   MICROPROCESSOR PROJECT MANAGEMENT

Carol Anne Ogdin

Software Technique, Inc.

1. ACQUISITION OF SKILLS

Most of what's been written on microcomputer design has implied
that all that's needed for successful project completion is judic-
ious mixture of hardware and software. But, the cook is as important to the outcome as the recipe or the quality of ingredients.
Microcomputer projects require a different set of skills from traditional data processing applications. Knowing what skills the designer or design team may need is an important first step to being
able to get the project done on time, within budget and within the
specifications.

Generally, the set of skills needed can be divided into four
major areas:

- Applications and system design,

- Hardware and electronics design,

- Software design and programming, and

- Project management

Many successful microcomputer projects have been completed by
one designer with all these skills, usually in varying depth. Most
of the earliest microcomputer applications were implemented by a
"converted" digital electronics designer, but his lack of software
experience often showed in the resulting design. A few projects
have been designed, managed and implemented by former programmers
with some aid from an electronics design team. Again, the designer's lack of experience with electronics often showed in the resulting design.

Systems designed by digital electronics engineers with little
software experience are usually characterized by an overabundance
of external logic to implement things that could have been done in
software. The input/output interfaces may contain extra capabilities that reduce the eventual software load to a point that it

149

spends more than 99% of its time waiting for external events. At the other extreme, these designers with limited software experience may implement very primitive hardware interfaces to reduce costs, leaving a job for the software that is just too large to handle. An unusual number of these kinds of projects have seen the hardware designer leave for another job just before the impracticality of the design was generally discovered! And, designers with this kind of background almost invariably underestimate the program storage size requirements, since they have no experience with the kinds of software overhead that are generally required.

When software people design microcomputer systems they must nearly always be aided by engineers or technicians with electronics experience. However, if the design is done by a designer with software experience and simply specified to the electronics design staff for implementation, the same set of problems above occur, in reverse. The designer may specify a rather complete software system and estimate the storage requirements rather precisely. But, the general system timing and input/output interfacing may suffer. Often, these kinds of implementations have started out with grossly erroneous assumptions which aren't detected until much later in the design process. Many microcomputers, for example, can operate at the maximum rated clock speed or operate with maximum capacity memories but not both. If the system designer, inexperienced with hardware design, is not aware of these trade-offs, he may expect the resulting configuration to be able to support 65K bytes of memory and operate at the maximum speed. Later, after being rudely surprised, he may find that the entire software design predicated upon that set of speed and storage size estimates may have to be scrapped.

Interdisciplinarians are essential. People who know both hardware and software design principles are rare; those who know them well are even rarer. And the educational system isn't geared to producing these wide ranges of skills. Electrical engineers don't learn much software design, and computer science majors are dissuaded from learning about circuitry. Even the new microcomputer courses in colleges and universities don't fill the bill; it takes a lot more than 100 hours to learn enough digital electronics or software design to be an interdisciplinarian.

Team Size

The design team responsible for a microcomputer system may consist of a single individual or an entire team of experts in different fields. The kinds of skills required must still encompass the required range in the four areas outlined above. But, the differences between an individual, a small team and a large team can be striking.

In assembling a team, a manager is trying to effectively create a composite individual out of many parts. If all of the required skills can be found in one individual, then the team arrangement may consist of little more than support staff for that individual. This is akin to the Chief Programmer Team approach used successfully in some projects in major software implementation. On the other, if no one individual has all of the requisite skills, a balanced team is necessary to prevent either hardware of software experience from dominating the design. In teams of two people, one of software and the other of hardware background, whichever of these two is placed in charge, the other will feel slighted. As major design decisions are made by the senior partner, the junior partner's inputs may be denigrated. In these cases, a separate manager of the project may be required as arbiter.

The ideal teams seem to be composed of either one or four members. The one-man team is just a special case of the four-person team, with all the skills in one body. The four team members need not be dedicated to the microcomputer design task full-time. Indeed, the four skill areas will interweave, as illustrated in Figure 1. During the initial weeks of a project, the applications and systems expert, the software programmer and the hardware designer must all cooperate together. Since this is the stage of the design where most of the critical (and often ill-founded) decisions are made, intercommunications among these people is essential. This is where so many one-man projects succeed in spite of later implementation difficulties. With a single coherent design, changes to the design necessitated by gross design errors are easier to make. But, many projects are simply too complex for one person to handle. Unless all of the team members have an appreciation of the other's skills and contribution potential, this part of the project can reduce to squabbling.

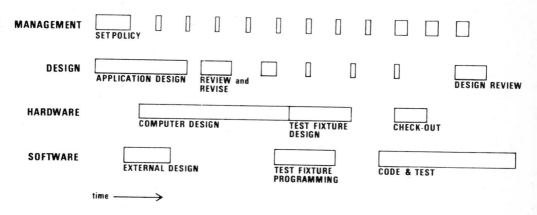

Figure 1. Project activities over time.

CAROL ANNE OGDIN

When a team is composed of many members, it is absolutely essential to have one key head of the team whose decisions are essentially final. The most acrimonious debates between team members will occur on the most trivial issues; the major issues will be decided by more rational logic. At some point, the strong leader must step in and make an arbitrary decision--and make it stick. Again, this points up the necessity to avoid appointing a team leader who has a dominant interest in either hardware or software, lest decisions always be based on that biased experience.

The key ingredient in the make-up of any microcomputer design team is the individual awareness of other team member's contributions. That implies software people understand the principles of hardware, and vice versa. Of course, if the team is composed of a group of one, then that individual must be intimately familiar with all the requisite skills.

Acquiring Skills

The decision tree for acquiring the necessary skills is relatively sparse (Figure 2). After inventorying the available skills and spotting the "holes" to be filled, a project manager should make the classic make-or-buy decision.

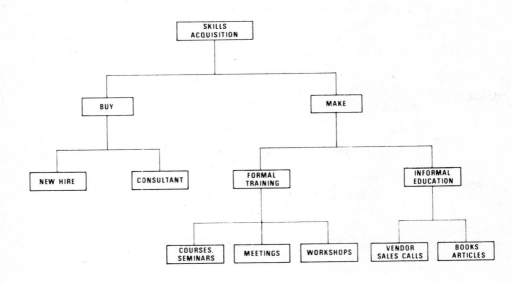

Figure 2. Alternative ways to acquire skills.

The easiest way to buy outside talent is to hire someone with experience. The advantages are clear: The new-hire has recent and relevant experience that can be brought to bear on the problem immediately. However, be prepared to spend a few months in the search--and lots of money. Microcomputer experience is much sought, so most of the good people are being very highly paid. In addition to high salary levels, the employer may have to hire a recruiting firm--at a 20% premium. And then there are relocating expenses, travel costs for interviews, and so on.

The new-hire has the potential for being an asset or a liability. Without some experience with other team members, the project manager can't be sure how this new-hire will work out. Of course, if one team member recommends someone outside for hiring, the likelihood of successful team cooperation is higher. Be prepared, too, to offer inducements other than money. In many cases, microcomputer designers have changed jobs because of promises made to better equip a lab. To others, the potential variety of applications can be an inducement.

If the needs are short-term and only transient, a consultant or design service firm may be the best way to acquire the skills. However, be sure that skills are really being acquired. The specific individuals with experience should be named in agreements, lest you get stuck with a trainee. Consultants are expensive, of course, especially if they're any good. Avoid the low hourly rate people; they're probably trying to gain experience to be able to boost their rates. If the project manager's objective is to acquire skills, then low-level experience won't help.

Often, the consultant can bring lots of equipment to the project as well as experience. If he's done very many microcomputer projects before, he probably has acquired a lot of the specialized equipment. If not, determine whether he has familiarity with the tools like Logic Analyzers and Development Systems. A lack of this kind of experience may point up a general lack of experience masked by repeated reimplementation of the same solution. Another disadvantage of consultants is that they may recommend the use of a particular microcomputer only because they are familiar with it-- whether it suits the job at hand or not.

Hiring Programmers

In general, computer programmers are spectacularly unsuccessful at programming microcomputers. That is not to indict all programmers--merely most. The vast majority of people who are called programmers don't understand electronics, computer architecture, input/output programming or small computers. There are many excellent programmers who do superb jobs in their fields but they will not be of use in applying a microcomputer.

153

Ideally, engineers should be able to design both the hardware
and software for microcomputer applications. However, that is not
always practical. So, if a programmer is inevitable (or forced
upon the team by management fiat), choose carefully. Be sure that
when the internal functioning of a component like a UART or a decoder is discussed the programmer understands what these parts do.
Experience with a minicomputer (the smaller the better) is a good
sign. A programmer with vast experience solely in COBOL or FOR-
TRAN or PL/1, or exclusively in data processing on large computers,
will be worse than useless--he'll be a definite hindrance in most
cases.

On the other hand, don't shy away from the programming people.
If someone who can take an interest in your project shows up, consider it as potentially valuable experience to tap. It is becoming a popular practice for programmers to read one-another's code;
have a qualified programmer read and critique the code produced
by the engineers. The novice programmer may be re-inventing the
software wheel and a qualified software expert can help show
easier and better ways to do the same job.

Creating the Skills

If motivated employees are already available but their
experience is limited, then they can often be trained to
take on the necessary tasks. Even if all the skills are
individually available, if a team is being assembled for the
first time it behoves the prudent manager to make sure all
the participants speak the necessary language. This approach
will tend to be less expensive than hiring new employees
or consultants, but it will likely take several months. If
a single product is planned with a micro, perhaps buying the
skills would be a better idea. However, if this is the first
in a whole series of projects, then in-house creation of the
skills pool is probably a better approach in the long run.

It is tempting to start going to all of the various
professional meetings being held in the U.S. and Europe,
but these require some initial knowledge before they are
useful. If the team members need to be brought up to speed
quickly, one of the three-to-five day "cram" courses is
probably the best bet. If more time is available, then
some of the college courses offered in Electrical Engineering or Computing Science departments may prove valuable.

The quick cram courses are offered by the various
microcomputer and microprocessor vendors, by colleges and
universities and by commercial concerns. The prices are
all about the same, so that is not often the reason for
choosing one particular course over another. Courses

given by traditional educational institutions may be taught by instructors with limited (or nil) industrial experience. Courses based on esoteric computers are usually an indication that the instructors are out of touch with industrial practice. The commercial courses are usually taught by designers with both hardware and software design experience--but not always. In either of these cases, you should call the seminar registrar and get the 'phone number of the lead instructor. Call him, ask him about his experience and judge whether the experience he'll relate to the class will be relevant to you.

The vendors offer general courses, too. However, you should be aware that only the specific products made by that vendor will be discussed; in some senses, you are paying for a sales pitch. If the selection of a micro has already been made, these are good courses. The participants will learn more about forthcoming products and the specific tricks and techniques. However, the quirks and deficiencies in the products won't be as frequently revealed as they will be in a commercially prepared seminar.

The three-day courses are a good training vehicle for a multi-member team. Each participant will gain some exposure to the other team member's problems and point out some of the areas that need to be learned in more detail. However, without some preparation beforehand, much of the new knowledge may be lost. A discussion of the microprocessor's status bus clocking may be completely over the head of a software designer who hasn't read up on the subject before attending the course.

Courses of the one-day kind, frequently offered by local chapters of the professional societies, are best as introductory media for project managers and applications analysts and system designers who won't need to know the electronic details or software structure. These very short familiarization courses will, at best, leave the participant with a knowledge of some of the jargon, and a general notion of how the pieces of a microcomputer system fit together.

A cram course of one week or less should be looked upon as a limited experience with limited value. The participant can't conceivably emerge from the experience with more than the ability to read selectively in the literature. But knowing what subjects need to be learned is an important accomplishment.

Of more value to creating interdisciplinarians are
the various workshops offered. The difference between
courses and workshops is in emphasis: courses and seminars emphasize the cerebral design activity, but workshops aim at giving the participant some practical skill.
The most successful workshops seem to be for digital designers and electronics technicians who go to workshops to
learn the rudiments of software. Even if the team will have
a high-powered software expert, the hardware designers and
implementers will need to be able to create some programs
just to test the hardware during fabrication. There are
a few workshops at which participants can learn how to
implement digital circuitry. The programs offered at various colleges and universities seem to be the best. The
expenses involved in setting up the equipment and developing the exercises seem to be too high to warrant many commercial ventures in this area.

The retail computer stores should not be overlooked
as sources for education, especially on the hardware side.
To supplement their incomes, many of the proprietors of
these stores are conducting relatively inexpensive how-to
courses on software and hardware implementation. For a
very basic introduction, these may serve the purpose adequately, although since they are done ad hoc, the quality
of education may be relatively low. On the other hand,
the ability to interact with a small group of people in a
hands-on setting and a knowledgeable instructor may make
up for the lack of formality.

Conventional college courses on software and electronics should be considered, especially if a designer
wants to become an interdisciplinarian. These may take a
year or more to complete, but the retention of the knowledge is more likely than with quick courses. The best
courses combine classroom education, homework and laboratory experience. The specific microcomputer courses should
probably be avoided, unless especially well done, since they
nearly all assume some knowledge on the part of the student.
The software designer who needs to know how to design simple digital electronics circuits will probably find that
these microcomputer courses will assume too much initial
knowledge. On the other hand, the prerequisites for a
digital logic design course may mean that that designer
must suffer through hours of lectures and lab experience
on analog basics; radio frequency circuits and the like,
just to learn the necessary "volts-and-amps" basics.
Often, a careful reading program supplemented with some
tutoring from one of the college instructors may be enough
to get started in the digital design course.

Similarly, the electronic designer with a yen to learn software may have to sit through hours of data processing fundamentals and introduction to RPG before he is ready to get down to the basics. Usually, the microcomputer courses are designed for digital designers with limited software experience. These may make a good entry point for the experienced electrical engineer. However, the single micro-computer course is not sufficient. The software engineer-ing curriculum, including courses on data structure and program structure, should be considered after the basic microcomputer course is finished. A course in FORTRAN or some other high-level language may be a prerequisite to these advanced courses, but could be taken concurrently with the microcomputer basics program.

The professional meetings offer a way to hone one's knowledge of the microcomputer subject. A variety of pro-grams, most of them offered under one wing or another of the IEE on the BCS, are offered regularly. The exhibits are often more educational than the technical papers, and sufficient time should be left to visit many of the booths. The technical papers can be reviewed from preprints avail-able at the conferences, and potentially important ones attended in the hopes that the author won't be merely reading the paper aloud to the audience. The panels and discussion groups are especially rich sources of practi-cal information; many of the opinions expressed are can-did--and unsuited for publication.

Self-Education

There are some people, especially impatient, who can-not sit through the lengthy formal education process but are self-disciplined enough to learn on their own. A self-education campaign can draw upon the resources of the vendors of products and services, good books, and the growing number of valuable publications in the field.

The vendors of microcomputers and microprocessors are eager to help educate you. The sales personnel themselves may not have enough experience to share, but they can pro-vide mountains of readable and informative literature. Furthermore, most companies have Applications Engineers available who can answer your questions.

The test equipment companies also form a cadre of informed sales people who can be drawn upon in the learn-ing experience. Demonstrations of Logic Analyzers and oscilloscopes and other paraphernalia can often serve as a mini-lab for software people. An experienced engineer or senior technician should participate, too, to pick up the kinds of questions that the novices ask; it will help cement the bonds of team.

The self-education version of workshops are available from several sources now. These usually include a small microcomputer (sometimes as a kit) and an accompanying educational text. It is wise practice to skim the book before you buy. If it is incomprehensible, the educational value will be wasted. Many of the "evaluation kits" assume entirely too much knowledge to be useful to the newcomer to micros. Instead, the products intended specifically as educational aids should be considered.

Most of the self-teaching microcomputer learning aids assume some knowledge of electronics and minimal exposure to computers and software. Before a software designer can effectively learn from these tools, he'll have to acquire the basic digital logic experience to be able to read and understand an electronics schematic diagram. There are many kinds of digital logic "trainers" available from reputable sources, and these can give the software designer the background needed to understand the details found in the microcomputer learning tool programs.

The hardware designer learning software will probably find the self-teaching tools quite adequate for learning about computer architecture, program coding and checkout. However, these texts seldom treat the difficult issues of software design (pre-coding), documentation or the myriad other necessary parts of competent software design activity.

When team members all have different skills to share these self-education experiences can have several beneficial effects. First, the learner will find that there is someone to whom questions can be addressed. Second, the expert in the subject on the team can be certain what other team members know, or will need to know; that can help set the proper level for internal documentation on the project. Finally, the joint experiences of learning can serve to knit the team closer together.

2. APPLYING THE SKILLS

Having acquired the necessary skills in the project, the manager is ready to embark upon a unique design effort. Before starting, it might be worthwhile to take one last look at the entire project process and to plan an attack.

Implementing systems with microprocessors isn't hard,
only different. It'll take some getting used to, especially the software part.

First, pick a small job. Ideally, the first job will
be much like some other design recently completed. If a
new application and a new technology are broached simultaneously, problems can expect to be compounded.

Second, carefully study and understand all the manufacturer's literature on the selected micro. If possible,
get some sample designs and understand them before starting
the actual design phase.

Third, invest in good tools. The microcomputer
development systems are important. Look into the new
logic state analyzers and other special microprocessor
test gear now being introduced. Working without adequate
test equipment is bound to get any team into trouble.

Fourth, plan the work carefully, Many engineers like
to plan projects with a Critical Path chart, like that
shown in Figure 3. This sample chart for a typical small
job shows what has to be done, and in what order. In this
case there are four major pathways through the chart:

1. Hardware, CPU, memory, etc.
2. I/O interface circuitry,
3. Software, and
4. Testing.

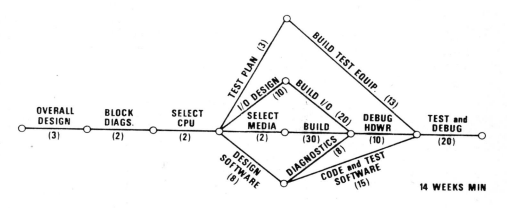

LEGEND: (n) ELAPSED WORKING DAYS

Figure 3. Plan for a typical micro project.

159

This example assumes the task is small enough to be
accomplished by one engineer. As an initial estimate,
it will require about 14 elapsed weeks. Shorter times
have been heard of, but only from experts with lots of
experience who had everything available at their finger-
tips.

In this project plan, it is evident that the designers
need to understand what the system is supposed to do before
programming or hardware design begins. Notice that the system is designed *before* the processor is selected, not after.
The pacing item in this small project is the time spent
awaiting parts ordered; most projects of this magnitude will
be based on one of the sets of pre-built cards. While waiting for the cards, the necessary application-dependent
input/output hardware can be designed and a test plan established. While a technician is fabricating the hardware
the engineer or programmer can be producing the software.

When the computer and memory boards arrive, a two-
stage testing phase can be entered. In the first stage
some small helpful diagnostic programs are loaded into
the computer so that the new special input-output hardware
can be debugged. Once the entire configuration is working,
the actual applications software is put in and combined
with the special test equipment so the whole system can be
tested.

Hardware Design

If the team opts to design and implement a unique
microcomputer, instead of using a pre-fabricated Single-
Board Computer, there are some logical steps to follow.
The step that is almost always taken first--because it is
the most exciting--is the design of the CPU module. This
is logical because the CPU can then be used to check out
other hardware subsystems.

The design of the CPU usually starts with the clock.
A good place to look for hints is the semi-conductor manufacturer's own application notes or schematics of boards
he sells. However, some of these clock circuits are designed for bench "diddling", not production line assembly.
Some of them even violate the manufacturer's own specs!
Note the characteristics that the specs call for and design the clock to operate for those; be sure to check it
under a dynamic load.

With the clock in operation, the CPU itself can be
fired up. Some outboard logic may have to be implemented
to support the CPU; start with the vendor's literature,
but use it as a guide, not a cookbook.

160

If the product is made up of more than a few integrated circuits and the program is expected to be bigger than a few hundred bytes, design and implement some kind of manual operator's panel. The packaging of the system will determine what shape that panel takes on. If the system is being composed of individual modular cards, then the panel ought to be an independent card. If the entire application is to be built on a small set of densely packed cards, then leave some socket space on those cards that an external, cable-connected panel can plug into.

The operator's panel should display the contents of address and data buses; if available, the other important signals at the CPU chip's edge should be brought up to LED's, too. Some switches to control stop, go, and single-step ought to be provided; single-step operation means that the CPU executes exactly one instruction each time the single-step switch is pressed. The panel should also provide some way of specifying an instruction from the panel itself, preferably from switches, and depositing that instruction into memory.

The operator's panel is used only during hardware and software debugging. However, in the latter stages of testing it will prove invaluable. A lack of an operator's panel on even a small project will cost at least one man-month in unnecessary wheel-spinning; it takes only a day or two to build.

Implementation Sequence

The first diagnostic program written should be one to write all one's or all zero's to memory and then read them back to assure operation. Write one diagnostic program that resides in the bytes lowest in memory and checks all the rest of the bytes. Next, write a diagnostic program that resides in a verified part of memory and checks the part previously occupied by the first program.

When designing and implementing the RAM and ROM parts of a microcomputer, be sure to leave plenty of room for expansion. If the design is limited to a fixed number of ROM's, for example, the software may become larger than can be accommodated. That might happen through poor program size estimating more often it happens because expanded services are demanded by the customer. It is almost a certainty that after the first production is underway, somebody will want to add a new feature for a new product and that will require more storage capacity. Leave room.

The first input/output facility on the budding microcomputer ought to be a simple UART-based interface to a
terminal. Many of the microprocessors now being marketed
have or will have UART-like chips in the family. Once a
terminal has been interfaced, pirate the ROM-based monitor that the manufacturer provides in the prototyping
system and plug it into the microcomputer. Now programs
can be easily inserted into RAM from the terminal and
debugged with on-line tools.

With the combination of the CPU and an operator's
panel, some RAM or ROM (with the monitor installed) and
a UART-based interface to a terminal, a complete and useful
microcomputer system exists. The team can now actively
engage in software development and hardware input/output
interface expansion.

Diagnostic Software

One of the easiest ways to check out hardware is to
use the microprocessor as a testing aid. Special programs are developed solely to set up known operating
conditions and verify behavior. Some of these programs
can actually diagnose some classes of faults and report
them automatically.

Programs to test RAM are well known. There have been
dozens of schemes published, although most of them are devoted to testing semiconductor chips themselves. Microcomputer designers are generally not interested in pattern
sensitivity and other sophisticated tests; these are used
in the characterization of the semi-conductor RAM's. By
writing (and then reading) all ones, all zeros and checker-
boards (alternating zeros and ones) one can usually determine
whether the memory is working or not.

Diagnostic programs are most useful when testing new
input/output equipment and interfaces. For input ports,
the diagnostics expect some preset external conditions;
the data present at a port is compared with stored patterns
or is printed out on the terminal for inspection. If the
incoming data rate is rapid and uncontrolled, a diagnostic
can be designed to "dump" the input data into RAM so that
the terminal can be used to print out selected portions.
Output devices are stimulated into action by programs that
use known patterns of data or input from teletypewriter to
control the port. Some observable phenomena must be watched
for to assure output port operation. Hardware designers
should get used to writing these little diagnostic programs at "the drop of a hat." Without software, the hardware is lifeless.

Once the diagnostic routines are operating and the hardware has been tested, all of the diagnostics ought to be combined together and stored in a ROM that is reachable from the debugging monitor. One entry point into the diagnostic package should cause it to run through all of the non-destructive tests (for example, read from RAM several times to assure repetitiveness, but don't write into RAM without first saving and later restoring contents). Other entry points should allow testing of specific input/output ports and equipment. This on-line diagnostic tool will be invaluable in deciding whether the hardware or software is at fault in certain instances. If an input/output port is suspected of faulty operation the diagnostic program can be invoked to check it out before continuing. The over-all system test can be run daily before any debugging begins to assure that the system is still there.

The existence and use of these diagnostic programs makes a significant, but perhaps unobvious, contribution to the design project schedule: They serve as a check, fairly early in the proceedings, that the characteristics of each interface are understood by both the hardware and software builders. This gets some common misunderstandings or oversights out of the way long before integration of the total system.

Software Design

Meanwhile, software is being designed. In a small project, hardware and software are designed together by the same system architect. In larger projects, the hardware and software designers are different people who must work together easily. In either event, software must be *designed*.

It is amazing to see that engineers who wouldn't think of starting a project by rushing to the bench are the same people who try to begin the software task by writing down assembly-language instructions. That isn't design, it is disaster. Most applications are characterized by an inexact problem definition. Although the major features of the desired product may be well-known, handling of error cases and special phenomena has not usually been well thought out. Software doesn't know the difference between normal cases and special cases; all of them have to be programmed and all of them have to be handled correctly. It is imperative, then, that all of the requirements of the job be understood at the outset.

Suffice to say that software development is just as hard as hardware development; not easier, not harder.

By understanding and following the same basic rules
applied to hardware in the design and implementation of
software, the designer won't go wrong. Paper designs are
cheap and easy to change. As with hardware, there is an
almost infinite variety of ways to design software;
choosing the right one is usually an exercise in economics.

How long software takes to write is virtually any-
body's guess. There are measures of programmer productivity like bytes-per-day, but these are all misleading.
It is a lot easier to write a 6,000-byte program to do a
particular job than to write a program for the same job
in less than 2,000 bytes. There is continuing effort
among computer scientists to identify and quantify the
important variables in software production costs but there
has been little progress. We can categorically state that
programming costs correlate well with inherent job complexity, number of people involved in the project,
inexperience of the programmers and instability of new
and developing hardware. In today's microprocessor applications, we tend to be constructing systems of moderate
complexity with few people, but the programmers are inexperienced (or totally devoid of experience) and the
hardware is in a state of flux during software development. It is not uncommon to spend several man-months in
development of a moderately complex microprocessor program,
especially if the entire microcomputer is being designed
from the chips up.

Totalling up the costs of programming man-power and
computer time and the costs associated with a software
development system shows that the software will cost about
as much as the hardware, and perhaps a little more. If the
project includes the design and fabrication of a unique
microcomputer, the software costs will about equal the
hardware development costs. If the project is developed
on a stock single-board microcomputer bought from a vendor, software costs will far exceed the hardware costs.
For rough estimating, you can use a cost of about $5 per
byte of code. However, remember that the actual costs
may range from $1 to $20, depending upon complexity,
skill and other important factors.

Test Plans

Before the design is too firm, it is a good idea to
establish some plan of attack on the problem of verifying
operation of the eventual system. Sometimes the designers
get too close to the design and lose sight of the original
intent of the product as a result, the test plan suffers.

Furthermore, as the project progresses and the deadline looms near there is pressure to shortcut the testing procedures. If they are written down that is harder to do.

Computer-based products are inherently more complex and harder to test than common digital logic systems. Because nearly everything is sequential, all of the combinations of inputs are multiplied by the time-scale; the potential number of discrete things to test becomes astronomical. Software people have a bad reputation for inadequate testing; the effects have been felt by many people. However, because of the nature of most program's environment, once the problem is detected it can be easily corrected by changing the program. However, with microprocessors that is no longer true. If a subtle program bug with catastrophic effects is discovered after several thousand models are delivered with mask-programmed ROM's, the cost of correcting the bug becomes astronomical. Thorough testing of the system, after it is "working", is the best insurance available.

A good test plan calls for initial software testing and debugging to be performed with the program stored in RAM. Later, as some parts of the software become trustworthy they are graduated into EPROM. Finally, the whole program is placed into EPROM for initial field trials. After this phase has been passed the program can be released for production use of mask-programmed ROM's.

The test plan must be designed from two different viewpoints: The end-user's and the designer's. The first tests should be planned before the product is completely designed; these tests are related to the normal and abnormal things that might happen in the field. Both usual and unusual input combinations should be tried. Remember: A debugged program is one for which the inputs that will make it fail have not yet been supplied. Try to compose test circumstances that will make the program fail. This is the crux of the testing issue: The programmer and engineer trying to debug an imperfect system try to develop test cases that will make the system work. A test plan must aim at making the system fail.

The second part of the test plan should concern itself with the testing of the design as it was finalized. The weakest points in the design should be probed so that the boundary conditions of performance are well understood. A classic example of the difference between user-oriented and design-oriented tests is in data rates. The application is probably designed for some nominal incoming data

rate. In the user-oriented tests, rates as fast as allowable and as slow as allowable must be tried. In the design-
oriented tests, extremely fast data rates should be tried
to determine the effects on the hardware and software. If
the design data rate can be exceeded only slightly before
the system goes wild, then the design is not very robust;
this is the time to correct it, not after several more
months of experience.

System Integration

There comes a time in every microprocessor project when
the hardware and software converge on the critical path of
the schedule and they have to work together. Here is where
most projects appear to fail; actually, the failures have
occurred earlier but they weren't noticed. If each of the
hardware and software components has been subjected to some
kind of unit test and passed, then the only remaining kinds
of errors should be misinterpreted interfaces. If adequate
unit tests have been conducted, system integration will be
painless, perhaps marred by one or two minor problems that
might take a day or two to iron out. If the hardware designer is depending upon correct software to test against
and the software designer has been waiting for debugged hardware, then integration can take literally months. It is a
good idea ·to leave plenty of slack in this part of the
schedule because the exact nature of the potential problems
is impossible to predict. However, this slack shouldn't
be considered a cushion to be absorbed by slippage in
earlier critical path items; if all the time isn't needed,
more elaborate tests can be devised to assure a more reliable end-product.

III.B   HARDWARE/SOFTWARE TOOLS FOR MICROPROCESSORS

Carol Anne Ogdin

Software Technique, Inc.

1. HARDWARE AIDS

Development of microcomputer-based products usually requires a support computer system. Products are seldom developed in the computer environment that will surround the eventual software. More often, a separate computer system is used to support software development efforts and to augment hardware testing. This is in sharp contrast with most minicomputer applications in which the mini is used for both development and production. Similarly, digital design engineers will find that checking out a microcomputer prototype requires more support than more traditional TTL or CMOS design efforts.

Small Support Environments

The most primitive kind of support system is based on the actual microcomputer being developed, or on another small system. Often, this small configuration is actually nothing but an evaluation kit from the semiconductor maker. The kit provides a micro, some small amount of data storage space and a debugging monitor in ROM or EPROM. The devices supported for I/O may be on-board or outboard. The on-board peripherals usually include a keyboard and some seven-segment LED displays used for hexadecimal data and address bus contents. Outboard devices are usually assumed to be a teletypewriter terminal of some kind operating at 10 or 30 characters per second.

These small systems are inexpensively priced, around $300. But, the features they provide are very limited. The limited program and data storage sizes of most evaluation kits prevent the use of an assembler, so all programming must be done in hexadecimal (or octal, depending upon the feature arrangement of the debugging monitor). The debug monitor is usually limited in size to what will fit in one or two ROM's or EPROM's. The interactive ability of the debug monitor may consist of little more than loading, executing, modifying and dumping a small program from memory.

The small read-write memory sizes included in the popular evaluation products, typically less than 1,024 bytes, mean that only the smallest of programs can be entered and tested without appreciably increasing memory size. And, that memory expansion may be complicated by the lack of space on the evaluation kit's printed circuit card and the lack of external bus buffering necessary to communicate with an outboard memory card. These products were designed for small evaluation exercises, not wholesale program development.

On the other hand, such evaluation kits can serve in the first project while designers and technicians are gaining familiarity with the micro. Some of the more elaborate systems, like AMI EVK series for the 6800, include adequate amounts of memory and other circuitry that some program development can be supported without investing in the more elaborate tools discussed later.

Most of the evaluation kits include displays that are solely under software control. Thus, they are not used for displaying the dynamic contents of the data and address buses. The first impulse, then, is to add a "front panel" capability. Storing and displaying the contents of the data and address buses is relatively simple, depending upon the micro. The circuitry to acquire, hold and show the status of control lines is also usually easy to implement. But, if the buses can only be displayed in real-time, little information of value is obtained. For maximum effectiveness, some controls must be provided that can stop the microprocessor, and to execute instructions one at a time under manual control.

Different microprocessors have different kinds of control characteristics. Some, like the 8080, have control signals that can be manipulated to cause the dynamic registers inside the chip to be constantly refreshed even while the execution is suspended. In the 8080, for instance, each time the processor refers to memory or I/O a control line (READY) can be held low for an indefinitely long period. During this time the processor refreshes its own registers. Appropriate logic can be inserted to allow execution to step one instruction or one memory cycle at a time. This can be especially valuable when debugging an input/output interface circuit. The processor can be "single stepped" by instruction until the input/output instruction, and then single-stepped by memory cycle until, mid-instruction, the data is on the bus. In this "frozen" condition, the signals can be easily traced from CPU to I/O device.

Processors with static registers, those that don't need any refreshing, like the RCA COSMAC or Intersil's 6100, can have variable rate execution. The clock can actually be stopped without affecting internal register contents. The single step capability is introduced in these kinds of processors by inhibiting clock pulses from reaching the CPU until the next machine cycle is to be executed. By reducing the regular clock (normally on the order of 1 MHz or so) down to a slower rate (say, 10 Hz) with a variable control, variable execution rate can be achieved. Faster rates can be used until the instruction sequence of interest looms near. At that point the rate can be manually slowed or stopped for finer control.

Some processors make this kind of detailed control more diffi-cult. The four-bit processors like the 4004 and 4040, and the other popular eight-bit machines like the 6800 and the F-8 are dy-namic systems. Suspension of execution within the machine cycles that make up an instruction is not possible without losing register contents. However, the circuitry that permits one instruction at a time to be executed can normally be provided. In this case, an ad-ditional switch is usually included in the front panel design to select between displaying the next instruction byte to be fetched and the last byte that was transferred on the data bus during the preceding instruction. The next instruction byte is usually the data bus contents because memory is being addressed; the prior last data bus contents are usually acquired and held in an eight-bit wide latch by clocking the loading of that latch coincident with the end of a memory read or write operation.

If these front panel controls are designed into a new micro-computer system they can be arranged together on an optional print-ed circuit card that can be plugged into the design as necessary. Not only can the front panel be used during the debugging phase of implementation, but it can be a useful diagnostic tool when fail-ures occur in the field. On the other hand, if these controls are to be added to an existing evaluation kit, printed circuit traces may have to be cut and circuitry patches inserted with wires to the external circuitry. The result of this kind of modification is usually a fragile Rube Goldberg that is only understood by the original designer.

Rather than design one's own, the generalized and processor-independent front panel systems can be adopted. When the design and debug time for a specialized front panel are considered, these off-the-shelf items of test equipment are usually less expensive and offer more features.

General Front Panels

Instead of developing a single special front panel interface circuit for each microcomputer product to be debugged, one of the different kinds of display/control devices can be purchased and connected. Typical product examples, both called Microprocessor Analyzers, are the Yucca International YA-1 and Systron-Donner's Model 50.

Both of these analyzers provide interfaces for the ever-popular 8080 and the 6800. The Model 50, in addition, can be interfaced to the MOS Technology 6502 with an off-the-shelf connector. Both systems display a sixteen-bit address bus, eight-bit data bus and eight bits of a control bus. For sixteen-bit microcomputers, half the data bus can be connected to the instrument's data bus input while the other eight-bits of the data bus can feed the control bus inputs. However, the discrimination between reading and writing is then prevented because all the inputs are consumed before control signals can be interfaced.

Operationally, both of these sophisticated front panel systems make use of the breakpoint as a major control. The Model 50 has front panel switches that can be matched with the address bus. The YA-1 can match the address, data and control buses. When the inputs match the switch settings, a breakpoint is said to occur. The reaction to this matching is different in the two devices. The YA-1 uses the match to strobe a 128-word memory; the Model 50 latches the input signals in the displays and halts the attached CPU.

The YA-1 has a 128-word memory, each word being 32-bits wide. When address, data and control bus inputs match the conditions set up in the YA-1's front-panel switches, the memory contents are frozen 96 cycles later. That means that the 32 bus contents prior to and the 96 after the match event are stored. Since the YA-1 has no output signals with which to control the CPU, it cannot suspend instruction execution. However, the memory can be examined to isolate the bug. The only annoyance is the need to step through the YA-1's storage contents one word at a time, watching the hexadecimal displays for significant changes.

The Model 50 can latch the bus contents at the time the match event occurs. Furthermore, if control circuitry has been provided in the monitored micro, the Model 50 can halt the system. Controls in the front panel of the Model 50 can then be used to single-step the microprocessor. Whether single-stepping is by instruction or by memory cycle depends upon the kind of interface circuitry the designer provides in the monitored microprocessor.

These sophisticated front panel devices have no software components accessible to the user; they typically cost in the $1,000 region. Because of the highly generalized design, they can be interfaced to almost any microprocessor, which means they are unlikely to become obsolete overnight.

A more sophisticated test instrument is the Intel μScope 820. This $2,500 instrument can be used to diagnose an 8080 system, although other micros can probably be interfaced. Certainly, Intel will provide interfaces for the rest of its own line -- but not likely its competitors'. Internally, the 820 includes a suitably programmed 8085 microprocessor, breakpoint logic and a logic state analyzer memory of 32 bits by 256 words. Provisions have been included for inserting a monitor or diagnostic program preprogrammed in EPROM into a front panel socket. This program can then be activated when the 820 is plugged into the system under test.

An even more dedicated analyzer from AQ Systems, the AQ6800, operates only with the 6800 microprocessor. Not only is data displayed in both binary and hexadecimal from the address and data buses, but detailed controls are included that can take control when the 6800 is being diagnosed. Monitoring features like other systems are provided, including a simple logic analyzer memory (which only records address bus contents, incidentally). But, because the CPU can be controlled, true front panel features like instruction insertion and program counter loading can be performed. The AQ6800 is priced under $1,000.

Simple Software Support

Even the evaluation kits have some software for aiding the debugging process. However, they nearly all require recourse to some computer terminal unless the kit's own hexadecimal keyboard and displays are used. If the internal "terminal" is used, operations are usually very limited and error-prone. If the computer's debug monitor permits the reading of programs from cassette tape (usually from an audio recorder), the lack of an external terminal may be mollified.

The debug monitor consists of some simple input/output software, plus a command interpreter to allow loading, modifying, executing and dumping memory contents. The more sophisticated monitors include the ability to perform hex-to-decimal conversions, insert software breakpoints which, when reached, cause control to return to the monitor, and the ability to display CPU register contents of programs that are being debugged.

When sufficient memory exists, say more than 8K bytes, an editor and assembler can be used on the small development environment. Ideally, these software objects are installed in ROM or EPROM and wired into the development system so that all of ROM is devoted to data space or program testing space. If the assembler and editor must be loaded into ROM each time they are to be executed, expect to spend a long time loading programs. It may take fifteen minutes to load in an assembler from paper tape at 100 baud.

Editing is a process that is interactive with a human in most cases, so while the input-output may be slow there is usually little notice taken. However, to read in a typical source program, make one change and write out a revised edited program on a Model 33 ASR Teletype may consume over an hour in the lab.

171

Assembly on a micro is usually input-output limited. The source program usually has to be read in twice, and the entire object and source code printed out and then the object code is punched out. Again, if the terminal is a 110 baud Model 33, an assembly of a typical 2K byte program may require well over two hours. By moving up to a faster terminal, say 300 baud, that time can be cut to about 45 minutes.

After adding all this software and hardware to an evaluation kit, along with the front panel circuitry for display and control, the designer may have several thousand dollars worth of test equipment. While the experience in designing it can probably be considered useful, that effort has not been expended in the direction of solving the employer's problem. Perhaps the investment in a more traditional development system would be more attractive after all.

Small Development Systems

The generalized front panel systems are designed with features to be exploited both during initial system debugging and later during field repair of the micro. There are, however, similar kinds of aids designed expressly for use during the development cycle. An example of this new kind of development environment is the PROMPT series from Intel. These are already available for the 8080 and the 8748. Features include a front panel with displays and controls, an EPROM programmer, and interface circuitry for connection to an even larger development system. The PROMPT 80 is based on an SBC 80/10 Single-Board Computer inside the instrument.

The PROMPT 80 looks much like a desk calculator, a calculated achievement by Intel designers who have appealed to those designers who'd rather not be intimidated by a larger development system. Programs are entered from the hexadecimal keypad; data are displayed on hexadecimal LED's. An EPROM socket is provided for the user's program, and interconnect cables to remote input-output circuitry are provided.

These kinds of test instruments are not quite large enough to be expanded to include assembler and editor features. However, as adjuncts to larger software support facility, they can be a useful debug control environment. The PROMPT 80 costs about $1,500.

Software Development Systems

Traditionally, microcomputer software design has been supported on large-scale computers, either through time-sharing or under the aegis of an operating system on an available computer, or on a microcomputer development system. The most popular of the latter genre are the Intel Intellec MDS and Motorola's EXORciser. To be sure, there are dozens of other suppliers of development systems with varying degrees of sophistication.

The simplest development systems are made up of a micro-processor, some limited input-output capability to a terminal, and a large amount of memory. Microcomputer development systems typically provide from 16K to 64K bytes of read-write storage, plus a small monitor. But, with larger memory sizes, the only reasonable way to exploit the capability is with more elaborate peripheral devices. After a higher-speed printer and a floppy disc is added (with the associated disc-based operating system), the price may have been driven to well over $10,000. The advantages, however, can be substantial. The Intel Intellec MDS with 64K and a disc, for example, can compile and execute PL/M programs without recourse to a larger computer system for high-level language translation.

Most microcomputer development systems depart from smaller systems by not providing any significant front panel capability. Since these systems are intended primarily for software development, they don't need these displays and controls, according to the vendors. One modest dissenter is muPro, whose model 80 includes all of the features of microcomputer development system in a surprising small box, the front of which is a full front panel for the 8080. Priced in the region of $4,000, the muPro 80 contains 16K bytes of RAM. Because of the integral front panel, a terminal is not required for initial development work.

In-Circuit Emulation

In-circuit emulation is a concept pioneered by Intel, although it appears to have been done by some Europeans before Intel announced their equipment. ICE (Intel has craftily trademarked that acronym) is a circuit that plugs into a socket replacing the 8080 CPU chip itself. The forty wires then lead to a small interface box back to the host microcomputer development system. The muPro 80E is a similar option for the muPro model 80.

An in-circuit emulator lets the host computer, with all of its additional memory and monitor software and peripherals, become a resource to support the operation of the system under test. ICE is a sophisticated tool that substitutes for the primitive features of a front panel. In the emulation mode, the operator can wrest control from the executing program by using monitor commands. The suspended program's register and memory contents can be examined and modified and execution resumed. Because there are no changes in the system under test except microprocessor replacement, all of this testing capability is transparent to the design. That means that the system under test can be a nearly completely finished system, packaged and ready to ship. Yet, the in-circuit emulator can be used to exorcise the last residual design blunders.

The in-circuit emulator option to a microcomputer development system typically costs in the region of $1,500.

Processor-Independent MDS

Until this year, virtually all microcomputer development systems were dedicated to supporting one particular vendor's microprocessors. However, sufficient operational experience has been gained so that respected instruments companies have designed and introduced development systems capable of supporting a variety of different microcomputers. The Tektronix 8002, for instance, is similar in feature list to the Intellec 888 system, but it supports the Z-80 and 6800 in addition to the 8080 and 8085. The basic cost for the 8002, which includes a dual floppy disc and a primitive front panel, is around $10,000. Software support includes editor and assemblers, in addition to the normal disc-based software monitor.

In-circuit emulation is provided in the 8002 Microprocessor Lab at three distinct levels. At the first level, a plug is provided to replace the microprocessor itself. This allows software emulation of the replaced micro. At the next level, a control probe is added to the system. With the control probe, input and output signals and other microcomputer control signals can be driven or sensed by the 8002 under its software control. Finally, an eight-bit input probe can be connected that permits the monitoring of eight control or data inputs to the system. The control probe and the real-time prototype analyzer interface go a long way toward satisfying the need for the general ability to stimulate inputs to the system under test and sensing outputs for comparison with predictions. The 8002 is well-suited to general testing of microcomputer systems, not just their emulation.

Another microprocessor-independent system is the Hewlett-Packard model 1611A. It is called a Logic State Analyzer, which will serve to thoroughly confuse designers trying to select among the various kinds of logic analyzers on the market. The $5,000 1611A is designed to support either the 8080 or the 6800. It is not clear what the cost might be to convert an 8080-supporting 1611A into a support tool for the 6800, but it appears possible by design. The 1611A has a forty-pin connector already installed for in-circuit emulation. However, the 1611A does not have the Tektronix system's expandability to a disc-based operating system with general software support.

Dynamic Tracing

The Tektronix 8002 Microprocessor Lab, Hewlett-Packard's 1611A Logic State Analyzer and Electronic Modules Corp.'s D9780 (for 8080 software development support) all have a novel set of interactive software tools that can save a significant amount of debugging time. The memory contents are decoded from binary back into a form resembling assembly language during system-controlled execution. This "disassembly" takes place whenever the computer is not being used in real-time.

With a disassembler in operation, ten or twenty lines of a CRT display are arranged in columns, much like an assembly program listing. The object code is shown in octal or hex. Next to that, on the same line, the mnemonic instruction is displayed, along with the addresses and other operands. If the operand portion of the instruction can be interpreted as a potential memory address, most of the dynamic tracers also show the contents of memory at that location. These systems only appear to show the instructions to be executed next; it would be nice to see the last few instructions just executed. In the Electronic Modules system, the right portion of the display is a complete array of the CPU's register contents, a selected part of memory, and the contents of the topmost terms in the pushdown stack. The Tektronix and Hewlett-Packard systems, on the other hand, show external input bit status levels to the right of the disassembled code.

Applications Oriented Equipment

In most practical microcomputer applications, some synthetic input signals are almost always needed during the testing phase. Just connecting the microcomputer up to a real-world environment is insufficient. Furthermore, it might not be practical for safety or cost reasons. All of the relevant inputs to the computer should be created synthetically, either with a special purpose test instrument built specifically for the purpose, or with a general purpose function generator.

The purpose of an input stimulator is to be able to create repeatable real-time conditions that can be used to test the software and hardware under worst cases. Too often, novices in microcomputer design simply use an available data source instead of creating one especially for the testing job. In a data collection application, for example, the special purpose test instrument is a manually controllable box that looks electrically like the eventual data points to be monitored. However, instead of the full complexity of real-time creation of the signals, manual operation is substituted. By manually controlling inputs to the microcomputer system under test, the designer can determine that all required features operate correctly, and that erroneous inputs don't cause erroneous outputs from the system.

Another microcomputer can be used for this task, too. When the inputs to the microcomputer must appear in a specific time order, the microcomputer test driver may be the only practical way to generate all those signals at the right time. Furthermore, if the software is to be tested under worst-case fastest-input conditions, only another computer can be entrusted with the task.

A microcomputer-based test input stimulator can also be turned around and used as an output validator. The outputs from the system under test can be read into the same microcomputer that drives the inputs. For each test, the given inputs to the system under test are associated with some expected output in a table. The test driver picks a table entry and places the specified signals on its outputs to drive the inputs of the system under test. The outputs from the system under test are read into the test driver computer and compared with the expected results stored in the same table entry. If the proper results are sensed, the next test in turn is conducted; if not, the test driving processor can alert the designer to the kind of error that occurred by displaying the presented input signals and the obtained output signals.

This kind of special test equipment may cost from a few hundred to a few thousand dollars to design and implement. If a software development system is handy, it can serve as the base for the microcomputer controlled version of the system, reducing the costs somewhat. In any event, some interface circuitry will usually have to be designed and constructed to emulate the eventual real-world electrical environment.

Logic Analyzers

If there's anything proliferating as rapidly as the microcomputers, it's got to be the wide range of Logic Analyzer instruments. From simple, microprocessor-oriented products like the Motorola MPA-1 to complex and sophisticated tools like the Hewlett-Packard 1600A, there is a huge array of features and benefits to pick from. And, to add to the confusion, there is a trend toward labelling some development aids that are specific to a particular microprocessor Logic Analyzer, like H-P's 1611A which is designed to support the 8080 or the 6800.

To the bewildered prospective customer, there just isn't any easy way to sort out all these products. An endless parade of salesmen, all proclaiming their product to be "vastly superior", can be a crashing bore after a few hours. The only way to make a rational choice is to ask what must be done and then see how the commercial products measure up. Rather than let sales presentations use abstract examples, the evaluator should dream up some problems faced in recent months and then ask for a demonstration of how the Logic Analyzer can be used to attack those problems.

The basic principle behind most Logic Analyzers is illustrated in Figure 1. The probes bring in signals from the equipment under development. The signals are matched with switches on the front panel so that some combination of them can be used to enable the memory to record all the inputs. The front-panel controls are usually toggle switches that can be set to recognize each input at 1 or 0, or to ignore that particular input. When the input conditions match the conditions specified in the switches, the memory is enabled.

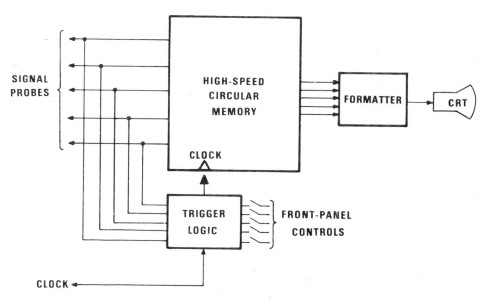

Figure 1. Organization of a logic analyzer.

The inputs are collected in memory, one for each clock pulse. As each new word is written, the oldest word is purged from memory. A display formatter then acquires data from the memory and produces the information on an internal (or, sometimes, external) oscilloscope.

Now, when debugging a digital system, technicians typically "freeze" everything when a fault appears. They are seldom interested in the current state of memory in the faulty system, nor do they care much about the future. They are most frequently interested in the past: "How'd I get into this mess?" So, normally, a Logic Analyzer is used as a digital historian; for each clock pulse a new set of inputs is recorded in memory, until the input condition that matches the front-panel switch conditions is detected. At that point, the memory is "frozen" (clock signals are not passed to the memory), and the display will show the most recent inputs.

The input probes are usually connected to bits of the address bus, and some of the control bus signals. It is often useful (but seldom absolutely essential) to have some record of the data bus contents too. The number of input signals that can be sensed and recorded in parallel is an important parameter of these devices. There are some very high speed Logic Analyzers with clock rates as high as 200 MHz, but these generally have very narrow (8-bit) memories. If debugging ECL or high-speed Schottky logic for a special application, these features may be important. However, for debugging microprocessors a sixteen-bit wide memory is about the minimum that can be tolerated. With a sixteen-bit address bus and only eight inputs, which address bus bits should be monitored?

An ideal word width would be about 40 bits. Then one could monitor a sixteen-bit address bus and data bus, and still have eight signals left over for control bus signals. The closest to that today is the Hewlett-Packard 1600A with the 1607A expander; these provide a total of 32 bits -- enough for an eight-bit data bus, the sixteen-bit address bus, and eight control signals.

Another feature found in many Logic Analyzers, especially the top-of-the-line models, is a second memory. The contents of the recorded data in one memory can be transferred to the auxiliary memory, and then more data recorded. Then, either memory contents can be displayed (usually side-by-side) or the logical difference shown. In the exclusive-or mode, the two memories' contents are displayed as one table; locations that are identical are displayed in normal intensity, locations that are different are displayed with high intensity. So, two different operating circumstances can be compared to see if they change important elements in the recorded data. For instance, supposedly benign input signals can be toggled to see if they affect the program's flow sequence.

The display formatter may be designed to reconstruct timing diagrams or present digital displays. Digital forms, sometimes called state tables, may be in binary, octal or hexadecimal. Ideally, the address and data bus would be in hex (or octal, if you insist), and the control bus in binary. Since the Logic Analyzer doesn't know which inputs are control bus, there is usually a limit of one format of digits.

Timing diagrams can be plain reconstructions of the digital states recorded in memory, or they may be augmented by "tick marks"; most people definitely prefer the extra marks so that the duration of a pulse can be easily determined from the display.

Another kind of display available is called a map. It can show, in one overall display, the general operation of a program. Generally, only the address bus is used to drive the map display, although other clever combinations could become popular some day.

The map display works by implementing two D-to-A converters, each typically eight bits wide, on the X- and Y- axis of the 'scope. The most-significant bits of monitored data are fed to the Y-axis, the least-significant bits to the X-axis. As the addresses are accessed, the beam moves about to show where in memory the program is operating.

Remember, with the map mode of display, both data and instruction fetches and stores are all displayed at once. Typically, the data is so dense that individual locations can't be picked out anyway. One clever trick is to only monitor the most-significant fifteen address bus bits; on the sixteenth input feed some signal that is true only when an instruction is being fetched. Then, the upper half of the display shows the sequence and pattern of data references, and the lower half is devoted to program references.

2. PROGRAMMING LANGUAGES

Newcomers to the programming craft are always faced with the perplexing array of programming languages. Unlike the language of schematic diagrams, which tend to have only a few basic styles and great similarity, the software notations are hard to understand at first. Furthermore, the skills acquired with one language are very often not transferable to another language.

Language Styles

It used to be said that high-level languages like FORTRAN, BASIC and COBOL were "free-form" languages. Statements in these languages could be written freely across the page. In contrast, assembly language was called a "fixed form" language, since individual statements had to be written in rigid vertical columns. Some assemblers, however, violate that distinction.

Later, high-level languages were called "one-to-many" languages. While assembly languages represent one computer instruction per source-code statement, high-level languages translated each statement into many equivalent computer instructions. Then macro processors with their vast "one-to-many" capabilities were added to assemblers and again the distinction was unclear.

In place of these historical definitions, perhaps a functional approach to the distinction between assembly language and high-level language would be useful: look at the translator for the language and determine how much work the programmer must do.

Think of the computer's hardware registers and storage locations as resources, and determine where the responsibility and authority for resource allocation lies. If the programmer must allo-

cate all of the registers in detail, then the language is at the
assembly level. If the translator, be it interpreter or compiler,
takes the responsibility for detailed allocation away from the
programmer, then it accepts a high-level language.

The use of an assembly language imposes some extra requirements
on the programmer. If there are two nested loops that must share
the same index register, for example, the programmer must keep
track of which loop variable is in the register at each point while
the program is being written. Plentiful opportunity is left for
programmer error. That problem is relieved in a high-level language, because the translator takes care of saving and restoring
loop variables in index registers for the programmer.

On the other hand, the compiler for a language may have only
one set way of saving and restoring registers. The procedure it
uses is safe, in that it always behaves predictably. A clever programmer, however, may take advantage of some special knowledge a-
bout the internal operation of the program and be more efficient in
the allocation of the index register. If the inner loop of the
nested pair never refers to one of the CPU's registers, the clever
programmer might save the index register's content there instead of
in main storage. The result is a program that is likely to execute
faster than the equivalent produced by a compiler.

Is the additional programming effort invested by the clever
programmer worth the savings in execution time? The answer is no
if this program executes only occasionally on a large-scale computer. However, if the program is part of a real-time microcomputer
task that consumes 90% of the CPU's "horsepower", then the answer
is clearly yes.

For High-Level Languages

Why do high-level languages allow programs to be produced so
much faster than assembly language? It is part of the folklore of
computing that productivity is constant for a given programmer in
the number of lines of debugged source code produced per day.
There is no merit in establishing productivity requirements like
"n-lines of code per day." What the project manager can do is
provide the programmer with the most powerful language available.
At a given programmer's productivity rate, this will contribute
the maximum amount of finished functional power to the eventual
applications program.

Typical high-level languages, as compared to assembly language, take fewer lines of source code to produce the same result.
A typical BASIC program might consist of a few hundred source
lines; the equivalent assembly language program might require a
thousand or more. An assembly language program typically requires

from 100 to 1000% more lines to achieve an application result than
the equivalent program expressed in a suitable high-level language.
The net savings is in program coding and testing cost, and the
program gets finished sooner.

For Assembly Language

But there's no such thing as a free lunch. Programs that result from a compiler are generally longer and require more time to
execute than those written by a highly skilled assembly language
programmer. An experienced programmer using assembly language
can be just as clever as the situation demands. By finding some
novel way to describe or process data, a good programmer can turn
a large, complex muddle of a program into a simple, elegant, small
and fast equivalent. A compiler, on the other hand, can only follow rote. It can produce code only of limited flexibility. The
compiler can only be as clever as was its original author. So,
the price paid for using a high-level language is lower efficiency
in the object program executed.

This traditional argument in favor of assembly language may be
out of date. The assumption of a good, experienced programmer, motivated to produce highly efficient code, was the benchmark. Most
programmers probably aren't that good. Using some of the most
sophisticated compilers, such as IBM's FORTRAN-H, it is hard for a
mediocre programmer to generate programs that are as efficient.
Even good programmers have a hard time beating that translator's
efficiency. Such optimizing compilers haven't yet been generated
for micros, though.

Typical compilers produce anywhere from 15 to 200% more code
than a good assembly language programmer. If the program is to run
on a single computer, there is little justification for increasing
programming costs to save money on storage. When production quantities are in the thousands or even hundreds, however, the number
of additional memory units required may constitute a substantial
cost, and make the potential savings worthwhile.

The execution time penalty introduced by a compiler is more complex to quantify, since it is highly dependent upon the application
or since the clever programmer might find a unique algorithm that
cannot be efficiently represented in the high-level language.
However, if we establish the rule that comparisons are based on alternative implementations of the same algorithm, a compiler can
produce code that takes 15 to 300% longer to execute than the e-
quivalent assembly-language version.

Finally, the cost of operating the translation system needs to
be considered. Typically, assemblers are available for micros that
require about 4K bytes of program space. The amount of data space

required is a function of the program being translated, but may be on the order of 4K with reasonable source programs. That means that the assembler may be supported on a very small configuration, often the very computer being used as the product prototype. High-level languages typically require larger systems to support them. The cross-compilers require access to a larger computer, either locally or through a time-sharing system. The service costs can be dramatic, especially if budgets aren't watched carefully. And native computer compilers require very large configurations -- typically 64K bytes plus a disc operating system. These configurations may cost well over $15,000; they rent for $1,200 per month. For a small one-shot project, the expense may not be justified.

The interpreters have the disadvantage that, although they don't generally require a large configuration, they must be installed in every copy of the product. Furthermore, execution time penalties of as much as ten-to-one may be experienced in some cases. That makes interpreters impractical for at least the real-time part of many applications.

The Choice

The essential trade-off a designer must make, then, is between the cost of program development and the life-cycle cost in production. It is well to note that there is a significant part of the cost of writing programs that is not affected by the language choice. The analysis of the application, algorithm selection and program design activities usually proceed without being affected by the language choice. Some outrageous claims of "10-to-1 reduction in programming cost" have appeared in print, but these refer solely to the coding and testing time, not design effort. In well designed programs, more than 2/3 of the dollars are spent before code is ever written, so the savings may not be as great as the seller would like to claim.

Microcomputers are frequently used in dedicated applications, where a single program is installed and executes during 100% of that computer's time. The designer may not be able to afford the execution time penalty imposed by a compiler. However, because only one or a small number of computers have this software installed, program size is not a terribly important issue. The savings in memory costs won't warrant developing the entire program in assembly language. To gain the execution time efficiency, then, the critical part of the software is typically isolated and written in assembly language. The bulk of the program is implemented in a suitable high-level language. Often, only a small fraction of the entire program need be rewritten in assembly language to effect improvements in performance of several hundred percent.

To achieve overall reductions in program size -- not just speed -- the entire program should be written in assembly language. Many microcomputer applications demand small program size. A typical Single-Board Computer, for example, has space for only 4K bytes of program storage. Exceeding this limit means that another memory card will be required to accompany the SBC. If the anticipated production volume is one or two, there is hardly justification for using assembly language. The memory card might cost an additional $500, but the added programming costs to save that money would be $2,000. If, however, five or more copies of such a program are required, extra programming effort to save the cost of five or more memory cards may be worthwhile.

The microprocessor, of course, represents the extreme case. The number of units of production may be in the hundreds or thousands, so the additional software development costs can be recouped rather quickly. If the use of a compiler requires an extra memory chip that costs $20, and you will be making 1,000 copies, then you can afford to spend up to $20,000 to program in assembly language in order to save that memory chip.

Translator Styles

The variety of styles of translators available complicates selection of the right programming languages. In the early days of computers, compilers produced object code equivalent to the assembler's output and these were the only kinds of translators made. Later, however, translators were developed -- especially on minicomputers -- that combined translation and execution into one step. These _interpreters_ do not generate the object program for each source statement to be saved for later execution. Instead, they actually execute some code each time the source statement is encountered. The advantage of an interpreter over a compiler is that the executing program can be easily interrupted, changed and resumed. Each source statement is translated anew each time it is to be executed. The disadvantage, of course, is the penalty in execution time that is usually paid. An interpreter may generate results 10 to 20 times more slowly than the equivalent compiled code.

Compilers require more completely-defined programs, but they produce entire programs that are relatively fast. Interpreters, on the other hand, need only have available the actual or condensed source code. In many applications, the total size of the interpreter and its source code will still be much smaller than the code produced by a compiler from the same language.

Although it is possible to construct interpretive assemblers, there is little reason to do so. Since the source code is a one-for-one representation of the object code, once it is translated it may as well be stored in memory for future execution. Some of the new software debugging aids, like HP's 1610A or Electronic Modules' D9780, use interpreters for assembly language so that complex interaction can be maintained between the programmer and his program. In production form, however, the final program is assembled into target-computer code for execution.

The popular programming languages like BASIC and FORTRAN could be implemented either way. In fact, most of the commercially available BASIC translators are interpreters. They are attractive for use in debugging and casual computer use, but execution times may be long. In those applications where the micro is "overkill" anyway, that additional execution time penalty may not even be important. If a typical process is being controlled with thermocouples, relays, and some modest amount of computation, the microcomputer is only "taxed" to perhaps 1% of its capacity; the balance is left for interpreter overhead, and the program will still spend most of its time in an idle loop waiting for something important to happen.

Language Trends

The trend toward high-level language adoption will continue, especially in light of recent U. S. Department of Defense (DoD) language standardization efforts and the continued increase in the size of program storage ROM's. DoD is evaluating future language options for standardization. The general acceptance of one particular language for real-time control applications will mean more compilers available for general use. And, larger ROM's mean that the incentive for assembly language programming will diminish, and compilers and interpreters may be distributed in ROM form.

The art of language development has matured over the past few years. Now, instead of merely throwing features that look attractive together, we can look back on large program families to determine what the problem areas were during implementation and maintenance. New solutions have been proposed and implemented. One of the most exciting languages is PASCAL.

The Defense Department has solicited proposals from industry to modify any one of three particular languages (PL/I, ALGOL-68, and PASCAL) to meet DoD requirements. The impact could be significant. If the DoD standardizes upon a particular language, then most computer companies will have to construct translators for it. As the user base broadens, more and more applications in the commercial sector will adopt the same language. The result, a la COBOL, can be staggering. Then, as compiler writers meet the challenge, successively better translators will be created. Comparison of today's FORTRAN translators with their forebears will reveal how good things may get.

But, even if DoD doesn't standardize, consider what the three languages they are proposing as the basis for a new language have in common. All three languages are based on block-structured programming, encouraging the adoption of proven structured programming discipline. Furthermore, these three languages (especially ALGOL-68 and PASCAL) are very strong in their ability to define complex data structures. The proper representation of data structures is emerging as an important design choice as algorithm selection; the proper data structure may mean the difference between an unsuccessful and a successful project. And languages that don't provide strong data description facility impede the development of sophisticated, reliable, maintainable programs.

There will likely never be one "ideal" language for all applications. But, for the real-time control problems endemic to the microcomputer milieu, one well designed language is a reasonable goal.

The minimization in the number of languages may make practical distribution of direct execution computers a reality. Imagine a microprocessor with PASCAL (or ALGOL, or FORTRAN) as its native language! The first steps are already being taken.

A small subset of BASIC has been implemented as a pair of ROM's by Electronic Arrays. These are designed to accompany an 8080; the resulting 8080 with the BASIC ROM's is functionally identical to a slow computer with BASIC as its native language. With 64K-bit ROM's now on the market, one can write an 8K-byte interpreter and be able to install it in a single memory chip for a price below $25.00. The vast majority of microprocessor applications (not in number of production units, but in terms of the number of different jobs micros do) are very slow. Most instrumentation, data acquisition and process control jobs could be done by a microprocessor one-tenth the speed of an 8080; the BASIC interpreter in a ROM will exhibit just that kind of performance. The resulting programs will be easier to write, debug and maintain.

Now, why can't an interpreter be written in microcode for one of the slice architecture computers? Furthermore, why not microprogram the entire microcomputer on a single chip? In fact, there is no real technical reason that it cannot be done. The only argument against at the moment is economics. No one's sure enough of the marketplace to risk spending the kind of money it will require to implement a true microprogrammed BASIC (or PASCAL, etc.) interpreter. But, we can realistically expect to see such products on the market before 1980.

The impediment to direct execution is responsibility. The semiconductor companies are unlikely to make the massive development investment required until the market materializes. And, no one customer is going to be large enough to warrant making the expense and then sharing the development with the world. Either some government facility (as in the Electronic Arrays case), or some independent developer is likely to be the catalyst in the development of direct execution microcomputers.

IV.A. AN INSTRUMENT DESIGN PROBLEM

David Dack

Hewlett Packard Ltd.

1. INTRODUCTION

There are of course many other areas of application for micro-processors than in electronic test instruments. It is certain however that the microprocessor revolution has hit instruments first and hardest in terms of the rapid changes in design skills required of the instrument designer. The opportunities for microprocessors range from the replacement of analogue modules by digital algorithms to the sequencing of whole series of measurements which formerly were done manually.

The most obvious result of the microprocessor takeover in instruments however is probably the appearance of the front panel and controls.

The traditional layout of front panel controls was largely dictated by the physical size of the modules connected to the controls. For example, a rotary switch connected to an attenuator had to appear on the front panel directly in front of the attenuator mounted on its control shaft. The final position depended much more on the internal structural constraints of the instrument than on the desire to provide an easy to use interface. Probably the best (and most expensive) solution to the problem of providing a good user interaction with an instrument is by using a computer terminal as the means for the Man-Machine Dialogue. Similar results can however be produced at a much lower cost by using a keyboard and seven segment or alphanumeric displays. The human interface to the instrument can now be considered quite separately from the design of the functioning instrument modules. An added benefit is of course that the designer of these modules is completely freed from the constraints imposed by the front panel (Martin, 1973).

To illustrate the new skills required, a complete instrument will be described. Neither space nor the reader's patience will permit a completely thorough description of a commercial instrument so a very simple power meter has been chosen which does however illustrate some useful points in the area of

keyboard software and in the replacement of analogue modules by
digital algorithms.

2. OVERALL INSTRUMENT SPECIFICATION

The objective of the instrument is to measure the power of an
input signal using full wave rectification for simplicity but
displaying the result in decibels.   The result should be
compared against a reference level and against previously entered
upper and lower limits so that an indication can be given of
signals higher or lower than expected.   A numeric keyboard will
be used for entering numbers and a seven segment display will be
used for results.

This seemingly innocent sounding specification could in fact
lead to all sorts of problems, particularly with regard to
operating speed, unless some unique software is created to exactly
match the problem.

3. SELF TEST

A less obvious but very important aspect of the inclusion of
microprocessors in instruments is that of self test.   In an
analogue power meter the logarithmic amplifier can only amplify
logarithmically.   A microprocessor programmed with a logarithmic
algorithm however is capable of being programmed to do many other
things including testing itself.   The extent of the application
of self test is limited only by the imagination of the designer
once the idea has been accepted but here are some examples of how
self test can be incorporated.

ROM Self Test

Each Read only Memory in the instrument contains a single
parity word in which each bit is chosen to give odd ones parity
on the columns of the ROM.   To test the ROM it is now only
necessary to write a simple routine to calculate the parity of
the ROM.   This is not a completely foolproof test but it does
pick up a surprisingly large proportion of expected ROM faults.

This test routine could be initiated at switch on and might
in fact form a useful wait loop if one is required in the program
rather than just incrementing a counter until it overflows.

RAM Test

A test of Random Access or Read/Write memory can of course
only be done when it contains no useful data which would be over-
written.   It would be possible at switch on however to load
every location in memory with test patterns and to read back the

results looking for errors. Some care needs to be taken in the selection of test patterns since if for example an address bit to the RAM were stuck then a word might be written into and read from RAM without it being realised that the wrong location had been addressed. A suitable test might be to load each location with its own address in a first pass and then to read the results back later. The test could then be repeated this time loading the complement of the address so that each memory cell is tested in its one and zero states.

Input-Output Test

A bidirectional bus is frequently used to handle the control and data paths of an instrument. In this case a write to the Bus could easily be followed as a matter of course by a read and a comparison with what was expected. Any failings in the Bus drivers or receivers could easily be detected in this way.

Memory Address Decoding Test

If the processor can be forced to execute a single instruction like a No Operation continuously, by disconnecting the ROM data lines for example and substituting a specially wired test plug, then the memory address lines will just count continuously. The most significant address line will oscillate at half the rate of the next most significant and so on.

This counting pattern is particularly easy to recognise with an oscilloscope and the whole memory address decoding circuitry can be readily checked out in this way.

The above self test ideas are directed at the processor testing itself. It is also possible of course to write special routines in which the rest of the instrument can be exercised in ways which are different from its normal operation but which enables faults to be found more rapidly. An example of this is the display of all possible numbers in a seven segment display.

4. KEYBOARD HANDLING ROUTINES

The pocket calculator has demonstrated how useful a keyboard is as a human interface. Even those models where each key can have up to three functions depending on the previous keys pressed are not difficult to use if the extra key functions are not frequently needed. Close on the heels of the calculators, however, are the electronic test instruments in which the traditional knobs and switches on the front panel are replaced by a keyboard.

Perhaps the most important reason for this change, at least in the eyes of the instrument designer, is flexibility. The specification of an instrument can change dramatically and frequently during the design phase and life is made much easier if a new keyboard overlay and a simple software change is all that is required compared with a complete new front panel layout.

Actually, no one who has had to process a design through to production will ever again believe that software change can be simple. The purpose of this section is to explain some techniques by which quite drastic changes in quite complicated instruments can be handled as simply as possible with a fair degree of confidence that the result will work.

The first step is to consider a routine whose sole job will be to look after the demands of the keyboard and the operator behind it. This routine will not be at all concerned with what an instrument does but only with the order in which it does it. As such it can remain unchanged throughout all the vagaries of the instrument design cycle and so, it is hoped, remain bug-free.

The job of the routine will be to inspect the incoming sequence of keyboard commands and to decide what must be done about them. This is analogous to the task of a parsing routine in a compiler and so such a routine is often known as a parser.

The routines which actually make the instrument perform its measurements, display selected results, etc., are written and tested separately and are simply initiated by the parser as appropriate. This simple distinction between what is done and when it is done is responsible for a great deal of the simplification of this approach.

Now if the parser routine itself is not going to change when a specification is changed, what is? The answer is a simple table which describes the desired results from every legal and illegal combination of key pressings. This parser state table is in effect a precise description of what the instrument does and it can be remarkably compact and easy to understand even for a complex instrument with many multifunction keys.

A parser state table for a simple power meter is shown in Fig.1. This table is not a program and could not be assembled into executable code. It is simply a description of what the instrument is expected to do, written in a form which is easy for the designer to manipulate. The translation into its final form in the memory of the microprocessor is, however, a purely mechanical task.

TABLE POSITION	KEY	SUB ROUTINE	PARAMETER	NEXT POSITION
TAB∅	REF	DISP	REF	TAB1
	XFER	NOP	–	TAB2
	MEAS	MEASS	–	TAB3
	REL	RDISP	–	TAB7
	ABS	ADISP	–	TAB7
	ULIM	DISP	ULIM	TAB4
	LLIM	DISP	LLIM	TAB5
	ANYKEY	NOP	–	TAB7
TAB1	DIGITS	NUM	REF	TAB1
	ANYKEY	NOP	–	TAB∅
TAB2	ULIM	XFR	ULIM	TAB7
	LLIM	XFR	LLIM	TAB7
	REF	XFR	REF	TAB7
	ANYKEY	NOP	–	TAB∅
TAB3	CONT	MEASC	–	TAB6
	ANYKEY	NOP	–	TAB∅
TAB4	DIGITS	NUM	ULIM	TAB 4
	ANYKEY	NOP	–	TAB∅
TAB5	DIGITS	NUM	LLIM	TAB 5
	ANYKEY	NOP	–	TAB∅
TAB6	HALT	DHLT	–	TAB7
	ANYKEY	NOP	–	TAB∅
TAB7	ANYKEY	NOP	–	TAB∅

Figure 1   Parser State Table

The TABLE POSITION column indicates the current state of the instrument with regard to the keyboard. The instrument will probably power up in state TAB0 and will progress through all the allowable states in an order depending on which keys have been pressed.

For each TABLE POSITION there are a number of keys which it would be sensible to press next.   It would be most unusual if for every state of the instrument then pressing any one key would take us to a new useful state.   What is much more likely is that for each state only a few keys have any real importance. The rest may be regarded as an error or may be ignored or may be treated as the start of a whole new train of events.

The KEY column of Fig.1 lists, alongside the TABLE POSITION, all the keys which are to produce unique results and for each of these keys which are pressed the NEXT POSITION column indicates the next state of the instrument.   Thus in Figure 1 if we are in state TAB0 and the REF key is pressed then we should go to state TAB1 and wait for another key to be pressed.   Certain actions should take place on the way but that is explained later.

If while in state TAB0 a key is pressed other than the first seven then we recognise this possibility by the entry ANYKEY which has a next position of TAB7.   We have therefore defined a path through the table for any sequence of key pressings.   No key sequence is ambiguous or undefined.

The next step is to define what shall happen when a key is pressed.   Again, if in state TAB0 and if REF is pressed then the SUBROUTINE column tells us that a subroutine called DISP should be executed before we go to TAB1 and wait for another key. Obviously we are here expected to display the reference level. It is very likely that a number of different items will have to be displayed at different points in the table so to avoid having to write a separate subroutine for each item to be displayed we will allow a PARAMETER column to indicate the item.   A single subroutine called DISP can then be used, each time taking its parameter from the table.

A useful technique to minimise the table size is to regard all the numeric keys, possibly including the decimal point and plus and minus signs, as digits and to deal with their occurrence with a single DIGITS entry in the table.   Thus if we are sitting in state TAB1 after having pressed REF and any digit key is pressed, then the subroutine NUM will be called, with REF as a parameter, to enter the first digit of the value of REF.   We then return to TAB1 to see if any more digits are coming along. If a non digit key is pressed, however, then the ANYKEY entry tells us to execute the NOP routine, that is to do nothing and to

192

go to state TABØ to await further instructions.

In fact, the interpretation of "go to state TABØ" really requires some further thought.   Suppose that after entering the value of the Reference Level as described above, we wish to do the same for the Upper Limit.   The non digit key pressed in state TAB1 would then have been ULIM.   With the present definition we would go to state TABØ and wait.   We would have to press ULIM a second time to obtain the desired action.   This could be tedious to say the least.   If, however, we treat TABØ as a special case so that we never actually wait there but simply pass through using the last key pressed as the key to look for in the KEY column then the problem is resolved.   If the instrument now powers up in state TAB7 rather than TAB1 then the definition is complete.

The table now is a specification of what the instrument will do under all possible circumstances.   It may not do exactly what the customer wants but it will certainly do what the designer intended and the loopholes for bugs to creep in have been practically eliminated.   To turn this human description of the table into a microprocessor description we need to translate the mnemonics of Figure 1 into numbers in the ROM of the processor. To do this requires a subroutine table, (Fig.2)   which simply gives a number to each subroutine, and a keycode table (Fig. 3) which does the same for each key.   Note that some keys have two labels.   This minimises the number of keys required but does not make the parsing task any more difficult.

As a convenience the digit keys have been given keycodes corresponding to their BCD values.   The measure and halt keys are easily distinguished from the rest by being the only ones whose keycodes begin with a 2.   Although it is not strictly necessary in this example, the technique of grouping together similar keys does make the job of recognising them much quicker when many more keys are used.   Since the digit keys are all treated in the same way in the table then it makes sense that we recognise a digit simply by looking for a keycode beginning with zero.   A portion of a completed table translation is given in Fig .4.

The standard routine to interpret the table can now be written.   A flow chart is given in Fig.5 where it can be seen that it is a very simple task.   It may be interesting to note that it is much more straightforward to define the table first and to write the subroutine afterwards than to start with the subroutine.

The application of the above techniques may seem tedious but each step is simple to apply and the result is a very flexible

D.DACK

SUBROUTINE NAME	SUBROUTINE NUMBER	ACTION
DISP	1	Formats number pointed to by parameter into display.
MEASS	2	Makes single measurement.
RDISP	3	Formats Relative Results into display area. Sets Relative Flag.
ADISP	4	Formats Absolute Result into display area. Sets Absolute Flag.
NUM	5	Build up decimal number into parameter and display it.
XFR	6	Transfer currently displayed number to location pointed to by parameter.
MEASC	7	Measure continuously.
DHLT	8	Display Halt Indication.
NOP	Ø	Do Nothing.

Figure 2   Subroutine Numbering

KEYLABEL	SECONDARY KEYLABEL	KEYCODE (Octal)
Ø		ØØØ
1	REF	ØØ1
2	ULIM	ØØ2
3	LLIM	ØØ3
4	REL	ØØ4
5	ABS	ØØ5
6		ØØ6
7		ØØ7
8		Ø1Ø
9		Ø11
.		Ø12
Xfer		1ØØ
MEAS		2ØØ
CONT		2Ø1
HALT		2Ø2

Figure 3   Keycodes

194

ROM ADDRESS	MNEMONIC	ROM CONTENTS
000	REF	001
001	DISP	001
002	REF	001
003	TAB1	040
004	XFER	100
005	NOP	000
006	–	000
007	TAB2	050
010	MEAS	200
011	MEASS	002
012	–	000
013	TAB3	070
014	REL	004
015	RDISP	003
016	–	000
017	TAB7	130

Figure 4 Part of Parser State Table ROM

A variable in RAM is also required to keep track of the current position in the table.

The parameter mnemonic takes as its octal representation the key number having the same name.

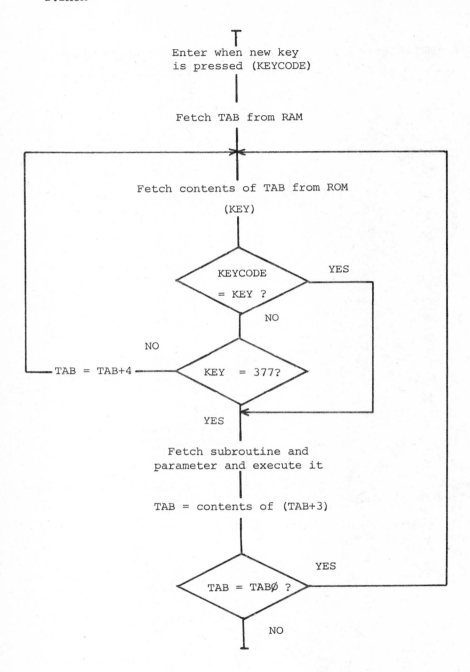

Figure 5 Subroutine to interpret Parser Table

structure which will survive bug-free any number of keyboard redefinitions.

5. NUMBER FORMATS

Most microprocessors have the facility to add or subtract binary numbers one byte at a time. In many applications, for example, in instrumentation, or in machines like point of sale terminals, a single byte is inadequate to represent the range of numbers to be handled.

The simplest way to handle larger numbers is to remain within the binary system and to use the carry or borrow flag also provided in most microprocessors to link together the several bytes needed to represent the required range of numbers.

The 'add with carry' or 'subtract with borrow' instructions of just about all microprocessors are used to add or subtract individual bytes and the carry/borrow flag will then be set up ready for the next byte.

Typically, the successive bytes of a number are stored in consecutive memory locations so the routine for adding or sub-tracting one pair of bytes would also increment a pointer to the next bytes.

Now, while microprocessors understand binary numbers perfectly well the average human operator is usually much happier when dealing with decimal numbers. If a result has to be dis-played after a lot of calculation then a decision has to be made whether to perform all the arithmetic in binary and to do a binary to decimal conversion at the end or whether to perform all of the arithmetic in decimal in the first place.

A feature found on some microprocessors like the Intel 8080 and the Motorola 6800 is the decimal adjust instruction which makes life much easier if decimal arithmetic is used throughout.

If two BCD digits are packed into an 8 bit word then after adding another pair using the normal binary add instruction, a decimal adjust instruction will convert the result back to BCD again, taking account of any carry from the right hand half of the byte to the left hand half. This feature certainly helps when doing decimal arithmetic but even when it is absent then decimal arithmetic is not too bad if a single BCD digit is stored in each byte. If it is stored in the left hand half of the byte then the conversion required after each binary add is to add 6 if the result is greater than 9. This will convert the result to BCD form again and also set the carry flag. This can be

D.DACK

inspected as the next bytes are added.

An interesting way of storing decimal numbers is used by
Motorola in their MPL high level language.   Each decimal digit
is again allocated one byte but it is coded in ASCll form rather
than BCD.   To add numbers now requires a subroutine with new
rules of arithmetic but since the ASCll version of a digit is
obtained from its BCD equivalent simply by adding 60 (octal) then
the rules are really no more complicated than those above and if,
as is often the case in instrumentation, a great deal of input and
output is involved then the ready availability of the ASCll
version of numbers is very helpful.

Perhaps if a lot of seven segment display is involved then
all digits could be coded in their seven segment form with one
bit per segment.   The arithmetic rules would be rather devious
but the digits could be driven directly without the need of a
seven segment decoder!

6.   MULTIPLICATION BY A CONSTANT

When numerical programs are run using a high level language
on a large computer then the program writer is unconcerned when
he multiplies A by B about the precise nature of A and B.   They
may both be random numbers, changing throughout the program, in
which case a general purpose multiplication routine will be
necessary.   On the other hand one of them may be a constant
which is unchanged throughout the program.   In this latter case
a quite different technique might be useful especially if the
same constant occurs several times in the program.

Of course a good high level language on a large computer will
recognise repeated constants during the compilation process and
will, for example, make sure that the constant is only stored
once, but it is unlikely that any further savings through special
software would be worthwhile on a general purpose machine.

In the world of microprocessors however it is often very
important to save memory space and processing time and often the
job to be done is very specialised.   In this environment
considerable savings can be made by a suitable choice of number
formats and algorithms.

A simple example is if numbers are stored in binary form and a
multiplication (or division) by a power of two is required.
Obviously this corresponds to a shift of the binary number by an
appropriate number of bits.

198

AN INSTRUMENT DESIGN PROBLEM

If a desired constant is close to a power of two then it would probably be worth investigating to see if the errors would be tolerable if the nearest power of two were used instead. In some cases, like the logarithm algorithm described below, then the entire process is designed to make use of the fact that division by a power of two is quick and cheap. Even if a simple power of two shift is not possible then there are better ways of multiplying by a constant than by involving a standard subroutine with a constant as one of the parameters.

What we do is to make use of the fact that a binary number usually has a lot of zeroes in it. As a first guess we might say that about half of the bits would be zeroes. Now the process of multiplying by this number is one of adding and shifting and the adding is only done for these locations containing a one bit. To make use of these facts we write a special purpose routine which will multiply a general number by our specific constant and no other. The constant is in effect stored as a specific pattern of program steps consisting of shifts and adds. Since on average we expect only about half of the bits of our constant to be ones then we will only have to code about half the number of adds that a general purpose routine would implement (half the time it would be adding zeroes, something which we do not do). The result of course would be a faster executing algorithm. An example is given in Fig.6.

The following subroutine will multiply the general number A by the constant 10110001.

At each shift the number A is truncated to its original number of bits so that the result will be truncated.

> Result = A
>
> Shift Result four places right
>
> Result = Result + A
>
> Shift Result one place right
>
> Result = Result + A
>
> Shift Result two places right
>
> Result = Result + A

Figure 6   A special constant multiplying routine

D.DACK

The above example only considered positive constants; when
negative numbers are considered then even more interesting
savings can be made.   Figure 7 lists all the numbers possible
using 4 bits in two's complement notation.   As expected, only
half of the bits are ones so a multiplication by a random
selection from these constants would involve only about half of
the adds of a more general routine.   Figure 7 also shows however
the same constants represented in a different form.   Here the
allowable bits are zero, one and minus one.   There is no problem
involved in storing the minus one digit since it just represents
a subtraction instead of an addition in the program and most
microprocessors will handle subtraction without any problem.

2's COMPLEMENT NUMBERS	COMPACT FORM NUMBERS	DECIMAL EQUIVALENT
0000	0 0 0 0	0
0001	0 0 0+1	1
0010	0 0+1 0	2
0011	0 0+1+1	3
0100	0+1 0 0	4
0101	0+1 0+1	5
0110	0+1+1 0	6
0111	+1 0 0-1	7
1000	-1 0 0 0	-8
1001	-1 0 0+1	-7
1010	0-1-1 0	-6
1011	0-1 0-1	-5
1100	0-1 0 0	-4
1101	0 0-1-1	-3
1110	0 0-1 0	-2
1111	0 0 0-1	-1
———	———	
32 ones	23 ones	

A four bit constant would require on average 1.4 times as
many ones to represent it as in the compact form.

Figure 7   An alternative to 2's complement notation
for constants

200

AN INSTRUMENT DESIGN PROBLEM

The interesting point here is that only 23 ones are required to represent the full range of numbers instead of 32, a ratio of nearly 1.4:1 against the two's complement form. It appears that as larger constants are considered, this factor rapidly approaches $\sqrt{2}$. A proof or otherwise of this is left to the reader! Suffice it to say that very significant speed advantages can be gained by looking carefully at the numbers we are dealing with and by being prepared to write special routines. This is really another example where speed and ROM space can be traded off against one another.

7. LOGARITHMS

A very frequent requirement in instrumentation is to display a result in decibels or dB's. All telecommunications test equipment must work in dB's and in the control world the characteristics of control loops are also required in dB's.

It is also very common for a result to represent the average of a series of readings rather than the instantaneous value of a signal. An example here is a simple power meter where the average power over a number of cycles of the input waveform is required rather than the rapidly changing instantaneous power.

Of course, analogue techniques for averaging, which is simply another way of looking at filtering, have been developed over many years. A good method of providing an average reading on an analogue instrument would be to stick a large capacitor across the moving coil meter while a logarithmic reading can be obtained by using a diode as the feedback element in an operational amplifier.

The first point to note here though is that the average of a logarithm is not the same as the logarithm of an average which is what we really want. In this case then the averaging must be done first, followed by a logarithmic amplifier. Even in analogue instruments however a digital readout is frequently required so an analogue to digital converter must follow the log amplifier.

At this point, we may be led to think that since we need an ADC anyway then why not use it to sample the signal rather earlier in the instrument and dispense with the log amplifier with its temperature drifts and trim pots.

This is a good approach if a fast enough, and cheap enough, ADC can be found and if more importantly the working out of the logarithms can be done quickly enough.

D.DACK

Very often the time over which the averaging has to be done is
specified by the requirements of the rest of the instrument,
particularly by the bandwidths of any preceding filters since for
a given error the smaller the bandwidth the longer the required
averaging time.

Let us say then that we need to compute in dB's the average of
a signal over one second.   An obvious attempt would be simply to
sample the signal with an Analogue to Digital Converter at a rate
greater than twice the highest frequency component of the signal
and to add them up over the one second period.   Having obtained
the sum and having divided by the number of samples (carefully
choosing the number of samples to be a power of two) then we
proceed to evaluate the logarithms by evaluating the power series
for log (1 + X).

$$\log (1 + X) = X - \frac{X^2}{2} + \frac{X^3}{3} - \frac{X^4}{4} \quad \text{etc.}$$

After all, most large computers use power series evaluations and
what is good enough for them should be good enough for us.

We may soon be daunted, however, by the number of multiplications required.   There are no multiplications by constants since
X is an unknown number, and the divisions are not all by powers of
two.

It would very likely take longer to evaluate the log than the
preceding one second averaging time when the microprocessor was
doing nothing more than adding numbers together.   There is
clearly something wrong here and a new approach is required.   It
would be desirable to minimise the log time which follows the
compulsory one second averaging so the time has come to apply
some lateral thinking and to reduce the log time to zero.

To see how this is possible consider the value of the average
result as it is built up during the one second averaging time.
As Figure 8 shows, for a constant input the result is a straight
line from zero to the final answer.   If the input was not
constant but a varying positive number then a straight line is not
obtained but the result still never decreases.

Now suppose we could arrange that instead of counting up a
straight line as in Figure 8, we could count up a logarithmic
curve, the output at the end of our averaging period would then
automatically represent the logarithm of the average: just what
we want.   By making the processor work a little harder in the
averaging period instead of just adding, then we can obtain our
dB answer immediately the compulsory averaging period is over.

To describe the algorithm for logarithmic counting in more
detail it is necessary to be more specific.   Let us assume that

AN INSTRUMENT DESIGN PROBLEM

a 0.1 dB resolution is required over a 30 dB range. This means that if a counter were to be implemented in software to represent the final result then every time the input increased by 0.1 dB the counter would be incremented.

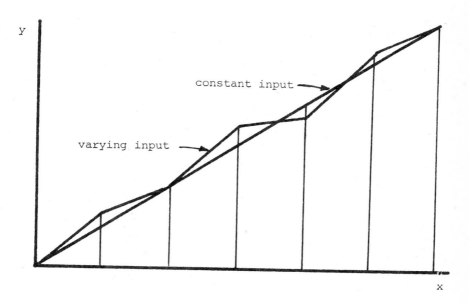

Figure 8. Averaging by counting linearly

As Figure 9 shows if a fixed X increment is used then the corresponding Y increment changes dramatically. Since, however, our instrument specification demands a fixed Y resolution then it is more sensible to start with this as in Figure 10 and to accept the necessity of calculating the corresponding X increment at various points on the curve.

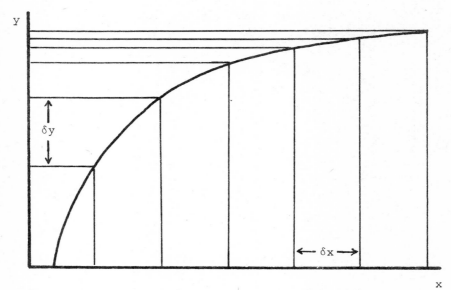

<u>Figure 9</u>. Averaging by counting logarithmically
Note how with a fixed x increment the
y resolution varies dramatically

As Figure 10 shows, the inputs required to generate this 0.1 dB increment get larger as the signal climbs up the logarithmic curve. It so happens that at each point on the curve corresponding to a further 0.1 dB increment then the input change required before we take the next 0.1 dB increment can easily be calculated.

With reference to Figure 10:

$$Y = 20 \log X$$ describes a particular point on the curve

so $$y + \delta y = 20 \log (X + \delta x)$$ describes the next point

$$= 20 \log x (1 + \frac{\delta x}{x})$$

so $$\delta y = 20 \log (1 + \frac{\delta x}{x})$$

now if δy is to be constant then $1 + \frac{\delta x}{x}$ must be constant

so $\frac{\delta x}{x}$ must be constant.

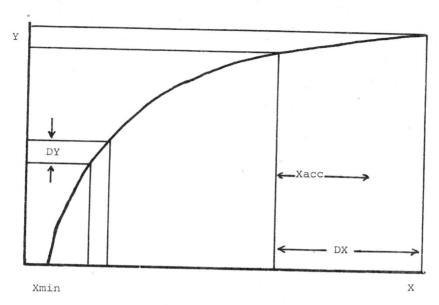

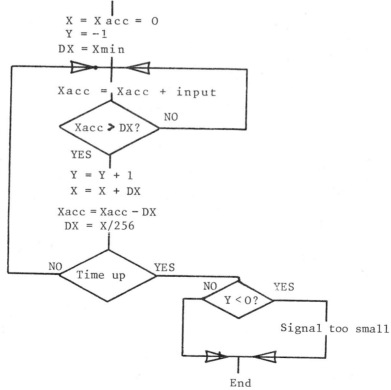

Figure 10   A logarithmic algorithm.

To achieve a δy of 0.1 dB or better, then $\frac{\delta x}{x}$ must be less than $\frac{1}{86}$. By choosing $\frac{\delta x}{x}$ to be $\frac{1}{256}$ then $\delta y = .0339$ dB and we will have achieved the specification with only a division of a power of two to deal with.

The algorithm is now very simple. Instead of incrementing the result counter by every input as we would when simply averaging, we work out (by shifting) the x input which must be accumulated before we are allowed to increment y. When this x input has been achieved we increment y and calculate the new x increment. After the one second period the Y counter contains the number of .0339 dB increments which must be accumulated to represent the result. This can either be done by accumulating .0339 dB Y times or by writing a special constant multiplying routine to multiply Y by .0339 as explained above.

We now have to consider how many samples need to be taken if the input were to be say a sine wave. If the power of the sine wave were A and only one sample were taken, then the result could lie anywhere between zero and 2A, depending on what part of the sine wave were sampled.

The central limit theorem, however, tells us that the variance in the result of an average of N samples is reduced by a factor of $\sqrt{N}$ (Jenkins & Watts, 1968).

If the error caused by taking insufficient samples is also to be less than 0.1 dB then

$$0.1 \;<\; 20 \log_{10} (1 + 1/\sqrt{N})$$

so N > 7458

It would be convenient to choose N to be a power of two so 8192 will be chosen.

A seven bit analogue to digital converter will be sufficient for the resolution contemplated so the maximum X value which will be accumulated will be 8192 x 128, i.e. 1048576. Since a 30 dB operating range is specified then the minimum value for X below which no results will be given is 33158.

All the relevant operating parameters have now been decided upon so it only remains to write the program to do the job.

With any numerical algorithm like this there is always the problem that if it does not work then it can be difficult to decide whether the basic algorithm is at fault or whether there is a mistake in the program writing.

AN INSTRUMENT DESIGN PROBLEM

If a general purpose minicomputer or programmable calculator is available then it is a very good idea to try out the algorithm first in a high level language before attempting any conversion to the microprocessor assembly language. Figure 11 shows a program written in ALGOL to perform this algorithm together with some results. As can be seen the specification is completely met, and so the basic algorithm and its design parameters can be trusted.

Now the maximum number to be expected during the course of the algorithm can be comfortably handled by a twenty-four bit word so arithmetic routines can be written using three byte binary numbers.

```
HPAL,L,"DEBE1"
BEGIN COMMENT THIS PROGRAM EVALUATES THE LOGARITHM OF AN INPUT
BY COUNTING UP A LOGARITHMIC CURVE FOR A FIXED NUMBER OF
SAMPLES OF THE INPUT;
INTEGER SAMPLENUMBER,SAMPLETOTAL,Y,INPUTX,TERMINAL:=7;
REAL X,DX,DXACC,XMIN,YINCREMENT;
& WRITE "?" AND READ THE INPUT
WRITE(TERMINAL,#("?"));
READ(TERMINAL,*,INPUTX);
& INITIALISE SAMPLETOTAL,YINCREMENT AND XMIN
SAMPLETOTAL:=8192;
YINCREMENT:=.0339;
XMIN:=33158;
& THIS IS WHERE THE STORY REALLY STARTS
DX:=XMIN;
X:=DXACC:=SAMPLENUMBER:=0;
Y:=-1;
WHILE SAMPLENUMBER<=SAMPLETOTAL DO
        BEGIN SAMPLENUMBER:=SAMPLENUMBER+1;
        DXACC:=DXACC+INPUTX;
        IF DXACC>=DX THEN
                BEGIN DXACC:=DXACC-DX;
                X:=X+DX;
                DX:=X/256;
                Y:=Y+1;
                END;
        END;
IF Y<0 THEN WRITE(TERMINAL,#(I3," INPUT TOO LOW"),INPUTX)
ELSE WRITE(TERMINAL,#(I3,2X,F5.1," DB"),INPUTX,Y*YINCREMENT);
END;
```

INPUT	RESULT
128	30.0 DB
64	24.0 DB
32	18.0 DB
16	11.9 DB
8	5.9 DB
4	INPUT TOO LOW

Figure 11   An ALGOL program to test the logarithmic algorithm

207

The final result, however, would be of more use if expressed in BCD, so a special constant multiplying routine can be written to multiply YINCREMENT by Y with YINCREMENT being stored as a BCD number and Y of course being binary.

If a high level compiler is available then the time and frustration saved by its use should more than compensate for any inefficiency in code generation. If such a compiler is not available then it will still be found very helpful to write the program first in pseudo ALGOL, obeying structured programming constructs.. The translation into assembly code then becomes more of a mechanical task which can be done without the distraction of worrying about the correctness of the algorithm.

It is obvious that the above technique would be useless in a general purpose computer to evaluate the logarithm of a wide range of numbers. In the special case of a power meter, however, it can make very good use of the dead time when the instrument has to average the signal.

8. SUMMARY

It would be impossible to completely describe all the thought processes and actions which go into the design of a microprocessor based instrument. What has been done though is to highlight some of the new areas in which the digital designer will find himself working.

The actual putting together of the processor chips will not differ very much from the putting together of LSI logic but that is the start rather than the end of the problem. When the software is contemplated it is soon realised that whereas hardware design is in many ways becoming easier, programming is just as difficult as ever it was. The widespread acceptance of Structured Programming techniques has brought some relief but at first sight it might not offer much consolation to the beginner at micro-processing, armed only with an assembler. Even the experienced programmer may be daunted when stripped of his high level languages and libraries of arithmetic subroutines.

Perhaps the best attitude to take is to realise that it has all been done before. High level languages are coming to micro-processors just as they did to minicomputers.

The keyboard parsing techniques discussed earlier are just a simple example of list processing in action, and computer science texts are full of numerical techniques which have just as much value in the microprocessor world as in other areas of computing.

9. APPENDIX

An implementation of a keyboard and display system of the type described earlier is given below to indicate the practical realisation of this part of a typical microprocessor application.

The keyboard matrix, alpha numeric display lights, and their interconnection to the input and output ports of a microprocessor are shown in Fig.12. The program listing is also given, and the comments within the listing should be sufficient to be self-explanatory. The design has been implemented and tested on an INtel S 1M 8 system.

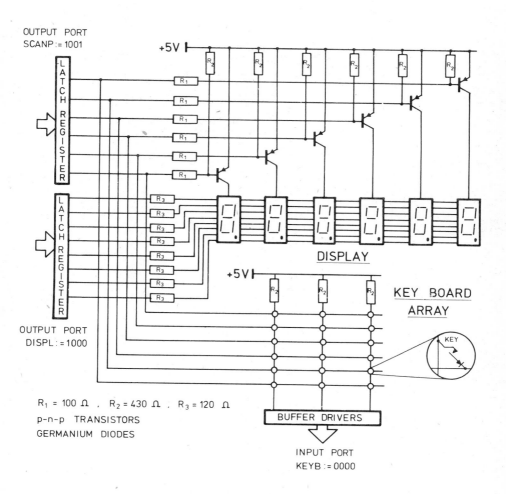

$R_1 = 100 \ \Omega$, $R_2 = 430 \ \Omega$, $R_3 = 120 \ \Omega$

p-n-p TRANSISTORS
GERMANIUM DIODES

Figure 12   Keyboard and Display System

```
  1                              CRG 000      SET ORIGIN TO ADDRESS 0 OF ROMO
  2                        ***************************************************
  3                        * THIS PROGRAM REPRESENTS THE KEYBOARD AND DISPLAY*
  4                        * HANDLING ROUTINES OF A SIMPLE KEYBOARD          *
  5                        * CONTROLLED INSTRUMENT.                          *
  6                        * IT CONTAINS A TABLE WHICH DEFINES EXACTLY THE   *
  7                        * RESPONSES TO ALL POSSIBLE KEYBOARD SEQUENCES    *
  8                        * AND PROVIDES LINKAGES TO APPROPRIATE ACTION     *
  9                        * ROUTINES.                                       *
 10                        * THE PROGRAM IS CONTAINED ON TWO 256 BYTE ROMS   *
 11                        * AND LINKAGES HAVE BEEN ARRANGED TO ENABLE THE   *
 12                        * PROGRAMS TO BE ASSEMBLED SEPARATELY.            *
 13                        ***************************************************
 14              TABPG ECU 000       THE KEYBOARD TABLE IS ON PAGE 0
 15              DISPG ECU 010       PAGE 10 IS RAM
 16              DISAD ECU 000       RAM DISPLAY AREA STARTS AT 0
 17              BCD   ECU 017       MASK FOR 4 LEAST SIG BITS
 18              SCANP ECU 011       COLUMN PULL DOWN IS PORT 011
 19              KEYBD ECU 000       KEYBOARD INPUT IS PORT 000
 20              DISPL ECU 010       SEGMENTS OUTPUT ON PORT 010
 21              TAB   ECU 031       CONTAINS THE TABLE POINTER
 22                        * WARNING ABSOLUTE ADDRESS CHANGE AT YOUR PERIL
 23              SUBS  ECU 400       LINKAGE TO SUBS ON PAGE 1
 24              RYCDE ECU 033       CURRENT KEYCODE STORED HERE
 25                        *WARNING ABSOLUTE ADDRESS CHANGE AT YOUR PERIL
 26              WAIT  ECU 447       LINKAGE TO WAIT ON PAGE 1
 27                        * HANG ABOUT UNTIL KEY IS RELEASED
 28                        * THIS PREVENTS A KEY BEING READ TWICE
 29                        * SET TAB TO TAB7
 30 00 000 056 010                  LHI DISPG    POINT TO
 31 00 002 066 031                  LLI TAB      TABLE POINTER
 32 00 004 076 130                  LMI 130      SET TAB TO TAB7
 33 00 006 101        KEYDN INP KEYBD      READ KEYBOARD
 34 00 007 054 377                  XRI 377      COMPLEMENT RESULT
 35 00 011 110 006 000              JFZ KEYDN    JUMP IF KEY DOWN
 36                        * START KEY AND DISPLAY SCAN
 37                        * THE KEYBOARD AND DISPLAY ARE SCANNED TOGETHER
 38                        * FROM LEFT TO RIGHT. AS EACH COLUMN IS PULLED
 39                        * DOWN BY OUTPUT E,A UNIQUE VALUE IS IN D
 40                        * THIS IS ADDED TO THE INPUT PORT VALUE TO DEFINE
 41                        * A CODE FOR EVERY KEY.
 42 00 014 066 000        STSCN LLI DISAD      POINT TO
 43 00 016 056 010                  LHI DISPG    DISPLAY AREA
 44 00 020 046 040                  LEI 040      SET BIT 5 OF E
 45 00 022 036 024                  LDI 024      INITIALISE D
 46                        * CONTINUE KEY AND DISPLAY SCAN
 47 00 024 307        CTSCN LAM            FETCH CONTENTS OF DISPLAY AREA
 48 00 025 121                  OUT DISPL    AND OUTPUT TO LED SEGMENTS
 49 00 026 304                  LAE          OUTPUT SCAN PULL DOWN
 50 00 027 123                  OUT SCANP    
 51 00 030 106 047 001              CAL WAIT     TO PREVENT DISPLAY SPILLOVER
 52 00 033 101                  INP 000      INPUT KEY ROW
 53 00 034 054 377                  XRI 377
 54 00 036 110 057 000              JFZ KEYPR    JUMP IF KEY PRESSED
 55 00 041 060                  INL          POINT TO NEXT DISPLAY LOCATION
 56 00 042 304                  LAE          SET UP NEXT
 57 00 043 032                  RAR          COLUMN TO BE
 58 00 044 340                  LEA          PULLED DOWN
 59 00 045 031                  DCD          SET UP
 60 00 046 031                  DCD          NEXT
 61 00 047 031                  DCD          COLUMN
 62 00 050 031                  DCD          CODE
```

```
63  00 051 140 014 000          JTC STSCN   JUMP IF SCAN COMPLETE
64  00 054 104 024 000          JMP CTSCN   JUMP IF SCAN NOT COMPLETE
65                       * CONVERT KEY ROW CODE INTO TWO BIT CODE
66  00 057 074 004      KEYPR CPI 004
67  00 061 110 066 000        JFZ KEY1
68  00 064 006 003            LAI 003
69  00 066 203        KEY1  ADD           ADD KEY ROW CODE
70                     *CONVERT KEYCODE
71                     * THIS SECTION USES A TABLE STRUCTURE TO
72                     * ARBITRARILY ASSIGN MORE USEFUL CODES TO KEYS
73                     * THAN THOSE DICTATED BY THE HARDWARE.
74                     * FOR EXAMPLE THE DIGIT KEYS ARE GIVEN BCD CODES
75                     * AT ANY TIME THE KEYS COULD BE RECODED JUST BY
76                     * CHANGING THE TABLE
77  00 067 056 000            LHI TABPG   POINT TO TABLE PAGE
78  00 071 004 211            ADI CONV    ADD TABLE BASE TO KEYCODE
79  00 073 360                LLA
80  00 074 307                LAM         FETCH NEW KEYCODE
81  00 075 056 010            LHI DISPG   AND STORE IT
82  00 077 066 033            LLI KYCDE   IN KYCDE
83  00 101 370                LMA
84  00 102 320                LCA         SAVE KEYCODE TEMPORARILY IN C
85                     * DISPLAY KEYCODE WHILE KEY DOWN
86                     * THIS IS AN EXTREMELY USEFUL DEBUGGING AID
87  00 103 121        KYDN  OUT DISPL
88  00 104 101                INP 000     WAIT UNTIL
89  00 105 054 377            XRI 377     KEY IS RELEASED
90  00 107 302                LAC         RELOAD A WITH KEYCODE
91  00 110 110 103 000        JFZ KYDN    JUMP IF KEY IS DOWN
92                     * THIS SECTION SCANS THE TABLE FOR A MATCH
93                     * WITH THE KEYCODE
94  00 113 066 031            LLI TAB
95  00 115 307                LAM         A HOLDS RELATIVE TABLE POSITION
96  00 116 056 010      SRCH  LHI DISPG
97  00 120 066 033            LLI KYCDE
98  00 122 327                LCM         C HOLDS THE KEYCODE
99  00 123 004 241            ADI TAB0    A HOLDS CURRENT TABLE ADDRESS
100 00 125 056 000            LHI TABPG   POINT BACK TO TABLE PAGE
101 00 127 360                LLA         L HOLDS ADDRESS OF KEY IN TABLE
102 00 130 317        SRCH1 LBM         B CONTAINS KEY FROM TABLE
103 00 131 010                INB
104 00 132 150 157 000        JTZ MATCH   IF ALL ONES ENCOUNTERED IN TABLE
105 00 135 302                LAC         A HOLDS KEYBOARD CODE
106 00 136 277                CPM         COMPARE IT WITH TABLE KEY
107 00 137 150 157 000        JTZ MATCH   JUMP IF MATCH FOUND
108 00 142 044 300            NDI 300     LOOK
109 00 144 277                CPM         FOR  DIGIT
110 00 145 150 157 000        JTZ MATCH   IF DIGIT
111 00 150 060                INL         MOVE TO
112 00 151 060                INL         NEXT KEY
113 00 152 060                INL         IN TABLE
114 00 153 060                INL
115 00 154 104 130 000        JMP SRCH1   SINCE NO MATCH WAS FOUND
116 00 157 060        MATCH INL           L-> SUBROUTINE
117 00 160 307                LAM         A HOLDS SUBROUTINE NUMBER
118 00 161 060                INL         L->PARAMETER
119 00 162 317                LBM         B HOLDS PARAMETER
120 00 163 060                INL         L-> NEXT TABLE POSITION
121 00 164 327                LCM         C HOLDS NEXT TABLE POSITION
122 00 165 056 010            LHI DISPG   UPDATE
123 00 167 066 031            LLI TAB     TAB
124 00 171 372                LMC
```

```
125                                 * FIND AND EXECUTE APPROPRIATE SUBROUTINE
126  00 172 106 000 001                 CAL SUBS
127                                 * JMP TO SRCH IF TAB=TAB0
128  00 175 056 010                      LHI DISPG
129  00 177 066 031                      LLI TAB
130  00 201 250                          XRA          THIS PECULIAR METHOD OF LOADING A
131  00 202 207                          ADM          FROM MEMORY ENSURES THAT THE 8008
132  00 203 150 116 000                  JTZ SRCH     FLAGS ARE SET
133  00 206 104 006 000                  JMP KEYEN    TO CONTINUE SCAN
134                                 * TABLE FOR CONVERTING KEYCODES
135  00 211 000                 CONV  DEF 000
136                                 *        NEWCODE   OLDCODE  LABEL
137  00 212 202                          DEF 202       1        HALT
138  00 213 201                          DEF 201       2        CONT
139  00 214 200                          DEF 200       3        MEAS
140  00 215 000                          DEF 000       NOKEY
141  00 216 202                          DEF 202       5
142  00 217 202                          DEF 202       6
143  00 220 100                          DEF 100       7        XFR
144  00 221 000                          DEF 000       NOKEY
145  00 222 012                          DEF 012       11       .
146  00 223 000                          DEF 000       12       0
147  00 224 202                          DEF 202       13
148  00 225 000                          DEF 000       NOKEY
149  00 226 003                          DEF 003       15       3,LLIM
150  00 227 006                          DEF 006       16       6
151  00 230 011                          DEF 011       17       9
152  00 231 000                          DEF 000       NOKEY
153  00 232 002                          DEF 002       21       2,UL
154  00 233 005                          DEF 005       22       5,AES
155  00 234 010                          DEF 010       23       8
156  00 235 000                          DEF 000       NOKEY
157  00 236 001                          DEF 001       25       1,FEF
158  00 237 004                          DEF 004       26       4,REL
159  00 240 007                          DEF 007       27       7
160                                 * TABLE TO DEFINE THE INSTRUMENT RESPONSE TO KEY
161                                 * SEQUENCES.
162                                 * SINCE THE TABLE CONTENTS FOR THE NEXT TAB VALUES
163                                 * ARE RELATIVE TO TAB0 IT MAY BE ASSEMBLED ANYWHERE
164                                 * IN ROM.
165  00 241 001                 TAB0  DEF 001          FEF
166  00 242 001                       DEF 001          DISP
167  00 243 010                       DEF 010          FEF
168  00 244 040                       DEF 040          TAB1
169  00 245 100                       DEF 100          XFR
170  00 246 000                       DEF 000          NOP
171  00 247 000                       DEF 000
172  00 250 050                       DEF 050          TAB2
173  00 251 200                       DEF 200          MEAS
174  00 252 002                       DEF 002          MEASS
175  00 253 000                       DEF 000
176  00 254 070                       DEF 070          TAB3
177  00 255 004                       DEF 004          REL
178  00 256 003                       DEF 003          RDISP
179  00 257 000                       DEF 000
180  00 260 130                       DEF 130          TAB7
181  00 261 005                       DEF 005          ABS
182  00 262 004                       DEF 004          ADISP
183  00 263 000                       DEF 000
184  00 264 130                       DEF 130          TAB7
185  00 265 002                       DEF 002          ULIM
186  00 266 001                       DEF 001          DISP
```

1o7	00	267	014		DEF	014	ULIM
188	00	270	100		DEF	100	TAB4
1o9	00	271	003		DEF	003	LLIM
190	00	272	001		DEF	001	DISP
191	00	273	020		DEF	020	LLIM
192	00	274	110		DEF	110	TAB5
193	00	275	337		DEF	337	ANYKEY
194	00	276	000		DEF	000	NOP -
195	00	277	000		DEF	000	
196	00	300	130		DEF	130	TAB7
197	00	301	000	TAB1	DEF	000	DIGITS
198	00	302	005		DEF	005	NUM
199	00	303	010		DEF	010	REF
200	00	304	040		DEF	040	TAB1
201	00	305	377		DEF	377	ANYKEY
202	00	306	000		DEF	000	NOP.
203	00	307	000		DEF	000	
204	00	310	000		DEF	000	TAB0
205	00	311	002	TAB2	DEF	002	ULIM
2o6	00	312	006		DEF	006	XFR
207	00	313	014		DEF	014	ULIM
2o8	00	314	130		DEF	130	TAB7
209	00	315	003		DEF	003	LLIM
210	00	316	006		DEF	006	XFR
211	00	317	020		DEF	020	LLIM
212	00	320	130		DEF	130	TAB7
213	00	321	001		DEF	001	REF
214	00	322	006		DEF	006	XFR
215	00	323	010		DEF	010	REF
216	00	324	130		DEF	130	TAB7
217	00	325	377		DEF	377	ANYKEY
218	00	326	000		DEF	000	NOP
219	00	327	000		DEF	000	
220	00	330	000		DEF	000	TAB0
221	00	331	201	TAB3	DEF	201	CUNT
222	00	332	007		DEF	007	MEASC
223	00	333	000		DEF	000	
224	00	334	120		DEF	120	TAB6
225	00	335	377		DEF	377	ANYKEY
22o	00	336	000		DEF	000	NOP
227	00	337	000		DEF	000	
22o	00	340	000		DEF	000	TAB0
229	00	341	000	TAB4	DEF	000	DIGITS
230	00	342	005		DEF	005	NUM
231	00	343	014		DEF	014	ULIM
232	00	344	100		DEF	100	TAB4
233	00	345	377		DEF	377	ANYKEY
234	00	346	000		DEF	000	NOP .
235	00	347	000		DEF	000	
236	00	350	000		DEF	000	TAB0
237	00	351	000	TAB5	DEF	000	DIGITS
238	00	352	005		DEF	005	NUM
239	00	353	020		DEF	020	LLIM
240	00	354	110		DEF	110	TAB5
241	00	355	377		DEF	377	ANYKEY
242	00	356	000		DEF	000	NOP
243	00	357	000		DEF	000	
244	00	360	000		DEF	000	TAB0
245	00	361	202	TAB6	DEF	202	HALT
246	00	362	010		DEF	010	DHALT
247	00	363	000		DEF	000	
248	00	364	130		DEF	130	TAB7

```
249 00 365 377              DEF 377      ANYKEY
250 00 366 000              DEF 000      NOP
251 00 367 000              DEF 000
252 00 370 000              DEF 000      TAB0
253 00 371 377     TAB7     DEF 377      ANYKEY
254 00 372 000              DEF 000      NOP
255 00 373 000              DEF 000
256 00 374 000              DEF 000      TAB0
257                         END
  1                         ORG 400      SET ORIGIN TO PAGE 1
  2                BCD     EQU 017
  3                CFLG    EQU 032
  4                DISPG   EQU 010
  5                DISAD   EQU 000
  6                KYCDE   EQU 033
  7                DPFLG   EQU 034
  8                DPNT    EQU 012
  9                DNUM    EQU 035
 10      * SUBS MUST BE THE FIRST LOCATION ON PAGE 1
 11      * SINCE PAGE 0 EXPECTS IT
 12 01 000 044 017  SUBS   NEI BCD        THIS SETS 8008 FLAGS
 13 01 002 150 056 001     JTZ SUB0    IF SUB CODE WERE 0
 14 01 005 330             LDA
 15 01 006 031             DCD
 16 01 007 150 064 001     JTZ DISP    IF SUB CODE WERE 1
 17 01 012 031             DCD
 18 01 013 150 057 001     JTZ SUB2    IF SUB CODE WERE 2
 19 01 016 031             DCD
 20 01 017 150 060 001     JTZ SUB3    IF SUB CODE WERE 3
 21 01 022 031             DCD
 22 01 023 150 061 001     JTZ SUB4    IF SUB CODE WERE 4
 23 01 026 031             DCD
 24 01 027 150 226 001     JTZ NUM     IF SUB CODE WERE 5
 25 01 032 031             DCD
 26 01 033 150 332 001     JTZ XFER    IF SUB CODE WERE 6
 27 01 036 031             DCD
 28 01 037 150 062 001     JTZ SUB7    IF SUB CODE WERE 7
 29 01 042 031             DCD
 30 01 043 150 063 001     JTZ SUB8    IF SUB CODE WERE 8
 31 01 046 007             RET         IF SUB NOT FOUND
 32 01 047 016 260  WAIT   LBI 260
 33 01 051 010      WAIT1  INB
 34 01 052 110 051 001     JFZ WAIT1
 35 01 055 007             RET
 36      * THE FOLLOWING STATEMENTS ARE DUMMY SUBROUTINES
 37      * DO NOTHING SINCE THIS SOFTWARE IS UNCOMPLETE
 38      * AS EACH NEW SUBROUTINE IS WRITTEN IT IS CALLED IN
 39      * THE ABOVE SECTION AND ITS DUMMY IS DELETED HERE
 40 01 056 007      SUB0   RET
 41 01 057 007      SUB2   RET
 42 01 060 007      SUB3   RET
 43 01 061 007      SUB4   RET
 44 01 062 007      SUB7   RET
 45 01 063 007      SUB8   RET
 46      * SUBROUTINE DISP
 47      * TAKES NUMBER FROM PARAMETER LOCATION AND CONVERTS
 48      * SEVEN SEGMENT FORM. PUTS RESULT IN  DISPLAY AREA
 49      * B HOLDS LOCATION OF NUMBER
 50      * E HOLDS ADDRESS OF DISPLAY AREA
 51      * C COUNTS DIGITS
 52      * B HOLDS BCD CHARACTER
 53      * A HOLDS 7 SEGMENT VERSION OF B
```

```
54                         * CFLG IS A FLAG INDICATING THAT THE NEXT
55                         * IF ANY IS THE START OF A NEW NUMBER
56                         * DPFLG REMEMBERS THAT THE DEC.POINT WAS PRESSED
57                         * SET CFLG,CLEAR DPFLG
58 01 064 056 010   DISP  LHI DISPG
59 01 066 066 032         LLI CFLG
60 01 070 076 001         LMI 001
61 01 072 066 034         LLI DPFLG
62 01 074 076 000         LMI 000
63                        * REMEMBER SOURCE OF DISPLAYED INFORMATION IN DNUM
64 01 076 066 035         LLI DNUM
65 01 100 371             LMB
66 01 101 361      DIS1   LLB          L -> NUMBER TO BE DISPLAYED
67 01 102 046 000         LEI DISAD    E->DISPLAY AREA
68 01 104 026 004         LCI 004      INITIALISE DIGIT COUNTER
69 01 106 307      DISS   LAM
70 01 107 044 017         NDI BCD      TO SET THE 8008 FLAGS
71 01 111 310             LBA          STORE NUMBER TEMPORARILY IN B
72 01 112 110 117 001     JFZ ONE
73 01 115 006 077         LAI 077          IF ZERO
74 01 117 011      ONE    DCB
75 01 120 110 125 001     JFZ TWO
76 01 123 006 006         LAI 006          IF ONE
77 01 125 011      TWO    DCB
78 01 126 110 133 001     JFZ THREE
79 01 131 006 133         LAI 133          IF TWO
80 01 133 011      THREE  DCB
81 01 134 110 141 001     JFZ FOUR
82 01 137 006 117         LAI 117          IF THREE
83 01 141 011      FOUR   DCB
84 01 142 110 147 001     JFZ FIVE
85 01 145 006 146         LAI 146          IF FOUR
86 01 147 011      FIVE   DCB
87 01 150 110 155 001     JFZ SIX
88 01 153 006 155         LAI 155          IF FIVE
89 01 155 011      SIX    DCB
90 01 156 110 163 001     JFZ SEVEN
91 01 161 006 175         LAI 175          IF SIX
92 01 163 011      SEVEN  DCB
93 01 164 110 171 001     JFZ EIGHT
94 01 167 006 007         LAI 007          IF SEVEN
95 01 171 011      EIGHT  DCB
96 01 172 110 177 001     JFZ NINE
97 01 175 006 177         LAI 177          IF EIGHT
98 01 177 011      NINE   DCB
99 01 200 110 205 001     JFZ DONE
100 01 203 006 147        LAI 147          IF NINE
101 01 205 316     DONE   LBL
102 01 206 364            LLE          POINT TO DESTINATION
103 01 207 370            LMA          STORE 7 SEGMENT CHARACTER
104 01 210 346            LEL          RESTORE DESTINATION ADDRESS
105 01 211 361            LLB          RESTORE SOURCE ADDRESS
106 01 212 060            INL          POINT TO NEXT SOURCE ADDRESS
107 01 213 040            INE          POINT TO NEXT SOURCE ADDRESS
108 01 214 021            DCC
109                      * REPEAT UNTIL C=0
110 01 215 110 106 001    JFZ DISS
111                      * CLEAR REMAINING DISPLAY
112 01 220 250            XRA
113 01 221 364            LLE
114 01 222 370            LMA
115 01 223 060            INL
```

```
116  01 224 370              LMA
117  01 225 007              RET
118                        *
119                        * SUBROUTINE NUM
120                        * ENTER WITH B AS PARAMETER
121                        * BUILDS UP NUMBER IN PARAMETER LOCATION
122                        * ENTER WITH L-> TABLE LOCATION
123                        * IF CFLG≠0 THEN CLEAR NUMBER
124  01 226 056 010   NUM    LHI DISPG
125  01 230 066 032          LLI CFLG
126  01 232 307              LAM
127  01 233 240              NDA                TO SET 8008 FLAGS
128  01 234 150 251 001      JTZ NFLG           IF CFLG NOT SET
129  01 237 250              XRA                OTHERWISE CLEAR CFLG
130  01 240 370              LMA
131  01 241 361              LLB                L-> START OF NUMBER
132  01 242 370              LMA
133  01 243 060              INL                CLEAR
134  01 244 370              LMA                NUMBER
135  01 245 060              INL
136  01 246 370              LMA                IN
137  01 247 060              INL
138  01 250 370              LMA                RAM
139                        * IF KEYCODE=DECIMAL POINT SET DPFLG
140  01 251 066 033   NFLG   LLI KYCDE
141  01 253 307              LAM                FETCH KEYCODE
142  01 254 044 017          NDI BCD
143  01 256 340              LEA                E HOLDS DIGIT
144  01 257 074 012          CPI DPNT
145  01 261 110 273 001      JFZ NODP           JUMP IF NOT DECIMAL POINT
146  01 264 060              INL                SET DPFLG IN
147  01 265 006 001          LAI 1              LOCATION FOLLOWING
148  01 267 370              LMA                KEYCODE
149  01 270 104 326 001      JMP ENUM
150                        * ELSE IF DPFLG IS SET THEN DO FRACTION
151  01 273 066 034   NODP   LLI DPFLG
152  01 275 307              LAM                FETCH DPFLG
153  01 276 240              NDA
154  01 277 150 312 001      JTZ NDPFG          JUMP IF FLAG NOT SET
155  01 302 361              LLB
156  01 303 060              INL                POINT
157  01 304 060              INL                TO FRACTIONAL
158  01 305 060              INL                PART OF NUMBER
159  01 306 374              LME                STORE DIGIT
160  01 307 104 326 001      JMP ENUM
161                        * ELSE DEAL WITH INTEGER PART
162  01 312 361   NDPFG   LLB
163  01 313 060              INL                SHIFT
164  01 314 307              LAM                2ND DIGIT
165  01 315 061              DCL                UP
166  01 316 370              LMA                ONE
167  01 317 060              INL                SHIFT
168  01 320 060              INL                3RD
169  01 321 307              LAM                DIGIT
170  01 322 061              DCL                UP
171  01 323 370              LMA                ONE
172  01 324 060              INL                LOAD NEW
173  01 325 374              LME                3RD DIGIT
174  01 326 106 101 001 ENUM   CAL DIS1        DISPLAY NUMBER
175  01 331 007              RET
176                        * SUBROUTINE XFR
177                        * REPLACES NUMBER IN PARAMETER
```

```
178                          * LOCATION WITH NUMBER IN
179                          * DISPLAY LOCATION
180                          * D IS NUMBER OF BYTES TO BE XFRED
181                          * C IS ADDRESS OF SOURCE
182                          * B IS ADDRESS OF DESTINATION
183                          * A IS USE FOR XFER OF BYTE
184                          *
185 01 332 056 010  XFER  LHI DISPG
186 01 334 066 035        LLI DNUM    FETCH POINTER TO NUMBER DISPLAYED
187 01 336 327            LCM
188 01 337 036 004        LDI 004     SET DIGIT COUNTER
189 01 341 362      XFR1  LLC         L-> SOURCE
190 01 342 307            LAM
191 01 343 361            LLB         L-> DESTINATION
192 01 344 370            LMA
193 01 345 010            INB         POINT TO NEXT DEST
194 01 346 020            INC         POINT TO NEXT SOURCE
195 01 347 031            DCD         COUNT DIGITS
196 01 350 110 341 001    JFZ XFR1
197 01 353 007            RET
198                       END
```

217

V.A.   MICROPROGRAMMABLE PROCESSOR COMPONENTS
                      AND ARCHITECTURES

                        Marco Vanneschi

                Istituto di Scienze dell' Informazione
                    University of Pisa, Italy

1. INTRODUCTION

Since microprogramming was introduced by Wilkes as early as
1951, it has been used in two different ways: as a hardware
design technique to implement the control unit of processors with
fixed instruction sets economically, and as a software technique
to emulate multiple instruction sets and programming languages.
The first way has been the predominant one until LSI technology
reached a stage where the construction of user microprogrammable
systems began to be a cost-effective task. In particular, the
developments of storage technology, table look-up logic and bit-
slice microprocessors have greatly contributed to a sensible
growth of interest in dynamic microprogramming. Moreover, not
only do microprogrammable microprocessors allow us to implement
efficient emulators, but they can be used advantageously as
flexible and powerful elementary components for complex systems.

In this work we shall analyze how, and what, LSI modules fit
to the implementation of dynamically microprogrammable processors,
together with a discussion of their architectural and structural
characteristics. Particular emphasis will be placed on the organization of the control unit and of the data path unit, and on
the architectural choices in the design of microprogrammable mi-
croprocessors.In the final Section we shall propose some modular,
parallel microprogrammable architectures well suited to the utilization of bit-slice microprocessors and other LSI components.

2. BASIC ORGANIZATION OF A PROCESSING UNIT

Two major subsets can be identified within a processing
unit: the Data Path Unit (DPU), or Operation Part, and the
Control Unit (CU), or Control Part. They are interconnected as
shown in Fig. 1. DPU performs a set of elementary (or primitive)
operations and communicates with other system units; for this
purpose it comprises a number of computational resources, such
as functional units, registers, interface buffers and mechanisms,

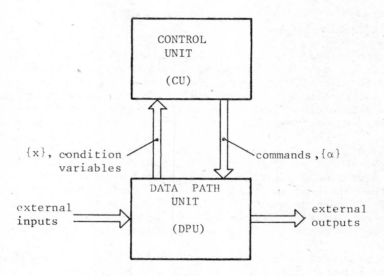

Fig. 1 - Basic organization model of a processing unit.

together with the gating circuitry and links for routing information between them. CU's task is: i) to ensure the correct flow
of information through DPU during the execution of any elementary
operation; this is done by sending a set of signals {α}, called
commands, which activate the proper data paths; ii) to sequence
the elementary operations according to the control algorithm of
the function to be performed; for this purpose, CU needs some
information about the internal state of DPU and it acquires it
through the value of a set of signals {x}, called condition
variables.

As an example, let us consider the portion of a simplified
DPU shown in Fig. 2, where: A is an accumulator register;
LS={R0,...,R7} is a Local Store; IB1, IB2 are input buffers; OB1,
OB2 are output buffers; ALU is a multipurpose arithmetic-logic
functional unit; MUX denotes a multiplexer. {α} signals are sent
to control the information flow through multiplexers, to enable
writing into registers, to specify the ALU operation, to produce
constant and mask values, to address the LS. {x} signals are
generated at the ALU outputs and/or at the outputs of specific
register bits (e.g. A[0]).

The activity of a processing unit, representing the control
algorithm, consists of a sequence of elementary steps, which are
elementary operations and/or tests. A well-defined configuration
of commands and condition variables corresponds to the execution
of every step. Therefore, the CU structure must be implemented in
such a way that the control algorithm is mapped onto it. We intend to show how LSI technology allows an easier, cheaper and
natural way of implementing the CU structure. For this purpose, it
is essential to remember that CU is a synchronous sequential circuit
in principle (see Fig. 3): besides the control register CR (i.e.
the set of internal state flip-flops), a complex combinatorial
network has to be implemented. Since the advent of LSI technology,
microprocessors and storage modules have received the greatest
attention from the manufacturers. The situation with logic circuits
is not as positive as with these modules, due to their specialized
nature. A solution to the implementation of logic circuits by
means of LSI technology might consist in the utilization of
storage modules. Although this idea is not new, it is of actual
application only now owing to the improved performance, reliability and cost-effectiveness of LSI storage modules, both of
the read-write (RWM) and read only (ROM) type or programmable
versions of ROM (PROM, EPROM). Moreover, some improvement has
been attained in the development of Associative, or Content
Addressable, Memories (AM). The LSI components obtainable by
combinations of these modules are described in the following
Section (Aspinall-Dagless, 77; Lipp, 76).

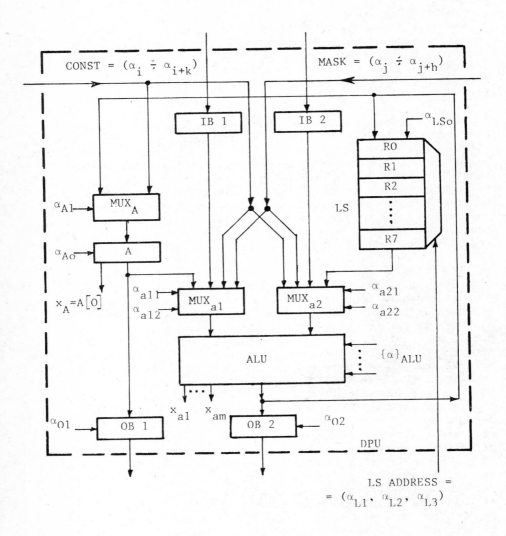

Fig. 2 - Example of DPU structure.

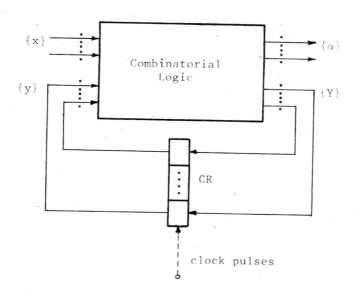

Fig. 3 - Sequential circuit representation of CU.

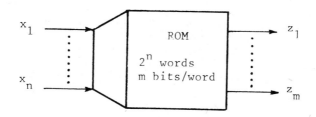

Fig. 4 - Combinatorial circuit implemented by a ROM.

3. IMPLEMENTATION OF CONTROL UNIT

3.1. Utilization of Table Look-up Techniques.

Let us consider a combinatorial function with n input variables $\{x_1,...,x_n\}$ and m cutput variables $\{z_1,...,z_m\}$. The most simple alternative to the classical implementation in terms of gates is represented by the utilization of a memory of 2^n words of m bits, for instance a ROM. As shown in Fig. 4 the address is given by the input vector, and each cell stores the corresponding output vector. This memory implements the truth table of the function in the most direct manner. However, we realize that there is a high ratio between the number of ROM bits and the number of gates to be replaced (usually, this ratio is $\geq$ 6-10). We can find more convenient ways to utilize table look-up techniques.

The first step is represented by the Functional Memory, an LSI module built through a combination of an Associative Memory and a ROM. As shown in Fig. 5, the AM replaces the ROM decoder. The number of ROM words can be reduced, for instance, by storing in it only the output configurations not containing all zeros: the bit patterns to be matched against the input vectors are the input configurations which produce a non-zero output.

A further step may consist in reducing the ROM size of a Functional Memory to the number of distinct (possibly non-zero) output configurations: in this case, the bit patterns in the AM are exactly the terms of the sum-of-products form of the function (i.e., we take advantage of the presence of "don't care" values). In other words, the AM and the ROM implement, in a table-look-up way, the AND-level and the OR-level of the logic circuit, respectively (see Fig. 6). The resulting structure is known as a Programmable Logic Array (PLA)

The described solutions are of direct application to the implementation of sequential networks too. The internal state flip-flops may be inserted separately into the feedback lines; alternatively, they may be implemented in the cells of the employed memories, as a flip-flop is described by a set of boolean expressions.

Let us consider a very simple example in order to illustrate the utilization of the previous solutions in the design of the CU (Gerace 68). The example refers to a processign unit performing two instructions, addition or subraction between the contents of an internal register A and of an input buffer B; the result is stored into A shifted left if the subtraction is performed. Two input flip-flops, P and I, signal the presence of the second operand and the instruction to be performed, respectively. The control algorithm is described in Fig. 7.a, the DPU is shown in

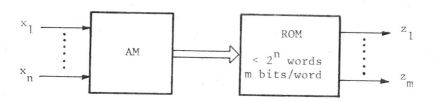

<u>Fig. 5</u> - <u>Functional Memory.</u>

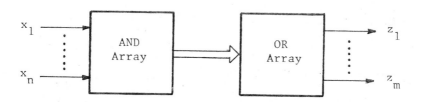

<u>Fig. 6</u> - <u>Programmable Logic Array.</u>

∅. if P=0 then go to ∅ else go to 1
1. if I=0 then go to 2 else go to 3
2. A + B → A, reset P, go to ∅
3. LSh(A - B) → A, reset P, go to ∅

a) <u>Control algorithm.</u>

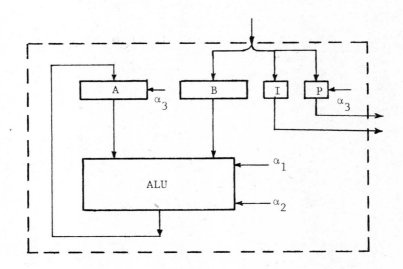

b) <u>DPU structure.</u>

	00	01	11	10	
∅	∅	∅	1	1	O_o
1	2	3	3	2	O_o
2	∅	∅	∅	∅	O_1
3	∅	∅	∅	∅	O_2

(table headed PI)

c) <u>CU flow table.</u>

<u>Fig. 7</u> - <u>Example of synthesis of a simple processing unit.</u>

	α_1	α_2	α_3
O_0: NOP	–	–	0
O_1: A + B → A, reset P	1	0	1
O_2: LSh (A – B) → A, reset P	0	1	1

d) <u>Command values for the elementary operations.</u>

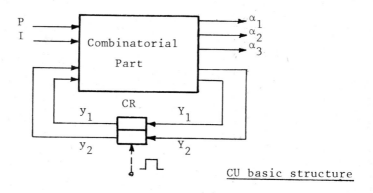

CU basic structure

P	I	y_1	y_2	α_1	α_2	α_3	Y_1	Y_2
0	0	0	0	–	–	0	0	0
0	0	0	1	–	–	0	1	1
0	0	1	0	1	0	1	0	0
0	0	1	1	0	1	1	0	0
0	1	0	0	–	–	0	0	0
0	1	0	1	–	–	0	1	0
0	1	1	0	1	0	1	0	0
0	1	1	1	0	1	1	0	0
1	0	0	0	–	–	0	0	1
1	0	0	1	–	–	0	1	0
1	0	1	0	1	0	1	0	0
1	0	1	1	0	1	1	0	0
1	1	0	0	–	–	0	0	1
1	1	0	1	–	–	0	1	1
1	1	1	0	1	0	1	0	0
1	1	1	1	0	1	1	0	0

e) <u>Truth table of the Combinatorial Part of CU.</u>

<u>Fig. 7</u> - (cont.) - <u>Example of synthesis of a simple processing unit.</u>

Fig. 7.b. The table of Fig. 7.d specifies the command values for
the execution of the possible elementary operations. The CU flow
table is shown in Fig. 7.c: by a synthesis procedure, we can
design a sequential circuit (of the Moore type). The combinatorial
part of CU is defined by the truth table of Fig. 7.e (the storage
elements of CR are supposed to be "register" elements). Although
this part could be advantageously synthesized as two distinct networks (the output - and the next-state network), we compare the
different solutions by implementing it as a unique network. The
ROM implementation requires 16 words of 5 bits = 80 bits. Using
a Functional Memory, we need a ROM of 14 words of 5 bits = 70
bits. A PLA is particularly suited for this application, due to
the characteristics of the truth table: it requires a ROM of 6
words of 5 bits = 30 bits (notice that 6 is the number of AND
terms of the function). Putting this example in perspective, we
can affirm that the implementation of CU through the synthesis
of a sequential circuit is alleviated by the existence of the
described LSI modules. Of course, this synthesis should in practice be done by decomposing the network into several distinct
parts in order to further simplify the design process. However,
this remains a complex and somewhat tedious task.

A further step in the utilization of table look-up techniques
leads to the microprogramming approach, which renders it possible
to map more directly the control algorithm onto the CU structure.
Nevertheless, the table look-up solutions proposed above will be
of outstanding importance in the implementation of specific parts
of both CU and DPU for microprogrammable systems.

3.2. Microprogrammed Implementation

The control algorithm described by a sequence of elementary
steps can be interpreted as a program, called microprogram,
written in a certain programming language, called microlanguage.
For instance, the description of Fig. 7.a is a simple microprogram. The microinstructions specify elementary operations of
arithmetic-logic type and/or of test-and-branch type. As both CU
and DPU are synchronous sequential networks and they are mutually
synchronized, every microinstruction is executed in a single clock
cycle (often from 100 to 200 nsec in bit-slice microprocessors).

The most direct way of mapping the control algorithm onto the
CU structure consists in storing the corresponding microprogram
into a memory, called Control Memory (CM): during every clock
cycle a microinstruction is fetched from CM and executed, part
in DPU (the arithmetic-logic operations) and part in CU (the test-
and-branch operations). Referring to the example of Fig. 7, we
need 4 words of CM to store the microprogram. Moreover, in order
to free the designer from the task of establishing an ad hoc
correspondence between input, output and internal state variables
of CU (as in the approaches described in Sec. 3.1), we need:

    i) to insert a separate logic, called Next Address Logic
(NAL), or Condition Network, which generates the address of the
next microinstruction;
    ii) to encode the microinstructions in the control words in
such a way that the command patterns are specified together with
the set of alternative microinstruction addresses and the corresponding logical conditions.

    The scheme of a microprogrammed CU is the one shown in Fig.
8.a. The symbols used within the control word are related to the
general structure of a microinstruction written in the transfer
structured (ts) microlanguage (Gerace-Vanneschi 74, 75):

$$\text{i.} \quad O_j \ (C_{i1}) \ k_1 \ ; \quad (C_{i2}) \ k_2 \ ; \ \ldots \ ; \quad (C_{ir}) \ k_r \tag{1}$$

whose meaning is the following: "execute microoperation O_j and
if the logical condition C_{i1} is true then go to microinstruction
k_1, else if C_{i2} is true then go to k_2,..., else if C_{ir} is true
then go to k_r". Of course, $C_{i1}, C_{i2}, \ldots, C_{ir}$ are mutually
exclusive logical conditions. An example of control word encoding
is shown in Fig. 8.b. The microoperation O_i (for instance O_0:NOP,
O_1:A+B→A, reset P of Fig. 7) may directly specify the complete
command pattern (as in Fig. 8.b), or this last may be (partially)
encoded to reduce word length: in such a case, a Decoding Network
on the CU outputs is needed. The Next Address Logic network
generates the address of the next microinstruction by selecting
first the condition variables pattern specified in the $\{C_i\}$
field(s) of the control word and then the next address corresponding to the verified logical condition. In general, a multiplexer
is present at the input of the control register CR (which behaves
as the "microinstruction counter"), as sometimes the next CU state
may be forced from DPU (for instance, the microprogram start
address) or in other ways (for instance, the return address from
microsubroutines).

    The implementation approach we have just described is the
classical microprogrammed implementation introduced by Wilkes
(Wilkes 51), and developed successively with few modifications
(see, for instance, Wilkes 69, Rosin 69, Husson 70, Agrawala-
Rauscher 77). Such an approach fits very well to the LSI characteristics: it utilizes a combination of table look-up (the CM)
and external logic (NAL, MUX, and Decoding Network if present).
It should be noticed that the external logic can be easily implemented by means of table look-up techniques too, for instance by
using Functional Memories or PLA's. The CM can be implemented by
a ROM or, for microprogrammable systems, by a PROM/EPROM or by a
RWM. Control stores of 256÷4K words, with access time of 40÷100
nsec, are presently available.

    Several techniques are used to limit the control word length,
especially with regard to the $\{C_i\}$ and $\{k_r\}$ fields. The logical

229

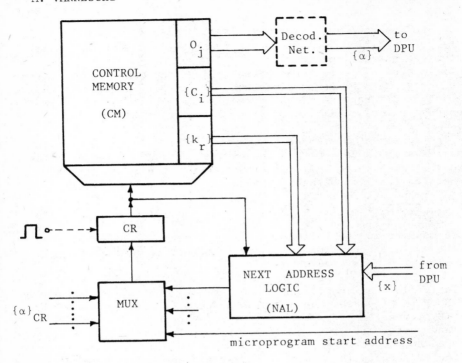

a) Microprogrammed CU scheme.

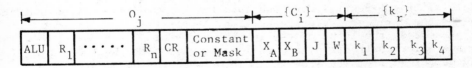

X_A, X_B : specification of two condition variables belonging to $\{x\}$.
J: conditional/unconditional branch; W: 2-way/4-way branch.
Absolute transfer: $\overline{k_1 k_2 k_3 k_4}$ (uncond. branch);
Long relative transfers (2-way branch): $\overline{k_1 k_2}$ (if $\overline{X}_A$), $\overline{k_3 k_4}$ (if X_A).
Short relative transfers (4-way branch): k_1 (if $\overline{X}_A \overline{X}_B$), k_2 (if $\overline{X}_A X_B$),
$$k_3 \text{ (if } X_A \overline{X}_B), \quad k_4 \text{ (if } X_A X_B).$$

O_j subfields contain commands for specific resources.

b) Example of control word encoding.

Fig. 8 - Microprogrammed implementation of CU.

conditions are often encoded by specifying the condition variables forming them (as in Fig. 8.b), thus enhancing the flexibility too. The next addresses are first   constrained in number; moreover, techniques of relative, base and implied addressing are used intensively (in the most simple case, address (CR)+1 is generated automatically). These considerations will be treated in Section 4.

3.3. Register Transfer Modules.

The microprogrammed implementation ensures high regularity, mantainability and (once certain conditions are verified) flexibility of CU, together with ease of design. The system processing speed, however, can be improved only by introducing a certain degree of parallelism in the microoperations (see horizontal microprogramming, Sec. 5.1). Alternative approaches can be used to map the control algorithm onto the CU structure in order to achieve higher speed: this can be done by exploiting the inherent parallelism of the control algorithm and by allocating a separate piece of hardware to each of the independent tasks thus obtained. These portions of CU, possibly controlled by a single sequential machine, may be organized either in parallel or in pipeline, or both.

An   approach of this type is represented by the Register Transfer Modules (Bell et al.72): a control module is made to correspond to each type of block in the control algorithm flow-chart, and the various control modules are associated to data-path modules.Although this approach is more expensive and less flexible than microprogramming, it is appropriated to build modular systems too, and the distinct modules may be implemented by means of table look-up techniques. In Section 6 we shall see how the microprogrammed approach can be generalized to cover the range of performances typical of Register Transfer Modules.

4. DYNAMIC MICROPROGRAMMING AND MICROPROGRAMMABLE MICROPROCESSORS

In the previous Section, microprogramming has been introduced as a hardware implementation technique which makes it possible to fully utilize LSI modules to implement the instruction set on a single processor economically. However, there is another way, perhaps more important, of looking at microprogramming: as a software technique to provide designers and programmers with an extra degree of representation; in particular, as an efficient tool to implement emulators, or interpreters, i.e. to develop multiple instruction sets each one appropriate for a particular application, both at the conventional assembler level and at the high level language level (Rosin 69, Chu 75, Iliffe 77). This type of application requires a form of dynamic microprogramming, that is a system which is user microprogrammable.

231

Once again, the state of semiconductor technology has a profound effect on the feasibility of microprogrammable processors, owing not only to the development of fast writable control stores but also to the evolution of bit-slice microprogrammable microprocessors. Not only does their utilization permit us to implement in a much more cost-effective way the next generation of small computers, but we can also think of them as elementary logic components to design special functional units and complex architecture systems. In this Section we analyze the structural characteristics of CU and DPU for microprogrammable processors, and refer them the present bit-slice families. Excellent sources are (Agrawala-Rauscher 76), (Fuller et al. 76), and (Edwards 76).

4.1. Control Unit Structures.

As sketched in Section 3.2, the control word encoding introduces several problems related to the word length reduction. In present microprocessors the microoperation field is often highly encoded and a Decoding Network is provided (possibly within the DPU chips) to generate the data path commands. However, user-definable fields are available to specify additional commands controlling optional resources and/or external logic added to the standard structure. Among the alternatives to reduce the microoperation field without considerably affecting the computing power, the following are worth mentioning:

i) Multiple microinstruction formats. Within a processing unit we can find groups of resources, regions, which are seldom used concurrently; therefore we can associate a distinct format to every region, at the expense of a greater complexity of the Decoding Network.

ii) Residual control. If additional registers are introduced (called "set up registers"), they can be used to store entire microinstruction fields during several clock cycles. In general, this technique is very useful in emulation to configure the target environment.

The structure and length of the logical condition and next addressing fields are of outstanding importance to improve both processing speed and microprogrammability. In order to examine the CU implementation needs, it is useful to refer to the programming control constructs adopted in writing microprogram (see Fig. 9).

a) The sequential construct is easily implemented in all microprogrammable microprocessors, as an incrementer within the NAL suffices.

b) The conditional and iterative constructs imply the existence of both a field to specify the condition variable and a next address field: relative and indexed addressing can be used where possible (as in the Intel 3001, MM 6710, Signetics 8X02, Texas 74S482). Of particular interest are: the Intel 3001, whose CM is

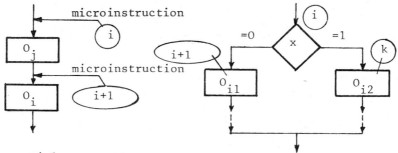

Sequential construct

Conditional construct

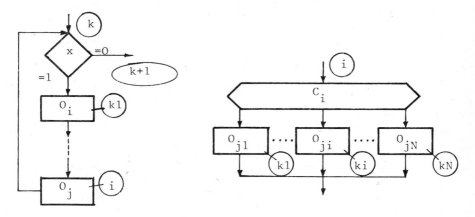

Iterative construct

Multiway branch

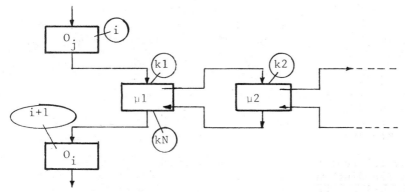

Subroutine nesting (hierarchical decomposition)

Fig. 9   Basic control constructs.

233

considered as a matrix of 32 rows x 16 columns allowing a wide range of addressing possibilities; and the Texas 74S482, whose NAL contains a full adder to perform several addressing modes in a powerful way.

Sometimes it is useful and/or cheap to implement the skip transfer in which the CR contents are incremented by two. An absolute microinstruction address, without specifying it in the control word, may be originated from a DPU register (loaded during a previous microinstruction, possibly in parallel with other elementary operations) or from the "CONSTANT" subfield of the microoperation field, if present (see Fig. 10). Absolute addresses are particularly useful to implement the iterative construct, as well as in other cases, for instance to jump to the fetch microprogram after an execution microprogram.

c) The multiway branch construct requires that many addresses are encoded in the control word together with the specification of complex logical conditions, unless this construct is simulated by a sequence of conditional branches. Often, this addressing scheme is restricted in range through short relative addresses, as in the Intel 3001 and Texas 74S482. The AMD 2909 is worth noticing due to the possibility of implementing a true "case" statement by means of a mask field.

In general, several techniques can be employed to derive the relative addressing; a simple solution for implementing a four-way branch is shown in Fig. 8. A frequently used way is to generate the least significant bits of the next microinstruction address depending on the values of the condition variables (see Fig. 10).

d) The subroutine nesting construct, a basic one in structured programming and of valuable importance in microprogramming to save CM words, implies the existence of a Push-Down Stack (see Fig. 10). The MM6710 has a single subroutine register; the Signetics 8X02, AMD 2909, Texas 74S482, Fairchild 9408 have a 4-level stack allowing a restricted form of hierarchical decomposition. The AMD 2930 has been announced with a 16-level stack.

A stack in the CU is also very useful for efficient interrupt handling, especially when the interrupt requests are very urgent. In these cases, the address (transmitted from an external unit or generated inside the DPU) of an interrupt handling microroutine can be forced automatically into CR while the CR contents, possibly incremented, are pushed onto the stack.

Other useful features of a microprogrammable CU would be the instruction decoding table and mechanisms for the dynamic microprogram relocation. The former (see Fig. 10) allows the mapping of the operation code of the fetched target instruction onto the address of the corresponding microprogram. Often this resource is simulated in the CM by forcing the (possibly shifted) opcode into

CR. However, the decoding function may be time-, or space-consuming: e.g., many microprograms may initiate with the same microinstruction. In these cases an Associative Memory (or a dynamically alterable Functional Memory), possibly associated with an automatic subroutine call, allows a more satisfactory solution. Moreover, no restrictions are imposed on the target language. The same resource may also be employed to efficiently specify various and complex I/O patterns causing an interrupt (Erwin-Jensen 72).

A dynamic relocation mechanism is useful to run large microprogram sets in comparatively little CM space. We can develop a caching scheme for this purpose, and devise special microprogram primitives to load microcode segments from main, or auxiliary, memory.

Fig. 10.a illustrates a simplified scheme of CU structure to exemplify the implementation of the constructs discussed in this Section. The control word encoding is shown in Fig. 10.b. The Control Memory is accessible, besides from CR, from external devices (e.g. Main Memory, DPU register file, I/O devices) in order to implement a dynamic microprogram loading, or to store constants if necessary. During this mode of operation, a CM address register (CMAR) and a CM data register (CMDR) are employed.

The size of the basic CM module is supposed to be 512 words. However, it can be extended to 2K by adding two bits in front of the microinstruction addresses, loaded by microprogram into the flip-flops E1,E2.

The basic microinstruction address is generated from one of the following sources: the Instruction/Interrupt Decoding Table (DT), the CONST field of the control word, the Microprogram Push-Down Stack (PDS), a Functional Unit (FU) and the concatenation of the k_r field (5 bits long) with the masked values of the condition variables. The FU behaves essentially as an adder (to perform $(CR)+k_r$) or as an incrementer (to perform $(CR)+1$).

A two-way branch, for which the alternative addresses are given by $(CR)+1$ and a generic k, is implemented by specifying the condition variable x (one of the four variables x_1,x_2,x_3,x_4) in the X field; the value x must assume to generate the k address (V bit) and the J bit (conditional/unconditional branch).

A multiway branch is implemented (setting the bit W to 1) by concatenating to k_r the masked values of the four condition variables. The mask is specified by $m_1m_2m_3m_4$ in the control word. In this way, we generate the least significant bits of the microinstruction address according to the values of the condition variables. An obvious alternative could be to use $(CR)+1$ in place of k_r.

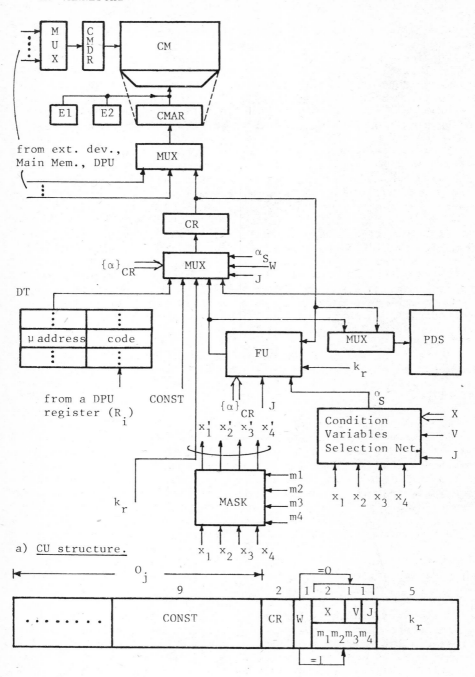

a) <u>CU structure.</u>

b) <u>Control word encoding.</u>

Fig. 10 - Example of CU organization.

An absolute address is obtained directly from the CONST part of the microoperation field.

The Push-Down Stack (possibly with 8,16 or more levels) may be loaded either with (CR), or with an address relative to (CR), say (CR)+1 or (CR)+k_r.

In conclusion, the programming constructs allowed by this CU organizations are expressed (with reference to Fig. 9) in the following ways.

a) Sequential construct:

i. O_j, i+1;

b1) Conditional construct:

i. ... (x=0) i+1; (x=1) k

where k is equal to i+k_r, or to CONST.

b2) Iterative construct:

k. ... (x=0) k+1; (x=1) k_1
.
.
i. O_j, k

c) Multiway Branch:

c1) i. ... ($x_1 x_2 x_3 x_4$=0000) k_r; ($x_1 x_2 x_3 x_4$=0001) k_r+1; ....

(example of 16-way branch) $\quad$ ...; ($x_1 x_2 x_3 x_4$=1111) k_r+15

c2) i. ... DP(R_i) → CR

d) Subroutine Nesting

i. O_j, kR → PDS, k1 $\qquad\qquad\qquad$ (call)
.
.
k_N. .... PDS → CR $\qquad\qquad\qquad\qquad\qquad$ (return)

where kR may be equal to i, i+1, i+k_r.

Of course, we confirm that the previous example should only help to see some solutions a designer has at his disposal to implement a microprogrammable CU. More efficient and powerful solutions can be used in practice to fit to both the specific needs and the designer's views.

4.2. Data Paths Unit Structures

The points of interest in the design of a microprogrammable

DPU are essentially: i) the structure of the ALU and the repertoire of operations it can perform, ii) the organization of
internal registers and their relationship to the ALU input and
output ports, iii) the interconnection structures between DPU
regions and external subsystems.

i) The operations performed by the ALU are in general restricted to simple arithmetic and logic functions (add, subtract,
and, or, exor, not, shift), executable in a very short time
(typically, < 50 nsec). However, more powerful (though expensive)
resources, like fast multipliers, could be used by employing an
asynchronous polyphase implementation (see Sect. 5.3).

As shown in Fig. 11, the shifter may be independent of the
remaining part of the ALU, or it may be attached to the ALU input/
output ports providing a preshift/postshift capability (see Intel
3002, Texas SBPO 400, MM 6701, AMD 2901). In addition, ALU inputs/
outputs may be masked (often within the multiplexers) to select
specific fields and/or transform operands (see Intel 3002).

An essential feature in microprogrammable systems is the
fast field-extraction, not only to produce operands, but also to
assist in decoding the target instructions, to fetch variable-
length instructions and data from main memory, to assemble condition variables to be tested in parallel, and so on. This function
can be performed by a very powerful LSI module, the high-speed
shifter: for instance, the Signetics 8243 shifts an input byte
left from 0 to 7 positions, zeroing out the leftmost bits, and
outputs the transformed byte. Using such a module as a building
block, larger shifters can easily be constructed.

Other target language-dependent functions should be performed
efficiently by means of flexible LSI modules. Examples of such
functions may be: character encoding, decimal arithmetic, main
memory accessing modes, interrupt management, multi-environment
emulation management. Often, PLA's, Associative and/or Functional
Memories can be used advantageously.

ii) The DPU registers, either of specific meaning or of general utility, may be organized in part in an independent way and
in part in local stores (LS). A module which is very useful in
microprogrammable DPU's is a program stack to save essential
machine status information in the presence of interrupts and
procedure calls, and to efficiently process arithmetic expressions.

The utilization of large local stores and stacks, as well as
of more high-speed working registers, are often desirable to make
it easier to microprogram emulators.

The organization of DPU registers and ALU affects the range
of microoperations which can be performed. The most frequent organizations are shown in Fig. 12 (I is an external datum and AC an
intermediate-accumulator-register). These organizations are typi-

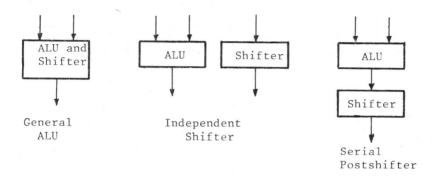

General
ALU

Independent
Shifter

Serial
Postshifter

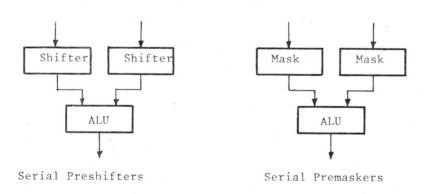

Serial Preshifters

Serial Premaskers

Fig. 11 - Types of ALU structures.

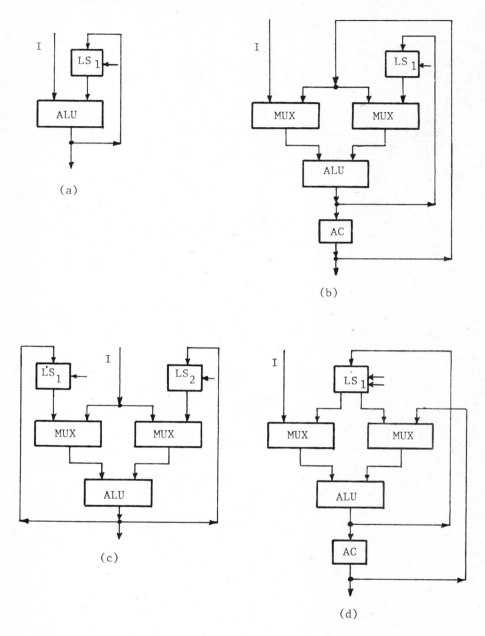

Fig. 12 - Organizations of DPU registers and ALU.

cal of Fairchild 9405 (a), Intel 3002 (b), SBP0400 (c), AMD 2901 and MM 6701 (d). Note the LS with double-read (single-write) access in organization d)

The repertoire of microoperations executable by these DPU organizations are now described (Aspinall, 1976 b). F denotes a generic function performed by the ALU, and R_i a register of local store LS_i. We list only the operations involving two or three registers: more assignment and unary operations can easily be derived.

a) $F(R1,I) \to R1$

b) $F(R1,I) \to R1$ $F(AC,I) \to R1$
 $F(R1,AC) \to R1$ $F(R1,I) \to AC$
 $F(R1,AC) \to AC$
 $F(AC,I) \to AC$

c) $F(R1,I) \to R1$ $F(R1,I) \to R2$
 $F(R2,I) \to R1$ $F(R2,I) \to R1$
 $F(R1,R2) \to R1$
 $F(R1,R2) \to R1$

d) $F(R1',R1'') \to R1'$ $F(AC,R1'') \to R1'$
 $F(R1',R1'') \to R1''$ $F(AC,I) \to R1'$
 $F(AC,I) \to AC$ $F(R1',R1'') \to AC$
 $F(AC,R1'') \to AC$ $F(R1',I) \to AC$

5. ARCHITECTURAL CHARACTERISTICS OF MICROPROGRAMMABLE PROCESSORS.

In this section we shall examine the architectural characteristics which, once the hardware resources and their performance have been selected, affect the performance of the processor. They are (Agrawala-Rauscher 76) the vertical-horizontal characteristic (microprogramming types), the serial-parallel characteristic (microprogramming models), the monophase-poliphase characteristic (microprogram timing).

5.1. Microprogramming Types.

This characteristic refers to the number of elementary operations that each microinstruction can execute. In vertical microprogramming a microinstruction contains a microoperation which in general consists of a single elementary operation; moreover a single logical condition per microinstruction is specified. Vertical microinstructions are very similar to classical machine language instructions; in particular, operative microinstructions and branch microinstructions are encoded by distinct formats. Their lengths lie in the range of 12 to 24 bits.

Horizontal microprogramming presents opposite characteristics:

a microinstruction can specify the parallel execution of several compatible elementary operations, and more than one logical condition, thus allowing multi-way branches simultaneously with microoperations. A horizontal control word has therefore greater length (typically, 48 or more bits).

The differences between vertical and horizontal microprogramming are obvious, in terms of cost (mainly affected by the complexity of DPU), processing speed and ease of microprogram writing. However, the dividing line is not well defined, and a number of mini-medium sized processors and bit-slice microprocessors have been designed allowing a limited capability to perform elementary operations and tests simultaneously. Often this compromise (sometimes called "diagonal" microprogramming) leads to optimize the performance/cost ratio in a wide range of applications.

Moreover, vertical and horizontal microprogramming may advantageously coexist in the same machine. The best known example is represented by the QM-1 minicomputer (Rosin-Frieder-Eckouse 72), where the vertical microinstructions are interpreted by sequences of horizontal microinstructions (called "nanoinstructions"). This allows an extra degree of flexibility in general emulation, as the microinstruction set (at the vertical level) can be modified by changing the corresponding nanoprograms. This concept will be more deeply discussed, and generalized, in Sect.6.

5.2. Microprogramming Models.

Looking at the execution of a microinstruction, we realize that it is performed in part in DPU - the microoperation - and in part in CU - the present microinstruction fetch plus the generation of next microinstruction address.

The serial-parallel characteristic measures the amount of overlap between the DPU and the CU activity. Let us analyze the opposite possibilities for implementing a microinstruction, through a modelling approach. Practical design techniques related to these implementation schemes can be easily derived.

In a serial implementation the three phases are executed sequentially during the same clock cycle, as shown in Fig. 13.a, where T_a, T_n, T_e denote the maximum times to fetch the microinstruction from CM, to generate the next microinstruction address within NAL and to execute the microoperation in DPU, respectively. Let us consider the following microinstruction:

i. $A+B \rightarrow A$ ($A[0] = 0$) k1 ; ($A[0] = 1$) k2   (2)

which tests the sign of the result of microoperation $A+B \rightarrow A$. It is executed in a single clock cycle of length

$$\tau_S = T_p + T_n \tag{3}$$

where $T_p = T_a + T_n$ is the total (maximum) CU delay. This implementation is possible provided that the condition variables are tested before the microoperation results are stored into the corresponding registers.

In a _parallel implementation_ the CU activity and the DPU activity are overlapped in order to obtain a shorter cycle time. A possibility is shown in Fig. 13.b, where the DPU clock pulses are delayed by a time interval T_a with respect to the CU clock pulses. This implies that a register pulsed with the DPU clock is inserted on the CU out its, and that the condition variables are tested at the output the corresponding memory elements. The resulting cycle length is given by

$$\tau_p = \max \{T_p, T_e\} \tag{4}$$

However, a microinstruction like (2) must be executed in two clock cycles, as if it were written

i. $A+B \rightarrow A$,   i+1

i+1. O_o $(A[0] = 0)$ k1 ; $(A[0] = 1)$ k2

We can implement a microinstruction like (2) on a parallel system by adding (within the NAL) a mechanism, which may be called "_implicit waiting mechanism_", which automatically forces the CU to wait while the correct value of the logical condition is formed. If an apposite bit is set in the control word, the following actions are taken when the microinstruction is fetched: the CR contents are left unchanged, and a flip-flop H is set to force the commands which are fetched during the next clock cycle to specify the "null" (NOP) microoperation O_o. During this cycle, the logical condition is tested, the corresponding next address is generated and H is reset.

Provision for both implementations is present in some microprogrammable processors. For instance, the Intel 3001 may behave in the parallel mode by inserting a "Pipeline Register" on the CU outputs; moreover the logical conditions, formed within the NAL, may be either stored in flag registers or tested immediatly. A similar feature is present in the AMD 2909 and in Fairchild 9408.

The convenience of the serial or parallel implementation, from the point of view of optimizing the processing speed, must be analyzed according to the specific control algorithm and to the timing characteristics of the system. It can be found (Redfield 71, Gerace-Vanneschi 75, Vanneschi 76.a) that the ratio between the (average) processing times needed by a parallel and a serial system (with the same CU and DPU organizations and

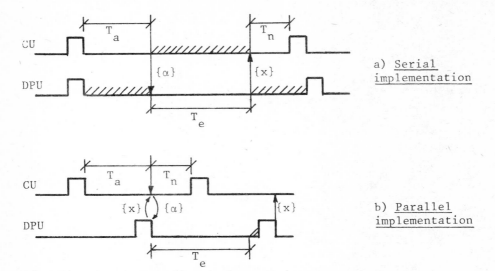

Fig. 13- Microinstruction implementations.

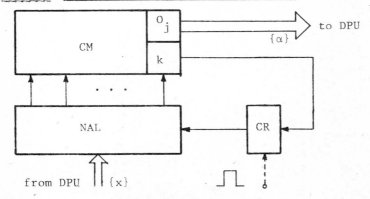

a) Mealy CU organization.

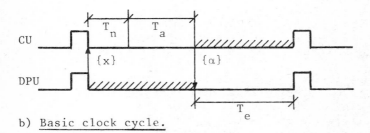

b) Basic clock cycle.

Fig. 14 - Phrase structured microprogramming.

identical resources) to perform the same control algorithm, is given by

$$r = \frac{T_p}{T_s} = \frac{1+\beta}{1+\beta_o} \tag{5}$$

where $\beta = N_A/N_S$ and $\beta_o = \min\{T_p/T_e ; T_e/T_p\}$. N_A is equal to the number of executed microinstructions containing "logical conditions of type A", i.e. conditions formed during the last microoperation performed (like in microinstruction (2)). N_S is equal to the total number of executed microinstructions. Therefore, the parallel approach is the most convenient if

$$\beta < \beta_o \tag{6}$$

β_o, called "unbalancing factor", takes into account the timing characteristics of CU and DPU. In "well-balanced" systems (where $\beta_o \simeq 1$), the parallel implementation is the most convenient independently from the characteristics of the control algorithm (i.e. the value of β).

Various techniques can be devised in order to improve the performance of the serial or of the parallel approach.

The parallel implementation can be made more sophisticated using the so called "guess technique". It consists in "guessing", in presence of logical conditions of type A, the next microinstruction address. This can be done according to some predictions (this is possible, for instance, in iterative constructs, or when exceptional conditions are tested). When the logical condition is actually formed, its value is verified: the microprogram goes on by fetching the guessed microinstruction if the prediction was correct; otherwise, the correct microinstruction address is generated and (only in this case) one clock cycle is wasted. Denoting by p the average "bad guess probability", the parallel approach is the most convenient if the following relation holds

$$\beta < \frac{\beta_o}{p} \tag{7}$$

The serial approach can be improved using a "variable cycle length" technique (see also Sect. 5.3), consisting in shortening the cycle by T_n when no logical conditions of type A are tested in the microinstruction. The "guess" parallel implementation is better than this kind of serial implementation if

$$\beta < \frac{\beta_o - \gamma}{p - \gamma} \tag{8}$$

where $\gamma = \min\{T_n/T_p ; T_n/T_e\}$. More information about these topics can be found in the cited references.

5.2.1. Phrase Structured Microprogramming. Until now we have taken into account microprogrammed systems whose CU is a Moore sequential machine. The corresponding microlanguage structure is the ts (see relation (1)). We have a Moore CU-Moore DPU or a Moore CU-Mealy DPU system according to whether a parallel or a serial implementation is chosen, respectively (Gerace-Vanneschi 75).

Let us give a short account of the microprogramming structures using a CU of the Mealy type. The general microinstruction form is called "phrase structured" (ps) and is the following

$$i. \ (C_{i1}) \ O_{j1}, k1 \ ; \ \ (C_{i2}) \ O_{j2}, k2 \ ; \ \ldots \ ; \ (C_{ir}) \ O_{jr}, k_r \qquad (9)$$

For instance, the ps microprogram for the algorithm of Fig. 7 is

$\emptyset.$ (P=0) O_o, $\emptyset$; (P=1) O_o, 1

1. (I=0) A+B $\rightarrow$ A, reset P,$\emptyset$; (I=1) LSh(A-B)$\rightarrow$A, reset P,$\emptyset$

The basic CU organization and the control word format are shown in Fig. 14.a. Notice that each control word encodes a "phrase", i.e. a pair O_{ji}, k_{ji}. The logical conditions are not specified in the control word: their values are taken into account directly in the NAL network. This CU structure resembles the hardware design techniques discussed in Sect. 3.1 much more than the microprogramming approach. In fact, a Mealy CU is not as microprogrammable as a Moore CU. However, it has a number of unique advantages:

i) the control word length is independent of the number of conditional phrases per microinstruction. This means that we can express an N-way branch with only one microinstruction, for any N;

ii) the control memory size is always less than the one of the corresponding Moore CU.

The NAL can be implemented through a table-look-up approach, possibly using writable LSI components, and this can improve the microprogrammability. It is the task of the microprogram translator to derive the configuration of the CM and NAL words.

Finally, a system with a Mealy CU (a Mealy CU-Moore DPU system) has a serial behaviour (see the basic timing in Fig.14.b). However, by the insertion of a "pipeline register" on the CU outputs and the implementation of the "implicit waiting" technique, we transform a Mealy CU into a Moore CU and can execute the ps microprograms according to a parallel approach too.

5.3. Microprogram Timing.

This characteristic refers to the number of phases, or minor cycles, required to execute a microinstruction.

In the most simple case, we have a monophase implementation, i.e. there are no distinct minor cycles in a clock cycle. When the execution of a microinstruction requires the activation of a cascade of elementary operations, then we need a polyphase implementation to ensure determinacy. It is possible to distinguish between synchronous and asynchronous polyphase according to whether the number of phases is fixed a-priori or it can be dynamically established through specific commands, respectively. A polyphase implementation, and in particular an asynchronous polyphase, renders it possible to achieve higher processing rates at the expense of a more complex timing control; moreover, it is suitable for a parallel implementation.

5.4. Microprogramming Efficiency and Computer Architecture.

The microprogrammable CU-DPU modules can be used as elementary components in complex computer architectures. This fact suggests that the system efficiency can be enhanced by choosing each microprogrammable module with its own microprogramming characteristics, according to the functions it must perform (Vanneschi 76.b). Therefore, additional efforts would be needed in the construction of bit-slice processors to increase their adaptability to the various microprogramming characteristics. In the following Section we shall examine a class of parallel architectures which, besides other features, are suitable to fully employ such characteristics.

6. ADVANCED MICROPROGRAMMABLE ARCHITECTURES

In this Section we shall give a short account of the possibilities offered by LSI modules, and in particular by the microprogrammable microprocessors, to conceive microprogrammable computer architectures characterized by high-performances, modularity and generality of emulation. The basic idea represents, in a certain sense, a generalization of the microprogramming concept, and of the QM-1 architecture in particular.

Let us think of a hierarchical microprogrammed system {CU,DPU}, where the DPU consists of a set of independent, active functional units {FU}: that is, every FU_i is itself a complete processing unit with its own CU_i and DPU_i. Once a microinstruction is fetched by the main CU, it is delivered for execution to an appropriate functional unit which in general interprets the microinstruction by a microprogram (or nanoprogram). Several functional units may be active simultaneously, thus enhancing the system performance. Moreover, every functional unit can be implemented optimizing the microprogramming characteristics (see Sect. 5.4). If convenient, it can be in turn organized in a hierarchical way. The general scheme of such a system is shown in Fig. 15 (Rietti-Tiriticco-Vanneschi, 1977 a).

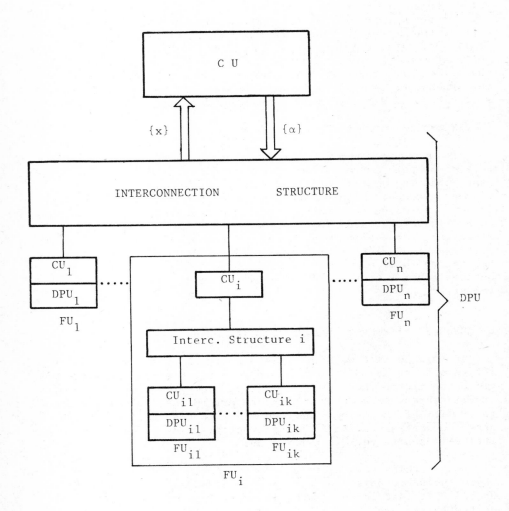

Fig. 15 - Hierarchical microprogrammable architecture.

The CU and the functional units can be advantageously implemented by microprogrammable LSI components. There are two main
problems to be solved:

i) A synchronization discipline must be established to ensure
the correct interaction among CU and functional units;

ii) the system can achieve high modularity and flexibility
provided that the Interconnection Structure and the set of condition variables {x} are independent of the specific computation.

To give a solution to these problems, let us analyze two specific organizations belonging to the proposed class of architectures.

6.1. Logic Machine.

This organization has been proposed and utilized in the implementation of several minicomputer-type systems by Kehl et al.
(Torode-Kehl 74, Kehl-Moss-Dunkel 75). A Logic Machine has the
following characteristics:

1) the Interconnection Structure is a bidirectional bus (MBUS),
through which the functional units exchange data under control
of CU and receive commands or data from CU;

2) CU is vertically microprogrammed. Few types of microinstructions are used: typically, transfers of data between two FUs,
one of which may be the CU itself; conditional   (unconditional)
branches on conditions which are internal to CU;

3) every time CU needs some information from a functional
unit, it executes a special microinstruction called DECODE. This
forces CU to wait for a microinstruction address sent by a functional unit through a separate bus (SBUS): this represents the
address of the microprogram which CU must execute.

The DECODE mechanism, together with the bus interconnection
structure, solves both problems i) and ii). All the condition
variables are eliminated at the CU-{FU} interface; they are tested inside the functional units only. Moreover, the DECODE is in -
serted in every point of the CU microprogram where it has to be
synchronized with the activities of the functional units. The
sequential access to the SBUS is ensured by an indirect interaction
mechanism (for instance, a daisy-chain or a polling).

As an example, let us consider a Logic Machine minicomputer
including at least the following functional units: a CPU, a
Memory Unit (MU) and several I/O units. Some microprograms performed by CU are shown below.

The microinstruction $FU_i(R_j) \rightarrow FU_i(R_j)$ means that the contents of the register R_j belonging to the functional unit FU_i are
transferred into the register R_j belonging to FU_i through the
MBUS. The microinstruction $FU_i(COMM)$ means that the command COMM
is sent from CU to FU_i through the MBUS.

M. VANNESCHI

```
       ©     Instruction Fetch Microprogram                    Legend:
START    : CPU(IC) → MU(MAR)                          IC:   Instruction
                                                            Counter
           MU(READ)                                   IR:   Instruction
                                                            Register
           MU(MDR) → CPU(IR)                          AR:   Operand
                                                            Address
           DECODE                                           Register

       C     Operand Fetch Microprogram
             CPU(AR) → MU(MAR)                        OR:   Operand
                                                            Register
             MU(READ)

             MU(MDR) → CPU(OR)                        MAR:  Memory
                                                            Address
       C     Instruction Execution Microprogram             Register
             CPU(EXECUTE)                             MDR:  Memory
                                                            Data Register
             GO TO START

       C     Interrupt Handling Microprogram
             .
             .
             .
             DECODE

       C     Operating System  Microprograms
             .
             .
             .
             DECODE
```

Once the Instruction Fetch Microprogram is performed, CU waits
for a microprogram address sent from CPU signaling that the
Operand Fetch and/or the Instruction Execution Microprogram must
be performed. This is done by means of the DECODE microinstruction. However, if a functional unit with higher priority than CPU
(e.g. an I/O unit) sends a microprogram address to CU (e.g. the
Interrupt Handling Microprogram address), this one is forced into
the CR of CU and the corresponding microprogram is performed. At
the end of this microprogram, a new DECODE allows to resume the
normal processing mode or to listen to other high-priority
requests. A number of microroutines can be added to the CU behaviour, including operating system functions. Specific functional
units can be included to process these tasks. The use of coroutines can help to implement the cooperation between the CU microprograms and the functional units microprograms.

6.2. Interconnection Mode Configurable Computer

This organization has been proposed in (Miller and Cocke 74)

and belongs to the class of data-flow systems   (Dennis 74,
Dennis-Misunas 75, Vanneschi 77). In a data-flow system an operation is enabled, and it can be executed, on condition that its
operands are "ready", i.e. they have been produced by other
operations: therefore the maximum parallelism inherent in the
computation is exploited. For instance, the data-flow representation of the multiplication of two complex numbers (a+jb), (c+jd)
is shown in Fig. 16.

In an Interconnection Mode Configurable Computer, a "segment"
of data-flow representation (like the one of Fig. 16) is encoded
in a "set-up instruction". Once-fetched, this instruction establishes a set of connections among the appropriate functional
units and fetches the initial operands. At this point, the segment is executed at the "natural" speed of the functional units,
without further references to the data memory except for storing
the final results. Once the execution of a segment is completed,
another segment is executed, and so on.

An Interconnection Mode Configurable can be implemented as
a hierarchical microprogrammed system architecture.The set-up
instructions are horizontal microinstructions stored in the CM.
Once CU fetches a set-up instruction, it sends a set of commands
to establish the connections among the functional units, one of
which is a data memory unit.

The Interconnection Structure must be a general one to connect
the functional units according to a great number of combinations.
In fact, the configuration of functional units must reproduce
the computation structure of the block to be performed. Although
the cost of the Interconnection Structure is high, the use of
LSI modules can help to achieve a satisfactory performance/cost
ratio. Another problem which has still to be fully solved concerns
the decomposition of the data-flow representation into blocks
in a way which is as efficient as possible.

The data-flow concept represents a noticeable step towards
unconventional (i.e. non-Von Neumann) computer system architectures which make it possible not only to exploit the maximum
parallelism of the computation through highly modular and uniform
structures,but also to have at disposal a high-level machine
language containing several advanced constructs of the programming languages. Unfortunately, the discussion of this topic is
no part of our subject; its study may begin from the cited works
of Miller-Cocke and Dennis.

The Logic Machine and the data-flow computer are examples
of system architectures which are suitable to efficiently
exploit both the LSI features and the microprogramming characteristics. Of course, great design and research efforts have to
be done with regard to other distributed architectures employing

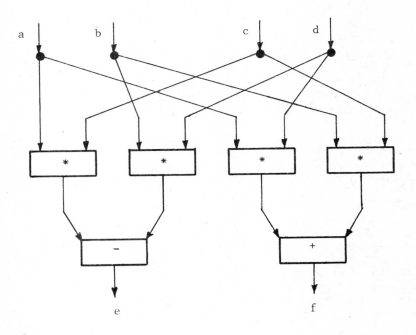

Fig. 16 — Data-flow representation of

(e + jf) = (a + jb) * (c + jd).

LSI microprogrammable components, as such as the multimicroprocessor systems and the local networks.

7. CONCLUSION

Semiconductor technology has reached a stage in which many cost-effective LSI components can be utilized in the design of computer systems. In particular, the bit-slice microprogrammable microprocessors offer some implementation solutions which were not feasible in the past generation. Several characteristics must be improved, however, like CU organizations allowing the efficient exploitation of all the structured programming constructs. An essential and interesting research field concerns the development of high level microprogramming languages and software support tools (translators, loaders, simulators, debuggers, and so on). In particular, the microprogram compiling is a complex and sophisticated task due to the required high efficiency of the object microcode. Some results in microprogram optimization are described in (IEEE 76); an implementation has been carried out at the University of Pisa (Rietti - Tiriticco - Vanneschi 77.b) leading to the development of an optimizing microprogram compiler suitable to a wide range of microprocessor organizations.

ACKNOWLEDGMENTS

I should like to thank Prof. David Aspinall and Dr. Erik Dagless for their very interesting discussions and valuable suggestions.

V.B.   INTERPRETIVE MACHINES

J. K. Iliffe

Visiting Fellow,
Queen Mary College,
University of London

These sections survey attempts to apply computers directly to
high level languages using microprogrammed interpreters. The
motivation for such work is to achieve language implementations
that are more effective in some measure of translation, execution
or response to the user than would otherwise be obtained. The
implied comparison is with the established technique of compiling
into a fixed general-purpose machine code prior to execution. It
is argued that while substantial benefits can be expected from
microprogramming it does not represent the best approach to design
when the contributing factors are analysed in a general system
context, that is to say when wide performance range, multiple
source language, and stringent security requirements have to be
satisfied. An alternative is suggested, using a combination of
interpretation and a primitive instruction set and providing
security at the microprogram level.

The early sections review the history and terminology of microprogrammable machines. Knowledge of conventional practice is
assumed. Readers already experienced in microprogramming should
skip rapidly to Section 3.

1. MICROINSTRUCTION DESIGN

If the conventional machine code is abandoned (at least temporarily) as a means of defining the computer's function set it is
necessary to fall back on the next level of description, i.e. the
microcode. A very extensive literature has grown up around that
subject in recent years, but I think it is true to say that no
commonly accepted theory or principles have emerged: that is the
consequence of rapid changes in the process of manufacturing
logical devices which force a continual revision of the economics
of design. In the introductory section, we shall study the
evolution of microprogrammed machines, but one can do little more
than present a collection of techniques. For detailed study of
application to machine language interpretation the student is
referred to Husson (1970), where an extensive bibliography to

255

1968 will be found, and to Boulaye (1971), for a shorter survey of techniques. The following notes do no more than provide an outline of design principles and introduce terminology.

The branch of technology that enables a raw microprocessor to interpret a given order code is termed 'microsystem design'. If one machine is to interpret one order code it is a very localised affair. If several machines must imitate two or three order codes the need for standard procedures and documentation arises: in the major application areas this is treated very much as an extension of the logic design. Tucker (1967) and Husson have written informatively on that aspect of microsystems. However, high level languages are not nearly as well defined as machine codes, they are generally more complex, subject to greater variation, and outside the control of any one laboratory. A survey by Rosin highlights some of the difficulties involved (Rosin 1969). We shall return to that subject in the last section, showing how it affects machine design. For the time being, let us recall how a microprogrammed machine handles the interpretation of a single 'target instruction set' or 'machine code'.

The first application of microprogramming as a formal technique is generally attributed to the designers of EDSAC-2 at Cambridge University (Wilkes et al. 1958). It is a systematic way of controlling the flow of signals through the data paths of a processing unit, each path, or in some cases each function of the processor, being determined by a bit in a microinstruction. If we regard the state of the processor as defined by the assembly of registers and control flip-flops, then a microinstruction determines a simple transition from one state to another. The attraction of the technique is that transformations of any complexity can be composed by applying a sequence of microinstructions: the limitations imposed by ad hoc control logic, which are apparent in the areas of machine definition and construction, are greatly reduced. At a time when relatively complex target instructions are thought to be the key to greater machine efficiency, the introduction of microinstructions obviously has great attraction.

The source of microinstructions is a store, which will be called the control memory in the present context. A single bit in the microinstruction can control the transmission of an entire field from one register along several parallel paths in one processor 'cycle'; another bit, or group of bits, will select a destination register and field. It is fairly easy to evolve a requirement for fifty or more bits in the microinstruction to control the possible data paths in the processor.

The second requirement of the microinstruction is to determine its successor. Application of a sequencing rule determines the string of actions carried out by the processor which, when properly defined, will interpret a target instruction. One of the simplest ways of sequencing is to place the next microinstruction address in the one currently being obeyed. To achieve conditional branching effects it is necessary to use the state of the processing logic in the calculation of at least part of the next address. The elements of the machine can be visualised as in Figure 1. The machine operates in three steps, i.e.:

1. Access control memory using the microinstruction address.

2. Use the microinstruction to control the state transition of the processor logic.

3. Use microinstruction digits and the result of step 2 to determine the next microinstruction address.

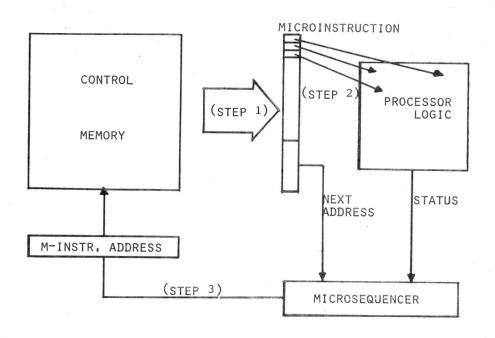

Figure 1:   Microprogram Control

J.K.ILIFFE

The development of microprogrammable machines from the above
principle of design leads to great elaboration of detail, the
main considerations being (a) optimising the use of control
memory, (b) achieving balanced timing of control memory and
processor logic, and (c) organising the registers and data paths
of the processor to suit the class of target machines of interest.
I shall discuss each aspect of design, giving examples from some
of the earlier microprogrammed machines.

1.1 Minimising the Cost of Control Memory

Exploitation of microprogramming was not widespread until
suitable techniques for loading and manufacturing control memory
had been developed. Such techniques are discussed by Husson
(Chapter 5), where it can be seen that the predominant forms of
construction allowed microinstructions to be read but not written
under program control. That is clearly sufficient for a well
defined and fixed instruction set. The later development of
semiconductor control memories with write capability has been
the main stimulus to further research in microprogram application.
With all memories, however, the main design requirement is to
deliver the information required at the right time and in as few
bits as possible.

Considerations of space lead to various forms of microinstruction coding. The form in which a single microinstruction bit
controls a unique processor gate (or data path) is termed direct
control. If we can find sets of mutually exclusive control
signals, such that not more than one is activated in a given
cycle, it is possible to encode them: a field of K bits will
activate one of 2^{K-1} control lines, or none at all. That is
obviously the case when one of, say, 8 registers can be gated to
one input of an adder. The same technique is used in machine
code design. It is illustrated below by the structure of the
IBM 360/30 microinstruction and by most of the 'first generation'
microcodes, all of which may be said to use encoded control, the
individual fields controlling microorders.

Three other common forms of coding deserve mention. In bit-
steering the particular control lines activated by a microorder
(or bit) are determined by another field of the microinstruction.
The second field directs the first to one or another set of control lines; it is appropriate when the processor logic can be
partitioned into sections that do not require activation on every
cycle (and can to some degree proceed in parallel). It has been
used in combination with other techniques, for example in the RCA
Spectra 70/45, Honeywell 4200 and IBM 360/25. Carried to the
extreme, the microinstruction ends up as a function group and a
number of operand fields, which would be difficult to distinguish
at first sight from a conventional machine code.

258

The second technique derives from the observation that over many sequences of microinstructions the values of certain control lines will remain constant, therefore they can be set in advance and taken as an implicit extension of the microinstruction. That technique will be referred to as <u>preset control</u>. It applies, for example, if particular carry or shift paths are fixed in advance, or if one of several possible register sets is being used.

Finally, it is easy to see that all 2^{100} versions of a 100-bit direct control microinstruction will not be used, and instead of attempting to encode individual fields it would be possible to list all the distinct microinstructions in a particular application and select those required by indexing a store containing the list. For example, in a particular application there may be less than 1024 distinct microinstructions. In that case a 2000 word microprogram can be compressed into 20 000 bits, a saving of 90%. All that is required is that the fully encoded microinstruction index another store 100 bits wide containing the 1024 fully decoded instructions (the second store is called the <u>nanostore</u>). The net saving in storage space is thus 40%.

It is more likely that some of the fields of the microinstruction will be fully used, leaving a residual field to be handled in the above way. The Nanodata QM-1 machine, Rosin et al. (1972), provides an illustration. The 16 bit microinstruction is loaded into one of the microregisters, a six bit field is then used to select a 342-bit <u>nanoinstruction</u>. The latter can use the remaining ten microinstruction bits as operand selectors, so it is appropriate to regard them as a form of preset nanocontrol (Figure 2). At this point the designer faces the same set of choices at nanomachine level as we have already discussed in connection with micromachines. He could use direct control: in fact, QM-1 does not, but obeys a far more elaborate sequence of nanoorders. The reader is referred to the literature for details.

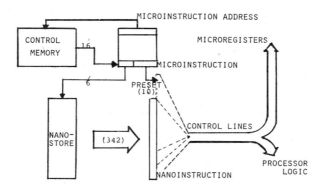

Figure 2:   Nanoprogram Control

259

1.2 Timing and Control Considerations

It will be shown later that interpreting one of the common target instructions takes approximately 20 microorders and two main memory cycles. If a premium is placed on memory utilisation it follows that the effective microorder rate must be ten times that of main memory: to achieve that the early machines use a horizontal or multi-order microinstruction that activates between five and ten processor paths in parallel. The microinstruction rate is synchronised to $\frac{1}{2}$ or $\frac{1}{3}$ the memory cycle time so that a 1.5 μsec core memory would be associated with a 750nsec or 500nsec microinstruction rate. Horizontal coding achieves speed at the expense of generality and ease of programming: in the next lecture we shall introduce a more 'relaxed' form of code in which each microinstruction contains only one or two microorders, which is naturally called vertical control.

The elementary steps of the machine execution cycle have already been indicated. If no overlap is attempted then the major components--control memory and processor--are alternately idle while the other completes its task (remember that read-only memories, and even writable semiconductor memories, may require very little time to recover for the next cycle). In order to achieve higher performance it is necessary to use faster and therefore more expensive components, or to overlap the elementary steps. The options are superficially the same as in machine code design. The main differences derive from the fact that micro-programs have been for the most part fixed, comparatively small, and have made extensive use of multiway branch or switch instruc-tions: the alternative of using a sequence of tests to decode a target instruction would simply be too slow.

A control memory address is frequently composed from several fields whose values are determined at different points in the machine cycle. The high order fields are normally known first, so the construction of an address reflects a gradual narrowing down of the alternatives until the exact microinstruction can be fetched.

In the IBM 360/Model 30, for example, a block address is found as part of the preset control, not normally affected by the current microinstruction; a functional branch is a field inserted directly from the microinstruction, and a switch is the low-order two-bit field of the control memory address, computed from the processor state. Thus, the successor to any instruction is within the current block of 256 (see diagram) and may be dependent on the outcome of one or two conditions or register values.

IBM 360/30 MICROINSTRUCTION ADDRESS	preset	from microinstruction	processor logic
	BLOCK	FUNCTIONAL BRANCH	SWITCH

We can now see more clearly when the overlap of processor and control memory cycles can be achieved. If the control address is determined by the processor state at the end of the current micro-instruction then although access might be initiated on the basis of block/functional branch fields the final decision has to be delayed until the state of the processor logic is known (the example given above falls into that category).

If the control address is determined by the processor state at the end of the previous instruction, then the control memory can be accessed while obeying the current instruction, e.g.

TIME

Previous μinst: ------OBEY / STATUS

Current μinst: ACCESS /   OBEY / STATUS

Next   μinst: ACCESS   /   OBEY------

The timing considerations just described are shared with very much more sophisticated processors: they result from any attempt to overlap one instruction with others and it is easy to see that the more 'changes in direction' in the flow of control the less effective are the overlap arrangements. It is true to say that microprogram is more afflicted by conditional and computed branches than machine language program, fcr which reason designers are reluctant to throw away the contents of the micropipeline and may ask the coder to deal with various 'run-on' conditions. What this means in practice is that one or two instructions in written sequence after a branch may be obeyed, e.g. in decoding a hypo-thetical target instruction the microsequence is written:

m_1 : Extract function field

m_2 : Branch to address + function

m_3 : Increment target instruction counter

Here, although the branch m_2 is taken, the following microinstruc-tion is still obeyed. It is in avoiding or dealing with such coding peculiarities and in taking account of critical memory or I-O timing constraints that microprogramming differs from conven-tional coding, or has done so in the past. Luckily, increasing hardware power has removed many of the characteristics of micro-program from modern machines, perhaps the only positive way in which a microprocessor can be distinguished from a 'mini' is in its dedication to the task of modelling processors rather than users' problems.

1.3 Highway and Register Organization

The basic requirements for imitating a given target instruction set are:

(a) arithmetic primitives for composing the arithmetic, logical and addressing functions of the target machine;

(b) memory mapping and resolution compatible with the store structure of the target machine;

(c) imitation of the internal control states, registers and register access requirements of the target machine;

and (d) peripheral interfaces that reflect the formats, status and timing expected by the target machine.

Within this field the degree of dedication varies with the performance/cost objective. Different design teams have gone about the same task in quite different ways: Husson (p414) makes the point that although the IBM 360 and RCA Spectra 70 achieve the same architecture the latter is a much more 'specific' design than the IBM models.

In this subsection I shall illustrate features of microprocessor design referring to the IBM 360/Model 30 which was one of the earliest models of the IBM 360 range and, as it happens, the subject of an early experiment in language oriented design that I shall refer to later. Further details will be found in Boulaye (1971) and Weber (1967).

Figure 3 shows the data paths in the central processor of the IBM 360/Model 30. There are twelve registers, each of one byte. Apart from the main memory address and data buffers (MN and R) no specific allocation of content is made by hardware. The data paths are uniformly 8 bits. The microinstruction is 60 bits long, encoded into the following microorder groups:

(i)	Store access:	Fields CM, CN, CU
(ii)	Data flow:	4-bit literal field CK
(iii)	ALU control:	CA, CF, CB, CG, CV, CD, CC, CZ
(iv)	Sequencing:	CH, CL
(v)	Status:	CS

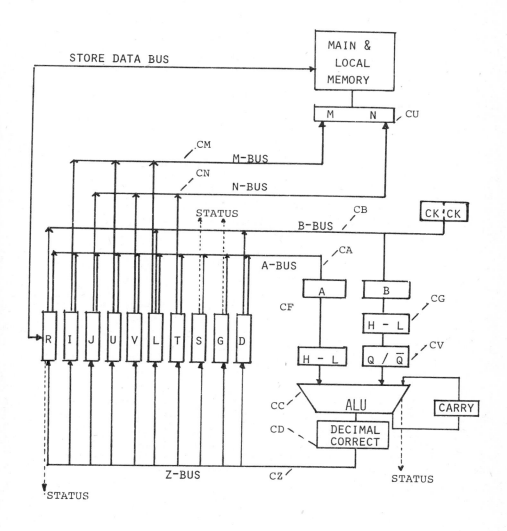

Figure 3: Simplified Data Flow of the IBM 360/Model 30 CPU

J.K.ILIFFE

For example, under group (i):

CM (3 bits) indicates: No action

Read from address IJ, UV, or LT to R

Regenerate

Write from R

CU (2 bits) selects main or local (register) storage.

Under group (iii):

CA (4 bits) selects one of 10 inputs to the ALU through the A register

CB (2 bits) selects one of R, L, D or the literal CKCK

CC (3 bits) selects the actual ALU function

CF (3 bits) modulates the A-input to ALU, i.e. high digit, low digit, none, low or cross-over

CG (2 bits) modulates the B-input to the ALU

CV (2 bits) selects true, complement or six-correct form of B

CZ (4 bits) gives the destination, one of ten registers.

Thus in one microinstruction, which takes 750nsec, an 8-bit arithmetic or logical operation is carried out, half a main store cycle is controlled, and the next microinstruction is selected. In the next cycle the main store operation must be completed while other operations are carried out.

If we consider the loop of instructions which interprets the target machine code it clearly consists of first fetching the instruction, then looking at the function/format digits and preparing each operand by computing an address and accessing the store when necessary, and then branching to the 'semantic' microsequence that interprets the target function. The instruction will normally terminate by servicing interrupts before proceeding to the next in sequence. Elementary IBM 360 instructions take between 15 and 30 µsecs in execution, i.e. 20-40 microinstructions: the large number reflects the fact that any address or arithmetic calculation involving operands of more than 8 bits has to be carried out serially by byte.

In order to achieve higher performance the microregisters and internal data paths must be more closely matched to those of the target machine, and supplementary functional units introduced to minimise the 'mismatch' between the microprocessor and the target system architecture.

2. GENERALISED HOST MACHINES

We have seen some of the ways in which specific features are built into microprogrammable machines to help in modelling particular order codes. However, our main objective is to consider systems at a level removed from machine code, where the target instruction sets can to some extent be chosen to suit the available hardware: in the last lecture we can attempt to answer the question of whether the need for specific adaptation will still arise.

I shall now discuss design generalisations that have been favored in recent years as the result of rapid reduction in the cost of storage and logical devices. In the latter context 'regularity' of hardware is at least as important as circuit or gate count, which is greatly to the benefit of the microprogrammer. I shall refer to the class of processors under discussion as host machines in order to suggest their role and to avoid undue emphasis on 'microprogram' or 'microprocessor' technology. In practice, the principal use of host machines has been in the form of instruc-set emulators (e.g. IBM 360 imitating the IBM 1401). The design objective of producing a 'universal emulator' became feasible with the introduction of writable control memories. It is clear from the outset that machines capable of imitating any instruction set at competitive speed could not be produced at competitive cost, nevertheless such a machine is invaluable as a vehicle for research into computer architectures. The ICL Research Emulator El, Iliffe and May (1972), the Standard Computer Corporation MLP-900, Rakocsi (1972), the Stanford University EMMY, Neuhauser (1975), and the Nanodata Corporation QM-1, Rosin et al. (1972), provide examples of generalised facilities, while in the commercial field the Burroughs Corporation B-1700 is particularly interesting from the point of view of memory allocation.

All the machines in this category use vertical instruction coding which allows much greater flexibility in function sequencing than the older horizontal designs, and at the same time a simpler and more familiar form of program input. The reader may compare the example of microprogramming given in Weber (1967) with the program style of any of the machines mentioned above, which bears comparison with a conventional assembly program listing except for the primitive nature of the arithmetic, the absence of address modification, and the elaborate field selection and branching functions.

In moving to vertical coding it is normally the case that the main memory system has a much higher data rate than the host needs, even with the fastest control store. The extra capacity is used in direct memory access by I-O devices, in dual processor configurations, and in many instances by using the main memory as a source of microinstruction. The last option is particularly attractive because it affords an escape from the rigid limitation

on microprogram that is imposed by a separate control store. On
the other hand it does impose a control structure which is
difficult to rationalise: perhaps the simplest view is to look
upon the interpreter as providing system standards, operating system interfaces, protection, etc, which are not normally present
at the microcontrol level.

The following subsections correspond to the main design areas
noted in the last lecture, with illustrations drawn from the
machines mentioned above. Further examples can be found in less
readily accessible specifications for many machines currently on
the market.

2.1 Generalised Arithmetic and Data Paths

One of the obvious ways in which MSI or LSI components affect
the arithmetic system is in allowing register lengths to be
standardised at a reasonably high value, rather than making use
of specialised lengths seen in earlier machines. The effects are
to speed up the machine and to save control memory, because
operations previously performed by a loop of microinstructions
can now be carried out in one.

The host is still specialised with regard to arithmetic width
and shift paths. Two methods have been employed for variable
precision arithmetic up to a prescribed field size:

(i) using a third input to the ALU, which is in fact a mask allowing carries to propagate. The SCC MPL-900 allows the microinstruction to select one of 32 possible masks which can be
used to propagate carry to the 'normal' sign position. A
mask may also be used to permit operations on unpacked fields
such as 6-bit characters stored in byte positions. One of the
difficulties of working with unpacked data, however, is that
it may eventually have to be aligned to an external interface
such as the store address bus.

(ii) allow the effective ALU width to be variable, i.e. taking
sign, carry and zero-test signals from any position of the
ALU. This method is used in the E1 emulator and the B-1700,
where the sign is part of preset control. If there are more
than one arithmetic widths in use concurrently it is desirable
to have more than one preset sign position, selected by microinstruction.

Variation in ALU width has an obvious counterpart in shift
functions. To reproduce exactly the shift patterns of a word of
arbitrary length it is necessary to preset the point at which end
connections are made, which is more difficult to engineer than
sign adjustment because a stream of bits is being handled. The
E1 emulator does allow shift lengths from one to 64 bits, but the

logic is expensive and most designers have settled for single or double length shifts and rotations. For high level language interpretation that is probably sufficient.

A final area where both the ALU and shifter are affected is in the type of arithmetic carried out. The predominant types are binary integer, decimal, and floating point. Generalised facilities for the last are usually complex and of limited value in either the commercial or research context. Decimal facilities can be built into the ALU in varying degrees, from fully signed operations down to facilities for detecting carries at the decimal digit positions. The choice rests entirely on the final cost/performance required. Although an important area of design it can be 'factored out' in comparative studies of language-oriented and fixed instructions set machines, for which reason I shall not extend the discussion at this point. It is important to remember that if a host has good arithmetic facilities then any lapse in handling the control or data access side of a language will be conspicuous, and conversely.

If the path from memory is not selective enough (and it usually is not) facilities are required for extracting fields from micro-registers for input to the ALU. Such facilities are expensive and may be confined to limited field selection or to particular registers (e.g. in the shift unit). Thus, the B-1700 provides full extraction on one 24-bit register and 6-bit subfield addressing on most others. The E1 emulator can extract any byte from the 15 microregisters for comparison or control purposes. The MLP-900 can conveniently use the third ALU input to select fields within registers. Apart from the obvious hardware cost of selecting any field in any register, space will be taken to identify the field in microinstructions. It does not appear that high level languages demand complete generality, and limitations could be accepted simply on the grounds of coding efficiency.

2.2   Memory Mapping and Address Translation

The unstructured nature of machine codes, allowing instructions to be used as data, and vice-versa, requires a strict correspond-ence to be maintained between the target machine and its represen-tation in the host. (There are exceptions: in mapping the IBM 1401 onto the IBM 360 it is more convenient for the latter to use EBCDIC character codes, converting to and from BCD in those instructions sensitive to BCD formats.) In most instances the target machine word is 'rounded up' when necessary to fit the host, not attempting to make use of every bit in store. However, the B-1700 goes to the length of resolving memory addresses to the bit level and allowing any string of up to 24 bits to be read or written, starting (or finishing) at a given position. In that case 100% memory utilisation can always be achieved.

J.K.ILIFFE

The memory word or part-word is made available for analysis
in the microregisters. It is an advantage to be able to select
from two or three potential data registers in order to avoid
extra 'move' microinstructions. At this point there is also the
opportunity to map the data into a more easily managed form. The
'crosspoints' of the E1 emulator and 'language boards' of the
MLP-900 both allow the choice by program of alternative hardwired
data paths to and from memory. They may be used, for example, to
prepare an instruction for decoding, to align 6-bit characters
to 8-bit byte boundaries, or to handle parity conventions on a
'foreign' data bus. The diagram shows the cross point paths used
by E1 to read ICL 1900 instructions, which enable function,
register and modifier fields to be accessed without shifting the

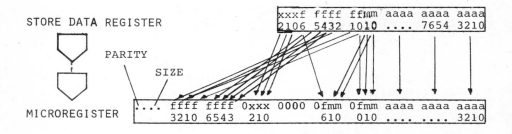

target instruction microregister. The effect of the crosspoint is
to save 5 or 6 steps in the typical interpretive loop of 25-30
microinstructions. It can be seen as complementing the internal
data selection functions: in a machine with powerful field
selection orders crosspoints would be less important.

Apart from data, addresses have to be matched to the conventions of the host. For example, if the target machine uses
decimal addressing and the host uses binary then conversion must
take place before accessing the store. Similarly, if the target
machine operates in virtual program space then virtual to real
translation is called for. If page and segment table accesses
are implicit in each memory reference the address conversion could
easily exceed the combined steps of instruction decode and instruction execution. The alternative of using hardware assistance--
allowing the host to work in virtual space--is expensive and still
leads to delay in memory access. Fortunately, in the environment
of high level language execution it is possible to work in a
virtual address space but avoid most of the overhead of address
translation.

2.3   Representing the Target Machine State

The primary data of an interpretive program are the registers,
the program counter, the instruction register, control flags,

channel status and control words of the target machine. A generalised host would expect to have room for the largest target machine state of interest, but even so it is unlikely to require more than a few hundred bytes of storage for that purpose, which often justifies a file of fast registers, the scratchpad (or local memory in IBM), in addition to the microregisters themselves.

It is a common requirement to access the scratchpad using an index value. For example, a target machine 'register-register' instruction contains two indices. Microinstructions do not admit the type of address calculation found in machine instructions sets, therefore it is necessary to carry out some preliminary scratchpad address calculation. That happens often enough--at least once in most target instructions--to justify building in predictive indexing hardware, which works in the following way. Certain microregister fields are designated (by preset parameters) as scratchpad indices. When any of those field values changes a scratchpad access is initiated (relative to a preset base), so that the corresponding scratchpad element is available for reading or writing in the next microinstruction (compare the main store address registers of the CDC 6600). The crosspoints for the E1 emulator are designed to place the target instruction

PRESET INDEX DESCRIPTOR

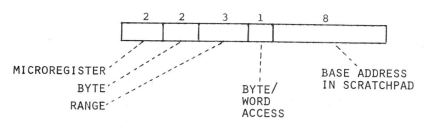

register and modifier digits in the position of predictive indices, allowing the register and modifier values to be used without delay.

The primary data of a high level language machine are the intermediate results, control flags, and the control, stack and environmental pointers that allow access to contextually relevant data. For the most widely used languages the 'state' can be mapped into a register file quite easily; moreover, its access patterns correspond closely to those of conventional target machines, hence the scratchpad organisation of a 'universal emulator' is equally applicable to the major programming languages. Whether there are alternative organisations suited to a wider class of languages is a question we shall consider later: it might be argued that a language is 'major' because it happens to fit onto conventional hardware, and that when that constraint is removed more attention can be given to problem-oriented languages.

2.4 Generalised Control of Peripherals

At this point we must draw a broad distinction between
emulation of the non-privileged users' instruction set and that
of the operating system. The latter would include instructions
for channel selection, requesting device status and sending
commands as well as receiving and sending data. It may also
include special addressing modes for channel control words, page
and segment table control, interrupt register and timer access,
handkeys, displays, fault indicators and so on. Full-scale
emulation, to the extent of running the target machine's peripherals, engineering test programs, channel commands and operating
systems involves at least twice the design effort of the non-
privileged instruction set alone and will almost certainly involve
physical adaptation of the peripheral interfaces.

In the present context, recognising that most languages are
non-specific with regard to the means of peripheral control, the
preferred approach is to match the I-O statements to the host
system using machine language and microcode procedures.

2.5 The Effect of Large Scale Integration

The level of complexity achievable in bipolar LSI devices has
reached the point of presenting complete slices (2 or 4 bits) of
control or arithmetic circuitry in a single package. However,
such circuits are only realised in favourable commercial/technical
situations, i.e. wide applicability and high functional content
in relation to edge connection. Some of the machine features
discussed above would fail on both counts. On the other hand, I
have indicated that language execution makes less stringent
demands than universal emulation, hence the 'generality' aimed at
by device manufacturers may well provide effective support for
the target instruction sets of interest in the context of high
level languages.

How much does generality cost in terms of performance? That
is impossible to say without detailed analysis of a range of
target machines. An indication can be given by comparing the
vertical encoding of the ICL register-store 'ORX' instruction on
the E1 emulator with the horizontal form for the 1904E. In terms
of microorders, the E1 obeys 30 compared with 14 for the specialised host. The difference is in sequence control (13:6), function
decode (5:2) and operand access (10:5). However, the most startling figure in each case is the ratio of support activity to 'useful' function: about 15:1. Our main concern in designing language-
oriented target machines must be to reduce that ratio.

3. INTERPRETATION OF HIGH LEVEL LANGUAGES

The existence of readily microprogrammed host machines naturally gives rise to speculation about the likely return from bypassing the normal instruction set. To do so succeefully involves the solution of a range of problems concerning definition, security, expansion, maintainability and so on, whose solution is taken for granted in conventional systems. Before looking at the broader problems it would be reassuring to have some measure of the potential advantage of microcoding, which is the subject of this section.

It is easy to find performance improvements in the region of 10:1 or more for a particular algorithm expressed in microcode compared with machine code. In evaluating such figures it must be remembered that they derive from three contributing sources: (i) the inherent speed of microcode which is the result of the simplicity of the instructions and the use of high speed control store; (ii) occasional advantages of the microfunctions over the target machine functions, especially in bit manipulation and control sequencing; and (iii) advantages gained from bypassing the architectural framework of the target machine, especially its protection mechanisms.

It would be meaningless to draw conclusions from isolated algorithms. The minimum basis of comparison is taken to be the combination of hardware and software supporting one of the major programming languages, which provides the syntax and semantics for a broad class of problems. The main parameters of performance are taken to be:

(i)   compile and load time

(ii)   execution time

(iii)   size of the support system

(iv)   object program size

(v)   diagnostic aids in (i) and (ii)

The two techniques used for performance comparison are benchmark testing, in which space and time measures are obtained for a representative sample of source programs, and factoring, in which performance is inferred from independent measures on artificially chosen statements. From the design point of view the second is much more useful, though except in the case of Algol 60 there do not appear to be any widely published sets of reference statements. Needless to say, the object of design is to optimise performance at a given system cost over a prescribed set of languages.

The weights attached to the measured parameters will vary from one class of use to another and no attempt will be made to determine them here. The aim is to show how variations in processor

function--specifically those brought about by microprogramming--
affect the parameters (i) - (iv). At the same time the qualita-
tive effect of diagnostic aids will be assessed. It will be seen
that the time measures depend partly on performance of a second
language which will be referred to as the system implementation
language (SIL), so whether the machine is good at compiling
Fortran, say, depends on what it has to do to produce executable
code, and how well it does it: as far as possible the second factor will be isolated by measuring the overall performance of run
time support modules. Similar comments apply to the execution
of primitive functions by stored microprogram or hardware because
that does not usually vary from one language implementation to
another and it can be measured in basic arithmetic speeds. It
would be relevant, however, if one implementation chose to use a
decimal radix, while another implementation of the same language
on the same machine used binary. Most of the language implementations reported in the literature have been rendered useless from
the design point of view by not keeping the executive algorithms
constant: in other words, if a performance gain P is generated
it is impossible to tell how much of P derived from the interpretive technique and how much from improved arithmetic or run-time
support.

The following subsections make a broad distinction between
procedure coding, illustrated by some of the scientific languages,
and data access, which is examined in the context provided by
Cobol.

3.1 Algol, Euler and Expression Evaluation

Factored measurements of Algol performance are reported by
Wichman (1973). In Table 1 I have abstracted some figures for
machines with roughly comparable arithmetic times. It is well
known that the Burroughs B-6700 uses a target instruction set
tailored to the representation of Algol: its effect can be seen
in the times for procedure entry. One would also expect it to be
effective in array assignment, but in this particular case the
compilers spot the indices [1,1] etc and generate optimised code
for the conventional machines. The advantage of the language-
oriented code is to simplify the compiler rather than speed up
execution.

The importance of individual statement times depends on the
weights attached to them in the final performance measure. In
general, arithmetic and array access operations have the highest
weights, procedure entry is an order of magnitude less important,
and array declarations an order of magnitude less than that. It
must be remembered that experimentally observed times reflect a
complex combination of hardware, software and support system.
Implicit in many decisions is the designers' assessment of
different language features, and his budget reflects an assessment

of the importance of the language as a whole.

TABLE 1:	SOME ALGOL STATEMENT EXECUTION TIMES		
Statement	Execution time in microseconds		
	B-6700	IBM 370/165	Univac 1108
x := 1.0	5.5	1.4	1.5
x := 1	2.7	1.9	1.5
x := y	3.9	1.4	1.5
x := y + z	5.5	1.4	3.4
x := y * z	11.3	1.4	4.0
e1[1] := 1	5.3	1.6	2.7
e2[1,1] := 1	7.7	1.7	5.8
e3[1,1,1] := 1	11.3	1.7	9.0
begin array a[1:500];end	408.	242.	918.
p1(x)	28.6	60.7	127.
p2(x,y)	30.5	83.6	137.

[Note: The times for the IBM 370 probably err on the low side because of the effect of the cache]

In comparing object code size, Wichman gives the following figures normalised with respect to Atlas:

Burroughs B-5500	0.16
Univac 1108	0.31
CDC-6600	0.56

The advantage of the Algol-oriented intermediate form in comparison with some of the best conventional systems is evident. To understand how such results are obtained we must examine some target machine states and the functions applied to them.

The advantage of language-oriented intermediate code is that, provided an 'expression-evaluation' mechanism is built in the interpreter, the details of register transfers that are usually found in machine code can be omitted. The compiler is simplified, the code is more compact. It is not inherently faster, because the data access is indirect, but in many instances that is more than compensated by savings in other parts of microprogram. The stack mechanism is the best known means of expression evaluation: the reader is no doubt familiar with the reverse polish form of code used in Burroughs B6700 and other machines and the various stack and environmental (display) pointers associated with it.

However, the apparent simplicity of the Burroughs representation leads to some complexity in the machine functions themselves. The value call operator (VALC) has to be able to detect and interpret all the operand types that can legitimately be presented in the course of computation, including indirect references through the stack and procedural definitions arising in parameter lists. In most applications the questions answered by examining tags could be answered in advance by the compiler: as a general rule unnecessary tests at execution time should be avoided except as deliberate backup for the compiler, the support system or data security.

In contrast, dynamic tag testing is essential to languages such as Euler and APL because the type of a variable is not predictable at compile time. Let us examine the Euler representation in greater detail and see how one of the target machine syllables fits onto the architecture of the IBM 360/Model 30 described in the first section (for greater detail, see Weber (1967)).

The representation of a variable is a [tag,value] pair, the tags having the following significance:

0	Null	5	Reference (m,loc)
1	Integer	6	Procedure (m, link)
2	Real	7	List (length, loc)
3	Boolean	8	(Unassigned)
4	Label (mp, pa)	9	Block mark (in stack)

The run-time environment consists of three storage areas: Program, which is indexed by pa (program address) and link (return address); Variable, indexed by loc (location), where all defined data is to be found, and the Stack, which consists simply of block marks giving static and dynamic chain links, references to parameters in the Variable space, and intermediate results. Operators exist to test the tag of a variable, e.g.

isn A   Is A an integer?

returns the boolean value true or false. Standard operators such as + - * / mod max abs can be applied to numeric values, yielding numeric results, and failing if illegal tags are encountered.

A list is an ordered set of values, each of which is either an elementary type or a list. Lists can be created dynamically, and operators exist for enquiring the length, detaching the tail, selecting an element and concatenating two lists. The existence of reference variables causes the variable space to be maintained by scanning pointers and recovering space which is no longer referenced, updating pointers when compacting the active store areas.

The Euler program area consists of sequences of operator syllables (bytes), each followed by the appropriate number of bytes giving literal values or indices. The program is represented in reverse Polish form, e.g. the statement:

'if v ≤ n or t = 0 then d else e'

would be represented by the following string of 27 bytes:

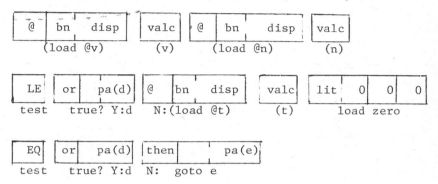

Note that the @ operator forms a reference on the stack, which valc converts to the corresponding value. The translation is thus a simple reordering of the input string, replacing variables by [block number, displacement] pairs. The latter are converted into [mark number, loc] pairs on loading to the stack. In the program the logical connectives give a destination to which control passes if the top of stack element has the required value. Figure 4 gives the microcode for the and, or and then operators. A Boolean variable has the binary form '0011000y', i.e. tag 3 and value y = 1 for true. The microregisters IJ are used as program counter, UV points to the top of stack. For simplicity, the address incrementing microorders, which are really byte-serial, have been written as 'IJ + 1' etc.

The sample microsequence checks the tag of the operand and interprets the logical connective in 8 microinstructions, 4 main memory cycles, or 6 μsec (7.5 if false). The corresponding IBM 360 target instructions would take the form:

```
CLI       0(STACK), LOGT
BE        ORTRUE
CLI       0(STACK), LOGF
BNE       TYPERROR
SH        STACK, ='4'
```

The interpretation of that sequence takes 32 μsec if 'true', 90 μsec if 'false'. It occupies 24 bytes of program as opposed to 3. That puts microprogram interpretation in its most favorable light: dynamic type assignment, minimal arithmetic content and naive compiling techniques. It is easy to see that even with dynamic type assignment it is often possible for the compiler to

J.K.ILIFFE

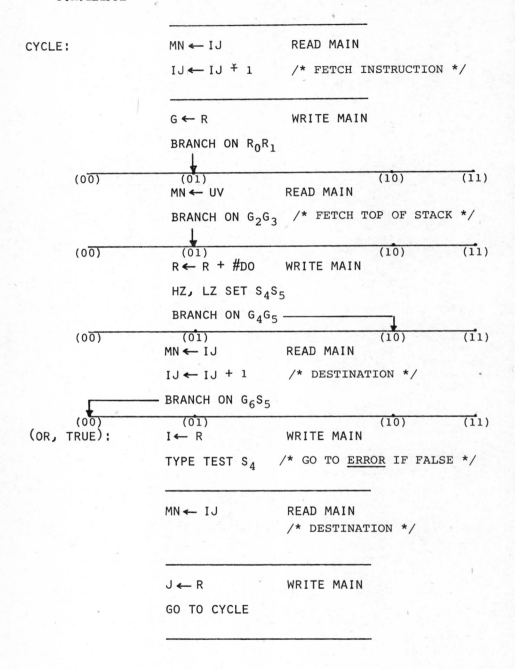

Figure 4: Microcode for Euler Logical Connectives

predict the result of an operation as far as type is concerned, and to omit further checks, as in:

$$\underline{if} \quad x = y \; \ldots$$

which must give a Boolean on top of the stack.

The advantage in space which results from the syllabic form of target instruction is a combination of two effects: the localisation of the operator/operand space implied by the source language, and the use of working registers implied by the stack. It would be possible to compress an operand 'address' to 3 or 4 bits, for example, provided changes of 'context', in which the full meaning of the operand is expanded, can be effected without excessive overhead. Unfortunately, very little is known about the consequences of one choice or another; it is not even clear that procedure boundaries should play a part in defining context. The use of a stack mechanism may not be optimal: we can see that some run-time maintenance activity is involved which a compiler could avoid, and it is known that the majority of expressions found in practice are of very simple forms which do not require the full generality of stack evaluation. Hoevel and Flynn (1977) suggest an alternative primitive form of instruction which recognises many important special cases. Space gains of up to 5:1 for Fortran compared with IBM System 370 optimising compiler are reported.

3.2 Cobol Interpretation

The major parts of a Cobol program are the Data and Procedure Divisions. The program operates on files of records and uses internal records for workspace. Each possible record format is declared in the Data Division: the same physical record may be mapped according to many different declarations, so there is no question of concealing representations or placing descriptive tags as parts of the record. The elementary items of data have a wide variety of representations with a dozen or so basic data types. The elementary items are named, and may be collected into named groups, which in turn may be grouped, up to the level of the record name itself. With the aid of PICTURE descriptions editing characters can be inserted in a field for output (and conversely for input) with the result that the 'type' code associated with a data item can be of almost any length.

Within a record individual items or groups of items may be repeated. The number of actual occurrences may vary, depending on a field in a fixed position in the same record. Repeated items are selected by following the repeated group or field name in the Procedure Division by one or more subscripts, or by using an implied Index value. The coefficients of the associated storage mapping function can be determined by the compiler.

J.K.ILIFFE

The Procedure Division is composed of a number of Segments, whose significance derives from the days of programmed overlays. A Segment comprises a number of labelled paragraphs, each containing one or more sentences. A sentence consists of one or more Cobol statements.

Individual statements have a fairly simple syntax, a verb followed by data names and Segment or paragraph names, e.g.

ADD P TO Q GIVING DAY_TOTAL ROUNDED

where P, Q and DAY_TOTAL are data names. The definition of Cobol implies strict observation of decimal rounding and truncation and is subject to the types of operands and the size of intermediate results (18 digits). The compiler is required to indicate if operands are incompatible, or if intermediate results are out of range. Some indication of verb frequencies is given by the following measures from a benchmark test:

VERB	DYNAMIC USAGE	STATIC USAGE
MOVE	30%	33%
IF	30%	18%
GOTO	11%	19%
ADD	10%	6%
PERFORM	7%	8%
WRITE	4%	3%
READ	3%	2%
Others	5%	11%

Thus for execution purposes seven verbs account for 95% of executed statements, while the same seven account for almost 90% of stored statements. The target code can be chosen purely as a compromise between compiler and microcode, without concern for reconstructing the source string (which affects APL coding for example). The final form depends on what are regarded as reasonable limits for field sizes in one Cobol source module. In the target instruction listed in Table 2 the maxima are taken to be:

Variables: 4096 ; Indices: 256 ; Files: 256 ; Data areas: 64

Procedure variables: 256.

In the design used here, which is based on a Cobol interpreter written for the ICL El emulator, each Cobol statement is represented by a sequence of 16-bit target instructions.

In the Data Division all names are mapped unambiguously into indices in the lists of data qualifiers (DQT), file and index table. Procedure variables are indexed in the Procedure Division. Information built up during the compilation phase can be carried over into execution without change in many cases. Figure 5 (p.289) shows the modular structure of Cobol as far as it affects the interpreter. The DQT contains a 64-bit descriptor for each variable, giving:

- the index of the base pointer for the record currently containing the variable
- offset and limit of the variable within the record area
- whether the debug option applies
- operand type and scaling information
- if subscripted, the index of mapping parameters in the subscript information table
  if edited, the index of editing parameters in the edit information table.

At runtime the data qualifier element DQT[n] is interpreted to give the address pointer to a sequence of bytes (or bits) within the area defined by the base. About 20 microsteps are required to extract the data attributes and place them in microregisters, followed by whatever is needed to extract the data itself and present it for the next operation. Hence the management of the DQT represents a significant part of the interpretive overhead.

In measuring Cobol performance the time and space requirements of a set of test statements were measured, and final figures of merit obtained by weighting the results according to dynamic or static usage. For space, a gain of 1:3 resulted in comparison with the ICL 1900 program requirements. It appeared possible to improve on that by adding to the function set. For time, an overall improvement of 1:2.5 was observed in comparison with the conventional compiler on the ICL 1900. That figure is disappointing. It is accounted for in part by the arithmetic complexity of Cobol. Nevertheless the average Cobol statement appears to need about 200 microsteps (as opposed to 500), and in several instances the conventional compiler generates code that runs faster than the interpreter, for much the same reason as we saw earlier in looking at Algol implementations. However, another factor proves to be significant: the time spent in the interface between the language interpreter and the supporting SIL.

TABLE 2:	A COBOL TARGET INSTRUCTION LANGUAGE

Format #1

4	12
f	n

f=0: Source operand at DQT[n]
f=1: Destination at DQT[n]
f=2: Operand at DQT[n]
f=3: Operand n
f=6: Branch within code area, offset n

Format #2

4	4	8
f	v	n

f=7:   n-byte literal operand, type v
f=8:   Scale operand, partial result,..., by n
f=9:   Arithmetic; scale first operand by n
       v[ADD, SUBTRACT, SUBTRACT-GIVING, MULTIPLY,
       DIVIDE, DIVIDE-REMAINDER, ..., etc]
f=10: Branch DEPENDING, via Procedure variable n
f=11: Branch n, depending on condition v
f=13: v[MOVE, COMPARE, SET INDEX, DEBUG, STOP,
       and call RUNTIME support]

RUNTIME: ACCEPT TIME, DATE, DAY, DISPLAY,
          OPEN, CLOSE, READ, WRITE, REWRITE, START, DELETE,
          CANCEL, CALL, EXIT, etc.

Cobol control structure is the source of some complexity because of the use of procedure variables and debugging options. Apart from the normal branching determined by GOTO statements it is possible to specify that a particular paragraph or sequence of paragraphs should be PERFORMed one or more times, or until a condition is satisfied (possibly varying some elements on each repetition). A simple compiler cannot tell in advance which paragraphs will be the subject of PERFORM, so it will insert a possible branch to a 'procedure variable' at the end of each paragraph: if PERFORM does not apply, the branch 'drops through' to the next paragraph in sequence. Further complication derives from the ALTER verb, which can be used to change the destination of a GOTO. Rather than change the stored object code the branch is again directed through the procedure variable table.

The complication arising from debugging is that any attempt to access a named data item, paragraph, file or index may be required to enter a debug procedure. In most compilers that means that the code generated for handling debugged elements is different from (and slower than) normal code, even when executing with DEBUG OFF. In interpretive systems the same target code is generated in all cases and the branch is taken in the interpreter.

4. INTERPRETIVE SYSTEM DESIGN

Improving on the range-defined instruction sets of fifteen years ago without meeting comparable system objectives is not particularly difficult. To present a realistic alternative it must be shown how programming standards can be maintained through a very wide power range; it must be possible to develop and maintain new languages and subsystems taking full advantage of the architecture without endangering system security; storage and control structures must be created to suit modern applications rather than those of the early 1960's. As far as I know, no 'microsystem' has been developed with the required properties. Even so, it is not sufficient to show that variable microcode achieves better results than fixed instruction sets: we also need to be convinced that it is the best way of using modern technology. In this section I shall draw together some of the results observed in language-oriented machine design and suggest two alternative system frameworks in which the demonstrated advantages could be retained.

4.1. The Effect on Language Parameters

As I have already indicated, many of the measures of language performance are affected strongly by the choice of supporting system, which we suppose to be reflected in the semantics of the System Implementation Language (SIL). For example, suppose the SIL is in fact a copy of the Executive package of a conventional machine range, and that a Cobol application package is obeyed (a) using the fixed instruction set and (b) using a Cobol target code such as discussed in the last lecture. Then the observable effect on storage requirements would be as follows (using typical figures for the ICL 1900):

	(a) Fixed Instr.	(b) Fixed+Cobol
Fixed instr. μcode	16 Kbyte	16 Kbyte
Cobol target μcode	0	9 Kbyte
Executive (kernel) functions:	16 Kbyte	16 Kbyte
System functions (spooling, command language, etc)	20 Kbyte	20 Kbyte
Cobol run-time support:	25 Kbyte	25 Kbyte
Cobol application – data (say)	9 Kbyte	9 Kbyte
– code (say)	9 Kbyte	3 Kbyte
Total	95 Kbyte	98 Kbyte

In other words, the reward for a great deal of effort and investment in control memory is negligible as far as storage is concerned. Of course, one can present the picture in other ways and use the speed gain to advantage if there is sufficient I-O capacity, but the point remains that unless the support system gains similar advantages from the interpretive techniques the improvement in language performance will be seriously diluted. Let us assume, therefore, that the SIL itself benefits from the use of micro-program. The effect may be seen as space reduction and a gain in speed; more probably it will be seen as improvement in function and flexibility. In reviewing the parameters listed earlier some of the requirements of the SIL will be noted.

(i) Compile and Load Time

Substantial (say a factor of 5) gains in speed can be made in the portions of a compiler concerned with lexical and syntax analysis, and to a lesser extent in code generation, by microcode interpretation of syntax tables. Where in-line coding has been used in the past the speed gain is smaller but significant saving in space is achieved by table-driven techniques. Compile time is indirectly affected by the choice of object code under (ii).

Load time is normally determined by the supporting system. If all programs have to be mapped into a (virtual or real) linear store the time and space overheads in starting a job step may be significant (comparable with the compiler itself in many conven-tional systems). Moreover, the operating inconvenience is significant and may result in such anomalies as separate 'batch' and 'load-and-go' language systems. There is no reason, however, why the SIL functions should not allow program execution with explicit structure. For example, the operating environment shown in Figure 5 can be maintained with no appreciable execution over-head on the part of the SIL. In that case, the load time is negligible.

(ii) Execution Time

Excluding arithmetic and I-O, execution time is governed by the time of access to variables and the change of control environ-ments, i.e. the subsets of the program space immediately available from particular points in the program. It is the 'localisation' of the environment which allows short addresses to be used and produces the greatest contribution to code compaction. The dia-gram shows the components of a generalised access chain. Data elements are assumed to be created in blocks (activation records or file areas) which are not necessarily contiguous in store, but selectable by an index n.   Data identifiers in the source text are mapped into indices m, which are used to refer to a table of attributes (cf. the DQT in Cobol) which give record pointer, off-set, size, type, and possibly other information derived by the compiler and required during execution. In general, several sets of attributes may refer to the same record, and one set of attributes can refer to several record areas (through dynamic adjustment of the control environment).

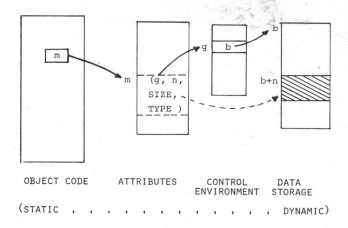

OBJECT CODE   ATTRIBUTES   CONTROL   DATA
ENVIRONMENT STORAGE

(STATIC , , , , , , , , , , DYNAMIC)

    Languages differ in the amount of attribute information
carried into the execution phase, the method of changing the control environment, the time at which attributes are assigned, and
hence in the ways of distributing components of the access chain
in storage. In Fortran, for example, attributes and record
pointers can be absorbed into the object code; in APL the object
code and attributes are dynamically assigned; in Algol the (g,n)
pair and size can be absorbed into the object code while the type
is sometimes attached to the data in the form of a tag. Where
explicit maintenance of attribute and environment is demanded by
the language there can be significant gains from using microcode.
The ratio of addressing and control instructions to arithmetic in
the output of a conventional compiler is in the region of 4:1, so
assuming a 5:1 speed increase from microcoding the former an overall speed gain of 5:1.8 or 2.8:1 is indicated. One would expect
more for the highly structured or 'dynamic' languages. Further
speed gains can be expected where specialised arithmetic functions
are called for, e.g. array, complex, controlled precision or
character string manipulation. A minimum overall gain of 3:1 in
speed of a 'production' compiler to range standards would be a
realistic objective for the languages in common use.

    A language allowing free assignment of pointers (reference
variables) entails potentially serious support overheads in the
assignment and recovery of space, not necessarily eliminated by
the provision of a large virtual store. Even if the SIL recognises
pointers it seems preferable for the language subsystem to undertake its own space management to take advantage of known local
characteristics. The language 'pointer' is evaluated in terms of
the underlying program structure at the time of use: that operation occurs frequently and benefits from processor adaptation to
the extent that once an evaluation has been carried out the result
can be used repeatedly on successive items of data. It is then
required of the SIL to allow language interpreters to work with

'absolute' as well as virtual addresses. In the next subsection
we shall see what that implies. (The alternative of having both
the SIL and the language microcode work in a virtual space supported by hardware can be disregarded because of the delay in accessing memory and the poor store utilization that results.)

Space management functions are principally concerned with
searching for and updating pointers and physically moving blocks
of data. They are time consuming and in many languages their use
is discouraged by artificial means, so the gain from making them
more efficient would be seen in program flexibility (in the user
language and the SIL) rather than in execution time.

(iii) Size of Support System

The SIL code benefits in two ways: in many situations, e.g.
in compiling to language-oriented code, it has to do less; and
it does it more efficiently than other high level system programming languages, or more elegantly than a macroassembler. Size
reductions in the region of 5:1 have been achieved for compilers.
Each language microcode represents a space overhead of at least
10 Kbytes, plus a similar amount for the resident SIL.

(iv) Object Program Size

Tailoring the object code to fit the source language shows the
clearest gains over conventional systems because of the elimination of unnecessary function, register and address bits. An
overall reduction in procedure size of 4:1 for large programs,
including attribute tables, would be a realistic aim. No significant gains in data mapping over a conventional system with word
and character addressing can be expected. Gains in space can be
seen as gains in main memory and channel capacity and to a smaller
extent in file space.

(v) Diagnositc Aids

As any APL user discovers, interpretive methods can give
exceptionally good diagnostic information, sufficient to overcome
eccentricities of the language itself. Unfortunately, diagnostic
quality is one that cannot be measured and is often overlooked in
favour of marginal improvements in the others.

4.2 Microsystem Problems

The use of microprogram brings its own problems, and raises
the question of whether the implied comparison with machines of
the mid-60's was the correct one to use. In the system context,
the obstacles to using interpretive microprogram are as follows.

INTERPRETIVE MACHINES

(A) Range Definition

The microprogram appropriate to a high performance machine is quite different from that of a slower microprocessor. There is also an absolute speed limitation: a machine executing target instructions at 10 MIPS is obeying microorders at least 10 times as fast, which is beyond the power of vertically encoded (i.e. easily programmed) host machines.

(B) Security

Microprogram derives part of its speed advantage by ignoring the security checks inherent in fixed instruction sets. For a small amount of microprogram under control of the manufacturer that is tolerable. The language performance figures obtained in practice give the interpreter responsibility for resources normally regarded as protected, i.e. absolute addresses, in which case the security of the system is in the hands of language implementors.

(C) Flexibility

Microprogram is a static form of code. It cannot easily be moved in store. Fast control memories and scratchpads are necessarily small, so the problems of sharing resources between interpreters and scheduling their use have to be solved.

Of the above, (B) alone is sufficient to prevent widespread use of microprogram in commercial systems. Four types of response can be recognised:

(1) Embed the Microprogram in a Conventional System

We have already noted that the space and time advantages are diluted in the context of a conventional system, nevertheless those that remain are obtained with minimum investment in redesign. The IBM APL Assist Feature running under DOS/VS, OS/VS1 and OS/VS2 has been made available on the System/370 Models 135, 138, 145 and 148 (Hassitt and Lyon (1976)). It consists of an additional 20 Kbytes of microprogram, resident in main store, which interprets APL statements. It carries out virtual--real address translation according to the rules of the host system, but returns control to the host to service interrupts and page faults. Hence system integrity depends upon correct use of addresses in the APL microcode.

(2) Extend Security Boundaries to the Microprogram Level

The in-line checks that can be used without impairing performance are restricted to key comparison, lockout on fixed sized

blocks of store, etc. The El emulator provides write protection
on 16-word frames of scratchpad, 64-word frames of control memory,
16 Kword frames of main memory and all I-O multiplex positions.
The main drawback to such schemes is their inaccuracy and the
difficulty encountered in handling dynamically changing or moving
programs, which occur quite frequently in modern systems.

(3) Control Address Formation in Microcode

An alternative, which can be seen as a generalisation of the
first approach, is to validate addresses when they are formed,
then to restrict their use so that further checks are unnecessary.
The SIL is responsible for forming addresses (from segment capabilities); the language microcode can modify them within given
limits and access the store directly. Addresses are distinguished
by tags so that the SIL can find and update them when necessary,
independent of the source language. This method is used in the
Variable Computer System(Iliffe and May (1974)) on the El emulator,
which makes provision for tag manipulation. For complete security,
however, specialised hardware support is necessary.

(4) Separate the Language Processors Physically

A special case of the second approach, which is attractive
because technology is available in the form of low-cost microprogrammable machines. The separation is conceptually physical,
in the form of multiple processor-memory pairs, but it could be
achieved by time-slicing.

From the general design viewpoint either of the last two
approaches can be used to provide a viable system model. Each
intends to cover a wide range of performance by using multiple
computers. From 3 it can be seen that because access to program
space is controlled the SIL and user programs can coexist in the
main memory and control store (if it exists), and that programs
can be distributed over the available memory space. This
'distributed program' model is well suited to the class of
applications with dynamically changing program requirements, or
which can be expressed in terms of cooperating parallel processes.

From 4 a more specialised 'dedicated language' model is derived.
Each program, together with its interpreter, has unrestricted use
of the local memory space of a processor-memory pair during
execution, but it is rolled in and out by the scheduler which forms
part of the SIL. The SIL microcode and system procedures can be
protected by holding them in read-only memory. Access to shared
data or to overlays must be through some form of secondary store
manager, which checks the rights of the user against declared
accessibility of the data, a relatively slow operation. The
disadvantages of the dedicated-language model are the sensitivity
of programs to physical store sizes, the amount of unproductive

traffic between central (i.e. secondary) memory and language processors, the poor utilization of processor and memory resources (if it is argued that processors and memory are give-away items, why bother with microprogram at all?). Nevertheless, such a system is in many ways the easiest to understand, it is least affected by failure of one of the processor-memory pairs, and it lends itself to the 'personal computer' mode of working in the same way that private cars lend themselves to private transport, however inefficient.

Each model presupposes the use of a system implementation language (SIL) whose aim is to provide a set of functions that can be used in all language applications to reduce development effort and code duplication at both micro- and target machine levels. In so doing it sets standards that can also be used in the variable part. There is no doubt that certain operations such as input-output and frequently used arithmetic procedures are properly part of the SIL. How far one can go depends on the type of system: if the integrity of system data cannot be guaranteed (which is the case for dedicated-language models) the amount of support the SIL can give is limited. On the other hand, commitment of the SIL to support facilities that are rarely used complicates the system and wastes resources. The interesting design area is thus the 'fringe' of functions just inside or just outside the SIL, which I can best illustrate by reference to the Variable Computer System developed on the E1 research emulator and later transferred to another host machine.

4.3 An Example of a SIL: The Variable Computer System

VCS is implemented at two levels of control: microprogram and the system target language (VCSL) in which all compilers and system utilities are written. The VCS procedures can be called either at microcode or at machine code level. It follows that if a microprogrammed procedure is called from machine level, or vice-versa, some code must be obeyed to adapt from one level to the other. It is undesirable to impose restrictions at this point because one cannot always predict whether a procedure will be committed to microprogram; the discrimination must be dynamic or immediately before task initiation, at worst. For that reason the list of procedure activations associated with any process contains both micro and machine level linkage information. Again, it is undesirable to impose limits on the depth of procedure call, therefore linkage information is stacked in main memory, the host machine link stack having very limited use.

Procedure activations form part of the process state vector (PSV), which also contains VCS registers, environment pointer, current program pointer and various flag bits that are mapped into the host registers. As calculation proceeds it is possible that other host registers will be used, but it is required that all

J.K.ILIFFE

state information will be contained in the PSV at points where a
change of procedure or process may occur. In that way the VCS
can effect process management without explicit knowledge of the
language state, and with a fair degree of independence of the
host machine. Similarly, by recognising tagged addresses the VCS
can carry out store management without explicit declaration of
the mapping used in current processes.

Procedure entry and exit is controlled through a dynamic chain
of marked links. The purpose of the marks is to distinguish task
initiation, system call and user procedure calls, allowing various
levels of restart to be employed and providing excellent diagnostics
at both control levels.

The interpretation to be placed on a program segment is
indicated by a control type assigned to a particular compiler.
Control type zero is used for pure data: any attempt to obey it
will fail. Control type 1 is for system use, type 2 for VCSL
target code, and type values for language extensions, e.g. to
Cobol, APL, etc, are assigned 3, 4, ... on a global basis. The
control type is examined on procedure call and return (in the case
of machine level code), branching to the appropriate interpreter.

It can be seen that the PSV's are key control structures that
must be protected if system security is to be ensured. The most
efficient and flexible basis for protection is a capability scheme
such as that of the Basic Language Machine. Many of the VCS
functions are concerned with creating and manipulating abstract
system objects in a consistent way, the PSV's being the representation of the abstract idea of a 'process'. In particular, we find
functions for:

(i)   setting up operating environments (bases) and defining
       the resources found in them;

(ii)   creating, starting and stopping processes;

(iii) entering and leaving procedures;

and (iv) controlling access to resources.

Here a 'resource' is a storage segment, PSV, I-O device, or a set
of resources. The recursive nature of this definition allows each
base to be constructed as a tree. Clearly, the integrity of any
object depends in the end on maintaining the integrity of its
representation, i.e. the store, and of the procedures that are
applied to it, i.e. the activation records contained in the PSV's.

Program structure is dynamic. A new base is able to share the
information available to its 'parent' at the time of its creation,
with the effect that a hierarchy of bases is set up with the
'system' at the apex. The base structure is important in building

language subsystems and dependent application environments:
Figure 5 shows a typical three-level base structure to which
one or more Cobol modules might be attached.

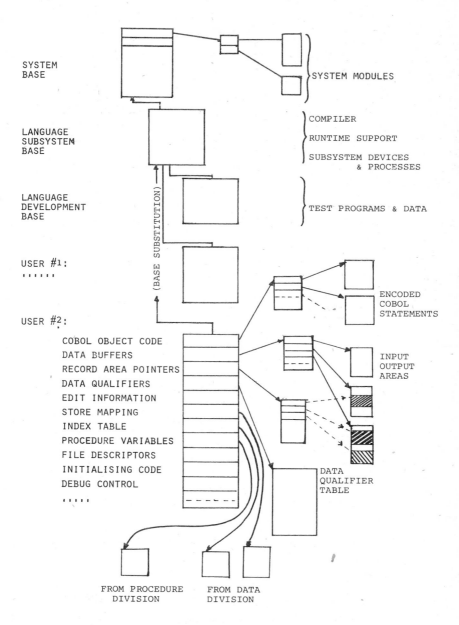

SYSTEM
BASE

SYSTEM MODULES

LANGUAGE
SUBSYSTEM
BASE

COMPILER

RUNTIME SUPPORT

SUBSYSTEM DEVICES
                  & PROCESSES

LANGUAGE
DEVELOPMENT
BASE

TEST PROGRAMS & DATA

USER #1:
......

(BASE SUBSTITUTION)

ENCODED
COBOL
STATEMENTS

USER #2:

COBOL OBJECT CODE
DATA BUFFERS
RECORD AREA POINTERS
DATA QUALIFIERS
EDIT INFORMATION
STORE MAPPING
INDEX TABLE
PROCEDURE VARIABLES
FILE DESCRIPTORS
INITIALISING CODE
DEBUG CONTROL
.....

INPUT
OUTPUT
AREAS

DATA
QUALIFIER
TABLE

FROM PROCEDURE
DIVISION

FROM DATA
DIVISION

Figure 5:   VCS Base Hierarchy

Resources are defined by various types of capability, found in capability segments at the branch points of the program tree. The most time-critical VCS functions are those concerned with forming addresses from segment capabilities (codewords), and with using them to access memory. For system reasons a codeword refers indirectly to store via a global segment table (GST). The corresponding address retains the GST index in order to check the accessibility and position of the segment, which happens each time an address is loaded into a register (from the PSV). The access code is used to control shared (read-only) access by several processes or unique (update) access by individuals. All such control and conversion together with the recycling of GST indices and memory is exercised by VCS microprogram, which provides a good example of the application of microcode to system problems.

The 'read', 'write' and 'modify' instructions which should strictly speaking be found on the VCS function list are too critical to handle by microsubroutine call. Users are therefore allowed to issue them directly for binary data and trusted to observe the limit and protection codes.

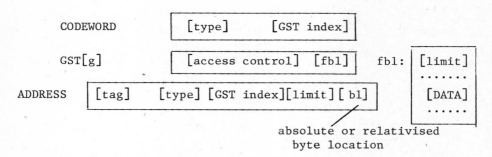

CODEWORD   [type]   [GST index]

GST[g]   [access control] [fb1]   fb1: [limit]
                                            . . . .
ADDRESS   [tag] [type] [GST index][limit] [b1]   [DATA]
                                            . . . . . .

absolute or relativised
byte location

In the course of design numerous candidates for positions in the VCS function list have to be considered. A fundamental problem in extending the system is to achieve valuable effect without degrading overall performance. Sometimes a microcode branch is obtained 'for free', while at other times a new facility entails extra tests in a critical path. The available control store in a range of host machines has also to be considered. Options considered in that light are:

(i)   selection of set elements by key rather than index value;

(ii)   provision of paging facilities;

(iii) static chaining in the procedure activation list;

(iv)   introduction of a third segment type consisting of a set of tagged elements;

(v)   use of semaphore variables for interprocess communication.

There are many possible variations of the addressing rule such
as (i) and (ii) but each entails a loss of space or time that
skilled programmers will try to circumvent. The best programming
environment appears to be a set of dynamically constructed,
variable sized segments: they make optimal use of store and
their access overheads are well understood. It is left to subsystem designers to map programs efficiently onto the tree structure, so that the store management implicit in a language such as
APL is carried out in part by the language subsystem (which is
aware of the details of APL usage) and in part by VCS functions
which provide the containers for the APL workspaces.

VCS procedures are not intended to represent high level control structures directly, though they happen to be adequate for
VCSL and simple languages such as Fortran. Recognition of static
levels involves extra work in procedure management and a variety
of actions dealing with special cases that could not be built into a fixed system, so it is intended that such structures be
mapped by the language microcode into simulated control stacks.
It seemed probable that mapping a display structure such as those
found in Algol-derived languages would benefit from the ability to
manipulate sets of addresses, but the practical implementations
studied so far have used indirect mapping techniques, i.e. a new
form of 'pointer' peculiar to the language is invented and mapped
dynamically onto the VCS structures (cf. the Data Qualifiers in
Cobol). The advantage of such techniques is that they can take
account of language parameters in the design of pointers, but we
noted earlier that 20 or more microsteps may be taken to reconstruct the absolute VCS address.

Finally, various forms of semaphore signalling were considered, but only a minimal 'busy' flag was implemented in the PSV.
The argument against greater elaboration is that the access
mechanism of the Global Segment Table already provides direct control over shared resources, associating the control variable with
the resource itself, so there is little point in providing more
obscure functions to the same end. The release of a segment for
rescheduling at the end of a critical section is not automatic:
to force it at procedure exit, for example, would again imply
intolerable overheads, so an explicit VCS Release function is
required.

The Variable Computer System provides support for language-
oriented microprograms in easily portable form: an investment of
about 8 Kbytes of microcode transfers the VCS functions, VCSL
support codes, compilers, utilities, etc to a new host machine.
It provides the type of support which is needed if the advantages
of microcode are to be fully realised for each language, and
although the function list could be improved in the light of

experience I think it is a sound method of exploiting the current generation of general purpose emulators, acknowledging that system security rests on the correct design of language interpreters.

4.4 Future Developments

Careful choice of words has left the most critical question unanswered: leaving aside short-term expedients, is a general pur-pose host machine with two levels of writable control the best starting point for processor design? I think not, for three reasons.

Firstly, the arguments that have been used are based on mea-sures of high level language implementation, whereas a substantial part of information processing still lies outside that well-defined area. Several systems of mediocre performance and limited applicability have resulted from the assumption that a high level language or set of languages would cover the field. On the other hand without the formality of high level constructs it is diffi-cult to see how to make use of writable control memory.

But even accepting the limitations of high level languages it can still be argued that the interpretive approach is not optimal in many instances and that the system problems outlined earlier have still not been solved. It has to be shown that there is a better approach to language implementation with the range and flexibility of conventional systems. We begin by drawing a distinction between the inherent coding advantages of micropro-grammed interpretation and the benefits which result from using fast storage or ducking behind the range architecture.

Microprogrammed interpreters have improved on fixed, complex target instruction sets to the extent that much of the redundant information in the instruction stream has been eliminated. The figures given earlier show a reduction from 500 to 200 microsteps for the average Cobol statement, or a reduction from 15:1 to 6:1 in the ratio of support steps to useful arithmetic and logic. That suggests there is still room for improvement, which might be found in a hybrid form of control in which in-line and interpre-tive methods can be mixed. After all, an interpreter is simply a means of calling a subroutine from the target instruction stream: its weakness is that the interpretive overhead is paid on every syllable. In other words, if we think in terms of an 8-bit function syllable, 128 codes might be assigned to hard-wired functions, the other 128 to procedure entries in a variable 'control environment'.

The starting point I suggest is that each language should be analysed from the point of view of minimising the product of micro-steps and space in the representation of programs, covering both instruction and descriptor decoding. I expect, though I do not know of a fully tested example, that the best code a compiler can produce will be a mixture of microsteps and monosyllabic procedure calls. In other words, the separation into 'interpreter' and 'target' code is no longer relevant.

The problem of presenting the control stream to the processor at high speed cannot be solved by committing the entire interpreter to control memory because it is now diffused through the program space. As it happens, it was not at all clear how to do that in a flexible manner for a general purpose multilanguage system. The conversion of 'microsteps' to 'nanoseconds' can best be treated in the broader context of speeding up memory access rates: look ahead, use cache buffers, or in the last resort pay more, but do not attempt to deal specifically with the restrictions of control memory or scratchpad. It will be noted in passing that for the multicomputer architectures envisaged the path from memory to processor is shorter than that of a centralised system with shared store highways, therefore the benefit of high speed control memory would be less marked.

Returning to system problems, we are left with (A) range cover which it was (and still is) hoped to achieve using multiple computers, and (B) security. The dedicated language system is not affected by the use of hybrid control: no assumptions are made about program security. The distributed-program system does depend on controlled address formation, which was achieved in the Variable Computer System by a policy of trusting the language subsystems. With hybrid control it becomes imperative to have hardware-enforced protection. It is also the case that many of the key VCS functions at present implemented by microsubroutine calls could be implemented by in-line code.

The above discussion has been based on vaguely defined 'microsteps' comparable with the vertical microinstructions of present-day machines. The reader may feel concerned at reverting to a processor style not far removed from that of twenty years ago. Is there a danger of inventing more and more complex microsteps and repeating the evolutionary cycle that led to the IBM System/360 and other 'range' architectures? The return in space that can be expected from more complex instructions depends on finding frequently repeated di-grams or n-grams that can be suitably packaged. They are more likely to occur in arithmetic, where 'hardened' floating point and decimal operations can be expected, then in control sequences. It would not be surprising to see the host arithmetic functions develop in the direction of current machine codes (with type interpretation placed on descriptor or tag fields), but the many modes of data access appear to benefit very little from complex addressing rules. I expect machine design to evolve from the 'restart point' of interpretive techniques, but there is no danger of reinventing the wheel after a few years.

SYSTEMS OF MANY PROCESSING ELEMENTS

David Aspinall

University College of Swansea

1. INTRODUCTION

When the microprocessor was introduced into the electronic engineer's component repertoire in 1972, it heralded a new era of electronic equipment implementation possibilities (Aspinall, 1976a).
Equipment for communications, instrumentation, and process control, for the enhancement of performance and to improve the ergonomics of domestic appliances (white goods) had previously been
based upon electrical circuits in which components were interconnected by simple conductors, usually copper wire.

The components include the transducers to translate the physical
values of mechanical or chemical properties into electrical
analogues or to convert electrical command signals into mechanical movement. Such components form the interface between the
host system to be served and the electrical system to serve it.
The service being to measure, process, or control, to gain
improved performance of the host. This information processing
service used to be based mainly upon electronic or electro-mechanical components; now it can be implemented by a combination of
interconnected programmable components plus the programs and data
structures within these components. In designing, commissioning,
and maintaining such equipment, the engineer finds himself requiring to adopt the attitudes of a computer engineer and to learn
from the experience of twenty-five years of computer system development and use.

These new attitudes will be incorporated into the well-proven
design methodologies of the electronics engineer and, hopefully,
modified to strengthen the design disciplines necessary to produce reliable and efficient products.

Consider, for example, the products of a manufacturer of electronic instruments. These range from basic measuring instruments
such as the voltmeter, through multirange meters to signal gener-
ators and signal processors for spectral analysis. The manufacturer should develop a strategy for specification, design, produc-

tion and maintenance which is common to all products in the range.
It has been recognised that the key to any such strategy is a
structured representation of the equipment requirements which can
be used as the basis for the documentation necessary for the subsequent stages in the product production use and maintenance
(Ross, 1977).

For a typical measuring instrument, the requirement definition
may appear as in Fig.1. On the front panel of the instrument will
be the controls to enable the user to set the desired range of
operation and select the facility required. Activity 1 must
interpret these commands and arrange for their display back to
the user, and also for them to control the other activities in
the instrument. The quantity to be measured will usually be in
an analogue or continuous form, and activity 2 is required to convert into digital form. The range and performance of the conversion is controlled from activity 1. The digital data then passes
to activity 3, where the measurement process is carried out.

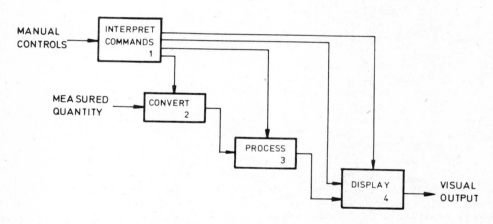

Fig.1   Activities in a Measuring Instrument.

The instrument may provide a range of different measurement capabilities which are pre-selected by the interpret commands activity.
The process activity must be matched to the rate at which data is
provided by the convert activity and can be accepted by the display activity which receives the processed data. The display
activity will further process the data to present it in a form
acceptable to the user. This may be on a CRT visual display
unit, or an array of light-emitting diodes, or a pen recorder, as
required. One important activity which is not shown in the diagram is that of self-test. The low capital cost of the instrument

cannot justify the expense of a team of on-site maintenance engin
eers. Facilities for rapid fault diagnosis by the user must be
included within the instrument to provide high availability. Such
facilities, together with further elaboration of the various activities in Fig.1, should be represented within the structured
requirement definition description.

On scanning the range of instruments, it is evident that the
sophistication of the equipment increases from the simple meter
through to the complex signal processor, and it is not surprising
that the cost of a piece of equipment rises with its sophistication,
as shown in Fig.2. A graph of this type is not unfamiliar to the
manufacturer of computing equipment in attempting to meet the
varying requirements of different users. The computer industry
realised that a range of computer mainframes, each based upon a
single sequential processor, could meet such a demand curve. At
the bottom of the curve, the processor is based upon low-cost
logic circuits. On moving up the curve, higher performance logic
circuits are used, and there is an increase in the parallelism of
each processing step. At all points in the range there is a single
processor which obeys a sequential program.

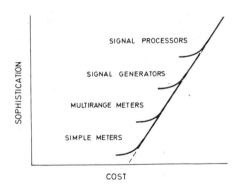

Fig.2   Range of Instruments : Sophistication versus Cost.

D.ASPINALL

An instrument manufacturer could adopt a similar strategy. The
activities of Fig.1 could be implemented as one program to be
processed in a single processing element. At the bottom of the
range, the processing element could be a single micro-computer
component comprising a 4-bit word processor plus ROM and
RAM. Moving up the range, the processor could become more
powerful, as demonstrated by its 8-bit or 16-bit word processing
ability. For the highest members of the range, specialised processors could be manufactured from the high performance bi-polar
semiconductor 'bit slice' components, supported by microprogram
controllers possibly exploiting the Uncommitted Logic Array
(UCLA) or Programmable Logic Array (PLA). At all points in the
range the activities are implemented as one sequential program in
a single sequential processor. The high performance processor
may be time-shared amongst several programs, but at any one instant
of time one, and only one, program step is being obeyed.

In adopting any strategy, the manufacturer should ensure that the
tools, such as language and development systems to fashion the
different instruments, should be common, to minimise the cost of
retraining the engineers and to maximise the use of portable programs up and down the processing elements of the range.

The cost of these programmable electronic components is directly
dependent upon the production volume achieved by the semiconductor
manufacturer. The highest demand and, hence, production, will be
for the less complicated micro-computers which find application in
the consumer market.

Thus, the component for the bottom of the range should be exceedingly low in cost. This economic factor suggests that the instrument manufacturer may have an alternative strategy. Instead of
basing the implementation upon a single sequential processing
element, the alternative is to use a plurality of low-cost processing elements interconnected to achieve the required instrument.
The number of such components employed depends upon the level of
sophistication. Whilst the simple meter may be implemented by a
single processing element, the multi-range meter may benefit by
using more than one element, and so on, until advanced signal
processing instruments may employ sixteen elements.

Before such a strategy can be adopted, the manufacturer needs to
be reassured of two significant points; first, that it is possible
to identify those activities which can be efficiently assigned to
separate processing elements, and secondly, that the physical
method of interconnecting the elements is reliable and does not
impose formidable overheads which cost too much when compared to
the alternative use of single, more powerful, processing elements.

2. LOGICAL DESIGN TO ACHIEVE PARALLELISM

The designers of the logic circuits within leading-edge mainframe computers have realised the value of concurrent operation of processing elements to achieve a high processing rate (Thornton, 1970). Circuit techniques were developed to provide the protocols at the interconnection of separate elements, to ensure correct synchronism and to guard against indeterminacy and deadlock. The analysis of these techniques can be based upon the contribution by Petri (1962), and Holt (1969), and have been well summarised by Noe & Nutt (1973) and Dennis (1970). The principle is that the forward flow of control, from element to element, must be associated with the backward flow of signals to acknowledge receipt of the forward command and completion of the required action.

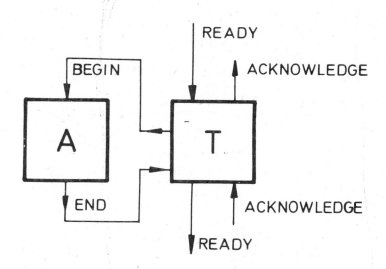

Fig.3   Use of Dennis T-Module.

An example of this technique is the T-module of Dennis (Fig.3). The processing element A is idle, in a dormant state, until it receives a command BEGIN from the T-module. On completing its task, the element sends an END signal to the T-module and returns to its dormant state. The T-module will only give the BEGIN command if it has received a backward ACKNOWLEDGE signal from the next T-module in the sequence and a forward READY signal

from the T-module which precedes it in the sequence. On receiving the END signal from the element, the T-module sends both a
backward ACKNOWLEDGE signal to the preceding T-module and a
forward READY signal to the next T-module in the sequence.
Such procedures ensure the reliable operation of concurrent actions.
A series of T-modules with their associated processing elements is
often termed a 'pipeline'. Within a pipeline, it is assumed that
there will be more than one token,indicating more than one action
occurring concurrently. Such a pipeline could be implemented by
using a number of separate processing elements, each based upon a
micro-computer. The T-module procedure and associated action A
could be programmed into the element. The Ready/Acknowledge circuits provided through input/output ports. A mechanism for passing data from element to element could also be devised.

Having found a technique for managing and implementing concurrency
the next problem is to identify those situations which naturally
spawn many tokens at once. The question is : How can a designer
identify parallelism in a sequential program ?

2.1 Evolution of Parallelism from Sequential Programs

The logic circuit engineers within the instrument manufacturers
have developed sound disciplines for the design of circuits
(Clare, 1973). When they were required to implement their design
in the programs and data structures of a micro-computer, they
accepted principles of structured programming, for they seemed a
natural extension of familiar procedures and disciplines. When
writing a programme, it is natural to think sequentially and produce a solution as a sequence of programme steps. It is natural
to turn to such programmes and attempt to identify parallelism
which can exploit more than one processing element to execute the
actions (Aspinall, Dagless & Dowsing, 1977). The parallel construct, par begin......par end, can be used where appropriate.
A single processing element will obey the main sequential thread
of the programme whilst an extra processor is added, to be invoked
whenever the parallel construct is encountered within the main
sequence. The number of extra processors is not equal to the
number of parallel constructs used within the sequential program,
but equal to the greatest number of extra parallel procedures
invoked within a parallel construct.

Techniques to provide concurrency,such as the pipeline or overlap,
do not naturally follow from the analysis of a sequential program.
The reason is that the single locus of control, or token, in a
sequential program cannot be readily replicated to provide the
many tokens within such concurrent systems. The parts of a programme which may provide an opportunity to replicate the locus of
control are the repetitive clauses such as While...Do or Repeat...
Until. By examining the flow of control through a repetitive
clause, such as that shown in Fig.4, it is possible to imagine

that, since the locus passes round the loop many times before passing to the next clause, the actions within the loop may be executed in separate processing elements, arranged in a pipeline. Consider what happens if each action Z_0 Z_1 Z_2 Z_3 Z_4 is assigned to a separate processing element. The locus of control enters the qualifier action within the main processing element. If the qualifier is true, then a token passes to processing element Z_0.

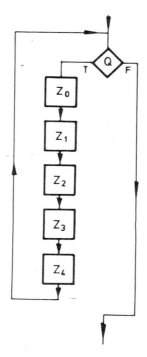

Fig.4   A Repetitive Clause.

On completion of the action Z_0, the token passes to processing element Z_1 while Z_0 pretends that it has received a second token and repeats its action concurrently with the action in Z_1, and so on. Many tokens will exist within the pipe until the token which leaves Z_4 and, on passing back to the qualifier action finds the qualifier false, causes the clause to be exited. The tokens behind it in the pipeline are invalid. At best, they have to be destroyed, by some mechanism, whilst there is a good chance that actions took place which should not have been allowed, and which may have corrupted data.

It seems that the only chance of finding concurrency within a
repetitive clause is if the sequence of actions within the loop
can be arranged so that the first one, Z_0, is the only one which
modifies the qualifier. It is then necessary to provide a new
construct Con begin.....Con end and invoke the use of the Dennis
T-modules to construct the loop, as shown in Fig.5.

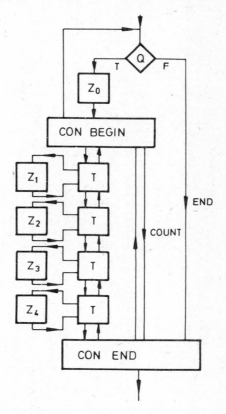

<u>Fig.5</u>   Pipeline Implementation of Repetitive Clause.

The operation is as follows: the locus of control of the main sequential program enters the qualifier action Q. If true, the locus
passes to Z_0. On completion of Z_0, the locus passes to the
CONBEGIN construct. The locus is immediately returned to the
qualifier action Q and two tokens are generated; the first
passes directly to the CONEND construct, to be counted. This
count will equal the number of tokens entering the pipe. The
first token will eventually pass through all the remaining actions
and finally emerge from the last T-module to enter the CONEND

construct. These tokens are counted to determine the number leaving the pipe. Meanwhile, the locus of control will have passed through the action Z_0 several times, until the qualifier is false; when the locus passes to the CONEND construct, where it waits until the total number of tokens leaving the pipe is equal to the number which entered. At this instant, the locus passes to the next action within the main programme sequence.

If the time to complete one traverse of the loop in Fig.4 is equal to T, and the total number of traverses is equal to n, then the time to execute the clause is nT. If the time to traverse Q and Z_0 is t, and the time to pass through the pipe Z_1, Z_2, Z_3, Z_4, and the constructs of Fig.5 is T', then the total time to execute the clause is $nt + T'$

$$\text{since} \qquad t \ll T$$

$$\text{then} \quad nt + T' < nT$$

Thus concurrency has enabled a reduction in the time to execute the actions of the repetitive clause.

At present, this seems to be the only procedure for optimising the repetitive clauses within a sequential program. It is a laborious process, and is not guaranteed to produce a significant increase in overall performance. This unsatisfactory situation suggests that the writing of the initial program should have been undertaken with a parallel implementation in mind. Programmers should learn ways to think parallel, before they think sequential.

2.2 Evolution of Parallelism by Functional Division

One can attempt the search for parallelism at the requirements definition stage of a product, before any implementation by programming is begun. Inspection of instrument descriptions such as that shown in Fig.1 suggests that it is possible to visualise each of the activities being implemented by program in a separate processing element. Depending upon the required performance, the elements may exist as separate physical entities, operating concurrently, or they may exist within one physical entity, being active one at a time. When the concurrent implementation is required, the solution involves the physical interconnection of the separate elements.

D.ASPINALL

3. DESIGN OF A CIRCUIT OF PROCESSING ELEMENTS

All circuits or networks may be considered in the abstract, as
node components interconnected by arc components. In electronic
circuits, the node components are physical electronic devices,
whilst the arc is usually a piece of wire or track on the surface
of a silicon chip or printed circuit board. In logic circuits,
the node components are logic gates or flip-flops, and the arc is
similar to that in electronic circuits. In circuits of processing
elements, the node component is a processing element comprising
processor and memory, real or virtual, and the arc component is a
data path which may be as real as a few pieces of wire or the complex Post Office data network, or as abstract as a pointer to memory.

The activities within a node component are shown in Fig.6. The
input data from the arcs are received and acknowledged by the
activity 1, and assembled as input data for the activity 2, which
carries out the necessary processing of these data to produce
results data to be passed to activity 3, which sends the data over
the output arcs and confirms that the transmission has been acknowledged.

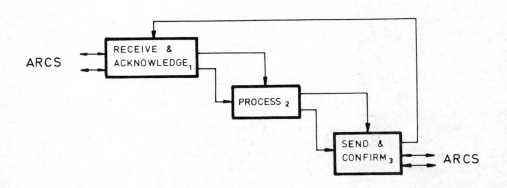

Fig.6   Activities in a Processing Element.

This total set of activities may be impemented in a processing
element, as shown in Fig.7. The element comprises the processor
and memory for obeying the programs of the three activities. The
input data arrives within a read only image memory, whilst the
output data flows from registers in the same image memory (memory
mapped input/output) (Aspinall & Dagless, 1977).

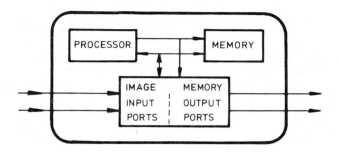

Fig.7   A Processing Element (Transputer).

The structure of the programme within the element is shown in
Fig.8. The single locus of control enters the Receive and
Acknowledge action, which monitors the input ports and accepts
input data, which it assembles as a message for the next action.
Each transaction through the input port must follow an agreed
protocol. Once the message has been assembled, the locus of
control passes to the Process action, which carries out the
necessary processing of the data and prepares a results message
for transmission to the next action. On completion of the process,
the locus of control passes to the final action, which sends the
messages over the output arcs. Each transaction through the output port must follow a protocol to enable confirmation of correct
transmission. When all arcs have been serviced, the locus of
control is passed back to the first action, to repeat the cycle.

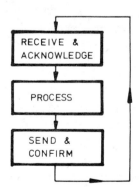

Fig.8   Program within Processing Element.

This sequence is similar to that which used to occur within a
large mainframe computer before time-sharing of input/output and
processing was introduced. The main reason for introducing time-
sharing, by interrupt or polling, was to maximise the use of an
expensive capital resource. The electronic programmable devices
are low in cost, and it is less important to time-share their use.
The inner process activity is independent of the interconnection
structure of which it is a component. The Receive-Acknowledge and
Send-Confirm actions are dependent upon the interconnection structure. The process component corresponds to a logic circuit component, whilst the other two processes correspond to the back
wiring or printed circuit board layout of a logic circuit. Thus
a standard process programme may be used as a standard component
within many instruments. The difference between instruments is
reflected in the choice of such components and in the programming
of the outer activities. Performance is governed by the time taken
to execute the inner process and the time to execute the overheads
of the outer processes. Just as in a logic circuit, their performance depends upon the delay of the logic components and the delay
due to the wiring between components. During the design stage,
the performance of different arrangements and numbers of processing elements must be assessed to arrive at an optimum solution.

4. IMPLEMENTATION OF A CIRCUIT OF PROCESSING ELEMENTS

The design process produces an abstract circuit showing the desired
interconnections between processing elements. The next step is to
map this circuit into a physical interconnection structure. Many
factors have to be considered before deciding upon an interconnection structure. These factors, and many structures, are covered
in the paper by Anderson & Jensen (1975), and Jensen (1976). A
variation of their taxonomy of interconnection structures, which
is applicable to the present discussions, is given in Table 4.1.
It shows eleven named varieties of interconnection structure.

```
TRANSFER
STRATEGY: DIRECT
                        PATH: DEDICATED

                                TOPOLOGY: LOOP              (DDL)
                                        : WIRED COMPLETE    (DDWC)
                                        : WIRED PARTIAL     (DDWP)

                        PATH: SHARED

                                TOPOLOGY: MEMORY            (DSM)
                                        : BUS               (DSB)
TRANSFER
STRATEGY: INDIRECT

            ROUTING: CENTRALISED

                        PATH: DEDICATED

                                TOPOLOGY: STAR             (ICDS)
                                        : LOOP             (ICDL)

                        PATH: SHARED

                                TOPOLOGY: BUS              (ICSB)

            ROUTING: DECENTRALISED

                        PATH: DEDICATED

                                TOPOLOGY: REGULAR          (IDDR)
                                        : IRREGULAR        (IDDI)

                        PATH: SHARED

                                TOPOLOGY: BUS              (IDSB)
```

Table 4.1   A Taxonomy (after Anderson & Jensen, 1975)

4.1 Summary of Selected Structures

Certain of the structures listed in Table 4.1 have been selected
for a brief description, since they warrant particular attention.

Direct Dedicated Wired Complete − DDWC (Fig. 9 (a)).   In this,
each element is connected to all others.   Provided that the number
of elements required is less than, or equal to, the number required,
the implementation is straightforward.   The addition of one extra
element affects all of the others.

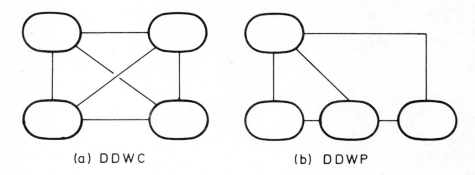

(a) DDWC   (b) DDWP

Fig.9   Interconnection Structures.

Direct Dedicated Wired Partial - D D W P   (Fig. 9.(b)). The interconnections are custom-built to suit the particular requirement.
Random wiring of this type was used in the patching of the elements
in an analogue computer.   The wires to interconnect the digital
processing elements are expensive to install and a potential
source of unreliability.

Direct Shared Memory - D S M (Fig. 9 (c)).   The registers in the image
memory of each processing element are contained within the shared
memory.   The Send and Confirm action in the source element sets the
output data in a register, whilst the Receive and Acknowledge
action in the destination element reads the register.   The low cost
of memory suggests that this is an appropriate structure for use in
closely-coupled systems.   Furthermore, the shared memory may be used
to hold common data, or to extend the local memory by adding to
that provided within a processing element.

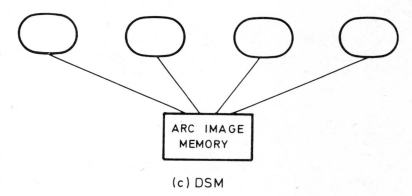

ARC IMAGE
MEMORY

(c) DSM

Fig.9   (continued)

Direct Shared Bus – D S B (Fig. 9(d)). Information transfer takes place by a processor in the source element writing, via the bus, into the memory of the destination element. Thus, the memory access mechanism within the element must allow two routes of entry; one from the local processor, and one from the bus. This interconnection structure is the one most favoured by the semiconductor component manufacturers since it offers a high degree of flexibility.

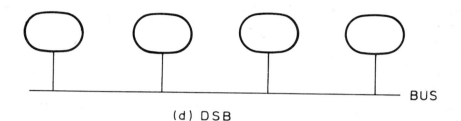

(d) D S B

Fig.9 (continued)

The Remainder. All members of the taxonomy are worthy of consideration (Anderson & Jensen, 1975). In particular the ID D R structure may come to the fore as the on-chip structure when very large-scale integration is in production.

5. A RESEARCH VEHICLE

The engineering implications of programmable electronic devices has been a subject for investigation in the Department of Electrical & Electronic Engineering at the University College of Swansea, since 1972. More recently, in collaboration with the Department of Computer Science, the investigation has turned to a study of the design and implementation of equipment, using many processing elements. As part of the investigation, a vehicle is under construction to undertake the complete production of an equipment to evaluate the design procedures and to establish design and development support facilities. The research vehicle, CYBA-M (Dagless, 1977), is based upon the D S M interconnection structure, as shown in Fig.10.

There are sixteen processing elements, each based upon the INTEL 8080 A microprocessors, plus 16 k bytes RAM of local memory. There are two shared memories. The Arc Image Memory, of 16 k bytes RAM, provides the input/output buffer registers for inter-element communication. The peripheral image memory is a 16 k byte area of memory mapped input/output registers for the communication of input and output data at the periphery of the equipment. Special semaphore facilities have also been included to permit inter-element communication in a time-shared situation.

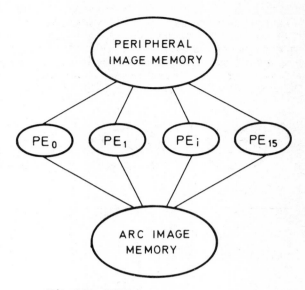

Fig.10 C Y B A - M

Most of the processor-memory access will be to the local memory
within a processing element which will contain the programme and
working space. The Arc Image Memory is reserved for the passing
of messages between elements. Nevertheless, the Arc Image Memory
must be of high speed to limit the congestion which can occur when
all sixteen processors request access to it at the same time.
There are many methods to resolve such contention problems, and
the C Y B A - M has been designed to accommodate different methods
of arbitration which will be evaluated as part of the research
programme.

In order to overcome the problem of the 'glitch' which can occur
at the interface between asynchronous processing elements, the
C Y B A - M has been based upon one single clock oscillator, which
provides the clock signals for each of the sixteen processors.

The view point of C Y B A - M which the designer of the concurrent
system has is that shown in Fig.10. The designer's task is to map
the different functionally-divided processes into the D S M interconnected processing elements. During the programme development
phase, when the actual implementation is being tested, the designer
has extra monitoring facilities, as shown in Fig.11. The console
processing element, C Y B A -80, is a separate INTEL 8080 A-based
computer system with extensive peripheral programme development
equipment. It has access into each processing element of C Y B A - M
and can read from and write to all the registers within the processors to provide full information and modification capability to
the designer of concurrent systems.

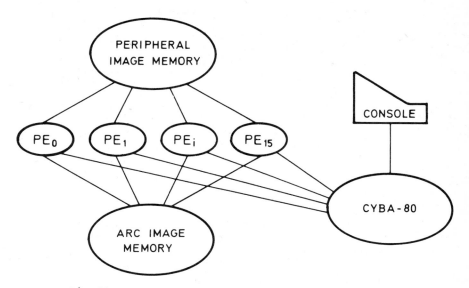

Fig.11   C Y B A - M Development System (Dagless, 1977).

The monitoring facilities will also be available for maintenance
of C Y B A - M, and have already proved invaluable during the
commissioning phase of the project. The total research vehicle
includes software aids to design and development, and will be used
in the implementation of several applications studies in the
provision of communications equipment, sophisticated instruments,
and in process control. The vehicle also provides an opportunity
to investigate the interconnection structures listed in the
Anderson & Jensen taxonomy

6.   CONCLUSION

The use of many processing elements to provide the circuit of a
piece of equipment is a subject for further research. This
approach will draw heavily on the accumulated experience of the
computer industry in its endeavours to provide multi-programming
and multi-computer solutions to the problems posed by its custo-
mers. It shares many concepts with the area of distributed processing in which the processing elements are scattered over a
wide physical area.

Before the advent of low-cost programmable electronic devices,
the designer, or programmer, could only design for a single processing element; just as the early composers wrote for a solo
instrument. Now that it is possible to contemplate a plurality of
elements operating in concert on a common task, the designer can
think of composing symphonies for orchestra.

311

COMMUNICATING SEQUENTIAL PROCESSES

C.A.R. Hoare

Programming Research Group, Oxford University

Summary: This paper suggests that input and output are basic primitives of programming; and that parallel composition of communicating sequential processes is a fundamental program structuring method. When combined with a development of Dijkstra's guarded command, these concepts are surprisingly versatile. Their use is illustrated by sample solutions of a variety of familiar programming exercises.

1. INTRODUCTION

Among the primitive concepts of computer programming, and of the high-level languages in which programs are expressed, the action of assignment is familiar and well understood. In fact, any change of the internal state of a machine executing a program can be modelled as an assignment of a new value to some variable part of that machine. However, the operations of input and output, which affect the external environment of a machine, are not nearly so well understood. Often they are added to a programming language only as an afterthought.

Among the structuring methods for computer programs, three basic constructs have received widespread recognition and use: a repetitive construct (e.g., the while loop), an alternative construct (e.g., the conditional if..then..else), and normal sequential program composition (often denoted by semicolon). Less agreement has been reached about the design of other important program structures, and many suggestions have been made: subroutines (FORTRAN), procedures (ALGOL 60; Naur, 1960), entries (PL/I), coroutines (UNIX; Thompson, 1976), classes (SIMULA 67; Dahl, 1967), processes and monitors (Concurrent PASCAL; Hansen, 1975), clusters (CLU; Liskov, 1974), forms (ALPHARD; Wulf et al., 1976), actors (Atkinson & Hewitt, 1976).

The traditional stored-program digital computer has been designed primarily for deterministic execution of a single sequential program. Where the desire for greater speed has led to the

313

introduction of parallelism, every attempt has been made to disguise
this fact from the programmer, either by hardware itself (as in the
multiple function units of the CDC 6600) or by the software (as in
an I/O control package, or a multiprogrammed operating system).
However, developments of processor technology suggest that a multiprocessor machine, constructed from a number of similar self-
contained processors (each with its own store), may become more
powerful, capacious, reliable, and economical than a machine which
is disguised as a monoprocessor.

In order to use such a machine effectively on a single task,
the component processors must be able to communicate and to synchronise with each other; and many methods of achieving this have been
proposed. A widely adopted method of communication is by inspection
and updating of a common store (as in ALGOL 68 (Van Wijngaarden,
1969), PL/I, and many machine codes). However, this can create
severe problems in the construction of correct programs; and it may
lead to expense (e.g., crossbar switches) and unreliability (e.g.,
glitches) in some technologies of hardware implementation. A greater
variety of methods has been proposed for synchronisation: semaphores
(Dijkstra, 1968), events (PL/I), conditional critical regions
(Hoare, 1972a), monitors and queues (concurrent PASCAL; Hansen,
1975), and path expressions (Campbell & Haberman, 1974). Most of
these are demonstrably adequate for their purpose, but there is no
widely recognised criterion for choosing between them.

This paper makes an ambitious attempt to find a single simple
solution to all these problems. The essential proposals are:

(1) Dijkstra's guarded commands (Dijkstra, 1975a) are adopted (with
    a slight change of notation) as sequential control structures,
    and as the sole means of introducing and controlling non-
    determinism.

(2) A parallel command, based on parbegin (Dijkstra, 1972), speci-
    fies concurrent execution of its constituent sequential commands
    (processes). All the processes start simultaneously, and the
    parallel command ends only when they are all finished. They may
    not communicate with each other by updating global variables.

(3) Simple forms of input and output command are introduced. They
    are used for communication between concurrent processes.

(4) Such communication occurs when one process names another as
    destination for output and the second process names the first
    as source for input. In this case, the value to be output is
    copied from the first process to the second. There is no auto-
    matic buffering; in general, an input or output command is de-
    layed until the other process is ready with the corresponding
    output or input. Such delay is invisible to the delayed pro-
    cess.

(5) Input commands may appear in guards. A guarded command with an input guard is selected for execution only if and when the destination named in the input command is ready to execute the corresponding output command. If several input guards of a set of alternatives have ready destinations, only one is selected, and the others have no effect; but the choice between them is arbitrary. In an efficient implementation, an output command which has been ready for a long time should be favoured; but the definition of a language cannot specify this, since the relative speed of execution of the processes is undefined.

(6) A repetitive command may have input guards. If all the sources named by them have terminated, then the repetitive command also terminates.

(7) A simple pattern matching feature, similar to that of Reynolds (1965), is used to discriminate the structure of an input message, and to access its components in a secure fashion. This feature is used to inhibit input of messages that do not match the specified pattern.

The programs expressed in the proposed language are intended to be implementable both by a conventional machine with a single main store, and by a fixed network of processors connected by input/output channels (although very different optimisations are appropriate in the different cases). Consequently it is a rather static language: the text of a program determines a fixed upper bound on the number of processes operating concurrently; there is no recursion, and no facility for process-valued variables. In other respects also, the language has been stripped to the barest minimum necessary for explanation of its more novel features.

The concept of a communicating sequential process is shown in sections 3-5 to provide a method of expressing solutions to many simple programming exercises, which have been used before to illustrate the use of various proposed programming language features. This suggests that the process may constitute a synthesis of a number of familiar and new programming ideas. The reader is invited to skip the examples which do not interest him.

However, this paper also ignores many serious problems. The most serious is that it fails to suggest any proof method to assist in the development and verification of correct programs. Secondly, it pays no attention to the problems of efficient implementation, which may be particularly serious on a traditional sequential computer. It is probable that a solution to these problems will require:

(1) imposition of restrictions in the use of the proposed features,

(2) reintroduction of distinctive notations for the most common and useful special cases,

C.A.R. HOARE

(3) development of automatic optimisation techniques,

(4) the design of appropriate hardware.

Thus the concepts and notations introduced in this paper (although described in the next section in the form of a programming
language fragment) should not be regarded as suitable for use as a
programming language, either for abstract or for concrete programming. They are at best only a partial solution of the problems
tackled. Further discussion of these and other points will be found
in section 7.

2. CONCEPTS AND NOTATIONS

The style of the following description is borrowed from ALGOL 60
(Naur, 1960). Types, declarations, and expressions have not been
treated; in the examples, a PASCAL-like notation (Wirth, 1971 a) has
usually been adopted. The curly braces { } have been introduced into
BNF to denote none or more repetitions of the enclosed material.
[Sentences in square brackets refer to an implementation: they are
not strictly part of a language definition.]

```
<command> ::= <simple command>|<structured command>
<simple command> ::= <null command>|<assignment command>
                      |<input command>|<output command>
<structured command> ::= <alternative command>|<repetitive command>
                      |<parallel command>
<null command> ::= skip
<command list> ::= {<declaration>;|<command>;} <command>
```

A command specifies the behaviour of a device executing the command, and it may succeed or fail. Execution of a simple command, if
successful, may have an effect on the internal state of the executing
device (in the case of assignment), or on its external environment
(in the case of output), or on both (in the case of input). Execution
of a structured command involves execution of some or all of its
constituent commands; and if any of these fail, so does the structured
command. [In this case, whenever possible, an implementation should
provide some kind of comprehensible error diagnostic message.]

A null command has no effect and never fails.

A command list specifies sequential execution of its constituent
commands in the order written. Each declaration introduces a fresh
variable, with scope which extends from its declaration to the end
of the command list.

2.1 Parallel Commands

```
<parallel command> ::= [<process>{||<process>}]
```

COMMUNICATING SEQUENTIAL PROCESSES

```
<process> ::= <process label> <command list>
<process label> ::= <empty>|<identifier>
            |<identifier>(<label subscript>{,<label subscript>})
<label subscript> ::= <integer constant>|<range>
<integer constant> ::= <numeral>|<bound variable>
<bound variable> ::= <identifier>
<range> ::= <bound variable>:<lower bound>..<upper bound>
<lower bound> ::= <integer constant>
<upper bound> ::= <integer constant>
```

Each process of a parallel command must be <u>disjoint</u> from every other process of the command, in the sense that it does not mention any variable which occurs as a target variable (see 2.2 and 2.3) in any other process.

A process label without subscripts, or one whose label subscripts are all integer constants, serves as a name for the command list to which it is prefixed; and its scope extends over the whole of the parallel command. A process whose label subscripts include one or more ranges stands for a series of processes, each with the same label and command list, except that each has a different combination of values substituted for the bound variables. These values range between the lower bound and the upper bound inclusive. For example, $X(i:1..n)::$ CL stands for

$$X(1):: CL_1 ||X(2):: CL_2||...||X(n):: CL_n$$

where each CL_j is formed from CL by replacing every occurrence of the bound variable i by the numeral j. After all such expansions, each process label in a parallel command must occur only once, and the processes must be well formed and disjoint.

A parallel command specifies concurrent execution of its constituent processes. They all start simultaneously; and the parallel command terminates successfully only if and when they have all successfully terminated. The relative speed with which they are executed is arbitrary.

Examples:

(1) [cardreader?cardimage|||lineprinter!lineimage]

This performs the two constituent commands in parallel, and terminates only when both operations are complete. The time taken may be as low as the longer of times taken by each constituent process, i.e., the sum of its computing, waiting and transfer times.

(2) [west::DISASSEMBLE||X::SQUASH||east::ASSEMBLE]

The three processes have the names "west", "X", and "east". The capitalised words stand for command lists which will be defined in

C.A.R. HOARE

later examples.

(3) [room::ROOM||fork(i:0..4)::FORK||phil(i:0..4)::PHIL]

There are eleven processes. The behaviour of "room" is specified by the command list ROOM. The behaviour of the five processes fork(0), fork(1), fork(2), fork(3), fork(4), is specified by the command list FORK, within which the bound variable i indicates the identity of the particular fork. Similar remarks apply to the five processes PHIL.

2.2 Assignment Commands

```
<assignment command> ::= <target variable> := <expression>
<expression> ::= <simple expression>|<structured expression>
<structured expression> ::= <constructor>(<expression list>)
<constructor> ::= <identifier>|<empty>
<expression list> ::= <empty>|<expression>{,<expression>}
<target variable> ::= <simple variable>|<structured target>
<structured target> ::= <constructor>(<target variable list>)
<target variable list> ::= <empty>|<target variable>{,<target
                                                        variable>}
```

An expression denotes a value, which is computed by an executing device by application of its constituent operators to the specified operands. The value of an expression is undefined if any of these operations are undefined. The value denoted by a simple expression may be simple or structured. The value denoted by a structured expression is structured; its constructor is that of the expression, and its components are the list of values denoted by the constituent expressions of the expression list.

An assignment command specifies evaluation of its expression, and assignment of the denoted value to the target variable. A simple target variable may have assigned to it a simple or a structured value. A structured target variable may have assigned to it a structured value, with the same constructor; and the effect of such assignment is to assign to each constituent simpler variable of the structured target the value of the corresponding element of the value list of the structured value. Consequently the value denoted by target variable, if evaluated after a successful assignment, is the same as the value denoted by the expression, as evaluated before the assignment.

An assignment fails if the value of its expression is undefined, or if that value does not match the target variable, in the following sense:

A simple target variable matches any value of its type. A structured target variable matches a structured value, provided that:

(1) they have the same constructor

(2) the target variable list is the same length as the list of components of the value

(3) each target variable of the list matches the corresponding component of the value list.

A structured value with no components is known as a "signal".

Examples:

(1)   x := x+1   – the value of x after the assign-
                                        ment is the same as the value of
                                        x+1 before.

(2)   (x,y) := (y,x)   – exchanges the values of x and y.

(3)   x := cons(left,right)   – constructs a structured value and
                                        assigns it to x.

(4)   cons(left,right) := x   – fails if x does not have the form
                                        cons(y,z); but if it does, then
                                        y is assigned to left, and z is
                                        assigned to right.

(5)   insert(n) := insert(2*x+1)   – equivalent to n := 2*x+1.

(6)   c := P( )   – assigns to c a "signal" with con-
                                        structor P, and no components.

(7)   P( ) := c   – fails if the value of c is not
                                        P( ); otherwise has no effect.

(8)   insert(n) := has(n)   – fails, due to mismatch.

Note:

   Successful execution of both (3) and (4) ensures the truth of the postcondition

   x = cons(left,right)

but (3) does it by changing x and (4) does it by changing left and right.   (4) will fail if there is no value of left and right which satisfies the postcondition.

2.3 Input and Output Commands

   <input command> ::= <source>?<target variable>
   <output command> ::= <destination>!<expression>

```
<source>    ::= <process name>
<destination> ::= <process name>
<process name> ::= <identifier>|<identifier>(<subscripts>)
<subscripts>  ::= <integer expression>{,<integer expression>}
```

Input and output commands specify communication between two concurrently operating sequential processes. Such a process may be implemented in hardware as a special-purpose device (e.g. cardreader or lineprinter), or its behaviour may be specified by one of the constituent processes of a parallel command. Communication occurs between two processes of a parallel command whenever

(1) An input command in one process specifies as its source the process name of the other process.

(2) An output command in the other process specifies as its destination the process name of the first process.

(3) The target variable of the input command matches the value denoted by the expression of the output command.

On these conditions, the input and output commands are said to correspond. Commands which correspond are executed simultaneously, and their combined effect is to assign the value of the expression of the output command to the target variable of the input command.

An input command fails if its source is terminated. An output command fails if its destination is terminated, or if its expression is undefined.

[The requirement of synchronisation of input and output commands means that an implementation will have to delay whichever of the two commands happens to be ready first. The delay is ended when the corresponding command in the other process is also ready, or when the other process terminates; in the latter case, the first command fails. It is also possible that the delay will never be ended, for example, if a group of processes are attempting communication, but none of their input and output commands correspond with each other. This form of failure is known as deadlock.]

Examples:

(1) cardreader?cardimage - from cardreader, read a card and assign
                             its value (an array of characters) to
                             the variable cardimage

(2) lineprinter!lineimage - to lineprinter, send the value of
                             lineimage for printing

(3) X?(x,y)   - from process named X, input a pair of
                             values and assign them to x and y

(4)   DIV!(3*a+b,13)   – to process DIV, output the two specified
                                values.

Note: if a process named DIV issues command (3), and a process
named X issues command (4), these are executed simultaneously,
and have the same effect as the assignment:

$$(x,y) := (3*a+b,13) \quad (\equiv x:=3*a+b; \; y:=13)$$

(5)   console(i)?c   – from the ith element of an array of con-
                               soles, input a value and assign it to c

(6)   console(j-1)!"A"   – to the $j-1^{th}$ console, output character
                               "A"

(7)   X(i)?V()   – from the ith of an array of processes
                               X, input a signal V(); refuse to input
                               any other signal

(8)   sem!P()   – to sem output a signal P()

2.4 Alternative and Repetitive Commands

<repetitive command> ::= *<alternative command>
<alternative command> ::= [<guarded command>{[]<guarded command>}]
<guarded command> ::= <guard> → <command list>
              |(<range>{,<range>})<guard> → <command list>
<guard> ::= <guard list>|<guard list>;<input command>
              |<input command>
<guard list> ::= <guard element>{;<guard element>}
<guard element> ::= <boolean expression>|<declaration>

A guarded command with one or more ranges stands for a series of
guarded commands, each with the same guard and command list, except
that each has a different combination of values substituted for the
bound variables. The values range between the lower bound and upper
bound inclusive. For example, (i:1..n)G → CL stands for

$$G_1 \to CL_1 [] G_2 \to CL_2 [] \ldots [] G_n \to CL_n$$

where each $G_j \to CL_j$ is formed from G → CL by replacing every
occurrence of the bound variable i by the numeral j .

A guarded command is executed only if and when the execution of
its guard does not fail. First its guard is executed and then its
command list. A guard is executed by execution of its constituent
elements from left to right. A boolean expression is evaluated; if
it denotes false, the guard fails; but an expression that denotes
true has no effect. A declaration introduces a fresh variable, with
scope that extends from the declaration to the end of the guarded

command. An input command at the end of a guard is executed only if
and when a corresponding output command is executed. [An implementation may test whether a guard fails simply by trying to execute it,
and discontinuing execution if and when it fails. This is valid because such discontinued execution has no effect on the state of the
executing device.]

An alternative command specifies execution of exactly one of its
constituent guarded commands. Consequently, if all guards fail, the
alternative command fails. Otherwise an arbitrary one with successfully executable guard is selected and executed. [An implementation
should take advantage of its freedom of selection to ensure efficient
execution and good response. For example when input commands appear
as guards, the command which corresponds to the earliest ready and
matching output command should in general be preferred; and certainly,
no executable and ready output command should unreasonably often be
passed over.]

A repetitive command specifies as many iterations as possible of
its constituent alternative command. Consequently, when all guards
fail, the repetitive command terminates with no effect. Otherwise,
the alternative command is executed once, and then the whole repetitive command is executed again. [Consider a repetitive command when
all its true guard lists end in an input guard. Such a command may
have to be delayed until either

(1) an output command corresponding to one of the input guards
becomes ready, or

(2) all the sources named by the input guards have terminated.

In case (2), the repetitive command terminates. If neither event
ever occurs, the process fails (in deadlock).]

Examples:

(1) [x≥y → m:=x[]y≥x → m:=y]

If x≥y, assign x to m; if y≥x assign y to m; if both x≥y and
y≥x, either assignment can be executed.

(2) i:=0;☆[i<size;content(i)≠n → i:=i+1]

The repetitive command scans the elements content(i), for
i=0,1,.., until either i≥size, or a value equal to n is found.

(3) ☆[c:character;west?c → east!c]

This reads all the characters output by west, and outputs them
one by one to east. The repetition terminates when the process
west terminates.

(4) *[(i;1..10)continue(i); console(i)?c →
        X!(i,c); console(i)!ack(); continue(i):=(c≠sign off)]

This repeatedly inputs from any of ten consoles, provided that
the corresponding element of the boolean array continue is true.
The bound variable i identifies the originating console. Its
value, together with the character just input, is output to X, and
an acknowledgement signal is sent back to the originating console.
If the character indicated "sign off", continue(i) is set false, to
prevent further input from that console. The repetitive command
terminates when all ten elements of continue are false. [An implementation should ensure that no console which is ready to provide
input will be unreasonably often ignored.]

(5) *[n:integer; X?insert(n) → INSERT
    []n:integer; X?has(n) → SEARCH; X!(i<size)
    ]

(Here, and elsewhere, the capitalised words INSERT and SEARCH
stand as abbreviations for program text defined separately.)

On each iteration, this accepts from X
either (a) a request to "insert(n)" (followed by INSERT)
  or (b) a question "has(n)", to which it outputs an answer back
        to X.
The choice between (a) and (b) is made by the next output command
in X. The repetitive command terminates when X does. If X sends a
nonmatching message, the containing parallel command fails.

(6) *[X?V() → val:=val+1
    []val>0;Y?P() → val:=val-1
    ]

On each iteration, accept either a V() signal from X and increment val, or a P() signal from Y, and decrement val. But the
second alternative cannot be selected unless val is positive (after
which val will remain invariantly nonnegative). [When val>0, the
choice depends on the relative speeds of X and Y, and is not determined.] The repetitive command will terminate when both X and Y are
terminated, or when X is terminated and val≤0.

3. COROUTINES

In parallel programming, coroutines appear as a more fundamental
program structure than subroutines, which can be regarded as a
special case (treated in the next section).

3.1 COPY

Problem: write a process X to copy characters out by

C.A.R. HOARE

        process west to process east.

Solution: X::☓[c:character;west?c → east!c]

Notes:

(1) When west terminates, the input "west?c" will fail, causing termination of the repetitive command, and of process X . Any subsequent input command from east will fail.

(2) Process X acts as a single-character buffer between west and
east. It permits west to work on production of the next character,
before east is ready to input the previous one.

3.2 SQUASH

Problem: adapt the previous program to replace every pair of consecutive asterisks "**" by an upward arrow "↑". You may
assume that the final character input is not an asterisk.

Solution: X::☓[c:character;west?c →
                [c≠asterisk → east!c
                ◻c=asterisk → west?c;
                                [c≠asterisk → east!asterisk;east!c
                                ◻c=asterisk → east!upward arrow
          ]]   ]

Notes:

(1) Since west does not end with asterisk, the second "west?c" will
not fail.

(2) As an exercise, adapt this process to deal sensibly with input
which ends with an odd number of asterisks.

3.3 DISASSEMBLE

Problem: read cards from a cardfile and output to process X the
stream of characters they contain. An extra space should
be inserted at the end of each card.

Solution: ☓[cardimage:(1..80)character; cardfile?cardimage →
          i:integer; i:=1;
          ☓[i≤80 → X!cardimage(i); i:=i+1]
          X!space
       ]

Notes:

(1) "(1..80)character" declares an array of 80 characters, with subscripts ranging between 1 and 80.

(2) The repetitive command terminates when the cardfile process terminates.

3.4 ASSEMBLE

Problem: read a stream of characters from process X and print
           them in lines of 125 characters on a lineprinter. The
           last line should be completed with spaces if necessary.

Solution: lineimage:(1..125)character;
           i:integer; i:=1;
           *[c:character;X?c →
                       lineimage(i):=c;
                       [i≤124 → i:=i+1
                       []i=125 → lineprinter!lineimage; i:=1
           ]   ];
           [i=1 → skip
           []i>1 → *[i≤125 → lineimage(i):=space; i:=i+1];
                   lineprinter!lineimage
           ]

Note:

When X terminates, so will the first repetitive command of this
process. The last line will then be printed, if it has any characters.

3.5 Reformat

Problem: read a sequence of cards of 80 characters each, and
           print the characters on a lineprinter at 125 characters
           per line. Every card should be followed by an extra
           space, and the last line should be completed with spaces
           if necessary.

Solution: [west::DISASSEMBLE||X::COPY||east::ASSEMBLE]

Notes:

(1) The capitalised names stand for program text defined in previous
sections.

(2) The parallel command is designed to terminate after the cardfile
has terminated.

(3) This elementary problem is difficult to solve elegantly without
coroutines.

C.A.R. HOARE

3.6 Conway's Problem (Conway, 1963)

Problem: adapt the above program to replace every pair of consecutive asterisks by an upward arrow.

Solution: [west::DISASSEMBLE||X::SQUASH||east::ASSEMBLE]

4. SUBROUTINES AND DATA REPRESENTATIONS

A conventional nonrecursive subroutine can be readily implemented as a coroutine, provided that:

(1) its parameters are called "by value" and "by result"

(2) it updates no nonlocal variables used in its calling program.

Like a FORTRAN subroutine, a coroutine may retain the values of local variables (own variables, in ALGOL terms); and it may use input commands to achieve the effect of "multiple entry points", in a safer way than PL/I. Thus a coroutine can be used like a SIMULA class instance as a concrete representation for abstract data.

A coroutine acting as a subroutine is a process operating concurrently with its user process in a parallel command:

[subr::SUBROUTINE||X::USER]

The SUBROUTINE will contain (or consist of) a repetitive command:

$*$[X?(value params) → ...;X!(result params)]

where ... computes the results from the values input. The subroutines will terminate when its user does.

The USER will call the subroutine by a pair of commands:

subr!(arguments);...;subr?(results)

Any commands between these two will be executed concurrently with the subroutine.

A multiple-entry subroutine, acting as a representation for data (Hoare, 1972b), will also contain a repetitive command, which represents each entry by an alternative input to a structured target, with the entry name as constructor; e.g.

$*$[X?entry1(value params) → ...
 []X?entry2(value params) → ...
 ]

326

The calling process X will determine which of the alternatives is activated on each repetition. When X terminates, so does this repetitive command. A similar technique in the user program can achieve the effect of multiple exits.

A recursive subroutine can be simulated by an array of processes, one for each level of recursion. The user process is level zero; each activation communicates its parameters and results with its predecessor, and calls its successor if necessary:

[recsub(0)::USER||recsub(i:1..reclimit)::RECSUB]

The user will call the first element of recsub:

recsub(1)!(arguments);...;recsub(1)?(results);

The imposition of a fixed upper bound on recursion depth is necessitated by the "static" design of the language.

This clumsy simulation of recursion would be even more clumsy for a mutually recursive algorithm. It would not be recommended for conventional programming; it may be more suitable for an array of microprocessors, for which the fixed upper bound is also realistic.

In this section, we assume each subroutine is used only by a single user process (which may, of course, itself contain parallel commands).

4.1 Function: Division with Remainder

Problem: construct a process to represent a function-type sub-
            routine, which accepts a positive dividend and divisor
            and returns their integer quotient and remainder. Ef-
            ficiency is of no concern.

Solution: [DIV::*[x,y:integer;X?(x,y) →
                  quot,rem:integer; quot:=0; rem:=x;
                  *[rem≥y → rem:=rem-y; quot:=quot+1];
                  X!(quot,rem)
               ]
            ||X::USER
            ]

4.2 Recursion: Factorial

Problem: compute a factorial by the recursive method, to a given
            limit.

C.A.R. HOARE

```
Solution:  [fac(i:1..limit)::
             *[n:integer;fac(i-1)?n →
                [n=0 → fac(i-1)!1
                [n>0 → fac(i+1)!n-1;
                    r:integer;fac(i+1)?r;fac(i-1)!(n*r)
               ] ]
             ||fac(0)::USER
             ]
```

Note:

This unrealistic example introduces the technique of the "iterative array", which will be used to better effect in later examples.

4.3 Data Representation: Small Set of Integers (Hoare, 1972b)

Problem: to represent a set of not more than 100 integers as a process S, which accepts two kinds of instruction from its calling process X:

      (1) S!insert(n) – insert the integer n in the set

      (2) S!has(n);...;S?b – b is set true if n is in the set, and false otherwise.

      The initial value of the set is empty.

```
Solution:  S::
             content:(0..99)integer; size:integer;size:=0;
             *[n:integer; X?has(n) → SEARCH; X!(i<size)
              [n:integer; X?insert(n) → SEARCH;
                        [i<size → skip
                         [i=size;size<100 →
                                content(size):=n; size:=size+1
                ]         ]
```

where SEARCH is an abbreviation for:

```
             i:integer; i:=0;
             *[i<size; content(i)≠n → i:=i+1]
```

Notes:

(1) The alternative command with guard "size<100" will fail if an attempt is made to insert more than 100 elements.

(2) The activity of insertion will in general take place concurrently with the calling process. However, any subsequent instruction to S will be delayed until the previous insertion is complete.

328

4.4 Scanning a Set

Problem: extend the solution to 4.3, by providing a fast method
for scanning all members of the set, without changing
the value of the set. The user program will contain a
repetitive command of the form:

```
        S!scan( ); more:boolean; more:=true;
*[more; x:integer; S?next(x) → ... deal with x ....
 []more; S?noneleft( ) → more:=false
 ]
```

where S!scan( ) sets the representation into a scanning mode; the
repetitive command serves as a <u>for</u> statement, inputting the successive members of x from the set, and inspecting them; until finally
the representation sends a signal that there are none left.

The body of the repetitive command is <u>not</u> permitted to communicate with S in any way.

Solution: add a third guarded command to the outer repetitive command of S:

```
...[]X?scan( ) → i:integer; i:=0;
                 *[i<size → X!next(content(i)); i:=i+1];
                 X!noneleft( )
```

4.5 Recursive Data Representation: Small Set of Integers

Problem: same as above; but an array of processes is to be used to
achieve a high degree of parallelism. Each process should
contain at most one number. When it contains no number,
it should answer "false" to all enquiries about member-
ship. On the first insertion, it changes to a second
phase of behaviour, in which it deals with instructions
from its predecessor, passing some of them on to its successor. The calling process will be named S(0). For efficiency, the set should be sorted, i.e., the ith process
should contain the ith largest number.

Solution: S(i:1..100)::
```
*[n:integer;S(i-1)?has(n) → S(0)!false
[]n:integer;S(i-1)?insert(n) →
     *[m:integer;S(i-1)?has(m) →
        [m≤n → S(0)!(m=n)
        []m>n → S(i+1)!has(m)
        ]
     []m:integer;S(i-1)?insert(m) →
        [m<n → S(i+1)!insert(n); n:=m
        []m=n → skip
        []m>n → S(i+1)!insert(m)
     ]    ]    ]
```

C.A.R. HOARE

Notes:

(1) The user process S(0) enquires whether n is a member by the commands

S(1)!has(n);...;[(i:1..100)S(i)?b → skip]

The appropriate process will respond to the input command by the output command in line 2 or line 5. This trick avoids passing the answer back "up the chain".

(2) Many insertion operations can proceed in parallel; yet any subsequent "has" operation will be performed correctly.

(3) All repetitive commands and all processes of the array will terminate after the user process S(0) terminates.

4.6 Multiple Exits: Remove the Least Member

Exercise: extend the above solution to respond to a command to yield the least member of the set, and to remove it from the set. The user program will invoke the facility by a pair of commands:

S(1)!least( );[x:integer;S(1)?x → ... deal with x ...
              []S(1)?noneleft( ) → ...
              ]

or, if he wishes to scan and empty the set, he may write:

S(1)!least( ); more:boolean; more:=true;
*[more; x:integer; S(1)?x → ... deal with x ...; S(1)!least( )
 []more; S(1)?noneleft( ) → more:=false
 ]

Hint: introduce a boolean variable b, initialised to true; and prefix this to all the guards of the inner loop. After responding to a !least( ) command from its predecessor, each process returns its contained value n, asks its successor for its least, and stores the response in n. But if the successor returns "noneleft( )", b is set false, and the inner loop terminates. The process therefore returns to its initial state (solution due to David Gries).

5. MONITORS AND SCHEDULING

This section shows how a monitor can be regarded as a single process which communicates with more than one user process. However, each user process must have a different name (e.g. producer, consumer) or a different subscript (e.g. X(i)), and each communication with a user must identify its source or destination uniquely.

Consequently, when a monitor is prepared to communicate with any of its user processes (i.e., whichever of them calls first), it will use a guarded command with a range, for example:

$$*[(i:1..100)X(i)?(value\ parameters) \rightarrow ...; X(i)!(results)]$$

Here, the bound variable i is used to send the results back to the calling process. If the monitor is not prepared to accept input from some particular user (e.g. $X(j)$) on a given occasion, the input command may be preceded by a boolean guard; for example, two successive inputs from the same process are inhibited by:

$$j:=0;*[(i:1..100)i \neq j; X(i)?(values) \rightarrow ...; j:=i]$$

Any attempted output from $X(j)$ will be delayed until a subsequent iteration, after the output of some other process $X(i)$ has been accepted and dealt with.

Similarly, conditions can be used to delay acceptance of inputs which would violate scheduling constraints, postponing them until some later occasion when some other process has brought the monitor into a state in which the input can validly be accepted. This technique is similar to a conditional critical region (Hoare, 1972a); and it obviates the need for special synchronising variables such as events, queues, or conditions. However, the absence of these special facilities certainly makes it more difficult or less efficient to solve problems involving priorities, for example the scheduling of head movement on a disc.

5.1 Bounded Buffer

Problem: construct a buffering process X to smooth variations in the speed of output of portions by a producer process and input by a consumer process. The consumer contains pairs of commands "X!more( ); X?p", and the producer contains commands of the form X!p . The buffer should contain up to ten portions.

Solution: X::
            buffer: (0..9) portion;
            in,out:integer; in:=0; out:=0;
            comment 0≤out≤in≤out+10;
            *[in<out+10; producer?buffer(in mod 10) → in:=in+1
            []out<in; consumer?more( ) → consumer!buffer(out mod10);
                                            out:=out+1
            ]

Notes:

(1) When out<in<out+10 , the selection of the alternative in the repetitive command will depend on whether the producer produces

C.A.R. HOARE

before the consumer consumes, or vice-versa.

(2) When out=in , the buffer is empty, and the second alternative cannot be selected, even if the consumer is ready with its command "X!more( )". However, after the producer has produced its next portion, the consumer's request can be granted on the next follow-ing iteration.

(3) Similar remarks apply to the producer, when in=out+10 .

(4) X is designed to terminate when out=in and the producer has terminated.

5.2 Integer Semaphore

Problem: to implement an integer semaphore S, shared among an array X(i:1..100) of client processes. Each process may increment the semaphore by S!V( ), or decrement it by S!P( ); but the latter command must be delayed if the value of the semaphore is not positive.

Solution: S::val:integer; val:=0;
       *[(i:1..100)X(i)?V( ) → val:=val+1
       [](i:1..100)val>0; X(i)?P( ) → val:=val-1
       ]

Notes:

(1) In this process, no use is made of knowledge of the subscript i of the calling process.

(2) The semaphore terminates only when all hundred processes of the process array X have terminated.

5.3 Dining Philosophers (Problem due to E.W. Dijkstra)

Problem: Five philosophers spend their lives thinking and eating. The philosophers share a common dining room where there is a circular table surrounded by five chairs, each be-longing to one philosopher. In the centre of the table there is a large bowl of spaghetti, and the table is laid with five forks (see figure 1). On feeling hungry, a philosopher enters the dining room, sits in his own chair, and picks up the fork on the left of his place. Unfortu-nately, the spaghetti is so tangled that he needs to pick up and use the fork on his right as well. When he has finished, he puts down both forks, and leaves the room. The room should keep a count of the number of philosophers in it.

332

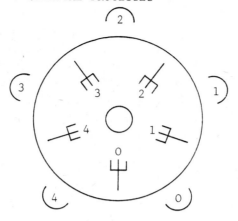

Figure 1.

Solution: The behaviour of the ith philosopher may be described as follows:

PHIL = *[... during i^{th} lifetime ... →
        THINK;
        room!enter( );
        fork(i)!pickup( ); fork((i+1) mod 5)!pickup( );
        EAT;
        fork(i)!putdown( ); form((i+1) mod 5)!putdown( );
        room!exit( )
        ]

The fate of the ith fork is to be picked up and put down by a philosopher sitting on either side of it

FORK =
        *[phil(i)?pickup( ) → phil(i)?putdown( )
        []phil((i-1) mod 5)?pickup( ) → phil((i-1) mod 5)?
                                                putdown( )
        ]

The story of the room may be simply told:

ROOM = occupancy:integer; occupancy:=0;
        *[(i:0..4)phil(i)?enter( ) → occupancy:=occupancy+1
        [](i:0..4)phil(i)?exit( ) → occupancy:=occupancy-1
        ]

All these components operate in parallel:

[room::ROOM||fork(i:0..4)::FORK||phil(i:0..4)::PHIL]

333

C.A.R. HOARE

Notes:

(1) The solution given above does not prevent all five philosophers from entering the room, each picking up his left fork, and starving to death, because he cannot pick up his right fork.

(2) Exercise: adapt the above program to avert this sad possibility. Hint: prevent more than four philosophers from entering the room. (Solution due to E.W. Dijkstra.)

6. MISCELLANEOUS

This section contains further examples of the use of communicating sequential processes for the solution of some less familiar problems; a parallel version of the sieve of Eratosthenes, and the design of an iterative array. The proposed solutions are even more speculative than those of the previous sections, and in the second example, even the question of termination is ignored.

6.1 Prime Numbers: the Sieve of Eratosthenes (McIlroy, 1968)

Problem: print in ascending order all primes less than 10000. Use an array of processes, SIEVE, in which each process inputs a prime from its predecessor, and prints it. The process then inputs an ascending stream of numbers from its predecessor and passes them on to its successor, suppressing any that are multiples of the original prime.

Solution:
```
[SIEVE (i:1..100)::
  p,mp:integer;
  SIEVE (i-1)?p;
  print!p;
  mp:=p; comment mp is a multiple of p;
 *[m:integer; SIEVE(i-1)?m →
      *[m>mp → mp:=mp+p];
       [m=mp → skip
       []m<mp → SIEVE(i+1)!m
  ]        ]
||SIEVE(0)::print!2; n:integer; n:=3;
           *[n<10000 → SIEVE(1)!n; n:=n+2]
||SIEVE(101)::*[n:integer; SIEVE(100)?n → print!n]
||print:: *[(i:0..101) n:integer; SIEVE(i)?n → ...]
 ]
```

Notes:

(1) This beautiful solution was contributed by David Gries.

(2) It is algorithmically similar to the program developed in the paper by Dijkstra (1972) pp.27-32.

334

6.2 An Iterative Array: Matrix Multiplication

Problem: A square matrix A of order 3 is given.
Three streams are to be input, each stream representing
a column of an array IN. Three streams are to be output,
each representing a column of the product matrix IN×A.
After an initial delay, the results are to be produced at
the same rate as the input is consumed. Consequently, a
high degree of parallelism is required.
The solution should take the form shown in figure 2. Each
of the nine non-border nodes inputs a vector component
from the west and a partial sum from the north. It outputs the vector component to its east, and an updated
partial sum to the south. The input data is produced by
the west border nodes, and the desired results are consumed by south border nodes. The north border is a constant source of zeroes; and the east border is just a
sink. No provision need be made for termination, nor for
changing the values of the array A.

Solution: There are twenty-one nodes, in five groups, comprising
the central square and the four borders:

```
[M(i:1..3,0):: WEST
||M(0,j:1..3):: NORTH
||M(i:1..3,4):: EAST
||M(4,j:1..3):: SOUTH
||M(i:1..3,j:1..3):: CENTRE
]
```

The WEST and SOUTH borders are processes of the user program; the
remaining processes are:

```
NORTH  = *[true → M(1,j)!0]
EAST   = *[x:real; M(i,3)?x → skip]
CENTRE = *[x:real; M(i,j-1)?x →
                M(i,j+1)!x; sum:real;
                M(i-1,j)?sum; M(i+1,j)!(A(i,j)*x+sum)
          ]
```

7. DISCUSSION

A design for a programming language must necessarily involve a
number of decisions which seem to be fairly arbitrary. The discussion of this section is intended to explain some of the underlying motivation, and to mention some unresolved questions.

7.1 Notations

I have chosen single-character notations (e.g. !, ?) to express

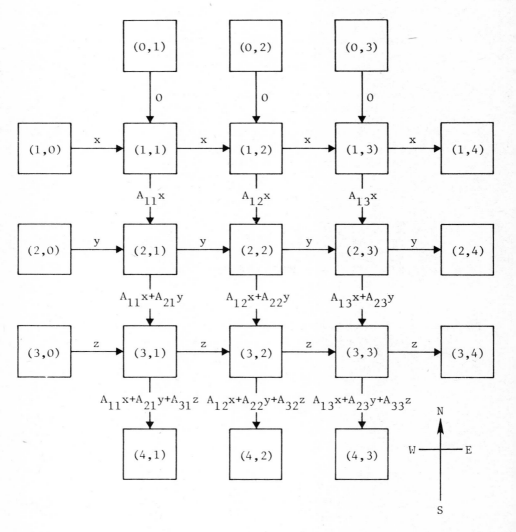

Figure 2.

the primitive concepts, rather than the more traditional bold-face or underlined English words. As a result, the examples have an APL-like brevity, which some readers find distasteful. My excuse is that (in contrast to APL) there are only a very few primitive concepts, and that it is standard practice of mathematics (and also good coding practice) to denote common primitive concepts by brief notations (e.g. +, ×). When read aloud, these are replaced by words (e.g. plus, times).

Some readers have suggested the use of assignment notation for input and output:

      \<target variable\> := \<source\>
      \<destination\> := \<expression\>

I find this suggestion misleading: it is better to regard input and output as distinct primitives, justifying distinct notations.

I have used the same pair of brackets ([...]) to bracket all program structures, instead of the more familiar variety of brackets (if..fi, begin..end, case...esac, etc.). In this I follow normal mathematical practice, but I must also confess a distaste for the pronunciation of words like fi, od, esac.

I am dissatisfied with the fact that my notation gives the same syntax for a structured expression and a subscripted variable. Perhaps tags should be distinguished from other identifiers by a special symbol (say #).

I was tempted to introduce an abbreviation for combined declaration and input, e.g. X?(n:integer) for n:integer; X?n .

7.2 Explicit Naming

My design insists that every input or output command must name its source or destination explicitly. This makes it inconvenient to write a library of processes which can be included in subsequent programs, independent of the process names used in that program. A partial solution to this problem is to allow one process (the main process) of a parallel command to have an empty label, and to allow the other processes in the command to use the empty process name as source or destination of input or output.

For construction of large programs, some more general technique will also be necessary. This should at least permit substitution of program text for names defined elsewhere, a technique which has been used informally throughout this paper. The COBOL COPY verb permits also a substitution for formal parameters within the copied text. But whatever facility is introduced, I would recommend the following principle, that every program, after assembly with its library routines, should be printable as a text expressed wholly in the language;

and it is this printed text which should describe the execution of
the program, independent of which parts were drawn from a library.

Since I did not intend to design a complete language, I have ignored the problem of libraries in order to concentrate on the essential semantic concepts of the program which is actually executed.

7.3 Port Names

An alternative to explicit naming of source and destination would
be to name a port through which communication is to take place. The
port names would be local to the processes; and the manner in which
pairs of ports are to be connected by channels could be declared in
the head of a parallel command.

This is an attractive alternative, which could be designed to
introduce a useful degree of syntactically checkable redundancy.
But it is semantically equivalent to the present proposal, provided
that each port is connected to exactly one other port in another
process. In this case each channel can be identified with a tag,
together with the name of the process at the other end. Since I
wished to concentrate on semantics, I preferred in this paper to use
the simplest and most direct notation, and to avoid raising questions
about the possibility of connecting more than two ports by a single
channel.

7.4 Automatic Buffering

As an alternative to synchronisation of input and output, it is
often proposed that an outputting process should be allowed to proceed even when the inputting process is not yet ready to accept the
output. An implementation would be expected automatically to inter-
pose a chain of buffers to hold output messages that have not yet
been input.

I have deliberately rejected this alternative, for two reasons:

(1) it is less realistic to implement in multiple disjoint processors

(2) when buffering is required on a particular channel, it can
readily be specified using the given primitives.

Of course, it could equally be argued that synchronisation can be
specified when required by using a pair of buffered input and output
commands.

7.5 Unbounded Process Activation

The notation for an array of processes permits the same program
text (like an ALGOL recursive procedure) to have many simultaneous

"activations"; however, the exact number must be specified in advance. In a conventional single-processor implementation, this can lead to inconvenience and wastefulness, similar to the fixed length array of FORTRAN. It would therefore be attractive to allow a process array with no a priori bound on the number of elements; and to specify that the exact number of elements required for a particular execution of the program should be determined dynamically, like the maximum depth of recursion of an ALGOL procedure, or the number of iterations of a repetitive command.

However, it is a good principle that every actual run of a program with unbounded arrays should be identical to the run of some program with all its arrays bounded in advance. Thus the unbounded program should be defined as the "limit" (in some sense) of a series of bounded programs with increasing bounds. Thus I have chosen to concentrate on the semantics of the bounded case, which is in any case necessary; and which is more realistic for implementation on multiple microprocessors.

7.6 Fairness

Consider the parallel command:

```
[X:: Y!stop( )||Y::continue:boolean; continue:=true;
              *[continue; X?stop( ) → continue:=false
              []continue → n:=n+1
              ]
]
```

If the implementation always prefers the second alternative in the repetitive command of Y, it is said to be unfair, because although the output command in X could have been executed on an infinite number of occasions, it is in fact always passed over.

The question arises, should a programming language definition specify that an implementation must be fair? Here, I am fairly sure that the answer is NO; otherwise, the implementation would be obliged to complete successfully the example program shown above, in spite of the fact that its nondeterminism is unbounded. I would therefore suggest that it is the programmer's responsibility to prove that his program terminates correctly, without relying on the assumption of fairness in the implementation. Thus the program shown above is just incorrect, since its termination cannot be proved.

Nevertheless, I suggest that an efficient implementation should try to be reasonably fair, and should ensure that an output command is not delayed unreasonably often after it first becomes executable. But a proof of correctness must not rely on this property of an efficient implementation. Consider the following analogy with a sequential program: an efficient implementation of an alternative command will tend to favour the alternative which can be most efficiently executed; but the programmer must ensure that the logical correctness of his program does not depend on this property of his implementation.

This method of avoiding the problem of fairness does not apply to programs like operating systems which are intended to run forever, because in this case termination proofs are not relevant. But I wonder whether it is advisable ever to write or to execute such programs. Even an operating system should be designed to bring itself to an orderly conclusion reasonably soon after it inputs a message instructing it to do so. Otherwise, the only way to stop it is to "crash" it.

7.7 Functional Coroutines

It is interesting to compare the processes described here with those proposed by Gilles Kahn (1974); the differences are most striking. Kahn's coroutines are strictly deterministic: no choice is given between alternative sources of input. His output commands are automatically buffered to any required degree. The output of one process can be automatically fanned out to any number of processes (including itself!), which can consume it at differing rates. Finally, his processes are designed to run forever, whereas my proposed parallel command is normally intended to terminate. His design is based on an elegant theory, which permits proof of the properties of programs. These differences are not accidental; they seem to be natural consequences of the difference between the more abstract applicative (or functional) approach to programming and the more machine-oriented imperative (or procedural) approach, which is taken by communicating sequential processes.

7.8 Output Guards

Since input commands may appear in guards, it seems more symmetric to permit output commands as well. This would allow an obvious and useful simplification in some of the example programs, for example, in the bounded buffer (5.1). Perhaps a more convincing reason would be to ensure that the externally visible effect and behaviour of every parallel command can be modelled by some sequential command. In order to model the parallel command

$$Z:: [X!2||Y!3]$$

we need to be able to write the sequential alternative command:

$$Z:: [X!2 \rightarrow Y!3 \ [] \ Y!3 \rightarrow X!2]$$

Note that this cannot be done by the command

$$Z:: [true \rightarrow X!2; Y!3 \ [] \ true \rightarrow Y!3; X!2]$$

which can fail if the process Z happens to choose the first alternative, but the processes Y and X are synchronised with each other in such a way that Y must input from Z before X does, e.g.

```
Y:: Z?y; X!go( )
||X:: Y?go( ); Z?x
```

7.9 Restriction: Repetitive Command with Input Guard

In proposing an unfamiliar programming language feature, it seems wiser at first to specify a highly restrictive version, rather than to propose extensions — especially when the language feature claims to be primitive. For example, it is clear that the multidimensional process array is not primitive, since it can readily be constructed in a language which permits only single dimensional arrays. But I have a rather more serious misgiving about the repetitive command with input guards.

The automatic termination of a repetitive command on termination of the sources of all its input guards is an extremely powerful and convenient feature; but it also involves some subtlety of specification to ensure that it is implementable; and it is certainly not primitive, since the required effect can be achieved (with considerable inconvenience) by explicit exchange of "end( )" signals. For example, the subroutine DIV (4.1) could be rewritten:

```
[DIV:: continue:boolean; continue:=true;
*[continue; X?end( ) → continue:=false
[]continue; x,y:integer; X?(x,y) → ...; X!(quot,rem)
]
||X:: USER PROG; DIV!end( )
]
```

Other examples would be even more inconvenient.

But the dangers of convenient facilities are notorious. For example, the repetitive commands with input guards may tempt the programmer to write them without making adequate plans for their termination; and if it turns out that the automatic termination is unsatisfactory, reprogramming for explicit termination will involve severe changes, affecting even the interfaces between the processes.

8. CONCLUSION

This paper has suggested that input, output and concurrency should be regarded as primitives of programming, which underlie many familiar and less familiar programming concepts. However, it would be unjustified to conclude that these primitives can wholly replace the other concepts in a programming language. Where a more elaborate construction (such as a procedure or a monitor) is frequently

C.A.R. HOARE

useful, has properties which are more simply provable, and can also
be implemented more efficiently than the general case, there is a
strong reason for including in a programming language a special
notation for that construction. The fact that the construction can
be defined in terms of simpler underlying primitives is a useful
guarantee that its inclusion is logically consistent with the remainder of the language.

ACKNOWLEDGEMENTS

The research reported in this paper has been encouraged and
supported by a Senior Fellowship of the Science Research Council of
Great Britain.

The technical inspiration was due to Edsger W. Dijkstra
(Dijkstra, 1975b), and the paper has been improved in presentation
and content by valuable and painstaking advice from D. Gries, D.Q.M.
Fay, Edsger W. Dijkstra, N. Wirth, Robert Milne, and its referees.

The role of IFIP W.G.2.3 as a forum for presentation and discussion is acknowledged with pleasure and gratitude.

VI.C.   THE TRANSPUTER

Iann M.Barron

The transputer is a computer on a chip - a processor, complete
with storage and standard external interfaces. It is a key technological development, because it enables information systems to
be designed at a higher level of abstraction than was previously
possible.

1. THE TRANSPUTER

Because of its importance, the word 'transputer' has been
coined to describe the computer on a chip. The word is derived
from the two words 'computer' and 'transistor'. The word 'computer'
is itself derived from the Latin 'putare' - to reckon; the 'com'
part is pure decoration, technically called an intensifier. The
word 'transistor' is a contraction of 'transfer resistor' and was
first used to describe an amplifier made from a crystal and two
cat's whiskers, even before it was discovered by Shockley. Apart
from its derivation, 'transputer' is a very appropriate name for
a computer on a chip, because unlike the conventional computer,
it is not what happens inside that is important, but what happens
at the interface. The transputer focuses interest on the transfer
of information across a boundary, rather than on the processing
of information within that boundary.

2. THE STATUS QUO

The concept of the transputer is almost as old as the idea of
the integrated circuit itself. In the mid 1960's, many forecasts
were made of the development of the computer on a chip in the
1980's.

Set against this background, the 'invention' of the microprocessor by Hoff in 1971 at Intel should not have been surprising;
after all, Robert Noyce, one of the founders of Intel, has been
amongst those predicting the development of the computer on a chip.
And yet no other company attempted to develop the microprocessor,
while the proposal from Hoff was a surprise to his own management.

IANN M. BARRON

The answer to this conundrum would seem to be that the semiconductor industry had not appreciated that even a very primitive processor was a saleable product, and that the microprocessor would find a very different class of application to the conventional computer.

Since the development of the Intel 4004, a large number of manufacturers have entered the microprocessor market, so that there are now more than 50 distinct microprocessor architectures available, and the number of separately identifiable products totals well over 100. Only a few of these are sold in any volume and the market is already exhibiting a strong tendency to "de facto" standardisation.

As well as the increased variety of microprocessors, the complexity and capability of microprocessor design has increased with the advance in semiconductor technology. At any particular time, measured by transistor count, the complexity of a microprocessor is considerably below that of a comparable storage circuit. There are two reasons :

The microprocessor requires 'random' logic, which achieves a much lower density than a regular array of storage cells, perhaps by as much as a factor of five.

The design and development of a microprocessor is considerably more difficult than that of a storage device, so that microprocessors take longer to develop and use older technology.

The increase in circuit complexity has been used in various ways in the microprocessor :

To increase the word length of the microprocessor, first from 4 to 8 and, more recently, from 8 to 16 bits.

To increase the variety of the instruction set; a somewhat questionable improvement.

To increase the facilities on the chip, and so reduce the amount of external circuitry required to make the microprocessor useful.

It is this last development which is the most important. The earliest microprocessors required a large amount of external circuitry to make them into useable devices. Typically, each microprocessor required 30 to 50 additional circuits before it was viable. The number of additional circuits has been reduced, firstly by bringing all the processor functions such as interface control and clock generation on chip,and secondly, by bringing other facilities on chip, like storage and interface. The advantages of this approach are that :

THE TRANSPUTER

It reduces cost by reducing the number of semiconductor components.

It reduces cost by reducing the associated packaging costs for the circuitry. In the ultimate, like a digital watch, these costs can be totally eliminated, a battery being mounted direct onto the plastic case of the integrated circuit.

It reduces the expertise necessary to design a product based on a microprocessor. This factor should not be underestimated since one of the main constraints on exploiting the microprocessor has been the wide range of expertise necessary to make it useful in a system.

The combination of these factors has meant that the cost of microprocessor based systems has fallen far more rapidly than is indicated by an examination of the component prices themselves.

At the present time, microprocessors are available in three basic varieties :

The microprocessor, which requires external storage and interfacing. Examples are the Intel 8080, Motorola 6800 and Texas 9900.

The combination circuit, in which the microprocessor is combined with storage or interfacing, thereby reducing the overall package count in a system. Examples are the Intel 8085, the Motorola 6802 and the Fairchild F-8.

The transputer, in which all the functions of a computer including processor, program store, data store and interfacing are combined on a single circuit. Early examples are the Intel 8048, the Texas 9940 and the Mostek 3870.

With the transputer, the semiconductor industry has truly achieved the goal of the computer on a chip, although with the present scale of integration the devices offered are extremely limited in their capability.

3. CURRENT PROBLEMS WITH MICROPROCESSORS

The use of microprocessors has proved difficult. In part, this is due to the unfamiliarity of many users with computing techniques, but it has also been caused by a variety of problems presented by the microprocessors themselves. These include: device testing, engineering, programming, and system development. Although there has been progress in some of these areas, the microprocessor still leaves a great deal to be desired. The design of microprocessor based products has often demanded a rare combination of skills -

knowledge of computer design and digital engineering techniques, the ability to program well and efficiently, and specialized applications knowledge. It is not surprising if large development teams have been required to assemble the necessary skills, nor if the results have been less successful than anticipated.

The testing of integrated circuits has always been a difficult matter, and the problem has been aggravated as the complexity of the circuits has increased. User testing is necessary, because the production techniques used by the semiconductor manufacturer mean that there is a significant probability, usually about 1%, that a device will not meet specification. The increase in the number of pinouts on a microprocessor, and the complexity of their signal specification, has meant that full testing requires an investment of the order of £100,000 in test equipment; the only alternative being "in situ" testing, which is not always practical, and which usually does not test the marginal characteristics of the device adequately.

The difficulties associated with engineering have been caused by the amount of additional circuitry required to build useful systems from microprocessors. To some extent, this difficulty has been reduced by the increase in complexity, enabling more functions to be performed on chip. Where it is applicable, the transputer goes far to alleviate these problems, since the engineering is reduced to standard digital interfacing of the transputer into the required application. The difficulty has also been reduced by the growth of peripheral circuits, providing relevant functions like interfacing to communication lines or to analog signals. Nevertheless, considerable difficulties still remain in the larger systems, because the system bus design of most microprocessors is poor, making the interconnection of multiple devices on a bus an inconvenient matter. It is also virtually impossible to interconnect several microprocessors to co-operate on a task, a technique coming increasingly into vogue as the cost of processing falls.

The increased component capability has been used to make microprocessors more complex. The variety of registers, instructions, and miscellaneous facilities is multiplying at an alarming rate. These things, however, do nothing to make the programming task easier. Indeed, the Intel 4004, given its obvious limitations, was extremely well conceived and organized. Subsequent architectural embellishments by Intel and other microprocessor manufacturers have done little more than increase the number of ways in which the programmer can make mistakes.

There has also been little progress in the area of assembly languages, which at present are the primary vehicle for most microprocessor applications. The ergonomics or, more properly, cognomics of assemblers is invariably poor, with ill defined expression formats and mnemonics, with the need for excessive

keying operations, and with poor diagnostics and legibility.
Assemblers also usually lack the facility for programming at the
module level, making it difficult to develop or debug a program
part by part.

There has been some attempt to provide standard high level
languages with microprocessors. In general, such languages do
not have relevant capabilities, being weak on input and output
and strong on numerical calculation, while they have been designed
(albeit not consciously) for long programs and for computers with
a long word length. Also, the architecture of every microprocessor is extremely irregular, so that programs compiled from
high level languages are very inefficient and fail to use the
'facilities' provided by the microprocessor. Perhaps the most
relevant of existing high level languages is Basic. This is
designed to operate with 8 bit characters, and has a very simple
structure leading to less inefficient programs, while its interactive characteristics could, potentially at least, help during
program development.

Most microprocessor manufacturers have opted to develop own
brand programming languages, usually highly modified subsets of
PL/1. This approach has almost nothing to recommend it. The
languages offered are strongly machine dependent, so that no
common standard could emerge, while they do nothing to overcome
the basic problem that the structure and facilities of the high
level languages developed for computers are not relevant to the
microprocessor environment.

Increasing attention has been paid to the problem of system
development, and most manufacturers now provide a wide variety
of aids.

The basic development aid is program development systems,
enabling programs to be written and debugged. If programming is
to be done efficiently, it is essential that the development
system can be used interactively, and that the relevant development software and the program under development can be held in
some form of readily accessible backing storage. The most satisfactory forms of development system are disc based (floppy disc
is adequate) and have a visual terminal to provide interactive
capability. It is also extremely desirable to have an output
printer to log the development progress, for management reasons
if nothing else.

It is unfortunate that most semiconductor manufacturers have
chosen to base their development systems on their own microprocessors, thereby restricting the user to the software and hardware facilities available with the microprocessor. This has meant
that it is only recently that disc based systems have become
available, and these are usually very limited in software capability

by comparison with minicomputers. In particular, such systems are usually deficient in filing and text editing, two key facilities for efficient program development.

Two types of hardware aid have evolved and become a sine qua non for the development system. The in circuit emulator provides a compatible replacement for the microprocessor in its target environment, enabling the development system to control and monitor the operation of the microprocessor. The logic analyser monitors and records the recent history of a set of digital signals, typically the system bus of the microprocessor. It operates under the control of the development system, so that the sequence of events leading to a failure can be analysed.

Progress on development aids has been hindered by the reluctance of the user to make the level of investment necessary to provide adequate facilities. As a result, there is a wide variety of low cost development systems on the market which save capital cost at the expense of extended development time and errors in the resulting product.

4. THE FURTHER DEVELOPMENT OF THE MICROPROCESSOR

The first microprocessors used a 4 bit word. As the technology has advanced, 8 and 16 bit devices have been introduced. Two alternative views have been put forward for the pattern of further development. The first is that each type of microprocessor has a natural market and will continue into the future :

        4 bits for control systems
        8 bits for information products
       16 bits as a minicomputer replacement

The alternative view sees word length as a limitation, and looks forward to the successive replacement of the 4 bit devices by 8 bit, 8 by 16, and in the future, 16 by 32, or even 64. The view taken by an individual manufacturer seems to depend on whether he is defending a long established product or promoting a new market entry.

In the short term, most semiconductor companies propose to introduce 16 bit products, which must necessarily be incompatible with their existing 8 bit products. The rationale behind this move seems to be based largely on competitive pressure. The technology allows this capability, and if the manufacturers do not introduce leading edge products, they feel they will lose out in future markets. In this respect, the American companies seem to be driven on by the fear of potential Japanese announcements. As yet, it would seem that few of the semiconductor manufacturers appreciate the high cost associated with creating and maintaining a computer architecture, and they are therefore still willing to write off early designs. Such products are planned to be announced in 1978, with deliveries starting in 1979 and volume in 1980.

As time progresses, the cost of supporting a microprocessor architecture is becoming more apparent to the manufacturers, and their attitudes are gradually changing. One company, Texas, already have a compatible range based on a 16 bit architecture, and it may well have established a commanding lead in the market. It would seem possible that the other manufacturers may eventually decide to decommit themselves from the 16 bit market and remain with their existing product lines, using the technology to enhance their capability in various ways.

The continuing improvement in semiconductor technology will make practical a complete 16 bit transputer with a 4K byte store, by 1980. Such a device would have a performance in excess of most present day minicomputers. While a variety of such devices may be announced, the competitive pattern of both the computer and the semiconductor industries suggests that there will be a rapid reduction in the number of accepted microprocessor architectures, leaving just one or two de facto standards. This has happened with the computer, with the IBM 360 has become the standard, with the minicomputer where the Digital PDP 11 is the standard, and in the semiconductor market with families like Series 74 TTL. This tendency to product monopoly can be explained by the high cost of product design, and by the advantages to the user of a well supp-orted standard, enabling interchangeability and purchase from multiple sources. The trend towards standard architectures does not preclude there being a variety of products with different capabilities and costs. It is expected that one or more micro-processor families will emerge to dominate the market, being offered by several - not necessarily compatible - second sources.

Because of the high cost of developing new architectures, semiconductor manufacturers will be increasingly attracted to the idea of copying existing computer architectures, thereby obviating the need to develop much of the support software. To date, this approach has not been practicable, because the complexity of even a simple minicomputer has been rather greater than could be achieved by semiconductor technology. This situation is now changing. In order of complexity, the three most obvious archi-tectures to copy are :

> The Data General Nova
>
> The Digital PDP 11
>
> The IBM 360

Neither the software, nor the organization of these computers is suited to microprocessor technology or application, but the advantages of a wide range of software and expertise are likely to overwhelm the disadvantages.

Fairchild has already announced a copy of the Nova, and Data General has initiated litigation to prevent the use of its architecture. Unfortunately, this is an extremely ill defined area of the law, and it is not clear whether, or to what extent, Data General can protect its architecture and the associated software. For the present, the threat of litigation has been sufficient to deter most would be copiers, but the pressure to copy is likely to increase. This is particularly so since the PDP 11 architecture has been adopted as a standard by the American DoD, and copying the IBM 360 architecture at the discrete logic level is already an accepted practice.

As a guide, the technology will have the capability to fully integrate existing computer architectures at the following dates :

1978	Data General Nova
1979	Digital PDP 11
1980	IBM 360

The microprocessor versions of these architectures are likely to offer higher throughput than the basic discrete versions, although they will not match the throughput of the higher members of the computer ranges.

5. THE TRANSPUTER AS A UNIVERSAL COMPONENT

The importance of the transputer is that it provides a new level of abstraction in the physical design of information systems. So far, there have been two levels of abstraction :

The electronic component. Here, the information is represented by an electrical signal and the design is carried out in terms of electrical properties, like voltage and capacitance.

The logical gate. Here, information is represented by logic levels, and the design is in terms of a logical calculus. The electrical details have largely been abstracted from the design process, although imperfections in the logical components mean that they must still be considered to some extent.

The transputer offers the potential for the design of the information systems in terms of a third level of abstraction, based on language, where the basic unit is the word, which can be given specific semantic connotations by the provision of an appropriate set of information operations. As yet, the transputer falls short of being an adequate information component for two reasons :

THE TRANSPUTER

It is a very imperfect abstraction from the logical and electrical levels, with the result that its use requires detailed
consideration of logical and electrical properties as well as
its information properties. The solution to this difficulty
is to formalise the communication between the transputer and
its environment, so that it operates correctly at the information level, communicating words of the information. This
means that communication with the transputer should only occur
through a rigorously defined interface.

Unlike the logical level, there is no ready made mathematical
calculus for design at the transputer level. Such a calculus
would provide the formalism for representing the interaction
between a number of intercommunicating information devices
which operate autonomously. Until such a calculus is developed,
the design objectives of transputers will remain intuitive
rather than scientific. Such a calculus is likely to take the
form of a program language, which has primitive operations
enabling communication between parallel processes. The primitive elements of such a language may be seen as akin to the
axioms of the mathematical theory, enabling a much wider
variety of user facilities to be constructed from the primitive
elements.

The significance of the transputer is not widely appreciated.
This is partly because the design technique for using this component has not been developed; it is also because the emergence of
the transputer has been obscured by the intermediate version of
the microprocessor which has been available with increasing capability in the early 1970's.

6. THE FUTURE OF THE TRANSPUTER

The semiconductor industry offers an increasing capability to
integrate circuitry. Potentially, the circuitry can be organised
in a wide variety of ways. It can be asked whether the transputer
will represent a large proportion of future semiconductor usage,
or whether it will represent a diminishing proportion as more
specialized circuits are developed for specific applications.

It is often argued that, as markets become better defined,
products initially developed using a transputer will be replaced
by custom circuits, with random logic designed specifically for
the purpose. In practice, the trend has always been in the opposite direction. Good examples are the calculator, the watch, and
car ignition systems. In each case, the original reason for using
custom logic was that a programmed version would cost more. However, as the level of integration has increased, it has been found
advantageous to move from the custom circuit to the microprocessor,
because the latter offers a much greater degree of flexibility and
a wider range of functions for the user.

It is expected that this trend will continue, and that most information products will be based on programmed transputers. There are a variety of reasons for this :

In terms of semiconductor area, the programmed transputer is very efficient, compared to custom logic. This is because a large amount of the information is stored in a compact regular array, rather than in the irregular low density patterns characteristic of random logic. Thus the advantage of custom logic over transputers is likely to lie in terms of performance rather than cost, and in most cases performance is not important.

The development of the programmed transputer is far easier, particularly where modifications are required, for example, when the specification has changed. This is true even now, when the development aids are relatively primitive. The advantage of the transputer is likely to increase in the future.

The use of a standard transputer architecture greatly simplifies the problem of testing the finished device. Indeed, it will often be economic to incorporate test programs into the product itself.

It is not expected that custom circuits will disappear, but rather that their nature will change. Instead of implementing custom logic, or a special application dependent microprocessor, such circuits will be based on the use of a standard architecture, and will provide a configuration specific to the application in terms of the quantity of storage used and the types of interface. In this way, the user of the custom circuit will be able to ensure that his component cost is minimized, whilst still being able to take advantage of the characteristics of a standard programmable architecture. Such custom circuits will be easy to develop because they will consist of standard sub masks interconnected, perhaps by a bus, to form the mask set for the device.

The volume necessary to justify customization may be expected to increase as the degree of production automation increases, and component costs fall. For the vast majority of applications, for example in process control, it may be more economic to under utilize a standard device rather than to use a device more closely matching the requirements. This argument could well apply to transputers themselves, leading to a reduction in the number of variants that were offered.

The characteristics of the transputer will be optimized around the requirements of the high volume markets, and not around conventional computer usage. For this reason, transputers may be expected to diverge increasingly from the established concept of the computer, and may not be an ideal component for conventional

computer design. Even so, their low cost will almost certainly
ensure that they are the basis for all future computer systems.

Four independent factors may operate to stabilize the development of the microcomputer in the medium term, and perhaps cause it
to ossify in the long term :

The simple transputer at the 1980 technology level will be
adequate for the majority of high volume applications that
are being proposed.

There is no obvious larger scale building brick than the
transputer. The elaboration of the concept of the transputer
by providing more complex configurations is likely to prove
self defeating, because the variety of such configurations
will be too large to be economic. (The same problem limited
the exploitation of small and medium scale integration during
the late 1960's and early 1970's.)

As the transputer market becomes more mature, the introduction
of new architectures will become progressively more difficult.
Further change may be inhibited by the market mechanism of
product monopoly, even though technologically feasible, or
desirable.

Semiconductor technology may be reaching the stage where the
financial return from further levels of integration may start
to decrease.

It will require a major shake up to overcome these stabilizing
factors. Although numerous technological advances can be foreseen,
none of these is likely to be of a magnitude to jusify its introduction, so that excluding any fundamental advance which obsoletes
current computer concepts, further change may not be possible
through normal market mechanisms.

7. ARCHITECTURAL DEVELOPMENTS

Present microprocessor designs are very unsatisfactory. They
have, in general, been developed without taking cognisance of the
design experience of computers and minicomputers and, as a result,
they repeat many of the early mistakes. It should be recognized,
however, that a microprocessor is not just a computer writ small,
and that copying good computer practice will not necessarily produce the optimum design for a microprocessor. There are a variety
of reasons for this; some of the more important are :

In a conventional computer, the emphasis is on internal computation rather than on external interaction. As the scale of
computer is reduced, first to a minicomputer, then to the

transputer, the importance of the internal operation declines
in comparison with the importance of the interface operation.
It is as though the computer could be represented by a circle,
with the interior for internal processing and the circumfer-
ence as the interface. As the size of the circle is reduced,
so the properties of the boundary come to dominate. This
consideration affects both the organization of the internal
architecture and the requirements for programming languages.

Measured in silicon area, the cost of processing is declining
in relation to the cost of storage, and not the converse - in
spite of the view of the majority of the computing industry.
A simple processor equates to about 0.5K bytes of storage, a
PDP 11 to 1K byte, and an IBM 360 to 2K bytes. On this basis,
it is not very good economics to associate a large storage
system with a single processor. It is better to find ways of
using more processors within the system, even if only for
trivial functions like address mapping. This relationship
between processing and storage appears intrinsic, and in the
long term it could lead to radical rethinking about the large
and monolithic programs which dominate conventional computing
today.

There is an even less favourable relationship between processing and interface capability, measured in silicon area. Because
of the space consumed by the drive transistors and the bonding
pads, 16 bits of interface occupies a similar area to a simple
processor, so that again, there is a strong rationale for
trading interface for processing wherever possible. This will
lead to a predominance of serial interfaces and information
compression techniques.

The cost of random logic is high in comparison with storage.
As a result, the most economic approach to microprocessor
design is to use a very simple logical organization, backed if
necessary by a microprogram level to provide the user instruction set. For reasons explained later, it may be advantageous
to give direct access to the simple instruction set rather than
provide the user with the complex instruction sets associated
with minicomputers or computers.

The range of applications is different. Conventional computers
have been dominated by numerical calculation. In the majority
of transputer applications, current and foreseen, numerical
calculation is not the dominant factor. Most transputers are
concerned with handling information, and within human organizations this is represented in alphabetic form.

The concept of word length is imprecise. Current 8 bit microprocessors like the Intel 8080 do provide some 16 bit operating
capabilities, while conversely, a 16 bit microprocessor like the

Texas 9900 offers 8 bit operations as well. This fragmentation of the concept of word length, with the microprocessor able to handle a number of different sized units, may be expected to increase. Thus, it is more relevant to ask what range of information units a transputer should be able to handle.

Within a conventional design philosophy, 16 bits would appear adequate, since this provides sufficient address space for the majority of applications, and gives a good balance between the store and processor in terms of silicon area. 16 bits are not adequate for numerical calculation, but then neither are 32 bits. A better alternative would be the use of multi-length decimal representation for numbers, and this approach has already been used on some microprocessors.

With a more advanced organization, the word length might be reduced to 8 bits or less, using hardware assistance for multi-length operations on numeric quantities.

The use of a linear address base to represent names is a primitive technique. It reduces the efficiency of representation and removes the contextual structure which is necessary for protection and for certain types of access. The direct support of structured names based on decimal or alphabetic strings appears a logical development for transputer architecture.

This approach is particularly relevant when the area relationship between store and processor is considered. Rather than constructing stores with large address spaces, it would seem better to fragment the store between a number of processors, which can provide structured access to the information at little additional cost.

One alternative often proposed is the use of content addressable storage. This is not considered to be as attractive an approach because :

The content addressable logic is badly under utilized.

It seems desirable to move away from the bit level approach to an information oriented approach, where the microprocessor has direct understanding of a character set.

Currently available microprocessor architectures are already fairly close to the limit of code compaction. It is probably not possible to reduce the size of code by more than another 30%, so that improved instruction set organizations will rapidly run into diminishing return.

By contrast, the storage of data is extremely inefficient. The use of 8 bit characters to represent text is extravagant.

355

Replacement of the 8 bit character by a 5 or 4 bit character, and the elimination of formatting redundancy, should cut the size of text storage by a substantial factor. Already much information is stored electronically and the volume will increase rapidly. It is to be expected that the storage of information will represent the major capital cost of information technology in the future, so that the adoption of a more efficient representation for information would lead to large scale savings in the longer term.

The handling of numerical information within computers is unsatisfactory. Numbers are normally mapped to binary fields with arbitrary constraints on size. A more appropriate method would be to use direct decimal representation, which can readily be implemented in a transputer.

A very attractive approach would be to set to primitive operations level of the transputer at the alphabetic level, so that it has direct concept of an alphabet and the associated primitive operations, like decimal addition, naming, and functions. If this were done, the concept of binary representation and binary operation would be totally eliminated from the instruction level of the transputer.

The use of computers designed for direct execution of high level languages has often been proposed, but has not been adopted in practice. The primary difficulty in the case of conventional computers has been the need to support a variety of languages on a single computer, which largely invalidates this approach. The transputer does not have the same need to support multiple languages, so that direct implementation of a high level language is more attractive. Such a system might either execute a compiled form of the language, or an interpreted form. In practice, there is a continuum between these two extremes, and the low cost logic would favour an approach biased towards the interpretive end, which in turn could affect the characteristics of the language used.

There is an inherent need for parallelism in a transputer, since it must support its internal operations and also operations at the interface. At present this is done by interrupts which time share the processor between internal and external operations. On some of the latest microprocessors separate register sets have been provided for internal and external operations, thereby reducing the overheads caused by interrupts. Given the cost of processing and storage, it may be expected that future transputers will use separate programmable processors for internal and external operations. These processors will communicate through common storage using some form of semaphore mechanism. In practice, there might be several external processors, one for each interface channel, so that the transputer of the future could contain multi- -ple processors.

It is also possible to envisage a higher degree of parallelism for the internal program operation, although the extent to which this is exploited will depend upon the development of appropriate languages and data flow concepts.

The pinouts of a transputer may be regarded as forming an interface. At present, the definition of the operation of these pinouts is far too irregular and uncontrolled to be regarded as a satisfactory interface. The definition of a proper interface for the transputer would greatly facilitate its use both singly and in assemblies, as well as reducing the pinout count. For most purposes, the transputer could use serial interfaces in place of parallel, and this would further reduce the pinout count. Pinouts represent a major cost in chip area and packaging, so that the development of improved transputer interfaces will lead to useful cost reduction.

The level of technical support for a transputer is improving as the need for development aids becomes more widely appreciated, and the cost of programming errors becomes apparent to the user. For the present, the programming languages available are woefully inadequate. Existing computer languages concentrate on the internal algorithmic structure rather than on the control of external events and, in consequence, are not appropriate for transputers. The attempts by the semiconductor manufacturers to adapt existing computer languages have been disastrous. If, and when, good programming languages are developed for transputers, the trend towards the use of high level languages may be expected to grow rapidly.

8. CONCLUSIONS

The transputer, which is a complete computer on a chip, is seen as a very significant development, both because it can cut the cost of many potential microprocessor applications, and because it represents a new level of abstraction for the design process.

In the medium term, the level of integration from the semiconductor industry will be adequate to achieve competent transputers, and there may be a trend for the semiconductor manufacturers to copy existing architectures like the PDP 11 or the IBM 360.

A variety of architectural developments are possible in the medium to long term, and many of these would be very desirable. Architectural change may, however, be inhibited by the pressure to "de facto" standardization.

VII   BIBLIOGRAPHY

AGRAWALA, A.K. & RAUSCHER, W.G. (1976). *Foundations of Micro-programming Architectures, Software & Applications.* Academic Press, New York.

ANDERSON, G.A. & JENSEN, E.D. (1975). Computer Interconnection : Taxonomy, Characteristics & Examples. A CM Computing Surveys, Vol.7, No.4 (Dec. 1975).

ASPINALL, D. (1976 a).Microprocessors : New Components for the Electronics Engineer. Electronics & Power, Vol.22, No.6, p.437 (July 1976).

ASPINALL, D. (1976 b).Microprogrammable Microprocessors. Proc. 1976 CERN School of Computing, pp.124-129. La Grande Motte, France.

ASPINALL, D. & DAGLESS, E.L. (1977) (Editors). *Introduction to Microprocessors.* Pitman, London. Academic Press, New York.

ASPINALL, D., DAGLESS, E.L. & BARTON, M. (1977). Comparison of Microprocessors : A Graphical Approach. Euromicro Newsletter, Vol.3, No.2, pp.84-71 (Apr. 1977).

ASPINALL, D., DAGLESS, E.L. & DOWSING, R.D. (1977). Design Methods for Digital Systems Including Parallelism. Electronic Circuits & Systems, Vol.1, No.2, pp.49-56 (Jan. 1977).

ATKINSON, R. & HEWITT, C. (1976). Synchronisation in Actor Systems. M I T, Room 813, Working Paper 83 (Nov. 1976).

BARDEEN, J. & BRATTAIN, W.H. (1948). The Transistor : A Semicon-ductor Triode. Phys.Rev. 74, p.230.

BARTON, M. & DAGLESS, E.L. (1977). Graphical Approach to Micro-processor Comparison. Microprocessors, Vol.1, No.6, pp.371-379 (Aug. 1977).

359

BIBLIOGRAPHY

BELL, C.G. & NEWELL, A. (1971). *Computer Structures : Readings and Examples*. McGraw-Hill, New York.

BELL, C.G. et al. (1972). The Description and Use of Register Transfer Modules (R T M's), I E E E Trans. on Computers, Vol.C-22, pp.495-500.

BOULAYE, G. (1971). *La Microprogrammation*. Dunod, and (English Translation) Macmillan, London (1975).

BOULAYE, G. & MERMET, J. (1972) (Editors). *Microprogramming*. Proc. of the International Advanced Summer Institute, San Raphael (1971). Published by Hermann, Paris.

BRINCH HANSEN, P. (1975). The Programming Language Concurrent Parcal. I E E E Trans. on Software Engineering, Vol.SE-1, pp.199-207.

BRINCH HANSEN, P. (1977). Experience with Modular Concurrent Programming. I E E E Trans. on Software Engineering, Vol.SE-3, pp.156-159.

BROWN, P.J. (1977) (Editor). *Software Portability*. Cambridge University Press, London.

CAMPBELL, R.H. & HABERMAN, A.N. (1974). The Specification of Process Synchronisation by Path Expressions. *Lecture Notes in Computer Science, Vol.16* (Editors, Goos, G. & Hartmanis, J.), pp.89-102. Springer Verlag, New York.

CARR, W.N. & MIZE, J.P. (1972). *M O S / L S I Design & Application*. McGraw-Hill, New York.

CATT, I. (1966). Time Loss Through Gating of Asynchronous Logic Signal Pulses. I E E E Trans. on Electronic Computers, Vol. EC-15, pp.108-11 (Feb. 1966).

CHANEY, T.J. & MOLNAR, L.E. (1973). Anomalous Behaviour of Synchronizer and Arbiter Circuits. I E E E Trans. on Computers, Vol. C-22, pp.421-422 (Apr. 1973).

CHENG, E.K. & MEAD, C.A. (1975). Single-Chip Cursine Character Generator. Proc. ISSCC Symposium, Philadelphia Conference Digest, 32, Vol.XVIII.

CHU, Y. (1975). *High-Level Language Computer Architectures*. Academic Press, New York.

BIBLIOGRAPHY

CLARE, C.R. (1973). *Designing Logic Systems Using State Machines.*
McGraw-Hill, New York.

COURANZ, G.R. & WANN, D.F. (1975). Theoretical & Experimental
Behaviour of Synchronisms Operating in the Metastable Region.
I E E E Trans. on Computers, Vol. C-24, pp.604-616 (June, 1975).

DAGLESS, E.L. (1977). CYBA-M : A Multimicroprocessor. *Information
Processing 77*, B.Gilchrist (Editor), pp.843-848. North Holland
Publishing Co., Amsterdam.

DAHL, O.J. et al. (1967). SIMULA 67, Common Base Language.
Norwegian Computing Centre, Forskningwien, Oslo.

DAVIS, C.G. & VICK, C.R. (1977). The Software Development System.
I E E E Trans. on Software Engineering, Vol.SE-3, pp.6--84.

DENNIS, J.B. (1970). Modular Asynchronous Control Structures for
a High Performance Processor. Record of Project M A C
Conference on Concurrent Systems & Parallel Computation,
pp.55-80.

DENNIS, J.B. (1974). First Version of a Data Flow Procedure
Language. Symposium on Programming I R I A , Paris, pp.241-271.

DENNIS, J.B. & MISUNAS, D.P. (1975). A Preliminary Architecture
for a Basic Data-Flow Processor. Proc. 2nd Annual Symposium
on Computer Architecture, pp.126-131.

DIJKSTRA, E.W. (1968). Co-operating Sequential Programming.
Programming Languages. Genuys, F. (Editor). pp.43-112.
Academic Press, London.

DIJKSTRA, E.W. (1972). Notes on Structured Programming.
Structured Programming. Dahl, O.J., Dijkstra, E.W. &
Hoare, C.A.R. (Editors). Academic Press, London.

DIJKSTRA, E.W. (1975 a) . Guarded Commands, Non-determinacy and
Formal Derivation of Programs. Comm. A C M, 18,8. pp.453-457
(Aug. 1975).

DIJKSTRA, E.W. (1975 b). Verbal Communication with Hoare, C.A.R.
at Marktoberdorf (Aug. 1975).

BIBLIOGRAPHY

EDWARDS, M. (1976). L S I Microprogrammable Microprocessors : An
    Analysis of the Data and Control Path Structures. Int.Report,
    Dept. of Electrical & Electronic Engineering, University
    College of Swansea (1976). (Since published : Edwards, M. &
    Dagless, E.L. L S I Microprogrammable Microprocessors,
    "Microprocessors" Vol.1, No.7, pp.407-414, Oct. 1977.)

ENGLAND, D.M. (1974). Capability Concept Mechanism and Structure
    in System 250. International Workshop on Protection in
    Operating Systems. Paris.

ERWIN, J.D. & JENSEN, E.D. (1972). Interrupt Processing with
    Queued Content Addressable Memories. Proc. 1972 A F I P S
    Fall Joint Computer Conf., pp.621-627. A F I P S Press,
    Montvale, N.J.

FITZGERALD, J.M. & FITZGERALD, A.F. (1973). *Fundamentals of
    Systems Analysis*. John Wiley, New York.

FULLER, S.H. et al. (1976). The Effect of Emerging Technology and
    Emulation Requirements on Microprogramming. I E E E Trans. on
    Computers, Vol.C-25, No.10, pp.1000-1009.

GERACE, G.B. (1968). Digitial Systems Design Automation : A Method
    for Designing a Digital System as a Sequential Network System.
    I E E E Trans. on Computers, Vol.C-17, No.11.

GERACE, G.B. & VANNESCHI, M. (1974). On the Processing Speed of
    Microprogrammed Systems. Proc.Euromicro Meeting, I R I A,
    Paris.

GERACE, G.B. & VANNESCHI, M. (1975). Flow Charting, Micropro-
    gramming & Processing Speed. Proc. 1st Euromicro Workshop.
    Zachs, R. & Hartenstein, R. (Editors). North Holland
    Publishing Co., Amsterdam.

GERHART, S. (1977). Unifieid View of Current Program Testing and
    Proving : Theory & Practice. Infotech State of the Art Report:
    Software Reliability. London.

GRAY, W. (1963). *Digital Computer Engineering*. pp.198-201.
    Prentice-Hall, Englewood, N.J.

GROVE, A.S. (1967). *Physics & Technology of Semiconductor Devices*.
    John Wiley & Sons, New York.

BIBLIOGRAPHY

HANSEN (1975)   See BRINCH HANSEN (1975).

HASSITT, A. & LYON, L.E. (1976). An A P L Emulator for System/370.
    I.B.M.Systems Journal, Vol.15, No.4, pp.358-378.

HETZEL, W.C. (1973) (Editor). *Program Test Methods*. Prentice-Hall,
    New Jersey.

HEWITT, C. (1974). Programming Methodology. Project M A C Progress
    Report XI, pp.254-255, M.I.T.

HOARE, C.A.R. (1972a). Notes on Data Structures. *Structured
    Programming*, pp.83-174. cf. Dijkstra (1972).

HOARE, C.A.R. (1972b). Towards a Theory of Parallel Programming.
    Operating Systems Techniques, pp.61-72. Academic Press,
    London.

HOARE, C.A.R. (1972c). Proof of Correctness of Data Representations.
    ACTA Informatica 1,4. pp.271-281.

HOARE, C.A.R. (1974). Monitors : An Operating System Structuring
    Concept. Comm.A.C.M., Vol.17, pp.549-557.

HOEVEL & FLYNN, M.J. (1977). The Interpretive Interface :
    Resources and Program Representation in a Computer System.
    Symposium on High Speed Computer and Algorithm Organisation.
    University of Illinois (April 1977).

HOLT, A.W. (1969). Information Systems Theory. Project Report,
    Applied Data Research Inc.

HOLT, A.W. (1977). Research on Information System Specification.
    Computer Associates Inc., Report CADD-7708-0911 (Aug. 1977).

HOWDEN, W.E. (1976). Reliability of the Path Analysis Testing
    Strategy. I E E E Trans. on Software Engineering, Vol.SE-2,
    pp.208-215 .

HURTADO, M. (1975). *Dynamic Structure & Performance of
    Asymptotically Bistable Systems*. D.Sc.Dissertation,
    Dept. of Electrical Engineering, Washington University,
    St.Louis, Mo.

HUSSON, S.S. (1970). *Microprogramming : Principles & Practices*.
    Prentice-Hall, New York.

BIBLIOGRAPHY

I E E E Trans. on Computers. Special issue on Microprogramming, Vol.C-22, No.10 (1971).

IGNALLS, D.H.H. (1971). F E T E - A FORTRAN Execution Time Estimator. Stanford University Report, STAN-CS-71-204.

ILIFFE, J.K. (1977). Interpretive Machines. *The Microprocessor and Its Application*. Aspinall, D. (Editor). C U P, London.

ILIFFE, J.K. & MAY, J. (1972). The Design of an Emulator for Computer Systems Research (Boulaye & Mermet (1972)).

ILIFFE, J.K. & MAY, J. (1974). A Machine Organisation Supporting Multiple Target Languages. Proc. A F C E T Conference: Machines Orientees Languages - Machines Orientees Systems. Alpe d'Huez (May, 1974).

JACKSON, K. & MOIR, C.I. (1975). Parallel Processing in Software & Hardware : The MASCOT Approach. Proc. Sagamore Computer Conference, pp.1-10.

JENKINS, C.H. & WATTS, G.C. (1968). *Spectral Analysis and Its Applications*. Holden Day Inc., San Francisco.

JENSEN, E.D. et al. (1976). A Review of Systematic Methods in Distributed Processor Interconnection. Proc. I E E E Conf. on Communications, Philadelphia (June, 1976).

JOHANSSEN, D. & MEAD, C.A. (1977). O M 2. Dept. of Computer Science Display File Memorandum 1111. California Institute of Technology (Sept. 1977).

KAHN, G. (1974). The Semantics of a Simple Language for Parallel Programming. Proc. I F I P Congress, 1974. North Holland Publishing Co., Amsterdam.

KEHL, T.H., MOSS, C. & DUNKEL, L. (1975). $L M^2$: A Logic Machine Minicomputer. "Computer", pp.12-22.

KNUTH, D. (1971). An Empirical Study of FORTRAN Programs. Software Practice & Experience, Vol.1, pp.105-134.

BIBLIOGRAPHY

LILIENFELD, J.E. (1928). U.S.Patent No.1900018, filed Mar. 1928. cf. Heil, O. British Patent No.937457.

LIPP, H.M. (1976). Array Logic. Proc. 2nd Euromicro Symposium. Editors: Sami, M.G., Wilmink, J. & Sachs, R., pp.57-64. North Holland Publishing Co., Amsterdam.

LISKOV, B.H. (1974). A Note on C L U. MAC Computation Structures Group Memo. 112, M I T.

LISTER, A.M. (1974). Validation of Systems of Parallel Processes. Computer Journal, Vol.17, pp.148-151.

LITTLEFIELD, W.M. & CHANEY, T.J. (1966). The Glitch Phenomenon. Computer Systems Laboratory, Washington University, St.Louis. Tech.Memo. 10 (Dec. 1966).

LONDON, R.L. (1975). A View of Program Verification. Proc.Intnl. Conf.Reliable Software, Los Angeles, pp.534-545.

MARS, P. (1968). Study of Probabilistic Behaviour of Regenerative Switching Circuits. Proc. I E E, Vol.115, pp.642-668 (May, 1968).

MARTIN, J. (1973). *Design of Man-Computer Dialogues*. Prentice-Hall, New Jersey.

McCOWAN, C.L. & KELLY, J.R. (1975). *Top-Down Structures Programming Techniques*. Petrocelli/Charter, New York.

McILROY, M.A. (1968). *Co-routines*. Bell Laboratories.

MILLER, G.A. (1956). The Magical Number Seven, Plus or Minus Two : Some Limits on Our Capacity for Processing Information. Psychol.Rev., Vol.63, pp.81-97.

MILLER, R.E. & COCKE, J. (1974). Configurable Computers : A New Class of General Purpose Machines. *Lecture Notes in Computer Science, Vol.5*, pp.285-298, Springer-Verlag, New York.

NAUR, P. (1960) (Editor). Report on the Algorithmic Language ALGOL 66. Com. A C M, 3,5. pp.299-314 (May, 1960).

NEUHAUSER, C. (1975). An Emulation Oriented Dynamic Micro-programmable Emulator. TN.No.65. Digital Systems Laboratory, Stanford University.

BIBLIOGRAPHY

NOE, J.D. & NUTT, G.J. (1973). Macro E-Nuts for Representation
of Parallel Systems. I E E E Trans. on Computers, Vol.C-22,
pp.718-727.

ORNSTEIN, S.M. (1966). Personal & Alarming Communication.
Computer Systems Lab., Washington University, St.Louis
(April, 1966).

PARNAS, D.L. (1972 a). A Technique for the Specification of
Software Modules with Examples. Comm. A C M, Vol.15,
pp.330-336.

PARNAS, D.L. (1972 b). On the Criteria to be Used in Decomposing
Systems into Modules. Comm. A C M, Vol.15, pp.1053-1058.

PARNAS, D.L. & DARNINGER, J. (1967). S O D A S and a Methodology
of System Design. Proc. AFIPS. Fall Joint Computer Conference, pp.449-474.

PAYNE, J.L. (1977). A Software Development Workshop for Programmable Microelectronics. Proc. I E R E Conference on Computer
Systems & Technology, Brighton, U.K., pp.25-34.

PETRI, C.A. (1962). Kommunication mit Automaten. (Translated into
English in Project MAC-M-212.)

RAKOCSI, L.L. (1972). Microprogramming the MLP-900 as a Fourth
Generation Computer System (Boulay & Mermet (1972) pp.329-340).

RAMAMOORTHY, C.V. & GONZALEZ, M.J. (1969). A Survey of Techniques
for Recognising Parallel Processing Streams in Computer
Programs. Proc. AFIPS, Fall Joint Computer Conference,
pp.1-15.

RAMAMOORTHY, C.V., SUI-BUN, F.HO. & CHEN, W.T. (1976). On the
Automated Generation of Program Test Data. I E E E Trans. on
Software Engineering, Vol.SE-12, pp.293-300.

RANDELL, B. (1975). System Structure for Software Fault Tolerance.
I E E E Trans. on Software Engineering, Vol.SE-1, pp.220-232.

REDFIELD, S.R. (1971). A Study on Microprogrammed Processors : A
Medium Sized Microprogrammed Processor. I E E E Trans. on
Computers, Vol.C-20, No.7, pp.743-750.

BIBLIOGRAPHY

REYNOLDS, J.C. (1965). C O G E N T Programming Manual. Argonne National Laboratory, Illinois. ANL-7022, 1965.

RIDDLE, W.E. (1973). A Method for the Description and Analysis of Complex Software Systems. A C M SIGPLAN/SIGOPS Interface Meeting, pp.133-136.

RIDDLE, W.E. (1974). Issues in the Development of Behaviour Specification Schemes for Software Systems. Report RSS M3, Computer Science Dept., Michigan University.

RIETTI, G., TIRITICCO, U. & VANNESCHI, M. (1977 a). Distributed Systems of Multiple Functional Units as Microprocessor Complexes (in Italian). A I C A Annual Congress. Editor: Lijtmaer,N., A I C A , Milan.

RIETTI, G., TIRITICCO, U. & VANNESCHI, M. (1977 b). Microprogram Translation Methodologies and An Implementation Scheme (in Italian). Internal Report, Istituto di Scienze dell' Informazione, University of Pisa.

ROSE, C.W. & BRADSHAW, F.T. (1971). The LOGOS Representation System. Internal Report, Case Western Reserve University.

ROSIN, R.F. (1969). Contemporary Concepts in Microprogramming and Emulation. A C M Computer Surveys, Vol.1, No.4, pp.197-212.

ROSIN, R.F., FRIEDER, G. & ECKHOUSE, R.H. (1972). An Environment for Research in Microprogramming and Emulation. Comm. A C M, Vol.15, pp.748-760 (Aug., 1972).

ROSS, D.T. (1977). Structured Analysis (S A) : A Language for Communicating Ideas. I E E Trans. on Software Engineering, Vol.SE-3, pp.16-34 (Jan. 1977).

ROSS, D.T. & SCHOMAN, K.E., Jnr. (1977). Structured Analysis for Requirements Definition. ibid pp.6-15.

SALISBURY, A.B. (1976). *Microprogrammable Computer Architecture*. American Elsevier Publishing Co., New York.

SAYNE, D. (1969). Is Automatic Folding of Programs Efficient Enough to Displace Manual? Comm. A C M , Vol.12, pp.656-660.

SCHNEIDERMAN, B. & SCHEUERMAN, P. (1974). Structured Data Structures. Comm. A C M , Vol.17, pp.566-574.

BIBLIOGRAPHY

SHANNON. C.E. (1938). Symbolic Analysis of Relay & Switching
Circuits. Trans. A M I E E E . Vol.57. pp.713-723.

SHOCKLEY. W. (1949). The Theory of P-N Junctions in Semiconductors
and P-N Junction Transistors. Bell.Sys.Tech.J., 28, p.435.

SUTHERLAND, I.E., MEAD, C.A. & EVERHART, T.E. (1976). Basic
Limitations in Microcircuit Fabrication Technology. Rand Corp.
Report R-1956-ARPA (Nov.1976).

TAYLOR, J.M., PARTRIDGE, M.J., NICHOLS, H.R. & HILLS, J.S. (1973).
H I V E : A High Integrety Virtual Machine for Complex Dedicated
Applications. Proc. I E E Conf. on Software Engineering for
Telecommunications Switching Systems, London.

TEICHROEW, D. (1972). A Survey of Languages for Stating Requirements for Computer-based Information Systems. Proc. AFIP,
Fall Joint Computer Conf., pp.1203-1224.

TEICHROEW, D. & HERSHEY III, E.A.) (1977). P S L / P S A : A Computer
Aided Technique for Structured Documentation and Analysis of
Information Processing Systems. I E E E Trans. on Software
Engineering, Vol.SE-3, pp.41-48.

THOMPSON, K. (1976). The U N I X Command Language. Infotech Conference 'Structured Programming', pp.375-384.

THORNTON, J.E. (1970). *Design of a Computer : The Control Data 6600*.
Scott, Foresman & Co., Glenview.

TORODE, J.Q. & KEHL, T.H. (1974). The Logic Machine : A Modular
Computer Design Concept. I E E E Trans. on Computers,
Vol.C-23, No.11, pp.1164-1169.

TUCKER, S.G. (1967). Microprogram Control for System 1360.
I.B.M. Systems Journal, Vol.6, pp.222-241.

VANNESCHI, M. (1976 a) . Implementation of Microprograms and
Processing Speed. Proc. 2nd Euromicro Symposium; Editors:
Sami,M.G., Wilmink, J. & Zach, R., pp.165-172., North Holland
Publishing Co., Amsterdam.

VANNESCHI, M. (1976 b). On the Microprogrammed Implementation of
Some Computer Architectures. Euromicro Newsletter, Vol.2,
No.2, pp.14-20.

BIBLIOGRAPHY

VANNESCHI, M. (1977). Models and Architectures for Data Flow
Computing Systems. Tecnologie di Informatica Olivetti,
Ivrea.

Van WIJNGAARDEN (1969) (Editor). Report on the Algorithmic
Language ALGOL 68. Numerische Mathematik, Vol.14, No.2,
pp.79-218.

WEBER, H. (1967). A Microprogrammed Implementation of EULER on
the I B M System / 360 Model 30. Comm. A C M, Vol.10, pp.549-558.

WICHMAN, B.A. (1973). *ALGOL 60 Compilation & Assessment*.
Academic Press, London.

WILKES, M.V. (1951). The Best Way to Design an Automatic Calculating Machine. Manchester University Computer Inaugural
Conference, pp.16-21. Ferranti Ltd., London.

WILKES, M.V., RENWICK, W. & WHEELER, D.J. (1958). The Design of
the Control Unit of an Electronic Digital Computer.
Proc. I E E, Vol.105-B, pp.121-128.

WILKES, M.V. (1969). The Growth of Interest in Microprogramming :
A Literature Survey. A C M Computing Surveys, Vol.1, No.3,
pp.139-145.

WIRTH, N. (1971a). Program Development by Stepwise Refinement.
Comm. A C M, Vol.14, pp.221-227.

WIRTH, N. (1971b). The Programming Language PASCAL Acta
Informatica 1, 1. pp.35-63.

WIRTH, N. (1977). Modula : A Language for Modular Multiprogramming.
Software Practice & Experience, Vol.7, pp.3-35.

WOLFF, M.F., (1976) The Genesis of the Integrated Circuit.
I E E E Spectrum, Aug.1976, pp.45-53.

WULF, W.A., LONDON, R.L. & SHAW, M. (1976). Abstraction and
Verification in ALPHARD. Dept.of Computer Science,
Carnegie-Mellon University (June, 1976).

Devices identified by numbers are given at the end of the index.

**Books are to be returned on or before
the last date below**